ConsumerReports®

Best Baby Products

TENTH EDITION

About this book

Best Baby Products comes to you from CONSUMER REPORTS, the testing and consumer-information source best known for product Ratings and buying guidance. We are also a comprehensive source of unbiased advice about services, personal finance, autos, health, and nutrition, and other consumer concerns. Since 1936, the mission of Consumers Union has been to test products, inform the public, and protect consumers. Its income is derived solely from the sale of CONSUMER REPORTS magazine, ConsumerReports.org and its other publications and services, and from nonrestrictive, noncommercial contributions, grants, and fees. Only CONSUMER REPORTS has secret shoppers throughout the country who buy all the products you buy. CONSUMER REPORTS accepts no ads from companies, nor do we let any company use our reports for Ratings or commercial purposes.

Other books from CONSUMER REPORTS

- Guide to Childproofing and Safety
- The Complete Guide to Reducing Energy Costs
- Smart Buyer's Guide to Buying or Leasing a Car
- Kitchen Planning and Buying Guide
- Annual Buying Guide
- Electronics Buying Guide
- Used Car Buying Guide
- New Car Buying Guide

ConsumerReports®

Best Baby Products

TENTH EDITION

Sandra Gordon
& the Editors of CONSUMER REPORTS

CONSUMERS UNION, YONKERS, NEW YORK

Consumer Reports Books

Editor, Books and Special Publications . . . . David Schiff
Author . . . . Sandra Gordon
Contributing Editor . . . . Susan Randol
Coordinating Editor . . . . Terese Christofferson
Contributing Researcher . . . . Maggie Keresey
Managing Editor, Health . . . . Melissa Virrill
Design Manager . . . . Rosemary Simmons
Contributing Art Director . . . . Vicky Vaughn Shea
Photo Editor . . . . Frannie Ruch
Director, Health and Family . . . . Ronni Sandroff
Associate Director, Health and Family . . . . Chris Hendel
Contributing Copy Editor . . . . Liz Wassell
Medical Editor . . . . Marvin M. Lipman, M.D.
Associate Director, Scheduling . . . . Nancy Crowfoot
Editorial Production Associate . . . . Terri Kazin
Technology Specialist . . . . Jennifer Dixon
Prepress . . . . Frank Collado, Wayne Lizardi, Tony Terzo
Web Associate Editor . . . . Artemis DiBenedetto
Editorial Associate . . . . Karen Grant

Consumer Reports

Director, Editorial and Production Operations . . . . David Fox
Design Director . . . . George Arthur
Creative Director . . . . Tim LaPalme
Product Manager, Retail Product Development . . . . Patricia McSorley
Senior Director, Product Safety Operations . . . . Carolyn Clifford-Ferrara
Senior Director, Product Safety and
    Technology Public Policy . . . . Donald Mays
Program Leader . . . . Joan Muratore
Project Leader . . . . Rich Handel

Consumers Union

President . . . . James A. Guest
Executive Vice President . . . . John J. Sateja
Vice President and Editorial Director . . . . Kevin McKean
Vice President and Technical Director . . . . Liam McCormack
Vice President, Publishing . . . . Jerold Steinbrink

First printing, May 2009
Copyright © 2009 by Consumers Union of United States, Inc., Yonkers, N.Y. 10703.
Published by Consumers Union of United States, Inc., Yonkers, N.Y. 10703.
All rights reserved, including the right of reproduction in whole or in part in any form.
ISBN-13: 978-1-933524-24-5
ISBN-10: 1-933524-24-3
Manufactured in the United States of America.

A-to-Z Guide (continued)

Contents

Introduction
Welcome! Here's how to use this book to get the best values and safest products for your new baby

A-to-Z Guide

About the Author

Sandra Gordon writes frequently about health, nutrition, parenting and baby products for books, leading consumer magazines, and Web sites including Parents, American Baby, Baby-Talk, ShopSmart, Prevention, Family Circle, and Kaboose.com. She has appeared on NBC's Today show and as a baby safety expert on The Discovery Health Channel's "Make Room for Baby." She lives in Connecticut with her husband and their two daughters.

PHOTO BY KVON

Introduction

Gearing Up for Your Baby

Congratulations! You have a new baby (or babies!) on the way. Of course, you'll want to welcome your offspring into the world with joy and love, in a secure and nurturing environment. You'll want to select the safest products and find the best values, and CONSUMER REPORTS Best Baby Products will help you do just that.

Gearing up: Use this guide to select the best products for your baby.

One of the first things you'll notice as a new parent is that this stage of life is filled with "stuff": car seats, pacifiers, bottles, breast pumps, strollers, developmental toys, cribs, swings, infant carriers, play yards, and baby gates—not to mention diapers, diapers, and more diapers. (You'll go through thousands by the time your baby is 2 or 3 years old.) Indeed, children's products are an $8.9 billion industry in the U.S., and hundreds of products are added to the lineup each year. As you'll soon discover (if you haven't already), stores cater to expectant parents with aisle after aisle of baby gear. Catalogs and Web sites offer everything from organic cotton diapers to hospital-grade breast pumps. And these retailers often offer helpful info, too.

Retailers and manufacturers are smart. They realize that new parents want the best for their baby and that they're willing to shell out for the privilege. In fact, a typical middle-income family with one child in the U.S. will spend an average of $13,590 on baby's first year alone! But you can spend less, get better value, and still buy high-quality, safe products. That's where Best Baby Products comes in. We know you want the best for your baby. But the good news is, you don't necessarily need to spend a bundle to get it.

Buying the Best for Less

To navigate the world of baby products and stick to your budget, you need to be prepared. Use this buying guide to do your homework before you spend, and shop with a list. That way, you'll have a firm idea of what makes and models of products to consider, and which items are a good fit for your lifestyle. If you don't take this strategic route, buying for your baby quickly can become an expensive and overwhelming undertaking, often eliciting more questions than answers. What makes one stroller $100 and another $750? Which car seat is best for an infant? How do you install it, anyway? What's the safest sleeping arrangement for a newborn? A crib? Bassinet? Co-sleeper? How many diapers will that diaper pail really hold? Are those baby bottles really free of bisphenol A (BPA)? And then there's the overarching question: What do I really need and what's nice but not necessary? True, you'll need some items, but many—as cute or as fashionable as they are—are purely optional. Others, even though they're sold in retail outlets, can be a safety hazard. In Best Baby Products, we'll help you determine which is which and

advise you on how to spot quality as well as the best and safest
brands and models.

Best Baby Products comes to
you from CONSUMER REPORTS,
the comprehensive source of
unbiased advice about products
and services, health, and personal
finance, published by the nonprofit Consumers Union. Since
1936, the mission of Consumers
Union has been to test products, inform the public, and protect consumers. We accept no advertising and buy all the
products we test.

To test strollers for durability, we use a machine to roll each model 19 miles over 150,000 bumps, with a 40-pound weight in the seat.

Our engineers, market analysts, and editors attend trade
shows, read trade publications, and visit stores to spot the latest
products and trends. The market analysts query manufacturers
about their product lines and update databases of model information.
Then staff shoppers anonymously visit dozens of stores or go online to
buy the selected models, just as you would. While shopping for a baby
can certainly be fun, we take it very seriously because, let's face it, there's
nothing more precious than your newborn.

The products we purchase are put to the test in CONSUMER REPORTS'
own labs in Yonkers, N.Y., or at a specialized outside laboratory under
the direction of our engineers (crash-testing of car seats, for example).
With baby gear, safety is always the key consideration, followed by convenience and usability. The findings of our baby-products experts—
based on unbiased, side-by-side testing—can guide you in your search
for safe products. Best Baby Products also can help you find the best
value and tell you when a bigger price tag means better quality—and
when it doesn't. We'll even help you decide when you need to buy new
and when used (or hand-me-down) is OK.

How This Book Can Help

Organized in a handy A to Z format, Best Baby Products covers a wide
range of essential baby (and parent) gear, with an emphasis on quality
and safety. We'll help you decide what to buy and what to steer clear
of—dubious products in the marketplace that aren't your safest options.

We'll also answer common questions about products that often are not addressed, such as, "Is it safe to borrow or buy a used breast pump, or use the same pump for baby #2, 3, or 4?" (See Breast Pumps on page 95 for our answer.) You'll also find sections on keeping your baby safe, ways to save money, tips on saving your own sanity and sidebar boxes that dispel myths about babyhood.

The baby products marketplace is always changing, of course. New models are frequently introduced and old ones are discontinued. We've tried to make sure that the products listed throughout this book will be available at the time of publication and that the prices will reflect what you'll pay. For the most recent product and pricing information available, be sure to also take advantage of your free 30-day subscription to *ConsumerReports.org.* If you haven't already registered for your free 30 days, go to *www.ConsumerReports.org/babyoffer.* With this book and the Web, you'll be set to go.

Trend Spotting

Several key trends are influencing the kinds of baby products you'll see in stores, in catalogs, and on the Web right now. Here's a quick peek at what you're apt to find:

More functional designs. Manufacturers, after studying the preferences of parents, have decided that functionality is essential to sales success, and they're right. The best products are not only safe, they're durable, user-friendly, and tailored to your busy lifestyle. You'll find ergonomic strollers with comfort features such as cup holders and compartments for your keys and cell phone. Some products today are developed with several uses in mind: high chairs that become toddler chairs and play yards that function as portable bassinets and changing tables. What product features do you really need? This book will help you decide.

More stylish choices. Manufacturers have upped the style ante. You'll find products from cutesy to sophisticated, items inspired by popular children's characters and television programs, and chic lines that fit your sense of style. You'll find all-terrain strollers, for example, with chrome or aluminum accents in today's hottest colors—chartreuse, periwinkle, orange, "cognac," and black. You'll also find baby products sold in collections: car seats, strollers, play yards, and high chairs all in the same fabric theme, designed to blend in with your home décor or just coordinate with each other. On the flip side, you'll also find lots of baby products in traditional pink for girls and blue for boys. Aesthetics are important to consider before and during your shopping trips. Although you may be tempted to buy the most stylish products on the market, remember that they will likely be more expensive, and that the most important factors to consider should be the products' utility and safety.

Eco-friendly. You'll find an array of "natural" and organic products for babies that are produced from organic or sustainable materials like hemp and bamboo, or are free of conventional chemicals typically used during manufacturing, such as dyes. Are these products really better for your baby and the environment, and worth any extra cost? Throughout Best Baby Products, we'll let you know.

Greater attention to safety. Safety is a major concern among product manufacturers. Overall, products marketed specifically for babies are generally safe, partly because of government regulations, which have recently been improved. The Consumer Product Safety Commission (CPSC, *www.cpsc.gov*) regulates toys and baby products and oversees recalls. In August 2008, the Consumer Product Safety Improvement Act of 2008 was signed into law, raising the bar on safety.

The law mandates that all "durable" nursery products, such as walkers, bouncers, and play yards, should be third-party tested and certified as meeting federal and industry safety standards. But implementation will be phased in gradually; currently, only cribs and pacifiers are required to go through the requisite testing and certification.

However, the statute also sets other standards for children's products. Beginning in February 2009, three types of phthalates—a compound found in plastics and cosmetics that may affect a child's development and reproductive system—are banned. Three other forms of phthalates are banned while under study and may also be prohibited. In August 2009, the permissible lead limit in paint applied to children's products will fall to 90 parts per million (ppm) from a current limit of 600 ppm; lead content will be lowered to 300 ppm from 600 ppm.

We test stroller brakes on this special ramp.

JUVENILE PRODUCTS MANUFACTURERS ASSOCIATION

CERTIFIED

AN INDEPENDENT TESTING LABORATORY VALIDATES THE MANUFACTURER'S CERTIFICATION OF THIS PRODUCT TO ASTM SAFETY STANDARDS

The JPMA seal is an added measure of safety.

So that children's products may be easily identified in case of a recall, the law requires permanent labels for all those manufactured after August 2009, whether domestic or imported. Tracking labels must list the manufacturer, and the location and date of production, as well as other information such as an identifying model name and number.

Until the testing-and-certification portion of the law is fully implemented, a simplified way to know that your baby product meets all standards and requirements is to look for the Juvenile Products Manufacturers Association certification seal. JPMA, a national trade association of 300 companies that make and/or import baby products, administers a program that certifies manufacturers. A JPMA seal means that the product has been tested by an independent facility and met the guidelines set by standards developer ASTM International. (Throughout this book, we note the products that are certified.) For more information about the JPMA certification seal, visit *www.jpma.org*.

Although JPMA certification is a handy product reference point, not all baby and children's products, such as crib mattresses, pacifiers, and toys, are included in the certification program. However, these must still meet federal standards—and can be recalled if they are not in compliance with the law. See those product chapters for more information.

In addition to the CPSC, more government agencies are at work to protect your baby. The Department of Transportation's National Highway Traffic Safety Administration (*www.nhtsa.gov*) sets mandatory safety standards for the crash performance of child car seats. The Food and Drug Administration (*www.fda.gov*) oversees baby formula and most baby food, and the Department of Agriculture (*www.usda.gov*) monitors baby food containing meat, poultry, and eggs.

As an even greater measure of safety, consumer organizations such as Consumers Union work to refine voluntary safety standards, and CONSUMER REPORTS regularly tests children's products. We often hold products to more rigorous standards than the government requires or that manufacturers must meet to comply with industry standards. You'll find results of our safety tests in specific chapters throughout Best Baby Products.

Recall Alert

Dozens of baby and children's products are recalled each year because of violations of safety standards established by the Consumer Product Safety Commission (CPSC). For updated recall information on infant products, consult monthly issues of CONSUMER REPORTS or visit the CPSC's Web site at *www.cpsc.gov*. Or sign up for free e-mail notices of future recalls at *www.cpsc.gov/cpsclist.aspx*. Also, many children's products may include a registration card; fill it out and send it in so you'll be notified directly by the manufacturer if the item is recalled. To report a dangerous product or a product-related injury, call CPSC's hotline at 800-638-2772, send an e-mail to *info@cpsc.gov*, or check out their Web site at *www.cpsc.gov/talk.html*. There you'll find forms to report an injury or file a complaint about an unsafe product. For information on child safety seat recalls, to register your seat, file a complaint, and to get e-mail notices of future recalls, go to the National Highway Traffic Safety Administration Web site at *www-odi.nhtsa.gov* or call 888-327-4236.

Getting the Right Return on Baby Products

If you end up with a malfunctioning or unsafe product, duplicate gifts, or something you're sure you won't use, don't hesitate to return or exchange whatever doesn't work. Here's how to get that refund or store credit with less hassle.

Before you buy or register, make sure the store or online vendor will let you return or exchange an item if there's a problem or you get a duplicate as a gift. This step is especially important if you buy the product online, since you can't inspect it in person before buying.

In-store return policies should be clearly spelled out on a sign near the register—if not ask. If terms are only on the store receipt, you won't know what they are until you've made a purchase. Any reputable Web site should also have a section that explains return procedures. You'll need to return the item before the retailer's return period runs out (usually 30 to 45 days from the date of purchase but sometimes longer). But if the return clock has run out, don't feel defeated. Persistence and politeness will often get you into overtime.

Save your receipt, gift receipt, or packing slip and the original packaging. Some retailers won't let you return an item or make an exchange without a receipt. Online retailers may let you return an item at their retail stores, unless the packing slip or the Web site terms state: "Not returnable in stores." Check the store's return policy regarding

A baby registry can take away the gift guesswork for friends and relatives. Hone your lists carefully.

receipts before making a purchase. When returning a product through the mail, send it back in its original package by certified mail so the item can be tracked if it gets lost.

If the baby product you buy is defective or damaged, contact the customer service department at the retailer before returning it or contacting the manufacturer. If the first representative you speak with denies you a refund, ask to speak with the manager. By selling you an item, a store gives an implied warranty of merchantability. That means that if the product you bought doesn't do what it's supposed to, or if it malfunctions or fails within an unreasonably short time for that type of product and price, the retailer is obligated to correct the problem, no matter what its return policy says. If you're told that you'll have to take your complaint to the manufacturer, stand firm. Tell the manager you're prepared to keep going—to the company's head office, the local Better Business Bureau and, if necessary, your state's attorney general. Keep records of all telephone conversations and the original paperwork, such as receipts, warranties, and e-mail correspondence; make copies if you need to send anything to the retailer's corporate headquarters.

If all else fails, contact the manufacturer. Many baby products are under manufacturer warranty. Send in the registration card and hold onto warranty information so you can refer to it. That small step can also help the manufacturer contact you in the event of a recall.

Money-Saving Strategies

A new baby can take a surprisingly big bite out of your budget. Throughout Best Baby Products, we offer specific money-saving strategies. (Look for our Budget Baby sections.) In the meantime, here are some general ways to save:

Take advantage of freebies and coupons. If you don't mind getting your name on mailing lists, call the toll-free customer-service lines or register at the Web sites of formula, baby-food, and disposable diaper companies for their parenting newsletters and new-parent programs, including coupons and free samples. Even if you don't register, you may get them anyway. Somehow, when you have a new baby, word gets out.

Consider a discount club membership. At places like Costco or BJs Wholesale Club, you'll reap discounts on everyday items you'll use a lot, such as disposable diapers, baby wipes, and laundry detergent. Sign on for the loyalty savings card program at your drugstore and supermarket and you'll receive discounts that can rack up savings.

Buy as your baby grows. Except for the basics listed on pages 18 and 19, don't buy baby products until you're sure you'll need them. The wait-and-see approach gives you time to ask friends about their experiences with specific baby products and ultimately can save you money. You may be able to borrow some items.

Watch for sales. Retailers such as Toys "R" Us, Babies "R" Us, and BuyBuyBaby routinely put out newspaper inserts and in-store fliers with big savings on brand-name baby items.

Go online. If you shop online, compare prices of bassinets, cribs, changing tables, and hundreds of other baby products quickly by visiting shopping Web sites found at *www.bizrate.com*, *www.epinions.com* (which also offers product advice from fellow parents), *www.nextag.com*, or *www.shopping.com*. For additional savings online, log onto sites such as *www.couponcabin.com* for online coupons from major e-tailers. Be mindful of shipping costs—they can sometimes wipe out any savings.

Consider buying some items used. Gently used baby clothes and toys can sometimes be found in thrift stores, online, and at yard sales at a small fraction of their original retail prices. But some items such as car seats and cribs always should be purchased new to ensure they comply with updated safety requirements and have no hidden flaws.

Weigh warranties. Hold on to warranty information so you can refer to it if there's a problem. You may find a warranty being used as a sales tool. Some less expensive but adequately firm baby mattresses, for example, offer no warranties, while top-of-the-line models may have a "lifetime guarantee." Is that protection you need to pay for? For a definitive answer, see Crib Mattresses, page 177.

Power your showers. Be sure you get the gifts you want and will use. Explore the marketplace yourself and then register with retailers that stock your choices, including major online merchants, like Amazon.com. Don't hesitate to request practical items. Although frilly baby clothes are often a gift-giver's first choice, a supply of diapers or formula can mean much more. Register for and request bigger-ticket gear too, like a stroller, play yard, or changing table.

■ **New Baby Basics**

A Master List for Moms and Dads

Here's a checklist of what you should have on hand before your baby arrives. Many of these products have their own chapters in this book.

Tooling Around
___ Car seat.
___ Stroller.

Nursery Essentials
___ Crib.
___ Crib mattress.
___ Two to three fitted crib sheets.
___ Four or more waffle-weave cotton or muslin receiving blankets for swaddling your baby.
___ Two waterproof mattress pads.
___ Baby monitor.

Diaper Duty
___ Diapers. Disposables: One 40-count package of newborn (birth weight under 8 pounds) or size 1 (birth weight over 8 pounds), then buy in volume after you find the brand you like best. Cloth: If you choose unfolded, prefolded, or fitted cloth diapers, you will need two to three dozen to begin with, plus six to ten waterproof covers. If you go the all-in-one or pocket diaper route, having 12 to 16 should be adequate in the beginning.
___ Diaper pail (with refills or bags as needed).
___ Diaper bag.

Dressing Your Baby
___ Four sleep sacks or one-piece sleepers with attached feet.
___ Six side-snap T-shirts.
___ Four to six one-piece undershirts that snap around the crotch.
___ A small baby cap (although the hospital will probably give you one).
___ Six pairs of socks/booties.
___ Two to three soft, comfortable daytime outfits. Get only a few items in the newborn size. Then, go for clothing in the 6-month size— your baby will grow into these quickly. But don't buy baby sleepwear that's too big— it's a safety hazard.
___ Cotton sweater or light jacket.

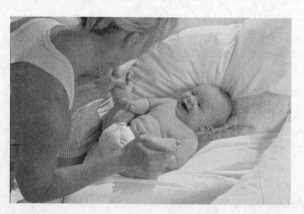

Summer Babies:

___ Brimmed hat.

Winter Babies:

___ Snowsuit with attached mittens or fold-over cuffs, or heavy bunting.

___ Heavy stroller blanket.

___ Warm knit hat.

Feeding Time

If you're planning to breast-feed:

___ Three to five nursing bras. Plan to buy a sleep/loungewear bra for the early days of nursing when you'll want to wear your nursing bra and pads 24/7 for leakage control.

___ A box of washable or disposable breast pads.

___ Breast pump if you expect to use one (manual or electric); go with a double electric breast pump if you'll be returning to work.

___ If you're supplementing breast-feeding with an occasional bottle, you may need only one or two bottles. You'll need six 4- to 5-ounce bottles if you are bottle-feeding exclusively.

___ Bottle-drying tree.

___ Bottle brush.

___ Insulated bottle holder for diaper bag (the hospital may give you one).

___ Three packs of cloth diapers or burp cloths.

If you're planning to bottle-feed:

___ Six 4- to 5-ounce bottles, plus nipples and rings.

Bathing/Grooming

___ Plastic infant bathtub.

___ Three soft hooded towels.

___ Two packs of baby washcloths.

___ Unscented baby body wash that doubles as shampoo.

___ Pair of blunt-tip scissors or baby-sized nail clippers.

___ Zinc-oxide-based diaper rash ointment.

___ Soft brush and comb.

___ Mild laundry detergent such as Dreft.

Medicine Chest Essentials

___ A pain-and-fever reducer recommended by your baby's doctor, such as Infants' Tylenol.

___ Cotton pads/swabs.

___ Nasal aspirator.

___ Digital rectal thermometer.

___ Rubbing alcohol.

___ Petroleum jelly.

Keeping Baby Happy

___ Pacifiers.

Extras: Nice but Optional

___ Changing table.

___ A rocker or glider.

___ Sling or strap-on soft carrier.

___ A doughnut-shaped nursing pillow designed to make holding baby during breast-feeding or bottle-feeding easier.

___ Nursing coverup. Attaches at your neck and allows for private breastfeeding when you and your baby are in public.

___ Infant swing.

___ Bouncy seat.

___ Night light.

Where-to-Buy Guide

The following list is an overview of places to buy and register for baby gear (and also, in many cases, products for older kids), from major retailers to more specialized outlets for items such as natural and organic baby products.

Company/ Ways To Shop	What You'll Find
Amazon.com *www.amazon.com* Online	You'll find a wide selection of baby products at competitive prices—from diaper pails and car seats to cribs and toys, with comments from fellow parents to inform your buying decisions.
Babies "R" Us *www.babiesrus.com* (888-222-9787) In store/Online	Babies "R" Us is the baby-outfitting component of the toy superstore Toys "R" Us, with almost everything you need to clothe and care for your baby, plus a baby registry. In addition, in advance of the new law governing children's product safety, the store stepped up "quality assurance" standards for its merchandise. (Click on the home page for details.) You can e-mail for help on orders using the online form or call the customer service number, 800-869-7787.
BabyAge.com *www.babyage.com* (800-222-9243) Online	You'll find thousands of baby products, from strollers and car seats to cribs and baby gates here. The site features a baby and gift registry, bedding finder, gift finder, new product arrivals page, an overstock center, special sales, and good deals on shipping, and also offers a customer rewards program.
BabyAnt.com *www.babyant.com* (866-609-0410) Online/One store in California	This Web site sells apparel, toys, and a large variety of gear from well-known manufacturers such as Evenflo, Gerber, Graco, Mclaren, and Peg-Pérego. You can shop by brand or category. You'll also find a baby registry, baby-care articles, a sale corner, and a "baby gallery" to which you can post a photo of your new family member.
The Baby Catalog of America *www.babycatalog.com* (800-752-9736) Catalog / Online	You'll find overall savings on baby and toddler products plus free ground shipping on orders of $45 or more, a low-price guarantee, an outlet store, and a closeout page for bargains. The company offers a 10% discount on almost any item in the catalog or at the Web site for their "Baby Club of America" members ($25 for a one-year membership, $50 for three years), as well as e-GiftCards, and a gift registry.
Baby Depot *www.babydepot.com* In store (Burlington Coat Factory) Online	Baby Depot is part of Burlington Coat Factory, a nationwide discount chain of stores that carry baby apparel and gear, among other merchandise. There is no phone number but the customer service page offers lots of help on order issues and there's an e-mail form geared to specific questions, such as shipping info. You'll need an ID number to return online purchases to a store.

Where-to-Buy Guide

Company/ Ways To Shop	What You'll Find
BabyEarth *www.babyearth.com* (888-868-2897) Online	BabyEarth offers a large selection of eco-friendly baby products and top-brand gear. What truly sets it apart is its BabyEarthLIVE demo-on-demand service, which uses webcam technology. After registering or entering your user name and password, you fill out a request indicating the baby gear you'd like to see demonstrated. A BabyEarth representative then calls you back prepared to do a live, online demo of your requested product. They will also recycle your baby gear; you pay shipping but get a $5 coupon.
babyGap *www.babygap.com* (800-427-7895) In store/Online	You'll find a good selection of fashionable baby clothes here—not just the basics but colorful, stylish T-shirts, separates, socks, dresses, jeans, sweaters, and outerwear plus toys and organic items. You can zoom in on patterns and details. There's $7 flat rate shipping and other deals, and you can print out a label for free returns.
Babyguard *www.babyguard.com* (866-823-2229) Online	This company sells a basic selection of latches (for everything from drawers to refrigerators), locks, and accessories for baby proofing your home. It also carries radiator covers, guards for TVs and VCRs, and a variety of safety gates. Shipping costs are based on order dollar amount, with a $6.95 minimum.
Babyworks *www.babyworks .com* (800-422-2910) Catalog/Online One store (Oregon)	This retailer's focus is on cloth diapering systems, including covers, with a variety of diapers (including unbleached flannel), accessories, and lots of tips. You'll also find a selection of cotton apparel, bedding, toys, natural skin-care and cleaning products, a baby registry, and a liberal return policy. You must register before ordering but the site doesn't share your info. Call for a catalog or download it.
Barefoot Baby *www.barefootbaby .com* (800-735-2082) Catalog/Online	You'll find mostly cloth diapers, diaper accessories, toilet-training items, and linens (cleaning cloths, bibs, and so on) from this company, as well as a selection of skin-care items, some swimwear, and potty training items. You must register to order and access your account info. There's $5 shipping for online orders over $55 and an online order form to request a catalog.
BJ's Wholesale Club *www.bjs.com* (800-257-2582) In store/Online	This warehouse store stocks a changing selection of gear, including child safety seats, strollers, cribs, high chairs, toys, bouncers, swings, and monitors as well as disposable diapers and wipes, often in large packages. Some items include shipping in the price. Membership required; you can sign up for e-mail offers and a rewards program too.
BuyBuyBaby *www.buybuybaby .com* (877-328-9222) In store/Online	Retail outlets of this baby superstore can be found in Illinois, Maryland, New Jersey, New York, and Virginia. Residents of other states can browse the store's online inventory of clothing, car seats, strollers, high chairs, furniture, bedding, diaper bags, toys, and more. You can return online purchases at stores (check the Web site for locations) or mail them back within 90 days. There's an online registry and you can shop the online circular for bargains.

Where-to-Buy Guide

Company/ Ways To Shop	What You'll Find
The Children's Place www.childrensplace.com (877-752-2387) In store/Online	This nationwide chain sells its own line of casual clothing for kids from infants through size 14 (ages newborn to 10). There's a wide selection of layette and infant apparel, including sleepwear and booties plus blankets and bibs, and some costumes. The Web site features a store locator (you can return online purchases to a store) and offers flat $5 shipping on any size order (shipping to some states is $8).
Costco www.costco.com (800-774-2678) In store/Online	You'll find budget-wise selections in a wide range of baby needs, from formula and diaper bulk deals to discounts on nursery furniture, bedding, and décor; travel gear and strollers; health and safety items such as monitors, humidifiers, and gates; baby gift sets; and toys. There are also limited-time online offers at this wholesale warehouse store. You must be a member to shop in the store or online. Items can be returned to any Costco store (locations are on the Web site) for a full refund, including shipping and handling; picked up for return (in original packaging); or sent back (e-mail customer service with the online form or phone 800-955-2292).
Ecobaby Organics www.ecobaby.com (800-596-7450) Online	You'll find a wide selection of organic baby items here, including diapers, apparel, and bedding, and other selections, such as a chemical-free pacifier, chemical-free crib mattress, and organic stuffed toys. The company also sells adult bedding, towels, and robes, and you'll find a clearance section.
Gymboree www.gymboree.com (877-449-6932) In store/Online	Known initially for its chain of activity centers offering playgroups and music classes for babies and toddlers, Gymboree offers apparel for newborns to age 12 (for girls) and age 10 (for boys), as well as toys and music CDs. There's a store locator online; no registry but you can ask for a store or online gift card.
Hanna Andersson www.hannaandersson.com (800-222-0544) In store/Online / Catalog	This company sells soft, comfortable, colorful apparel for babies, toddlers, and older kids, as well clothing for Mom and Dad and some family collections of coordinated outfits. You'll also find toys and dolls, plus a good selection of backpacks. Once European, sizes are now American, and there's a measurement chart to help. The Web site has a store locator.
J.C. Penney www.jcpenney.com (800-322-1189) In store/Online Catalog	This department store offers a wide range of baby apparel, gear, and furniture. It sells its own apparel label, as well as other well-known brands. You'll find a good selection of child safety seats, strollers, high chairs, diaper bags, and more, and you can shop by brand or category. A gift registry is also available, as is the free JCP rewards program, that earns you points for in-store, online, and catalog purchases. Also expect lots of sales and discounts.

Where-to-Buy Guide

Company/ Ways To Shop	What You'll Find
KMart *www.kmart.com* (866-562-7848) In store / Online	You'll you'll find apparel, gear, diapering supplies, high chairs, baby care and safety products, and nursery furniture on this Web site. You can sign up for Kmart e-mail updates on in-store and online savings, and there's also an online weekly circular, as well as gift cards and a registry. Returns can be shipped back or taken to a Kmart store—check the store locator on the Web site.
Lands' End *www.landsend.com* (800-963-4816) Catalog / Online	Both the catalog and Web site offer bedding, apparel, diaper bags, outerwear, and footwear. You can get live help by chatting via phone or text with a rep while you shop and Lands' End makes returns easy by letting you print return forms and labels online ($6.50 is deducted from your refund for use of the label), which is handy if you've lost yours. You can also return Internet and catalog orders at Sears.
L.L.Bean *www.llbean.com* (800-441-5713) Catalog / Online	Both the catalog and Web site of this outdoor/casual wear outfitter offer bicycle trailers, jogging strollers, and a selection of apparel, including outerwear and footwear, even Bean booties. There's live help when ordering via chat with a customer service rep—or just e-mail for help. If you've lost your return and exchange form, you can print one out online, along with a prepaid shipping label from UPS or the post office ($6.50 is deducted from your refund).
Macy's *www.macys.com* (800-289-6229) In store / Online	Macy's sells a selection of baby apparel, including special-occasion outfits, and has a range of bedding items, diaper bags, and shoes. Also look for nursery furniture. You can shop by brand, get in on lots of sales, including one-day events, and find clearance items. Online purchases can be returned at Macy's stores (locator and hours on the Web site).
One of a Kind Kid *www.oneofakindkid .com* (866-404-2927) Online	This Web site features European and American designer baby clothes and children's clothing, christening gowns, special-occasion clothes like flower-girl dresses, and costumes as well as custom baby bedding, cribs, furniture, room décor, and gifts. There's a gift registry, gift certificates, and a "specials" button for deals.
Peapods *www.peapods.com* (866-966-3869) Online	Peapods sells a selection of slings, as well as cloth diapers and diaper covers, blankets, crib mattresses, feeding bottles, music CDs, and toys made from recycled materials. The site specifies that products are made from all-natural materials, with no plastic, petroleum by-products, batteries, or cartoon characters. You'll find a gift registry and gift certificates.
Pottery Barn Kids *www.pottery barnkids.com* (800-993-4923) In store/Catalog/ Online	The kids' line of this housewares and home-furnishings retailer features bedding, window treatments, toys and gifts, lamps and lighting, and furniture. There's a gift registry, and some items may ship for free. Some prices may be steep—but there are sales and gift cards are available.

Where-to-Buy Guide

Company/ Ways To Shop	What You'll Find
Safe Beginnings www .safebeginnings.com (800-598-8911) Catalog/Online	This company sells babyproofing items such as safety locks and latches, outlet covers, gates, furniture straps, crib tents (to bar pets from the crib), hearth guards and padding, even planter covers to keep a curious toddler out of the dirt. A gift registry is also available.
Sears www.sears.com (800-MY-SEARS) (800-697-3277) In store/Catalog / Online	You'll find the wide range of baby products you'd expect from a department store here. Apparel, furniture, monitors, and more are offered through all of Sears' shopping venues. The Sears Web site has a special baby section, which allows you to browse its inventory of baby items. There's a price-matching policy, plus an additional 10% off, and lots of deals. Online items may be available for pick-up at a Sears store, and may be returned there too, saving shipping costs.
Target www.target.com (Stores: 1-800-440- 0680; online orders: 800-591-3869) In store/Online	Target stocks a huge variety of baby items in-store and online. Furniture, strollers, child safety seats, other gear such as play yards and swings, apparel, and bedding are among its offerings. You'll see deals and bargains, coupons and specials, some free shipping offers, plus a baby registry and gift cards. You can find a store online—or if a certain store carries an item you want. Some online items may be returned to the store; you can print a in-store Receipt online.
USA Baby www.usababy.com (800-323-4108) In store/Online / Catalog	This nationwide chain sells furniture, including nursery ensembles, bedding, gates, monitors, feeding supplies, gliders, strollers, child safety seats, play yards, and more. Promising not only a huge selection but super low sale prices, USA Baby offers a "once a trimester sale," a "twins policy" — 10 percent off on a duplicate item—a registry and gift certificates. Online orders have a 30-day money back guarantee, plus free shipping if you spend over $100. The site has a store locator, but stores can't accept online returns and you must contact customer service by e-mail.
Wal-Mart www.walmart.com (800-966-6546) In store / Online	This retail giant offers a generous selection online—furniture, bedding and décor, gear from safety seats to diaper bags, gates, monitors, and gifts, as well as diapering supplies, including "earth-friendly" diapering, and feeding accessories (but formula isn't available online). You can shop by brand or category, register for gifts. Check the "Special Offers" section for sales, clearance, shipping deals. Look for the "Site to Store" logo, which indicates an item can be picked up in-store to save shipping. Returns are by mail or in-store.

chapter

Autos: Kid-Friendly Vehicles

Whether you're in the market for a new car or evaluating future needs now that you have a baby, consider the size of your family, the age of your kids, and your family's activities to choose the vehicle that's best for you.

The Honda Accord rates tops in our tests for family-friendly vehicles.

Before buying a family vehicle, you'll also need to factor in safety, reliability, and practical concerns such as ease of access to the backseat where the kids will be sitting, child-seat compatibility, and the size of the cargo area. It's a lot to consider. "But finding the right family vehicle doesn't have to be a difficult or long process if you invest some time to research your options before you go out shopping," says David Champion, director of CONSUMER REPORTS' Auto Test Center in East Haddam, Conn.

Can you get by with a sedan, or do you need the extra passenger space of a minivan, wagon, or sport-utility vehicle? That, of course, is the $14,000 to $40,000 question. "Parents need to think about how they'll be using the vehicle, what type of cargo they intend to carry, and how their needs may change during the years they own the vehicle," Champion says.

Shopping Secrets

Focus on vehicles with a roomy and versatile interior, plenty of cargo space, ease of access, and windows that make it easy for kids to see outside. "If they can't look out the window, that can trigger boredom and bickering among siblings," Champion says. If you've got children who are old enough to bicker, consider taking them with you when you're vehicle shopping to see how the window height in the back seat measures up compared to their viewing height.

Minivans are an excellent choice for families because the windows are lower to the ground in relation to seat height, giving kids a better view out. They also offer easy access for passengers through big sliding doors and cargo areas that are easy to reach.

Sport-utility vehicles are popular in part because many have big, roomy interiors and four- or all-wheel-drive systems to better handle bad weather and unpaved roads. But young children may have a tough time getting into larger SUVs because these vehicles stand higher off the ground and sometimes have door handles that are difficult for youngsters to operate.

Four-door sedans and smaller wagons are fine for families with one or two children. Bigger families (and those needing the family car for long road trips or carrying friends) should consider a vehicle with a larger cargo area and/or more seating capacity. All minivans and many SUVs and wagons can carry seven passengers. Some accommodate eight.

Loading groceries, strollers, and other items into a large SUV can be more difficult because the cargo area is elevated. Remember, too, that taller vehicles such as SUVs have a higher center of gravity, which makes them more top-heavy and more susceptible to rolling over than lower vehicles, such as sedans and wagons. Fortunately, the recent trend toward car-based, all-wheel-drive SUVs, sometimes called crossovers, has provided a greater range of choices, including models that are more family friendly than traditional versions because they're lower to the ground, which makes it easier for little kids to get in and out. Car-based SUVs also typically provide better handling and fuel economy than truck-based SUVs.

Minivans like this top-rated Toyota Sienna are great for families because kids can get in and out easily through big sliding doors, and the well-positioned windows give kids a better view out.

What Kind of Car Should You Buy?

To zero in on what type of vehicle is right for your family, consider these questions:

How many people will you be carrying? If you have one or two children, a small or midsized sedan, which is usually less expensive and more fuel efficient than a larger car, will suffice. Keep in mind, though, that while most cars are equipped to accommodate five people, the center rear position is often uncomfortable. Check out the rear-seating quality of any vehicle you're considering.

There are still a few—but not many—larger sedans that can be equipped with a front bench seat, which allows them to carry six passengers, but it's a tight fit and the center passenger has only a lap belt. A roomier solution would be a minivan, or seven-passenger wagon or SUV. All seven-passenger vehicles include a third-row seat that can either be removed or folded down when not needed for passengers. (The latter is the better solution because you don't have to struggle to get the bulky seat in and out, and because it's always there when you need it.) No matter what type of car you choose, check out how easy it is to get in and out of all seats. That can vary a lot from one vehicle to another.

How old are your children? Plan ahead. If you intend to keep a vehicle for a number of years, your family's space needs will change as your children grow. If you've got small children now, consider how much room you'll need for child safety seats. Take the seats with you when you shop to see how easily they fit and install in the car you are considering buying. They can take up a lot of space, and having your seat kicked from the rear gets annoying.

How much cargo space do you need? For smaller families, the trunk of a sedan may provide adequate cargo space. A vehicle with more space may be a better choice for large families or those involved in outdoor activities, who tend to travel a lot, or who need extra room for home-improvement supplies or baby gear such as a stroller. There's a wide range from which to choose, from small wagons to SUVs.

How adaptable is the vehicle? In addition to cargo size, consider its versatility. Does the rear seat fold down? If so, is it a split design that allows one side to be folded separately from the other side? For carrying extra-long items, can the front passenger seat also fold down? If you're considering a seven-passenger vehicle with a third-row seat, check whether the third seat needs to be removed completely when not needed or, better, whether it can simply be folded out of the way. Finally, remember that vehicles that sit lower to the ground are typically easier to load and unload.

What conditions will you be driving in? The area of the country in which you live may influence the type of drivetrain you need. For most conditions, including very light snow, a two-wheel-drive vehicle will likely work fine. Front-wheel drive with traction control is the preferred setup for slippery conditions. All-wheel drive (AWD), however, can provide more traction to help keep you from getting stuck when conditions are slick, but doesn't improve braking. AWD is always active so you don't need to turn it on when conditions get slippery. Four-wheel drive (4WD) requires that you activate it and often is accompanied by low-range gearing and additional ground clearance that can help you get over larger rocks and more deeply rutted roads. If you drive a lot on snow and ice, switching to a set of winter tires will provide additional grip—and added safety for both steering and braking—with any vehicle. Both AWD and 4WD will reduce a vehicle's fuel economy.

How important is fuel economy? As a general rule, the larger the vehicle, the lower the fuel economy. Small, lightweight sedans typically

Family-Friendly Tips From Our Tester

"The safety and functional aspects are most important, but the niceties make travel

CONSUMER REPORTS auto tester Jennifer Stockburger is the mom of two.

enjoyable. When choosing a new vehicle, take your family along to make sure everyone fits comfortably and has easy access to what they need. For little ones, look for cup holders in the backseat, especially ones that can accommodate a juice box, and storage areas such as pockets in the seats, which can keep plenty of toys and books stowed within easy reach," says CONSUMER REPORTS auto tester Jennifer Stockburger. "For older kids, you may also

want 12-volt power ports for plugging in games, and rear DVD players, which can keep your child occupied and can help limit distractions, such as sibling squabbles during long drives." A good sound system helps, too, since children can be lulled by music or can spend hours listening to a recorded book. Some systems let your children listen to their music on headphones while you listen to yours through the car's audio system.

get the best economy, while large, heavy SUVs get the worst. If you need more cargo room than a sedan can provide, consider a wagon. Some models provide as much usable cargo space as an SUV, but usually get better fuel economy. If you need a seven-passenger vehicle, keep in mind that minivans typically get better mileage than seven-passenger SUVs.

What safety equipment is included? By law, every new passenger vehicle comes equipped with dual front air bags. But some sophisticated systems have occupant sensors to determine if the air bag should deploy and at what strength. An increasing number of vehicles have side air bags and head-protecting side curtain bags that deploy to protect occupants in both the front and rear seats. (In general, the safest place to put a car seat is in the center rear seat of the automobile, whether or not your car has air bags. For information on installing infant car seats, see the Car Seats chapter, page 111.)

Our auto experts also highly recommend a feature called electronic stability control (ESC), especially on SUVs. It selectively applies the brakes to the appropriate wheel when it senses the vehicle is sliding out of control and helps to keep the vehicle going in the direction in which you are steering. It can help you avoid an accident in all kinds of weather and is especially valuable in slippery conditions and when swerving to avoid an accident. It can also prevent an SUV from getting into a situation where it could roll over.

Vehicle Picks

In choosing the best family vehicles, CONSUMER REPORTS looks at a range of factors, including performance, comfort, ease of access, safety, fuel economy, roominess, and reliability. Here are our top recommendations in several categories. The price ranges were current at the time of publication and may, of course, change. Even so, they'll give you a ballpark idea and are useful for comparison. More detailed car Ratings and current pricing information are available online at *www.ConsumerReports .org.* To activate a free 30-day trial membership to the site, see the inside of this book's front cover.

Best Family Sedan: Honda Accord

The Accord is one of the best family sedans on the market. It has a roomy cabin, agile handling, and a steady, compliant ride. Most controls are logically arranged. The driving position is excellent, the seats are supportive, and visibility is impressive. The automatic shifts very smoothly and responsively. The four-cylinder engine is smoother than some V6 engines and you can expect fuel economy of 23 mpg. The new V6 model is very quick and polished, but fuel economy of 21 mpg overall is slightly less than the four-cylinder version. Road noise is a bit noticeable, however. All models have standard ESC.

Base MSRP price range: $20,905 to $30,905.

The Honda Accord is a roomy, well-rounded sedan.

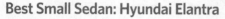

The Hyundai Elantra gets 27 mpg.

Best Small Sedan: Hyundai Elantra

The Elantra is a pleasant small sedan with a comfortable ride and low road noise, though it isn't as agile as a Mazda3 or Honda Civic. The engine booms at high revs but returns good fuel economy at 27 mpg overall. The relatively roomy interior is put together nicely. It also has more standard safety equipment than some competitors. ESC is standard on the SE trim and, combined with wider tires and a tighter suspension, makes the car very secure. Its reliability has been above average.

Base MSRP price range: $14,120 to $17,820.

Best Large Sedan: Toyota Avalon

The Avalon is a lot of car for the money. It has a limolike rear seat that can even recline. The quality of the cabin materials is very good. The Avalon rides very comfortably and quietly. But because of its relatively soft suspension, the car tends to float a bit when encountering road dips at highway speeds, less so in the Touring model. Handling is responsive but far from sporty, with overly light steering. The 268-hp, 3.5-liter V6 feels smooth, punchy, and quiet. Crash-test results are impressive and ESC is standard for 2009. Reliability has been above average of late.

Base MSRP price range: $27,845 to $35,185.

The Toyota Avalon is a lot of car for the money.

The Toyota Highlander has a roomy second-row seat and the flexibility of a fold-down third-row seat.

Best Three-Row SUV: Toyota Highlander

The Highlander scores high for its refinement, quiet interior, ride comfort, and flexible and roomy second-row seat. Its 3.5-liter V6 delivers solid performance and 18 mpg overall. The hybrid model gets 24 mpg and drives similarly, and can propel itself on electric power alone at low speeds. Handling is sound and secure, but not particularly agile and the steering feels vague. The third-row seat is tight and doesn't fold in a 50/50 split. The easy-to-use controls and good fit and finish make the interior pleasant. Cabin access is easy.

Base MSRP price range: $25,705 to $41,020.

Best Small SUV: Toyota RAV4

The RAV4 has a flexible, well-designed interior. It is fairly quiet, has a comfortable ride, and, with its standard ESC, handling is agile and secure. The rear seat is relatively roomy, and a tiny third-row seat is optional. For 2009, the RAV4 got a slightly larger 2.5-liter four-cylinder engine, which is quieter and gets a good 23 mpg overall. The optional 3.5-liter V6 makes the RAV4 quicker and quieter, and it returns only 1 mpg less than the four-cylinder, but in Limited trim it pushes the price to about $30,000.

Base MSRP price range: $21,500 to $27,810.

The Toyota RAV4's backseat is relatively roomy for a small SUV. It gets 23 mpg overall.

Best Minivan: Toyota Sienna

Our top-rated minivan is comfortable with well-designed features. The strong, fuel-efficient 3.5-liter V6 engine is mated to a smooth five-speed automatic transmission. The interior features a 60/40-split rear seat that folds flat into the floor. Handling is secure, predictable, and responsive, but isn't as agile as the Honda Odyssey. Fuel economy is a relatively good 19 mpg. All-wheel drive is optional but results in 18 mpg overall, a firmer ride, and more road noise because of the run-flat tires that come standard with the AWD model. Crash-test results are impressive.

The cargo-friendly Toyota Sienna features a 60/40-split rear seat that folds flat into the floor.

Base MSRP price range: $24,540 to $37,865.

Best Mini-Minivan: Kia Rondo

One of the most overlooked small vehicles, the Kia Rondo has an impressive amount of room for its compact size and affordable price. With seating for up to seven, it has minivanlike utility with the dimensions of a small car. Built on the same platform as the Kia Optima family sedan, the Rondo also shares its 2.4-liter, four-cylinder engine, as well as the optional 2.7-liter V6. Expect fuel efficiency of 21 mpg from the smooth V6. Fit and finish are very good and access is easy. Lots of glass makes it easy to see out. Handling isn't particularly agile, but it is secure. ESC and curtain air bags are standard. Reliability has been above average.

Seating for up to seven gives the Rondo minivanlike versatility.

Base MSRP price range: $17,495 to $22,295.

Family Vehicle Concerns to Consider

Blind zones. Every vehicle has a blind zone immediately behind the rear bumper. It can be five feet, or 50 feet, depending on the vehicle's size and styling. In that space might lurk a toy, pet, or even a child.

Every year, children are injured and killed because drivers backing up don't see them. In general, pickups and larger SUVs have longer rear blind zones than sedans.

To check a vehicle's blind spot, sit in the driver's seat of the parked vehicle and have someone stand directly behind

Rear cameras allow you to see into the blind spot behind your vehicle.

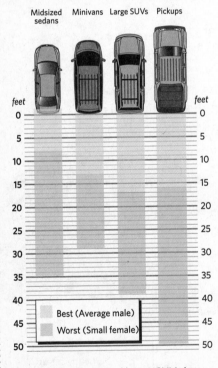

In general, pickups and larger SUVs have longer rear blind zones than sedans.

the car, next to the bumper, and hold out a hand at about waist level. Have the person walk back slowly until you can see the hand through the rear window. This will give you an idea of how big the vehicle's blind spot is. The chart at left shows the length of the blind spot for an average-height driver (5 feet, 8 inches) and a shorter driver (5 feet, 1 inch).

Rear cameras are powerful tools that allow you to see into that otherwise-hidden area behind the car. Happily, cameras are now becoming available on more and more vehicles, although to get it on some models you also have to get additional options, such as a navigation system. Aftermarket cameras are also available and their cost and ease of installation has been improving. Even a small screen, like one in a rearview mirror (found in the aftermarket and on Fords, GMs, Hondas, and Mazdas), can alert you to unseen hazards. We recommend that you purchase the technology, but you still need to make sure that you check the screen and use your rearview mirrors before you start backing up, every time—no exceptions.

Child safety seats. Child safety seats save lives and should be used until a child is big enough to wear a regular safety belt (typically when he is 57 inches tall). The traditional method of attaching a child seat is to use the vehicle's safety belts. But incompatibilities among the car's safety belts, the car seats, and the child safety seats often have made it difficult, and sometimes impossible, to get a tight fit. Most vehicles made after September 1, 2002, are required to have the Lower Anchors and Tethers for Children (LATCH) system. LATCH-equipped vehicles have built-in lower anchors and ready-to-use tether attachment points, so compatible child safety seats can be installed without using the vehicle's safety-belt system.

The system doesn't work equally well in all vehicles. In many cars, the attachment points are obscured or difficult to reach, so it's not easy to use them even with some of the newest child seats. Try your child seat in the vehicle before you buy. See the Car Seats chapter, page 111, for more information.

Power-window switches. At least 32 children have died from injuries involving power windows during the past decade, according to KidsAndCars.org, a national nonprofit organization that works to prevent injury and death to children in non-traffic, auto-related events. Typically, the child has her head out the window of a parked car, often but not always with its engine left running, and accidentally leans on the window switch. The glass moves up with force, strangling the child.

Two types of switches are inherently riskier than others, particularly if they're mounted horizontally on the door's armrest: Rocker switches move the glass up when you press one end of the switch, down when you press the other; toggle switches work when pushed forward or pulled back. The National Highway Traffic Safety Administration has banned power window rocker and toggle switches in all passenger vehicles manufactured for sale in the U.S. on or after October 1, 2008. A third type, the lever switch, is safer because it makes it harder to raise the window accidentally. Lever switches must be pulled up to raise the glass. They generally haven't been implicated in fatal injuries, according to KidsAndCars.org. However, there have been cases in which the driver or a passenger has inadvertently raised the window, without checking that children were safely away from it. Switches of any design mounted vertically or on an upswept armrest are harder to activate by accident, but this design isn't typical. In the meantime, there are millions of older vehicles that still have the riskier designs. Be on the lookout for them if you're shopping for a used family vehicle and avoid them if you can, particularly if you have young children. And never leave children alone in a car or the keys in the car when kids are nearby.

A good alternative to an SUV, the Subaru Outback offers a comfortable ride and a useful cargo area.

Best Midsized Wagon: Subaru Outback

Comfortable and versatile, the Outback is similar to the discontinued Legacy wagon but with slightly more ground clearance. While the base 2.5-liter four-cylinder engine is a bit sluggish, the XT's 2.5-liter, turbocharged engine offers much more power, but fuel economy suffers. The 3.0-liter, six-cylinder engine is less responsive than the turbocharged one and returns 19 mpg. The base car gets 21 mpg overall. Handling is agile with good steering feel, and the ride is supple. The wagon has a useful cargo area, but the rear seat is snug. The Outback tends to slide its rear end a bit too readily at its cornering limits. ESC, standard for 2009, keeps the Outback secure, but the system was slow to react in our emergency handling tests. AWD is standard.

Base MSRP price range: $22,295 to $34,095.

chapter 2

Baby Bottles & Nipples

Even if you breast-feed your baby, you may need bottles for pumped breast milk or supplementary formula. Bottles are a must if you'll be using formula full-time. There's a variety of bottle types to choose from, many of which also may be healthier for your baby and the environment.

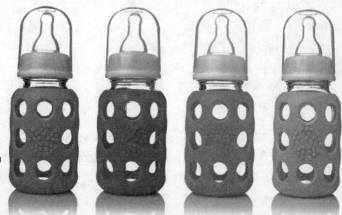

Unless you're breast-feeding exclusively and never away from your baby, you'll need bottles.

Styles and colors of bottles abound, but your mission should be to find bottles that don't leak or cause excessive spit-up, burping, or gas. The bottles should also be easy for your baby to hold and for you to clean and, equally important, be made without bisphenol A (see below). You'll use a bottle the most in your baby's first year. After that, you may decide to transition to a sippy cup. In fact, that's an ideal time to wean your baby from the bottle, or at least start attempting to do so. At that point, cow's milk will likely be a diet staple, possibly with breast milk.

The Buzz on BPA

Concerns about the chemical bisphenol A, or BPA, which is found in baby bottles made of polycarbonate, a hard, translucent plastic that can be clear or colored, have prompted some manufacturers to switch to other types of plastics. When it's heated, washed in the dishwasher, or exposed to acids such as those found in juice, polycarbonate tends to break down and leach BPA into food and drinks, according to Frederick vom Saal, Ph.D., a BPA researcher at the University of Missouri-Columbia. Polycarbonate containers don't get better with age; older polycarbonate items leach more than newer ones, says vom Saal. Based on the latest research, the National Institutes of Health concluded there was some concern for the effects of BPA on the brain, behavior, and reproductive system of fetuses, infants, and children at current human exposures.

The Food and Drug Administration has long maintained that BPA exposure levels are below those that may cause health effects. The agency continued to hold that position even after an FDA-requested peer review concluded that its safety margins for exposure were inadequate. However, the FDA has announced it is moving ahead with research to address the potential low-dose effects of BPA. For now, polycarbonate baby bottles are still on the market in this country, although Canada has begun the process of banning them.

The Siliskin by Silikids is a silicone sleeve, made without BPA in sizes to fit standard Evenflo glass bottles.

If you're concerned about BPA, use bottles made without polycarbonate (No. 7 plastic). Many stores and Web sites now sell plastic baby bottles labeled "without BPA," or "Bisphenol-A Free." They're made of polypropylene, polyethylene, polyethersulfone, or Tritan, a polyester-based material. Bottles not made from polycarbonate can be a little more expensive, but it depends on the brand. Glass, including bottles sold with protective silicone sleeves, is also an option. Silicone sleeves for glass bottles are also sold separately. Silikids, for example, sells silicone sleeves for 4- and 8-ounce bottles for $6.95 and $8.95, respectively. But glass is still breakable. And it's heavier for you and your baby to hold than plastic, which gives plastic bottles made without BPA the edge in terms of ease of use.

Bottles That Pass the Test

CONSUMER REPORTS used an outside lab that specializes in plastic analysis to test for BPA in several brands of plastic baby bottles that were labeled as "without BPA" or "Bisphenol-A Free." We found that the BPA levels were negligible. These five bottles we tested are a better choice than polycarbonate, if you don't want to use glass but still want to limit your baby's exposure to BPA: BornFree, 9-fluid-ounce or 5-fluid-ounce twin-packs; Evenflo Classic without BPA CustomFlow, 8-ounce, tinted; Medela Breastmilk Feeding and Storage Set, 5-ounce; Nûby Non-Drip, multicolored, by Luv n' Care, 10-ounce or 7-ounce; and MAM BPA-free Anti-Colic Bottle, by Sassy, Inc., 9-ounce.

These tested baby bottles have negligible levels of BPA.

What's Available

The market is flooded with a range of bottle brands and styles. Your main baby bottle choices are standard, angle-neck, wide, disposable (drop-ins), natural-flow, and premium. According to manufacturers, bottles and nipples are constantly being improved to reduce the chance of a baby's ingesting air bubbles, which may contribute to colic, spitting up, burping, and gas, and the negative effect of suction, which is fluid in the ear. Some makers of baby bottles are, in alphabetical order: Adiri (*www.adiri.com*), Baby Life (*www.gobabylife.com*), Born Free (*www.newbornfree.com*), Dr. Brown's (*www.handi-craft.com*), Evenflo (*www.evenflo.com*), Gerber (*www.gerber.com*), Green to Grow (*www.green togrow.com*), Nûby by Luv n' Care (*www.nuby.be*), Medela (*www.medela.us*), Munchkin (*www.munchkin.com*), Nurture Pure (*www.nurturepure.com*), Philips Avent (*www.avent.com*), Playtex (*www.playtexbaby.com*), Sassy (*www.sassy baby.com*), Silikids (*www.silikids.com*), Second Nature (*www.regallager.com*), Think Baby (*www.thinkbabybottles.com*), and The First Years (*www.learningcurve.com*). Here's the lowdown on the types of bottles available:

Standard bottles

There are two basic sizes of this classic shape with straight or slightly curved sides: 4 or 5 ounces for infants and 8 or 9 ounces for older babies, in glass or plastic, including non-polycarbonate plastic. Some brands come in 7 or 11 ounces as well.

The MAM Anti-Colic "BPA-free" Bottle from Sassy has a valve to help ensure a natural flow and air-free feeding.

Pros: These bottles are easy to fill and hold, can be used repeatedly, and allow you to accurately gauge formula amounts. Most breast pumps and baby-bottle warmers are designed to be used with standard bottles, although you can easily transfer pumped breast milk from a standard bottle to a disposable, if you like.

Cons: Many bottles such as the MAM Anti-Colic bottle by Sassy, a standard polypropylene bottle, have a valve on the bottom and vents in the nipple that manufacturers claim minimize air intake during feeding ($11.99 for three 9-ounce bottles, *www.target.com*). We found no independent evidence that such designs actually minimize gas in a baby's tummy.

Price range for 4-, 5-, 8-, or 9-oz 3 packs: $2.99 to $27.99.

Angle-neck bottles

These bottles are bent at the neck, making them easier for you to hold in a comfortable position.

Pros: Their shape causes formula or breast milk to collect at the bottle's nipple end, so your baby is less likely to swallow air, according to manufacturers. The shape may work well for feeding your baby while she lies semi-upright; this position may help prevent fluid from collecting in her ear canals, which can lead to ear infections. One type, the Playtex VentAire Advanced angle-neck bottle, has a patented, micro-channel vent at the removable bottom of the bottle. The vent is designed to keep air out of the liquid so your baby drinks virtually bubble free.

The Purely Comfi is Evenflo's "BPA-free" plastic angled bottle.

Con: Angle-neck bottles can be awkward to fill—you must hold them sideways or use a special funnel to pour in liquid.

Price range: $6.49 to $10.99 for 6-, 8-, or 9-ounce bottle 3-packs. As with other bottle styles, you may pay more for "BPA-free" plastic, depending on the plastic. Playtex VentAire Advanced Crystal Clear 3-packs, for example, will run you up to $18.99. Playtex "Crystal Clear" is a shatterproof baby bottle line made of Tritan and without BPA. All Playtex baby care products are now being made without BPA, so check labels.

Wide bottles

Many baby bottle brands, such as Playtex VentAire, Dr. Brown's, and BornFree, make a wide-neck bottle, which is slightly shorter and broader compared to a standard bottle and used with a corresponding wide nipple.

Pros: Wide-neck bottles and wide nipples are marketed to feel more breast-like to babies and are considered a good choice for "combo moms," those who plan to switch back and forth from breast- to bottle-feeding. "A small nipple makes a harder transition from the bottle to breast-feeding," says Laura Dihel, the mom of a 12-week- old and a 2½-year-old, from Bartlett, Ill., who knows from experience. Wide bottles are available in 4, 5, 8, and 9 ounces and come in glass and plastic made without BPA, in angled or straight sides, with and without bottom venting. Wide nipples are available in slow, medium, fast flow, and Y-cut.

Wide bottles use wide nipples, which have a broader base than standard nipples.

Bottle Bargains

The best prices we've found on major-brand baby bottles were at Wal-Mart and Target. Major baby stores also offer sale and coupon mailers and newspaper inserts, so watch for them. The latest Babies "R" Us mailer we've seen gave a 15 percent discount on bottles and feeding accessories from Philips Avent, Dr. Brown's, Born-Free, MAM, Evenflo, and Playtex. It also offered discounts on hundreds of other baby products.

Cons: You'll pay 50 to 70 cents more for a wide plastic bottle compared to a standard plastic bottle, both made without BPA. And even with a wider feel, there's no guarantee your baby will take to this style of bottle and nipple. But it's worth a try, especially for "combo moms."

Price range: $13.99 to 19.99 for 5- to 9-ounce plastic 2- and 3- bottle packs, made without BPA.

Disposable-liner bottles

The Philips Avent Tempo disposable system Natural Feeding Nurser uses collapsible liners, as does the Playtex Drop-Ins bottle.

In these bottles, a disposable plastic pouch, or liner, fits inside a rigid outer holder, called a nurser. The top edge of the liner fits on top of the nurser's rim. You pour in formula or breast milk and hold the liner in place by fastening the lid (a nipple and bottle ring). The liner collapses as your baby drinks, reducing the tendency for air bubbles to form. The makers of Playtex Drop-Ins and Philips Avent Tempo nursers (two brands that make nurser systems) claim their liners are BPA-free, as is the Playtex nurser (the bottle), but Philips Avent Tempo nurser currently is not. The liner prevents breast milk or formula from making contact with the nurser though, so BPA transfer to your baby might not be an issue.

Pros: Collapsible liners are designed to prevent air from collecting as your baby sucks. Cleanup is easy: You just remove the liner, wash the nipple, and you're done.

Con: You'll need to buy liners continually, which adds to the cost of the system.

Price range: Expect to pay about $13.50 for a starter set with 4- and 8-ounce holders and 10 liners. An 8-ounce nurser costs roughly $3.59 (Playtex) to $7.99 (Philips Avent). Liners will run you another $7.99 to $10.00 for 100 4-ounce or 8- to 10-ounce sizes.

Some Like It Warm

Formula or breast milk is fine right out of the refrigerator, but many babies prefer it warmed up. The best way to heat the bottle is to hold it under a stream of warm water from the faucet or to place it in a bowl of warm water for several minutes. Shake the bottle gently to help distribute the heat. For about $20, you can buy an electric bottle warmer, which has a chamber you fill with water to produce steam heat. That's fine for glass bottles, but BPA researcher vom Saal doesn't recommend such high heat for plastic bottles because of the possibility of additives leaching into the formula or milk. (See Basic Bottle Dos and Don'ts, starting on page 44.)

Don't use a microwave to heat formula or breast milk. It can cause uneven hot spots you may not be able to detect. It can also destroy valuable immunological components of breast milk. And never put disposable bottles in the microwave—the plastic liner could explode when you take it out, possibly scalding you and your baby.

Natural-flow bottles

These bottles, made by Dr. Brown's, have a patented two-piece internal strawlike vent system that's inserted into the center of the bottle. The company says it's designed to eliminate the vacuum that can form when a baby sucks, so there are no air bubbles, reducing the possibility of colic and gas. Dr. Brown's makes polycarbonate, polyethylene, and glass baby bottles with its strawlike vent system.

Pro: The patented design may just work. A recent study published in Gastroenterology Nursing of 36 colicky infants found that using these bottles over a two-week period reduced the infants' crying and fussing. "When my first son was born in 2004, we tried every bottle on the market because he was colicky from day one, and Dr. Brown's worked like a charm," says Cathy S. Hale, a mom of two from Austin, Texas. She now uses Dr. Brown's plastic bottles made without BPA for baby number two because the bottle system worked so well the first time around.

Cons: Compared with other bubble-reducing bottles, such as angle-neck models, these have an extra piece or two to wash. The straws can be hard to clean. You'll need a tiny bristle brush, which comes with the bottles. Replacement

Dr. Brown's bottles come in polycarbonate, polypropylene, and glass.

Most bottles are made to be "more like mom," but the Adiri Natural Nurser truly looks the part.

brushes ($8.99 for a 4-pack) are available where baby bottles are sold.

Price range: $12.99 to $24.99, respectively, for Dr. Brown's 2- or 3-packs and the standard starter kit, which includes one 4-ounce and two 8-ounce bottles, each with a level-one (slow flow) nipple, plus two level-two (medium flow) nipples.

Premium Bottles

These eye-catching bottles, such as the Adiri Natural Nurser, are a class unto themselves, characterized by their unique design. The Adiri, which is a single nipple-bottle unit made from a soft plastic made without BPA, looks and feels breast-like, and has a "petal" vent at the bottom of the bottle designed to reduce colic. The natural shape and feel also help reduce "nipple confusion." Breast- and bottle-feeding each require their own technique—milk flows easily from a bottle, so a baby need only suck with his lips rather than his whole mouth. Trying to switch back and forth from bottle to breast may cause a baby to balk at breast-feeding.

Pros: The nipple and bottle come as a unit, so there are fewer pieces to clean and keep track of. The 8-ounce bottle/nipple comes in three color-coded flow rates: white (stage 1, 0-3 months, slow flow), blue (stage 2, 3-6 months, medium flow), and orange (stage 3, 6+ months, fast flow). To change the flow, you change bottles.

Cons: At $12.99 per bottle, stocking up will cost you a bundle. And because babies have their own preferences, this bottle type may not work for your baby. Despite its design, "My daughter wasn't able to latch onto it," says Courtney Fox, the mom of a 5-month-old and a 3½-year-old from Arlington, VA.

Price range: $12.99 for one or $24.99 for a 2-pack.

Basic Bottle Dos and Don'ts
DO
▶ Wash your hands before preparing your baby's bottle.
▶ Have someone else introduce your baby to the bottle about four weeks into your nursing regimen if you're breast-feeding but want to begin using a bottle. Your baby may associate mom with breast-feeding and may resist if you try to give her the bottle yourself.

- Get tough with glass. Thoroughly clean glass bottles by washing them in the top rack of the dishwasher, or wash bottles in hot tap water with dishwashing detergent and rinse them in hot tap water. You can also use a sterilizer or boil glass bottles in water for 5 to 10 minutes.
- Pamper but still thoroughly clean plastic bottles. Bottles may be termed "dishwasher-safe," but numerous studies have shown that polycarbonate bottles can leach BPA after being exposed to high heat. And researcher vom Saal cautions against putting any plastic product in the dishwasher, a bottle sterilizer, or microwave. Wash plastic baby bottles by hand, not in the dishwasher, using hot, soapy water.
- Wean your baby from a bottle by 12 months of age, if possible. By that time, he will be ready to drink from a sippy cup—just make sure it's not made with polycarbonate. Prolonged bottle use (after 14 months) can cause your baby to consume too much milk and not enough food, and may delay the development of feeding skills. It can also lead to baby-bottle tooth decay, which is painful, difficult to treat, and can cause problems for permanent teeth.
- If you choose formula, protect your baby's teeth by wiping them off with a washcloth or gauze pad after every feeding so that a layer of dental plaque doesn't get the chance to form. For more information, see Protecting Your Baby's Teeth (in the Formula chapter, page 219).

DON'T

- Heat formula or breast milk in the microwave. (see Some Like It Warm on page 43 for details.)
- Give your baby a bottle of milk or formula to suck on during the night or at naptime. The habit can cause baby-bottle tooth decay. Give your baby a bottle only at feeding times and don't mix bottles and bed.
- Prop up your baby with a bottle. This feed-yourself practice can lead to choking, ear infections, and tooth decay (yes, again), as well as less cuddling and human contact, which all babies crave.
- Give your baby a bottle, especially a glass bottle, even with a silicone sleeve, to carry around and "nurse." Not only is it dangerous (babies have been known to throw their bottles), this practice can lead to tooth decay, drinking too much, and sharing bottles with little friends, increasing the risk of colds and other infections. The contents of the bottle can spoil, which can cause food-borne illness, such as bad tummy bugs, which are no fun for your baby or for you.

The Nuances of Nipples

The bottle you choose is important, but as we mentioned, sometimes the nipple, rather than the bottle, makes all the difference to your baby. Some bottles, such as the Second Nature bottle by Regal Lager, are all about the nipple. The Second Nature baby bottle has a silicone nipple that features a thin membrane with multiple microholes. As the baby suckles, the membrane flexes and the holes open, getting larger the more strongly the baby pulls so the baby controls the flow, which mimics what happens during breast-feeding. The First Years/Learning Curve makes the Soothie bottle, which has a nipple that has the same shape and feel as the Soothie pacifier your baby is likely to get in the hospital. (They're distributed through hospitals and sold in retail outlets.) If your baby takes to a Soothie pacifier, you might consider a Soothie bottle. Learning Curve also makes the Breastflow bottle, which has a nipple with a two-part design that requires both suction and compression. It's designed to better mimic breast-feeding, which is the ultimate aim of most bottle/nipple combos, especially for breast-feeding moms. Philips Avent makes the Natural Feeding bottle and nipples, which uses the Airflex technology. As a baby feeds, the skirt on the nipple flexes to allow air into the bottle, preventing any vacuum buildup, so air is released into the bottle, not the baby's tummy.

The Breastflow bottle by Learning Curve has a double nipple system, requiring both suction and compression, that mimics breast-feeding.

Nipples are sold with bottles or as part of a feeding-system starter kit, which usually includes 6-ounce and 9-ounce bottles with both slow-flow and fast-flow nipples and an extra nipple or two for good measure. Nurser kits usually include 4- and 8-ounce bottles, disposable liners, a breast-pump adapter ring, sealing disks, and nipple rings. Nipples are also sold separately, usually in packs of two, for $1.99 to $6.99. Some bottle nipples, such as Munchkin's Tri-Flow Standard Nipple, which gives you a choice of fast, slow, and a medium flow rate by turning the nipple ring, are compatible with different brands of standard bottles so you can mix and match. But most bottle nipples are designed to be used with the same brand of bottle.

Overall, there are no hard and fast rules about how to choose the right bottle/nipple combo for your baby. What works for a friend's baby might not work for yours, which is

■ **Chemical Caution**

Stick with Silicone

Most nipples are made of latex or silicone. Buy silicone nipples only; they're clear or brightly colored, not brownish. Silicone is safer than latex, since some babies may develop a sensitivity or allergy to latex. Clear, odorless, taste free, and heat resistant, silicone is also less porous than latex, so a silicone nipple may be better at resisting bacteria, which can settle into any textured material. Neither silicone nor latex are made with BPA.

why word of mouth or even advice from a lactation consultant on what bottle or nipple to use isn't always helpful. You'll need to be flexible, and experiment until you find a bottle brand and nipple that make feeding your baby a smooth operation.

Features to Consider

Shape. Nipples come in several shapes: the traditional "natural" bell, or dome, shape; a slightly bulbous "orthodontic" design; or a flattened shape. As we mentioned, there are also wide nipples, with a wider base, especially for those babies who switch between bottle and breast. Most nipples are smooth. An exception is the Playtex NaturaLatch, a silicone (best) or latex nipple that's slightly textured instead of smooth around the perimeter of the nipple, to feel more like mom. It's intended to promote latch-on and a slower flow, thus reducing nipple confusion for babies who are both breast- and bottle-fed.

Flow rate. Nipples generally come in three standard flow variations with different-sized holes appropriate for the baby's age: newborn or slow flow (for newborn to 3 months), medium flow (for newborn to 12 months), and fast flow (for babies over 3 months). A nipple should offer some resistance, but not so much that your baby has to struggle to get milk. Generally, younger babies prefer a slower flow; older babies, a faster one (although that's not always the case).

Dr. Brown's also makes a slightly faster, level-four nipple for "more aggressive eaters," usually 6 months-plus, and a Preemie Flow nipple for feeding babies born prematurely. Dr. Brown's and other brands, such as Gerber, also offer a Y-cut (a tri-cut or cross-cut) nipple for cereal or thick juices, but the American Academy of Pediatrics doesn't recommend giving a baby "food" through a bottle because it can lead to excessive weight gain. And it's good for a baby to get used to the eating process—taking bites, resting between bites, and setting an eating pace.

How to Make Sure Nipples are Safe

◆ Before the first use, boil nipples and accessories, such as the vent on Playtex VentAire bottles, according to the manufacturer's directions—usually five minutes.

◆ After each use, wash nipples and accessories in hot, soapy water for about a minute and rinse thoroughly.

◆ Use the nipple with the bottle it's designed to be used for (typically the same brand). Mixing and matching bottle and nipple brands and types can cause the nipple to feed too fast or too slow.

◆ Whichever type of nipple you choose, inspect it regularly, especially when your baby is teething. For safety's sake, replace the nipple at the first sign of tearing, cracking, stickiness, or other signs of excess wear. Your baby could accidentally inhale small pieces, which could cause injury.

◆ Never try to enlarge a nipple hole with a pin. That could cause the nipple to tear and become a choking hazard.

Recommendations

There are pluses and minuses with every nipple and baby bottle. Be prepared to try out bottles and nipples to find a combo your baby likes and that is easy for you to use. To save money while you're experimenting, start with a lower-priced bottle made without BPA, such as Evenflo, and see if your baby likes it. If so, you've got a winner. Some babies accept any bottle. If feeding doesn't go smoothly, you can always switch to a slightly more expensive bottle made without BPA such as Playtex Drop-Ins or Vent-Aire Advanced or Dr. Brown's Natural Flow polyethylene bottles.

If you're having a baby shower, register for a variety of starter kits, which have several bottles of various sizes and nipples in one set. If your baby keeps spitting out or battling with a bottle, or is especially fussy after eating, offer a slower or faster nipple. If that doesn't work, try a premium bottle, such as BornFree or Adiri, which costs over $10 per bottle.

If your baby shows signs of intolerance, such as gas, a rash, persistent vomiting, diarrhea, or any other unusual symptom, talk to your pediatrician. You'll probably need to switch formulas, not the bottles or nipples, if your baby is formula-fed . If you're predominantly or exclusively bottle-feeding, six 4- to 5-ounce bottles will be a good start. If you're supplementing breast-feeding with an occasional bottle, you may need only one or two bottles. Once you settle on a nipple, buy about half a dozen.

chapter

Baby Food

When your baby is 4 to 6 months old, a whole new world of tastes and textures opens up. That's when most babies are ready to start mouthing and chewing "solid" food. It's mushy and messy, but it's an important and exciting milestone.

Baby food manufacturers usually divide their product lines into age-related stages.

Your baby is ready for a real-food fest when he meets some key developmental markers—he sits up with support, holds his neck steady, and shows good head control—and he reaches twice his birth weight. If you eat with your 4-to-6-month-old baby at meals, you'll begin to notice entrée envy: He may reach out and grab for the food you're eating. And you'll be able to spoon-feed your baby without resistance. At about 4 months, most babies lose the tongue-thrust reflex, the tendency for an infant to push his tongue against the roof of his mouth when a spoon is inserted. Still, your baby has a way to go before he is nibbling from your plate.

The first solid food your baby will eat is likely to be a soupy mixture of a tablespoon or two of dry infant rice cereal combined with breast milk or formula. Breast milk or formula will still be on the menu until your baby is a year old or so and makes the switch to cow's milk. If your baby doesn't demonstrate an allergic response— rashes, repeated vomiting, diarrhea, or constant fussiness— after three to five days, you can gradually make the cereal thicker. When your baby is 6 months or so, you can begin to introduce, one at a time, yogurt, oatmeal, barley, wheat, and puréed fruits, vegetables, and meats that you buy in jars or make yourself.

Infant cereal will be your baby's first "solid" food.

When your baby is 7 to 10 months old, you can try bite-sized foods, such as Cheerios, pieces of bread, well-cooked pasta, avocado, cheese, and meats cut up for easy chewing. Your pediatrician will be your best source of advice about what to feed your baby and when, and what to do if you hit a snag—if, say, your baby rejects certain foods or suddenly starts eating less (not unusual when a baby is teething). At each well-child visit, starting at about 4 months, you'll probably get a new list of foods your baby can eat and a list of what to avoid, such as peanut butter. (It's generally a no-no until at least age 2.) You may be told to introduce foods one at a time to make sure your baby isn't allergic to them. Always supervise your child when he's eating.

■ Safety Strategies

Keeping Baby's Food Safe

To keep baby food free of bacteria and other food-borne pathogens that can cause illness:

◆ Wash your hands with soap and water before handling baby food or preparing formula or bottles of breast milk. Not only will you be keeping your baby safe, but regular handwashing also helps protect you from getting sick. Take an alcohol-based sanitizer or baby wipes with you when you take your baby to places like the park so you can clean your hands if soap and water are unavailable.

◆ Don't feed your baby from the jar (or yogurt container) and then put the uneaten portion in the refrigerator. Harmful bacteria from your baby's mouth can multiply in the jar. Solution: Throw it out. If your baby is likely to eat less than a full jar, spoon a portion into a bowl and put the jar in the refrigerator for later. You generally can keep opened jars in the fridge for up to three days in the case of fruits and vegetables, one day for meats, and two days for meat and vegetable combos. Date open jars with a permanent marker.

◆ Don't leave perishable items, including breast milk and infant formula, out of the refrigerator without a cold pack for more than two hours. Throw them away if they've been sitting out longer.

◆ Watch expiration dates on baby food. Listen for the pop of vacuum seals of jarred foods. Don't feed your baby anything that has expired and throw out jars with chipped glass or rusty lids, or that are leaky or without a label.

◆ Don't feed your baby or older child home-canned food; dairy products made from raw, unpasteurized milk; partially cooked or raw meat, poultry, fish, eggs, or foods that may contain them, such as homemade ice cream or eggnog. And no cow's milk before one year of age.

◆ Transport food and filled bottles in an insulated cooler with frozen packs when you're traveling.

◆ Don't give your baby honey if she is less than a year old. It could contain bacteria associated with infant botulism, a potentially life-threatening disease. Also, avoid egg whites and nuts, also not recommended for babies less than a year old.

◆ To freeze homemade baby food, put the mixture in an ice-cube tray. Cover with heavy-duty plastic wrap and freeze. Later, you can pop the frozen food cubes into a freezer bag or airtight container and date it. Store vegetables and fruits up to three months, and meat, fish, and chicken up to eight weeks.

◆ Use dishwashing detergent, hot water, and a clean dishcloth to wash and rinse all utensils that come in contact with the baby's food, including the can opener. Just wiping them with a paper towel isn't enough.

◆ When your baby gets to the finger-food stage, as early as 7 months, cut food into bite-sized pieces. But don't offer your baby nuts, raisins, grapes, popcorn, cherry or grape tomatoes, or hot dogs; they're all choking hazards and not appropriate for infants or toddlers. And always supervise your baby when he's eating. Don't give him food while he's in his car seat, which can be a blind spot, especially if he's still facing rearward.

Shopping Secrets

Besides scouring supermarket circulars, joining a food co-op, or buying in bulk at a wholesale price club, try these money-slashing tactics many new parents swear by:

Consider homemade. Although commercial baby food is convenient and has a certain official, this-is-what-babies-eat quality about it, baby food is something you can make yourself from scratch, except for rice and other instant infant cereal. All you need is a fork, for example, to mash bananas. You can process fibrous foods such as sweet potatoes or meat in a baby-food grinder (found in baby stores), food processor, or blender. Before preparing food, always wash your hands and the food thoroughly, and wash your knives and cutting board with soap and water after you've cut meat, to prevent cross-contamination of other foods with meat juices. Buy the freshest fruits and vegetables and use them within a day or two. Remove peels, seeds, and cores. Boil, bake, or steam them until soft, then purée them well.

A time-saving tip: Pick one day a week to make a big batch, then freeze individual portions in ice-cube trays. (Transfer puréed food from blender to ice-cube tray with a turkey baster.) Or try the cookie sheet method: Place 1- or 2-tablespoon-sized dollops of cooked puréed food on a clean cookie sheet, cover with plastic wrap and place in the freezer. Once the food is frozen solid, remove it from the cookie sheet or ice-cube tray and store it in plastic freezer bags in the freezer. Frozen fruits and vegetable purées will last three months; puréed meat, fish, and chicken will last up to eight weeks. You can mix them together before you freeze them if you'll be using the whole mixture within eight weeks. Good veggies to start with are squash, peas, potatoes, sweet potatoes, and winter squash. Excellent first fruit choices are apples, apricots, bananas, peaches, pears, plums, and prunes. Homemade food can go right from freezer to microwave, but make sure it's just barely warm before serving. Add water, breast milk, or formula to smooth the texture, but omit butter, oil, lard, cream, gravy, sauces, sugar, syrup, salt, and other seasonings. And don't use honey as a sweetener for babies under a year old. It can harbor bacteria related to botulism. Give the food a good stir to dissipate any hot spots before serving.

One other caveat: According to the American Academy of Pediatrics (AAP), fresh beets, turnips, carrots, collard greens, and spinach

■ **Budget Baby**

Cashing in with Coupons

When you come across a valuable baby food coupon, stock up on it. "If I see coupons in the Sunday paper, I not only save them, but order more through a clipping service such as The Coupon Master (*www.thecouponmaster.com*)," says new mom Elizabeth Schomburg, senior vice president of Family Credit Management in Rockford, Ill. "On average, I pay about 10 percent of the value of the coupon for the service. But if I don't count the cost of obtaining the coupon, I often get free jars of baby food if I redeem the coupon during a sale at a grocery store that doubles coupons," she says. Be sure to total up your costs for getting the coupons to know you're actually saving.

Sometimes it can be worth buying extra copies of the newspaper for valuable coupons. You can download coupons from *www.coolsavings.com* and *www.smartsource.com*, but might have to supply personal information, so check privacy policies.

Combining store sales with manufacturer's coupons is the ticket to maximum baby food savings, and it works for other items too, such as diapers and baby wipes.

In addition to coupons in newspapers and magazines, most major baby food manufacturers post offers on their Web sites. These offers are worth checking out, but know that your e-mail address may end up on lists sending junk e-mail you don't want.

may be high in nitrates, chemicals that are rich in the soil in certain parts of the country and can cause an unusual type of anemia (low red-blood-cell count) in infants up to 6 months of age. Unfortunately, you can't solve this problem by buying organic produce. Because organic produce is raised without synthetic fertilizer, it can sometimes be lower in nitrates. But unfortunately there are too many variables to know for sure.

The AAP recommends buying commercially prepared forms of these foods, especially when your child is an infant. Baby food companies screen the produce for nitrates and avoid using vegetables with high levels of these chemicals.

Shop outside the baby-food aisle. If you compare the prices of commercial baby foods to the stuff you eat yourself, you're apt to find that ounce per ounce, baby food costs significantly more. Fresh and canned fruits and vegetables are easy, economical alternatives to commercial baby food. Canned pumpkin, for example, is well puréed, as are many types of applesauce (buy one without added sugar). You can purée the food more at home. Baby-food cookbooks have suggestions and recipes. You might also ask your pediatrician for advice.

Get a store card. With a preferred-shopper card, you receive the sale prices published in the weekly circular, in the newspaper, or online on products like baby food without clipping coupons.

Shop online. Shopping online for baby food may not save you money because shipping or delivery charges factor into your total costs, but it could save gas, time, and a trip to the supermarket, which isn't always easy to pull off when you've got a new baby on board. If your local supermarket doesn't offer online shopping, go to the source. Some manufacturers, such as Earth's Best, have an online store where you can order baby food at prices comparable to what you'd pay at a brick-and-mortar store. Amazon.com also offers a limited variety of baby food.

What's Available

The major brands of baby food are Beech-Nut (*www.beechnut.com*) and Gerber (*www.gerber.com*). The major organic lines are Earth's Best (*www.earthsbest.com*) and Gerber Organic (*www.gerber.com*).

Most pediatricians recommend starting your baby on commercial infant rice cereal. It's easy to digest and mixes easily with breast milk or formula. Some cereals have fruit, which is appropriate after your baby has mastered the plain stuff. Commercial makers of jarred baby food usually divide their product line into three stages: beginner (stage 1), intermediate (stage 2), and toddler (stage 3). Stage 1 foods are made for babies just starting on solids. They're usually a single food, puréed for easy swallowing. Beginner vegetables in jars are peas, carrots, green beans, squash, and sweet potatoes. Fruits are applesauce, bananas, peaches, pears, and prunes.

> **Most pediatricians recommend starting your baby on infant rice cereal."**

Stage 1 foods have the plainest formulations without sauces or flavorings. Sweet potatoes are sweet potatoes and peas are peas. Intermediate (stage 2) foods are for more experienced eaters (at about 6 to 8 months). At this point, the choices are more interesting because foods are combined to improve taste and offer new textures, such as apples and chicken, or turkey and rice—and you don't have to open two jars. Stage 2 foods have a smooth texture, but are not as fine as beginner foods. Stage 3 foods are for children 7 to 9 months and older, babies who are learning to chew and mash. At this stage, chunkier, larger portions, such as Gerber Organic's Herbed Chicken with Pasta, keep up with growing appetites. Some parents never bother with stage 3 but simply start giving their baby normal fare, still mashed and cut up

■ **Chemical Caution**

Go with Glass or Ceramic

When heating baby food in the microwave, heat it right in the glass jar according to package directions (if your baby will eat the entire portion), or use a heatable glass dish (Pyrex) or any microwaveable ceramic dish instead of a plastic bowl or the plastic tub the food comes in. Even if plastic bowls are labeled microwave safe—meaning they can withstand heat—some bowls may be a source of chemicals that may impact a baby's development and reproductive system.

According to the Environmental Protection Agency, chemicals in some types of plastic containers may leach into foods when the container is heated. In addition, studies suggest that washing plastic in the dishwasher can also degrade it over time, increasing the possibility of leaching. So handwash any plastic dishes and utensils your baby uses for dining with soap and moderately hot water. Discard any clear plastic containers that no longer look clear, indicating the plastic is permanently damaged and more prone to leaching.

for easy chewing and swallowing. Infant juices are available, but many are no different from the kind marketed to adults. Avoid citrus juice until your pediatrician gives you the go-ahead, usually when your baby is around 6 months old. It can upset little stomachs.

In addition to basic juices such as apple and white grape, there are many combinations, some of which contain yogurt or are fruit-vegetable blends. Some also have added calcium and vitamin C. Go easy on the juice, though. Too much can cause diarrhea and gas, and contribute to tooth decay. And when babies drink juice, they may take in less breast milk or formula, which contain the nutrients they really need. The AAP recommends limiting fruit juice to no more than 4 to 6 ounces per day from 6 months to 6 years of age, and making it part of a meal, not a snack. Fruit drinks aren't nutritionally equal to fruit juice. Check the label to be sure you're giving your child 100 percent juice. The juice your child drinks should be pasteurized (flash-heated to kill pathogens). Fresh-squeezed juice isn't pasteurized.

Once your baby graduates to cow's milk at the one-year mark, keep in mind that juice fortified with calcium and vitamin D isn't a milk substitute. Milk has a whole package of nutrients, including riboflavin, phosphorus, zinc, and essential amino acids that help form strong bones. Fortified juice doesn't. And don't put your baby to bed with a bottle of juice or milk; that can lead to tooth decay.

Food Additives

Just as supermarket shelves are becoming increasingly complex for adults to evaluate (think vitamin-fortified Diet Coke, eggs enriched with omega-3 fatty acids, and bread spreads that supposedly reduce cholesterol), the baby food aisle is following suit. Here are the most common additives you'll find:

Yogurt and infant formula with probiotics. Research suggests that probiotics—"good," live bacteria—may help improve the health of the digestive tract. Friendly bacteria normally reside in the gut, where they help break down foods and medicine and keep disease-causing bugs in check. Antibiotics and certain gastrointestinal illnesses can trigger diarrhea by killing off or overwhelming our normal microbes. Probiotics can help counteract those effects. Several studies now suggest that infants on antibiotics or suffering from diarrhea may get some relief when they're fed yogurt with probiotic strains.

To produce the clinical benefit, however, a serving of any probiotic yogurt needs to contain at least 100 million live cultures. Typically, products contain 1 billion to 10 billion per dose or serving, says Mary Ellen Sanders, Ph.D., a probiotic consultant in Centennial, Colorado. Check the container to see if the ingredients list includes live cultures. At least one infant formula also contains probiotics. For more information, see the Formula chapter, page 217.

Should you try it/buy it? The jury is still out about the benefits of probiotics. So before giving your child food or formula containing them, talk to your pediatrician. If you're considering probiotics as a cure, your doctor can also evaluate what is actually causing any possible stomach upsets and diarrhea. Likewise, don't try a probiotic-fortified infant formula without discussing the issue with your pediatrician. If you supplement infant formula with breast-feeding, a probiotic formula probably isn't necessary since breast milk is a natural source of probiotics.

Baby food with added DHA or ARA. DHA and ARA are omega-3 fatty acids found in breast milk and certain foods, such as fish and eggs. DHA and ARA may be important for infant eyesight and brain development. Beech-Nut and Gerber each offer a line of foods—including fruits, vegetables, cereals, yogurt blends, and even wild salmon, brown rice, and macaroni

Beech-Nut DHA Plus+ Sweet Potatoes & Wild Alaskan Salmon gets its DHA from the salmon.

and cheese—that contain DHA. Other manufacturers may follow suit. The lines currently available tend to cost a few cents more per ounce than regular baby food, but less than most organic options. DHA is now added to most brands of infant formula.

Should you try it/buy it? According to the Food and Drug Administration, which approved the addition of DHA and ARA, the scientific evidence is mixed as to whether the addition of these substances is beneficial. Some studies of infants suggest that including these fatty acids in infant formulas may have positive effects on visual function and neural development over the short term. Other studies of infants don't confirm these benefits. There are no currently published reports from clinical studies that address whether any long-term beneficial effects exist. Again, talk to your pediatrician. However, if you continue to breast-feed after your baby begins eating solid food, these additives aren't necessary because they're naturally found in breast milk anyway. If your pediatrician approves of giving your baby DHA-fortified foods, you can find them in stores nationwide.

Prebiotics. The Beech-Nut DHA line also contains prebiotics, including fructooligosaccharides (FOS) and, in some instances, inulin, which is derived from chicory root, among others. Prebiotics are non-digestible ingredients that work with your native beneficial bacteria to help them do their good work in the digestive tract. They may also improve calcium absorption.

Should you try it/buy it? Again, ask your pediatrician for a recommendation. The costs are roughly the same for baby food with and without this additive. If you're breast-feeding, you can skip this purchase (and buy regular baby food) since breast milk is a natural source of prebiotics.

Fiber and whey protein. Protein is essential for growth. Some manufacturers are also adding soluble fiber and extra protein to their products. Beech-Nut's Good Morning and Good Evening lines of jarred baby food and infant cereal, for example, contain oat bran and whey protein, respectively. The addition of fiber slows digestion, so energy is released steadily following a meal.

Should you try it/buy it? You'll need to consult two experts here: your pediatrician and your baby. Chances are if your baby is eating regularly and normally, she won't need these extras. And sometimes it all boils down to what your baby likes and what agrees with her tummy.

That might take a fair amount of trial and error, regardless of whether your child is a picky eater or not.

Is Organic Better for Your Baby?

Children may be at risk of higher exposure to the possible toxins found in nonorganic food because baby food is often made up of condensed fruits

If you want to go organic, there are plenty of organic baby food options.

or vegetables, potentially concentrating pesticide residues. Children's developing immune, central-nervous, and hormonal systems may be especially vulnerable to damage from toxic chemicals. Do organically grown foods contain fewer pesticide residues than conventionally grown foods? According to our evidence, the answer is yes. A study published in the peer-reviewed journal Food Additives & Contaminants and co-authored by a senior scientist at Consumers Union showed that organic foods had residues of fewer pesticides that were present at lower levels than those found in conventionally grown foods. In general, foods produced organically or conventionally contain the same kinds and amounts of vitamins and minerals.

Given the health concerns associated with levels of many pesticide residues, it makes sense to buy organic food for your baby when you can, especially those fruits and vegetables that typically carry the highest residue levels. We've found that it can be worth paying more for organic apples, peaches, spinach, milk, and beef to avoid chemicals found in the conventionally produced versions of those items.

You'll find a cornucopia of organic options in the baby food section from two major brands: Earth's Best and Gerber Organic. Natural and organic food markets often carry their own organic lines as well as exclusive premium brands. Plum Organics (*www.plumorganics.com*) and Happy Baby (*www.happybabyfood.com*) are frozen organic baby food lines, and Homemade Baby (*www.homemadebaby.com*) can be found in the chilled dairy section. Some local businesses also offer home deliveries of their own organic baby food. To find other organic options in your area, visit *www.theorganicpages.com* and *www.eatwellguide.org*.

Baby food labeled "USDA organic" must meet standards set by the United States Department of Agriculture and be at least 95 percent organic, meaning that all but 5 percent of the content was produced without conventional pesticides and fertilizers. Organic food can't be irradiated (a one-time exposure to radiation intended to kill pathogens such as salmonella, listeria, or *E. coli*), genetically modified (a technique that alters a plant's DNA), or produced with hormones or antibiotics. Animals used in meat products must be fed organically grown feed.

USDA's National Organic Program accredits certifiers and they, in turn, certify organic producers and processors. Other terms found on food labels, such as "natural," "free-range," and "hormone-free," don't mean organic. Only food that has been certified to meet the USDA organic standards can be legally labeled "organic."

Organic for Less

If you buy organic food for your baby, or your whole family, it will cost you. In our informal research, we paid as much as 48 percent more for jarred organic baby food than for nonorganic versions (60 cents more for each 4-ounce jar of baby food). Still, there are ways to save. Try these thrifty tips:

Supermarket comparison-shop. Check several local grocery stores to find the lowest prices on frequently purchased organic food. We found a 4-ounce jar of organic baby food in the New York area for as little as 69 cents a jar. Also, stock up on sale items. We found 4-ounce jars of store-brand organic baby food on sale for 49 cents each at a national organic foods supermarket, a 28-percent discount. And keep in mind that fresh organic produce is often cheaper in season.

Hit the farmers' market. Price organic produce at your supermarket so you know you're getting the best buy, and see if you can bargain. Check *www.localharvest.org* for organic growers and market listings.

Join the farm team. Buy a share in an organic farm structured as a community supported agricultural (CSA) operation. The produce almost always is cheaper than at a farmers' market and often costs less than the same nonorganic items at a supermarket. For a list of CSA farms, go to *www.localharvest.org/csa* and then contact the farms in your area to ask if they are certified organic. If so, they should be able to produce evidence of certification. If they sell less than $5,000 worth of produce a year, they may not be certified but should have documentation showing that they follow organic growing practices.

Buy in bulk. Some organic baby food lines sell variety packs of 12 4-ounce jars at a savings of a few cents a jar over single-jar purchases. Stock up when variety packs go on sale and you can save even more.

Recommendations

Let your pediatrician be your guide about what to feed your baby and when to move to the next stage. Compare the ingredients and nutritional value of commercial baby food and always check "use-by" dates listed on the label or lid. If the date has passed, don't buy or use the food. All baby food jars have a depressed area, or "button," in the center of the lid. Reject any jars with a popped-out button—an indication that the product has been opened or the seal broken. Do the same for any jars that are sticky, stained, or cracked. If budget is the bottom line, buy the cheapest baby food according to your baby's age and stage by comparing unit prices in the store and stocking up on sale items.

chapter

Backpack Carriers

A backpack carrier lets you travel in ways you never thought possible with a baby, including a rugged, backcountry hike or snow-shoeing. It can often let you go where a stroller can't, give your baby a new perspective on the world, and offer you hands-free mobility.

If you'll be venturing into the wilderness, you'll need a "backcountry" baby carrier like this Rumba SS 08, which is rated to carry up to 70 pounds.

Backpack carriers aren't just for the great outdoors, though. Many parents report that they also use backpack carriers for less exotic trips to the beach, the mall, the zoo, or even Disney World. Most backpack carriers are only intended for children old enough to sit up independently, and who have full head and neck control, usually by at least 6 months of age. Although some carriers feature moldable head and neck support for children as young as 3 months, we don't recommend using a backpack carrier until your child has full head and neck control. Backpack carriers can typically be used for a child and gear totaling 30 to 50 pounds, although some models are rated to carry as much as 70 pounds. The weight of the pack itself can add another 4 to 7 pounds to your load, so consider that when choosing a pack. A heavy carrier might make it more difficult to carry your child.

A mirror helps you keep an eye on your little one. This Kelty KIDS child view mirror, sold separately, attaches with a hook and loop to Kelty KIDS carriers.

Most backpack carriers have an aluminum or aluminum alloy frame, which together with the waist or hip belt distribute a baby's weight along your back, shoulders, and hips, rather than putting it all on your shoulders and neck as do some front soft infant carriers, especially ones without a waist belt. Although the weight is on your back, "your entire upper torso is supporting it," says Anne Coffman, a physical therapist from New Berlin, Wis., and a member of the American Physical Therapy Association as well as the mother of two. This tot-toter is a superior choice when your child can sit up completely by herself, has full head and neck control, and fits comfortably into the pack. But don't expect a backpack carrier to make your load light. A 25-pound child will still feel heavy after a while, even if her weight is distributed evenly over your hips with maximum padding.

Most backpack carriers come with a built-in stand that make loading and mounting easier, but they definitely aren't stable enough to be used as a baby seat on the ground or any other surface. Seats and shoulder harnesses are made of moisture-resistant fabric. Many models have multiple positions for the wearer and the child. Carriers usually have densely padded shoulder straps and hip belts, storage compartments, sun/rain hoods, and toy loops. Parent extras may include a changing pad, a removable diaper bag, a rearview mirror so you can watch your baby without removing your pack, a removable insulated bottle holder, a detachable pillow so your child can nap on the go, and multistorage compartments for all the baby gear you'll be carrying on your back, too.

Backpack carriers, though, can be cumbersome and expensive. Many are designed for the great outdoors, and may be more pack than you need if your idea of an adventure is a trek to the grocery store with your baby on board. Some, such as the Deuter Kid Comfort III (approximately $239), have a substantial aluminum frame that takes up a lot of storage space. Still, some backpacks are now better designed for everyday use. These "urban" carriers look more like a regular backpack, but still have a structured frame to support your child. They're less bulky than some of the more traditional backpack carriers and are more packable for short trips that are part of your daily routine.

With urban backpack carriers like the Kelty TC 1.1 shown here, think everyday, not expedition.

Shopping Secrets

Bring your baby. When your baby is the right age and weight, take him shopping for a backpack carrier and if he is game, do test runs in the store. Try a backpack with a coat on you and your bundled-up child in the pack if you expect to wear it during colder months.

Practice, practice. With the help of a knowledgeable salesperson, practice putting the carrier on and taking it off. Have your partner do the same to make sure it fits you both comfortably. If you and your partner will be switching the pack back and forth, try adjusting the straps to fit your torso to see if it's easy to do. Walk with the backpack to be sure the frame doesn't hit the back of your head, that it's not too long for your height, that the straps fit properly so they won't slip off your shoulders, and that the frame doesn't start to dig into your lower back after a few minutes. "You should be able to walk comfortably with your arms at your sides," says Coffman. Carrier directions should be clear and easy to follow.

Look for a snug-fitting safety harness. The safest backpack carriers have a five-point harness for the child that connects the shoulder straps with the crotch, torso, and hip restraints for a snug fit. Don't purchase a carrier that relies on a lap belt that's separate from the shoulder and crotch straps, leaving openings at the side that could potentially be big enough for a child to slip through. Such slips can sometimes occur when children pull their legs up and subsequently put both feet and legs into one opening; they've been the reason for the recall of several models. We consider that style of harness inadequate for a small child.

Be wary of secondhand equipment. Many parents pick up a backpack carrier at a tag sale. If you decide to buy used, check for recalled brands first at *www.cpsc.gov*. Inspect carriers for excessive wear, which can dangerously weaken straps and seams. Make sure the instructions/owner's manual comes with the used backpack carrier. Don't use a carrier for which you have no instructions, no matter how simple it might seem. Accidents can happen too easily.

What's Available

Some brands of backpack carriers, in alphabetical order, are Baby Trend (*www.babytrend.com*), Chicco (*www.chiccousa.com*), Deuter (*www.deuter.com*), Evenflo (*www.evenflo.com*), Kelty Kids (*www.keltykids.com*), Macpac (*www.macpac.co.nz*), Phil & Teds (*www.philandteds.com*), REI (*www.rei.com*), and Sherpani (*www.sherpani.us*). You'll find the widest selection of these major brands at camping/outdoor outlets, specialty Web sites—such as *www.childcarriers.com*, which has a handy brand comparison chart—and catalogs and mass merchandisers—such as Target (*www.target.com*)—rather than in baby stores. Prices range from $50 to $320.

As of January 1, 2008 the Juvenile Products Manufacturers Association (JPMA) began certifying framed backpack carriers that meet requirements set by standards developer ASTM International, including strength, stability, and leg-opening safety. To date, only two brands of framed carrier, Chicco and Kelty Kids, are JPMA-certified.

The Chicco Smart Support Backpack is JPMA-certified.

Features to Consider

Important factors to consider in evaluating backpack carriers are how much you'll use a backpack carrier and your baby's comfort and safety (not to mention yours). Many models differ by only a feature or two, which can add to the cost (or reduce it). Some features may be more important to you than others. Your best bet is to make a list of must-have features, such as those we cite below, and then try on and compare the various models.

The cockpit. Higher-end backpack carriers tend to offer a roomier ride for a baby and may include stirrups so a baby's feet don't dangle. That support may help reduce the chances your baby's feet will fall asleep as you're plodding along. Padding is key. Some parents say that their children seem happier in a cushier ride. On framed and urban backpack carriers, look for an adjustable five-point harness (two straps over the shoulders, two for the thighs, and a crotch strap), sometimes also called a "chest plate."

Fabrics. Backpack carriers are likely to be made of durable nylon similar to what's used in suitcases. Fabrics vary from lightweight to heavy-duty. The material should be sturdy, moisture-resistant, and easy to clean by wiping with a mild detergent. (Let the carrier air out a few days when it gets wet.) Light-reflecting piping or stripes can help drivers see you, but keep a safe distance from traffic. Avoid using a carrier after dark or anytime visibility is poor.

Fasteners. Carriers have a variety of buckles and fasteners for shoulder and waist straps and the baby's seat. Buckles that hold shoulder and waist straps should be easy to adjust and should hold the straps tightly so they can't work loose when the carrier is in use. Snaps and buckles should be sturdy and difficult for babies to unfasten.

Foldability. A framed backpack carrier that can easily be folded flat to fit in the trunk of your car or in a closet is a plus.

Kickstand. The kickstand should lock firmly in the open position and have hinges with spacers so fingers don't get pinched. When the carrier is on your back, the kickstand should close so it doesn't snag on objects as you walk. When the carrier is on the ground with the kickstand open, it should be hard to tip over. However, as we mentioned, never use a carrier with a stand as a baby seat.

Leg openings. These should be fully adjustable to fit snugly around your baby's legs.

Padding. Look for a backpack carrier with padding that covers the metal frame near your baby's face. You'll want padding that's firm rather than mushy.

Seats and seat belts. Look for a seat that adjusts to different baby sizes, so your baby can see over your shoulder from the beginning, but not so high that your child could fall out. The cockpit should be padded for comfort and have enough depth to support your baby's back. It should have leg openings that can be adjusted to be small enough to prevent your baby from slipping out. Check all buckles and other securing hardware and be sure seams won't tear and straps won't slip.

Shoulder, waist, and chest straps. Shoulder-strap padding should be firm and wide. Putting your baby in and strapping the carrier on should be fairly simple. Shoulder straps should have an adjustable chest buckle that keeps straps on your shoulders and prevents chafing at the neck. They should also be adjustable even while you're carrying your baby. Overall, look for as much flexibility in the straps as possible. The chest strap should be adjustable in height and length; the waist belt should be vertically adjustable. But don't be swayed by fancy-looking padding, particularly on shoulder straps, which shouldn't take a lot of stress anyway. Fit and firmness are more important than padding thickness, especially at the shoulder. In the lumbar area, well-made carriers may have a large pad in the middle of the waist strap for adults that helps distribute the baby's weight from your shoulders to your hips and pelvic area, and prevents strain on your lower back. Carrying the weight lower is definitely more comfortable. In the store, fasten the belt to see if it's long enough and neither too high nor too low when the carrier is in place.

> "Carrying the weight lower is definitely more comfortable."

Storage pouches. If you can't leave your house without lots of toys, an extra bottle, snacks, and a diaper stash, or you'll be traveling with your baby on overnight expeditions, you'll need a carrier with ample storage. Some models have only a small pouch for a cell phone or bottle. Others are loaded with pockets, pouches, and toy loops, with handy ones built into the waist belt. Zippered pouches or ones with a Velcro closure are better because things can't fall out. Plastic-lined pockets are good for damp items. Some heavy-duty carriers for serious hiking have removable pouch accessories so you can choose what to add or remove. But be mindful not to exceed the weight maximum of the carrier you choose.

Sun/weather shield. Since a baby's eyes and skin are sensitive, you'll need to protect her from the sun and bad weather. Most backpack carriers come with a sun/weather shield or offer them as an accessory. If the carrier you select doesn't come with a shield, buy one separately on the spot. Not all sun/weather shields are created equal. The better shields are "hoods" that provide full coverage. Even with a good shield, be sure

Carrier Cautions

When using a backpack carrier, follow these safety tips:

◆ Buckle and tighten all straps on the safety harness so that your child isn't tempted to climb out when you're on the go. Serious injuries, including skull fractures and concussions, can occur when children fall from carriers.

◆ Doublecheck that buckles, snaps, straps, and adjustments are secure before each use. Snaps can open and adjustments may be incorrectly made, which pose safety hazards.

◆ When your child is in the carrier, especially as he gets older, his head could be higher than yours. Be mindful of obstacles at your child's height, such as door frames and tree branches.

◆ Keep your baby's fingers away from the frame joints, especially when you're folding the backpack.

◆ Check on your child from time to time. Children can become overheated in warm weather or be exposed to harmful rays from the sun. See that your child's legs and arms are secure in the leg and arm openings, but also that his circulation isn't impaired in any way. Since your baby can't tell you if his legs are falling asleep, take frequent breaks as a precaution.

◆ Check the backpack periodically for ripped seams, missing or loose fasteners, and frayed seats or straps. Stop using a carrier with frayed seams, which can give way suddenly.

◆ Don't lean over when using a backpack carrier. Bend your knees, not at your waist, to keep your baby from falling out when you're reaching for something low.

◆ Never carry the child in a pack while in a moving vehicle or on an airplane, and never use the carrier as a substitute for a certified child car seat. When you're traveling by car or plane, always secure your child in the appropriate child seat.

◆ Even though a backpack carrier can give you the freedom to venture where a stroller can't, don't use one in areas where you won't have firm footing, such as hiking on wet rocks, big boulders, icy terrain, or wet, leafy trails. Don't hike after dark when visibility is poor.

◆ Don't leave your child unattended in a backpack carrier. Your child shouldn't be in a carrier unless the pack is on your back. In other words, don't place your baby in a backpack carrier and then perch her on a kitchen counter, couch, bed, or picnic table, even for a moment. Babies can fall or suffocate much faster than you might think.

◆ Don't carry more than one child in a backpack carrier at a time.

◆ Only use the carrier for walking, not sporting activities.

◆ Metal heats up. If your backpack has been in the sun, let it cool before putting your child into it.

to have protective clothing for your baby—a hat with a 3-inch brim or a bill facing forward and a long-sleeved shirt and long pants made from tightly woven cotton.

Recommendations

Before buying a backpack carrier, think about how much you'll use it. That will help you determine what to spend. We've found that price, however, isn't necessarily a reliable indicator of quality. Consider sharing with neighbors if you expect to use a backpack carrier only occasionally.

If you plan longer or more frequent outings with your baby, consider models that will have more storage features, better padding, and a more comfortable fit. As we mentioned, don't use a backpack carrier until your child can sit up unassisted (usually at 6 months) and has full head and neck control.

Before you venture out, become familiar with your backpack carrier. If the directions are unclear, for example, about how to secure your child in a carrier seat, use a carrier seat's lap belt, or assemble an accessory such as a rain hood, call the manufacturer. Keep all instructions for future reference. Don't wing it. Unclear directions and a lack of understanding can be dangerous since both your and your child's safety depend on setting up a backpack carrier and adjusting the straps properly.

Make sure your backpack carrier has a good sun shield like the one on this Kelty FC 3.0 hiking model.

Be sure to send in the registration card so you'll be notified in the event of a recall.

Finally, before doing a lot of walking with a carrier, be in good physical shape. It's easy to underestimate, but you'll need a strong back, hips, and quadriceps to lug around a baby. Stay within the recommended weight limits. When your child outgrows the backpack carrier, stop using it.

5

chapter

Bathtubs

Forget about the towel-lined sink you may have been bathed in as a baby. Although that's certainly still an option, there are plenty of portable bathtubs on the market these days that make bathtime a whole lot easier—and more fun for you and your baby.

A baby bathtub like this one from Primo makes bathtime easier.

A baby bathtub provides an appropriately compact place for bathing. It can be placed in a sink, in a regular bathtub, on a counter or kitchen table, or on the floor. However, no matter where you bathe your baby, be sure to keep a hand on her at all times to prevent her from sliding underwater.

Many tubs have a removable mesh or fabric inner cradle so a baby can't move around inside too much. Others have a foam-lined contoured interior that allows a baby who can't sit up yet to relax in a semi-upright position. In any case, you'll use a baby bathtub for less time than you may think. At about 6 months, when your baby can sit up, she'll probably be too big to be bathed in an infant tub that sits in the sink. Although there are tubs on the market that are designed for babies from newborn to toddler or up to 25 pounds, she'll probably outgrow this style of baby bathtub too, when she's about 9 months old. Then it's time to move your baby to a regular bathtub that contains only a small amount of water.

Bath Basics

Before we get into the specifics of what's on the market, here are a few bathtime tips. For starters, don't worry about giving your baby an official bath right away. Except for sponge baths, bathing shouldn't start until the stump of your baby's umbilical cord falls off (between one and three weeks post-delivery). After that, you can give your baby a bath every day if you find it necessary, although two to three times a week is better because daily bathing can dry out a baby's tender skin. In addition to the tub, you'll need a soft towel (preferably hooded to cradle your baby's head), a baby washcloth, and an unscented, hypoallergenic baby body wash that doubles as shampoo.

There are a variety of baby bathtubs on the market. Keep in mind that just about any tub you buy will be awkward to use at first, mainly because bathing a wiggly baby—who may dislike temperature changes and being put in water—is awkward and daunting for even the most experienced parent. In other words, at first you'll just want to get the job done—and fast. Expect your baby to protest the first couple of times. After that, she will probably grow to enjoy bathtime—and so will you. But remember, when your baby is in the bath, you should always have a hand on her.

- **Safety Strategies**

Don't Buy a Baby Bath Seat

The Juvenile Products Manufacturers Association has certified two brands of baby bath seats: Safety 1st and Learning Curve/The First Years and there is a voluntary industry safety standard. Even so, we don't recommend them or any other bath seats.

Based on Consumer Product Safety Commission data, 138 deaths and an estimated 650 hospital-treated injuries linked to baby bath seats occurred between 1994 and 2005, the latest year for which figures are available. Baby bath seats can tip over, toddlers sometimes slip through the leg holes, and kids often try to climb out of or over the seat. In addition, the suction cups at the bottom of a baby bath seat must be attached to a smooth surface, and if the tub is a slip-resistant or nonskid model, the suction cups will not adhere and the bath seat will slip. Even if the seat seems secured to the bottom or side of the tub, it can dislodge and tip, and keep a helpless baby's face underwater. And despite warning labels, the seats can induce a false sense of security, leading parents to think they can turn their back on the baby for a short time. In many

A baby bath seat, even one that attaches to the tub, is not recommended.

drowning cases, parents had left the room only momentarily. Given the troubled history of baby bath seats, we continue to believe parents should avoid this product. Avoid using any baby bath seat, including the kind with a support "arm" that attaches to the side of the tub.

What's Available

Some brands of baby bathtubs are, in alphabetical order: Fisher-Price (*www.fisher-price.com*), Juvenile Solutions (*www.juvenilesolutions.com*), Kel-Gar (*www.kelgar.com*), 4moms (*www.4momsonline.com*), Learning Curve/The First Years (*www.learningcurve.com*), Primo (*www.primobaby.com*), Prince Lionheart (*www.princelionheart.com*), Safety 1st (*www.safety1st.com*), and Summer Infant (*www.summerinfant.com*). You'll see basic tubs that are flat on the bottom, tubs with contoured interiors or inserts that help position a baby's head above water, and tubs with supportive, internal nylon mesh slings featuring padded headrests that cradle newborns. You'll also see inserts that don't include a tub; they're little more than a sling that can be used in both a baby tub and a sink to prop your baby up. You'll also find tubs designed to fit in the sink, then

Make the Most of Tubtime Fun

By the time your baby is 9 to 10 months old, she'll begin to understand the notion of object permanence—that if you or an object is out of sight, you or it still exists. To reinforce that concept and add an element of surprise, try this take on peek-a-boo: "During bathtime, have toys disappear under a washcloth, then magically reappear," suggests Stacy DeBroff, founder of MomCentral.com. Or cover your face with a towel, and then uncover it—again and again.

convert to a tub that can be placed in a regular bathtub when your baby can sit up. Some tubs are designed to fit in a regular tub from the start. You can even find tubs with many of these features that fold for more compact storage.

One of the newest tubs on the market is the WashPOD by Prince Lionheart; it's a baby bath bucket with a foam insert on the bottom that holds your baby vertically in the water, to simulate the womb, according to the company. (Of course, babies are normally upside down in the womb.) Since your baby is upright and the design is compact, it can be tough to reach knee crevices, or scrub off diaper rash cream. Your baby may also outgrow it quickly. Although we haven't tested the WashPOD, we're not convinced this new tub type is practical or superior to conventional baby bathtubs. Bathtubs range from $7.99 (for a bath sling) to $40 (for an infant tub—with a built-in digital thermometer—that allows "dirty" water to drain and fresh water from the faucet to circulate as baby bathes).

The WashPOD holds your baby upright.

Bath seats designed to be used in a regular tub by a baby who is able to sit up are available, but we don't recommend them. (See Don't Buy a Baby Bath Seat, page 71.) There are also inflatable tubs that fit inside a regular bathtub to give your baby a padded space to bathe in, but we don't recommend those either because they can be dangerous: Parents might put these in a regular bathtub with water in it. The inflatable tub can then float and tip.

Features to Consider

Contoured design with padded lining. In lieu of a sling, a contoured design is a must for keeping a baby from sliding around too much.

A drain with an attached plug. This can make the tub easier to empty. A large drain plug allows for quicker post-bath cleanup.

Temperature indicator. Some models of bathtubs, such as The First Years Sure Comfort Deluxe Newborn-to-Toddler Tub, have a temperature indicator—a drain plug or a temperature strip changes color when the water is too hot for a baby. In our tests, we found these features to be impractical. It's too difficult to keep track of a temperature strip or the shade of a plug when you're bathing a baby. Don't bother with these high-tech extras when you're shopping.

The 4moms Cleanwater Infant Tub ($40) goes a step further in gauging water temperature. It has a built-in digital thermometer that changes color when baby bath water is too hot, too cold, or just right (95°F) and an audible alert sounds when water temperature is too high as well. We haven't tested the accuracy of the thermometer on this model. The tub is designed to fill from the faucet and continuously drain during bathtime and needs an ample sink to accommodate it.

Even with a temperature indicator, double-check the temperature by testing the water with your elbow before putting your baby in the tub or rinsing him off; it should feel comfortably warm. Your elbow is more sensitive than your hand, so it will give you a better sense of whether the water temperature is in a good range for your baby's sensitive skin.

Convertibility. Many tubs, such as the Fisher-Price Aquarium and Rainforest Bath Centers, The First Years Sure Comfort Deluxe Newborn-to-Toddler Tub, and Primo's EuroBath, are made to last from newborn to toddler. The Aquarium and Rainforest Bath Centers include a hammock-like padded infant cradle that you take out when your baby can sit up unassisted. The EuroBath is molded to support a baby under both arms; a crotch post keeps babies from slipping forward in the water. With this model, babies can be bathed in a reclining position from birth to 6 months. Then, from 6 to 24 months, they sit upright facing the other direction;

Some baby bathtubs have a digital temperature indicator, but use "an elbow test" as well. Water should feel warm, not hot.

the older-baby end of the tub has less infrastructure and more wiggle room. A convertible tub, though, probably won't last you as long as manufacturers claim. As we mentioned, a convertible tub will probably buy you three additional months or so, but not much more.

Foldability. Some tubs, like the Summer Infant Newborn-to-Toddler Fold Away Baby Bath, fold in half for easy storage or travel. The downside? Some foldable tubs can be compact; your baby may grow out of it quickly. To make sure a foldable tub won't leak, practice at first with a small amount of water.

An internal mesh sling/cradle. It's cozy and supportive, especially for a newborn. Some models, like the Mother's Touch Large Comfort Bather by Summer Infant, come with a two-position backrest for added comfort. Some fabric slings have steel rods that support the infrastructure. We think steel rods might become uncomfortable when your baby kicks his legs or moves from side to side. Other slings are hammock-like and don't have steel rods. Look for those.

Bathtubs with slings like the Sure Comfort Deluxe Newborn-to-Toddler Tub from The Learning Curve/First Years help contain a slippery newborn.

Fresh-water rinse. Some tubs, such as the Newborn-to-Toddler Bath Center and Shower by Summer Infant, feature a separate, battery-powered shower unit that lets you rinse your baby with fresh water from the sink instead of using bath water. The style can be unwieldy because you may need more hands than you have—one hand on the baby, another to wash him, then two additional hands to use the shower feature. In our tests, we found that a showerhead may deliver water too slowly to get the job done fast and efficiently.

There are also shower units that sit inside the tub, but some parents report that these units get in the way, crowding their baby's leg room. They ended up using the spray attachment from the sink or a plastic cupful of water at rinse time, which can be the best way to go anyway, in our opinion.

With the 4moms Cleanwater Infant Tub, fresh water flows from the sink or tub faucet into a collection area on the tub, over a temperature sensor and into a reservoir, and then departs through a sidewall drain. The design gives soapy water an exit route so it's easier to rinse a baby,

Bathtub Tips

In addition to not buying a bath seat, follow these bathtub safety tips every time you give your baby a bath:

◆ Never leave your baby unattended during bathtime, even for a second, even when you're just filling the tub with water. To play it safe, stay within arm's reach of your child when he's around water, whether he's in an adult or toddler tub. If your baby can't sit up on his own yet, always keep a hand on him at bathtime, too. Plan ahead. Make sure you have everything on hand before you start the bath. You don't want to have to scurry off for a washcloth or towel while your baby is in the tub.

◆ When bathing your baby, fill the tub with as little water as possible. Two inches is a good amount. Place the baby bathtub on a flat, level surface that doesn't allow it to slip and makes it easy for you to handle your baby. Don't add more water while your baby is in the tub, and never put the baby bathtub in a larger tub that is filled with water because it can float around and tip.

◆ Be careful about scalding water. The water should feel warm, not hot. Before you put your baby in the tub, test the temperature with your elbow. Don't rely on a tub with a temperature indicator, such as a drain plug that changes color to indicate too hot, too cold, and just right. If you're using a thermometer with a read-out, baby bath water should be between 90°F and 100°F. But again, use your elbow as your main guide.

◆ If you need to leave the bathroom, take your baby with you. Don't rely on older children to watch the baby for you. If the phone rings, let the answering machine or voice mail pick it up. If there's a knock on the door, ignore it. Make that rule as stringent as strapping your baby into her car seat every time you drive.

◆ When using a baby bathtub in the sink or in a regular tub, always turn the hot water off first and watch out for hot metal spigots. Get a cover for the bathtub's spout to protect your child from its heat-conducting metal and hard edges. Some covers are soft plastic in the shape of an animal, such as a moose or an elephant. Others are inflatable plastic. Swoosh tub water around with your hand so that any hot spots even out. To play it safe, reduce the setting of your hot-water heater to 120° F. An infant's skin burns much more easily than an adult's.

◆ Use washcloths instead of sponges. Either one will end up in your baby's mouth, but washcloths are safer because tiny pieces of sponge can easily break off and become a choking hazard. And washcloths can go through a washer and dryer so they can get really clean, while sponges have to air dry and can harbor harmful bacteria.

◆ Always empty the bathtub immediately after bathtime. Babies can drown in as little as one inch of water.

◆ When your baby graduates to a regular bathtub, attach rubber strips to the bottom of the tub to prevent slipping.

◆ Remind caregivers, your partner, and your baby's grandparents about these safety tips. Better yet, if they're new to bathtime, tell them not to give your baby a bath while you're away, if possible.

but you'll pay more for the privilege. At $40, this tub is among the most expensive on the market.

Easy storage. Some models have a handle or hook on the back to hang the tub up for draining or storage. That's a feature to look for if space is tight. Hang the tub upright from its hook in your shower, so water doesn't drip on the bathroom floor.

A smooth, overhanging rim. This feature makes it much easier to carry a heavy, water-filled tub (without your baby in it, of course) from the sink to another location.

Nonskid surface. Some models have a nonskid surface on the bottom to keep the tub from sliding in a regular bathtub.

Recommendations

For a baby 6 months or younger, buy a bathtub that has a contoured design or an internal sling that cradles the baby in the water. A mildew-resistant, padded foam lining is also a plus, although to prevent mildew and soap-scum buildup, you'll still have to clean the tub and dry it after each use. If you're short on space, buy a unit that folds. You can also buy one that doesn't fold and can be stored in your shower (ideally) or a closet. Don't buy an inflatable bathtub or a bath seat, even if your pediatrician recommends it. (One new mom we know of was even offered the chance to try out a bath seat at the pediatrician's office.) Be consistent and a stickler when it comes to bath-time safety. Follow the safety guidelines we outline every time you give your baby a bath.

chapter

Bicycle-Mounted Child Seats & Trailers

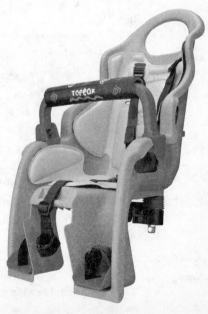

Chasing around a toddler wannabe certainly qualifies as exercise. Still, if you get the feeling it's not enough, a bicycle-mounted child seat or a bicycle trailer can help you cover some ground in the name of fitness and fresh air.

A bicycle child seat like the Topeak BabySeat can be a fun way to explore the great outdoors with your toddler.

To make shopping easier, you'll first need to decide which type of tot toter is right for you. Here's the wheel deal:

Bicycle-mounted seats are mounted behind or in front of a cyclist's seat and can transport one child age 1 to 5 or so. In both seats, the child faces forward. They're potentially less safe than trailers, which have two bicycle-type wheels and a long hitching arm that fastens to a bicycle from behind and ride low to the ground. In an accident, a child would fall about three feet from a mounted bike seat, compared with a fall of about 6 inches from a trailer. With the added weight of a little passenger at the back or front, a bicycle with a mounted seat might be harder to handle, which can be unnerving or just annoying, depending on your cycling experience. Getting on and off a bike with a baby in a mounted seat can also be difficult.

Trailers attach to a bike's rear axle or frame, and can carry children from age 1 through 6 or so. They provide some protection to passengers since children are seated, strapped in, and usually enclosed in a zippered compartment. Trailers have a rigid frame enclosed in durable fabric, which offers some protection for young passengers if the unit rolls over. But children still must wear a bike helmet. (For our helmet ratings, see page 85.) As we mentioned, because a trailer is closer to the ground, it's potentially safer than a bicycle-mounted seat in an accident. Some designs have a hitching arm that allows the bike to fall without tipping the trailer. But bicycle trailers pose safety problems because their low profile makes them difficult for motorists to see, especially in limited light. They should have a 3½-foot- to 7-foot-tall, high-visibility orange flag. Trailers are also wider than the bike, so they take up more of the roadway. If you're riding on the shoulder,

This InStep Take 2 trailer has a 100-pound total child capacity and easily seats two.

which we don't recommend because we consider trailers "off-road" vehicles, the trailer can stick out into the road if you're not careful. And trailers can tip

Rent a Step-Through Bike

Renting bikes on vacation? If you'll be getting one with a rear-mounted child seat, try to get a "step through" model—sometimes referred to as a "woman's bike." This eliminates the need to swing your leg around the back of the bike to mount and dismount, as you usually do with a bike that has a top tube—and won't be able to do with a child seat in the way. With a step-through frame, mounting and dismounting will be easier and safer.

over if you turn abruptly or turn when one wheel is going over a bump. As you speed up, braking becomes harder, especially on wet surfaces. Trailers can become snagged on bushes or other objects.

Although both types of bicycle carriers have safety issues, the American Academy of Pediatrics states that it is preferable for a child to ride in a bicycle trailer rather than a front- or rear-mounted bicycle seat because "a young passenger on an adult's bike makes the bike unstable and increases braking time." The AAP believes that a mishap at any speed on a bicycle-mounted seat could cause significant injury to a child.

Shopping Secrets

Take a trailer or a bicycle-mounted seat for a test ride. Put some weight in it if you test it at the store. Don't test-drive it with your child in it. Save that for home, after you've selected a seat, installed it according to the manufacturer's directions, and feel comfortable with it. Bring your child along when you shop, though, to see if the seat is a good fit. If you can't test-drive at the store, borrow a friend's bicycle trailer or mounted bicycle seat and take it for a spin with weight in it, such as a sack of potatoes (not your child).

Buy for your bike. In our tests, some bicycle trailers couldn't be mounted on bicycles with disc brakes, and some bicycle-mounted seats couldn't be used on bicycles with oversized tubes. So keep compatibility in mind when you're shopping.

Shop online only after you've cased the store. Avoid buying a trailer or bicycle-mounted seat that you're not able to examine carefully, such as one sold exclusively over the Internet. Keep your receipt and the trailer or mounted seat's packaging in case you discover a fitting problem when the seat arrives, just as you would if you had bought the item at a walk-in store.

■ **Budget Baby**

Be Wary of Secondhand Seats

Bicycle child seats and trailers are popular items at tag sales, but before you buy a used model, check the Consumer Product Safety Commission Web site, *www.cpsc.gov*, to make sure you don't buy a defective product. Fortunately, there have been few recalls in recent years. Also, inspect the seat or trailer to check for excessive wear and tear or missing hardware. The safety harness should be like new, or a close approximation. Ideally, a used seat is sold with an owner's manual. If not, visit the manufacturer's Web site for that information, so you can install the seat properly.

What's Available

Some major brands of mounted bicycle seats are, in alphabetical order: Bell (available at *www.target.com*), Kettler (*www.kettlerusa.com*), Topeak (*www.topeak.com*), and WeeRide (*www.weeride.com*). Prices range from $26.99 to $135. Some mount behind the bike's seat, while others mount in front, accommodating one child from 40 to 50 pounds (it varies by manufacturer).

Some major brands of bicycle trailers are, in alphabetical order: Baby Jogger (*www.babyjogger.com*), Burley (*www.burley.com*), Chariot Carriers (*www.chariotcarriers.com*), InStep (*www.instep .net*), Schwinn (*www.schwinnbike.com*), and Wee-Ride (*www.weeride.com*). WeeRide also makes the Convertible Coach, which converts from a bicycle trailer to a jogging stroller. Prices range from $160 to $600 for one- and two-passenger models, and the trailers can hold up to 100 pounds.

Cushy ride: The WeeRide Kangaroo LTD features a padded pedestal as well as thick pads on the seat back and harness.

Features to Consider

Assembly. If you plan to buy a bike trailer or a bicycle-mounted seat and put it together or install it yourself, you'll need clear instructions because assembly and installation can be a challenge. If you need help understanding the owner's manual, consult the manufacturer's Web site. Many have tutorial videos that can help you get the gist of assembly. You can also call the manufacturer or consult your local bike shop.

Convertibility. Some manufacturers offer conversion kits (typically sold separately) that allow you to transform your bicycle trailer into a jogging or hiking stroller or a cross-country skier. The skier lets you haul your tot behind you with the aid of a waist belt, two aluminum tow bars, and two lightweight skis that replace the wheels.

Cross bars. Some rear-mounted bicycle seats have a cross bar that goes across the lap in addition to a five-point harness, an added safety feature in case of a fall. It also gives children something to hold onto, which may make them feel more secure.

Some bicycle trailers, like the Cheetah by Chariot Carriers, are multitaskers. With a conversion kit, they can be used for jogging or even cross-country skiing.

Pedestal support. Some front-mounted bicycle seats have a pedestal support designed for a child to hang onto, which may be padded on top-of-the-line models.

Protection from the elements. Many trailers come with a plastic shield, which protects against sun, wind, and rain. A zippered front shield will keep water or mud from splattering your child. But if the shield encloses the entire cabin, make certain there's ventilation, such as breathable mesh windows. Your kids may appreciate tinted windows, which aren't available on all models. They protect your child from sun glare, and keep the "cockpit" cooler.

Folding mechanism. Some trailers feature quick-release wheels and fold easily for storage (even in a hall closet), which can be an advantage if you don't have a garage.

Frame. Trailer frames generally are made of steel, but in more expensive models they may be aluminum alloy, which is lighter. The frame should be sturdy. Better models offer a roll cage—a perimeter frame—to better protect passengers in the event of a rollover. However, these roll cages are not strong enough to protect against a collision with a vehicle.

Harness. With either a bicycle-mounted seat or a trailer, a padded, adjustable five-point harness is ideal: two straps over the shoulders, two for the thighs, and a crotch strap, much like the restraints on a child's car seat.

Hitching arm. A trailer's hitching arm should have a backup to prevent the trailer from breaking loose. Check the wheel mounting to be sure that it will hold. Look for a universal hitch, which can be used with almost any bicycle. Some hitching arms are designed to help keep the trailer upright even if your bike goes down.

Certification

There is no certification program by an independent organization for these products, although standards developer ASTM International has established a voluntary standard for rear-mounted bicycle child seats and one for bicycle trailers designed for human passengers. A manufacturer may test to the requirements of that standard and certify that the product meets it. Our advice is to buy a trailer or a rear-mounted seat that meets all ASTM standards. And be aware that although some bicycle seats will accommodate a child up to 50 pounds, the standard covers child carriers with a maximum weight load of 40 pounds.

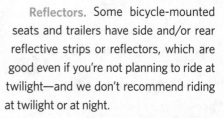

A roomy cabin like this one in the Schwinn Joyrider Trailer can make for a more enjoyable ride.

Reflectors. Some bicycle-mounted seats and trailers have side and/or rear reflective strips or reflectors, which are good even if you're not planning to ride at twilight—and we don't recommend riding at twilight or at night.

Safety flag. If you're buying a trailer, a safety flag—a high-visibility pennant on a whip tall enough (3½ feet to 7 feet) to make it visible to drivers—is a must.

Seating. The interior of a trailer should offer comfortable seating with adequate leg room and good back support. The seat's protective cavity should be free of protrusions. Roominess is a plus, as are storage pockets for toys and such. But don't let your child play with toys while riding because they can distract you if your child throws them, which could cause an accident. At the higher end of the price range, you'll find seats that recline, cushier padding, and, on two-passenger trailers, a seat divider. On bicycle-mounted seats, look for a padded seat cushion for a smoother ride. Seats with a reclining backrest and an adjustable foot- and headrest are common at the top of the price range.

Seat location. If you're shopping for a bicycle-mounted seat, consider whether you want a seat that mounts in the back or the front. In our tests, with an 18-month-old and a 30-month-old, the kids seemed to prefer riding up front, and we found the tested front-mounted seat did not affect the bike's handling as much. Front and center, kids can enjoy an unobstructed view. In the rear position, they have to look at your back and turn their head and possibly shift their weight to catch the scenery, which can be unsafe because it may throw off your balance. However, our parent testers had to bow their knees out slightly to avoid rubbing against the front-mounted seat or the occupant, which isn't necessarily a safety issue, but it can be uncomfortable. A front rider can grab the handlebars while using this type of seat, which could cause an accident.

Side protection. Some bicycle-mounted seats offer side protectors, which help shield a child in the event of a fall.

Wheels. Trailer wheels usually are made with steel rims, which can rust, or aluminum rims, which don't rust and are lighter than steel. The wheels should also have one or more reflectors. Look for high-quality rubber tires. Also, consider wheel size. In our tests, larger wheels rolled over bumps better, but smaller wheels made maneuvering easier.

Recommendations

Don't buy a bicycle trailer or a bicycle-mounted seat until your baby is at least 1 year old. We don't recommend bicycle trailers and bicycle-mounted seats for children younger than that because they may not be physically equipped to withstand the forces they'll be exposed to when riding in them. Children younger than age 1 can't support their heads properly with a helmet on, which all riders should wear. Choose based on your needs, riding ability, and where you're riding. Trailers are "off-road vehicles"; use them only in parks and on safe, smooth trails where there's no risk of encounters with cars. Follow the manufacturer's recommendations regarding the maximum weight, which is usually up to 100 pounds.

The better bicycle trailers have sturdy construction, tinted windows, a comfortable interior, and a wide wheelbase. But before you buy, ask yourself if you will use the trailer enough to justify the price. If you think you'll use it only occasionally, buy the most durable trailer you can find at the low-end price. Also, consider how much weight you'll tow. If the weight of the bicycle trailer plus the passenger or passengers exceeds 50 pounds, you may start to feel like a beast of burden. Pedaling uphill

Bike Helmets

A helmet that fits properly helps protect your child from injury.

A bike helmet can reduce the risk of bicycle-related head and brain injuries by up to 88 percent, and of facial injuries by two-thirds, according to data analysis published in the Annals of Internal Medicine. So of course you'll want to make sure everyone— yourself as well as your child— is protected with a properly fitted helmet whenever you ride.

A bike helmet should sit level (left) on the head, not titled back (right).

Before you buy a helmet, try it on your child in the store—preferably a bike shop or a store where the salesperson can help you choose the right size and adjust the helmet to your child's head (or your head, if you're also shopping for yourself). A helmet should fit snugly and sit level on your child's head, not tilt back like a hat. Not all helmets match all heads, and your child will resist an uncomfortable helmet, or one she doesn't like, so pick a color or design he approves of. And make sure you can return it.

Replace a helmet that has absorbed impact in an accident, advises the Bicycle Helmet Safety Institute. Some manufacturers will replace a crashed helmet for a nominal fee.

To be sure the helmet you choose for your child is safe, look for a label inside the helmet that states that the helmet meets the CPSC's mandatory safety standard.

All of the bike helmets in our Ratings passed our impact and strap-retention tests.

can be especially difficult. At that point, maybe it's time for kids to get their own bikes.

Take your cycling ability into consideration. If you opt for a bicycle-mounted seat, you might find a rear-mounted seat with a child in tow unnerving and exhausting to operate. If you're a novice or not in top shape, you'd probably be better off with a front-mounted seat. If you go with a bicycle trailer, ride with only one child at a time if you're an infrequent rider. Keep your receipt in case you need to return your bicycle trailer or seat for any reason, including the possibility that the trailer or seat doesn't fit your bike, or impedes your ability to pedal or turn the handlebars comfortably. Many bicycle trailers and mounted seats are also under manufacturer warranty. Send in the registration card and hold onto warranty information so you can refer to it. That small step can also help the manufacturer contact you in the event of a recall. Finally, have your child wear a lightweight, well-fitting bike helmet.

Ratings • Bike Helmets

	Excellent	Very good	Good	Fair	Poor
	⊖	⊖	○	◔	●

Within types, in performance order.

	Brand & model	Price	Overall score	Test results			
				Impact absorption	Retention system	Ventilation	Ease of use
	ADULT						
✓	**Bell** Citi	$45	79	⊖	⊖	⊖	⊖
✓	**Bell** Slant	50	79	⊖	⊖	⊖	⊖
	Giro Atmos	175	68	○	⊖	⊖	⊖
	Specialized Air-8	60	67	○	⊖	⊖	⊖
	Louis Garneau Equinox	40	64	○	⊖	⊖	⊖
	Louis Garneau Chrono	100	48	○	⊖	◔	⊖
	YOUTH						
	Bell Trigger	35	65	○	⊖	⊖	⊖
✓	**Schwinn** Intercept	17	60	○	⊖	○	⊖
	Uvex Cartoon	40	54	○	⊖	◔	⊖
	TODDLER						
	Bell Boomerang	30	63	⊖	⊖	◔	⊖
	Giro Me2	30	51	○	⊖	◔	⊖
	BMX STYLE						
	Bell Faction	35	44	○	⊖	◔	◔
	Mongoose BMX Hardshell MG-119	17	38	○	⊖	◔	◔

✓ **CR Best Buy** These models offer the best combination of performance and price. All are recommended.

Guide to the Ratings

Overall score is based primarily on impact absorption, retention-system strength, ventilation, and ease of use. **Impact absorption** refers to how well the helmet absorbed the forces of an impact; it's based on tests at various impact speeds and on various impact surfaces. **Retention system** refers to how well the helmet's straps, buckles, and other hardware met our strength criteria. **Ventilation** is our evaluation of vent design and how well air flows through the helmet to provide cooling while riding. **Ease of use** is our judgment of how easy the various buckles and adjustments were to use. **Price** is approximate retail.

7

chapter

Bouncer Seats

Babies like to be where the action is. A bouncer seat—also called a "bouncy" seat—gives your baby a place to hang out near you and the rest of the family during his first six months or so. It can also help your baby doze.

The Svan Bouncer has a frame made from bent wood instead of metal.

A bouncer seat generally consists of a lightweight frame made from metal wire, tubular metal, heavy-gauge plastic, or lightweight wood. Covered with a soft, removable, washable pad that conforms to a baby's shape, bouncer seats are somewhat springy and bounce or rock when your baby moves to keep him relaxed and amused. The fabric seat is rounded to support a baby's still-fragile spine, and the semi-upright tilt gives him a view of the surroundings. For babies who need a little help falling asleep, a bouncer seat that vibrates can be invaluable because it imitates a lulling car ride. (Keep in mind, however, that the safest place for a baby to sleep is on his back in a crib on a firm mattress.) Many parents report that their babies love to nap in a bouncer seat. The sitting angle also appears to be more comfortable for some babies than lying in a flat crib after they've had a big meal.

Most models have a detachable, bent-wire play bar (sometimes covered with padding) or an overhead mobile of plastic toys for your baby to kick, bat, or gaze at. Some models have a set of colorful lights and sound effects that respond to a baby's movements and/or vibrate at two or three speeds to lull the baby to sleep. Some simulate nature sounds or a heartbeat or play computer-chip-generated classical music. Others transform your child's smallest movements or your fancy footwork (they have a foot-bounce you step on to activate bouncing) into a soothing rocking motion, sans batteries. The latest versions on the market, such as the Zen Collection Infant Seat by Fisher-Price (*www.fisherprice.com*, $100), fold compactly for travel and aesthetically coordinate with other baby gear. You can expect to use a typical bouncer until your baby can sit up unassisted or reaches the weight or age limit, whichever comes first. The typical weight maximum is 18 pounds, about the upper average for infants at six months, which is the usual age limit. However, some models top out at 28 or 30 or 40 pounds, and so are made to function as toddler chairs too, with the seat back raised to a comfortably upright position and any toy bar or restraint system removed.

It's a match! The Zen Collection Infant Seat by Fisher-Price coordinates with a cradle swing, gliding bassinet, and high chair.

Consider a Rocker-Bouncer That Vibrates

Instead of a bouncer, consider an infant rocker-bouncer, which is like a bouncer seat, only it rocks.

Pricewise, a rocker-bouncer is in the same ballpark as a bouncy seat—around $40—but you can get more mileage out of it. Infant bouncers such as the Fisher-Price Infant-to-Toddler Rocker can typically be used until your child reaches 40 pounds, which could be until age 3 or so.

Tip: Get one that vibrates. You'll use that mode a lot initially, especially since a young baby won't be big enough to actually rock in the rocker. The rocking function kicks in as your baby becomes a toddler (in no time). Then, she'll have her own little chair to enjoy.

The Fisher-Price Infant-to-Toddler Rocker can be used for babies and toddlers.

Shopping Secrets

Keep this product's short life span in mind. Your baby will probably use a bouncer as a bouncer for only five or six months. Once he can sit up unassisted, he'll likely move on to more interesting things, like playing and rolling. With that in mind, an inexpensive, lightweight model (provided it's stable), such as the Bright Starts Bouncing Buddies Cradling Bouncer (www.brightstarts.com, $19.99), may serve you as well as a top-end design like the BabyBjörn Baby Sitter 1-2-3 (www.babybjorn.com, $100), which is designed to become a chair for a child up to 29 pounds. In general, more money will get you a seat that's made to last and one that may be decked out with toys, reclining and vibrating features, realistic (not tinny) music, and plush or designer fabric. Still, more isn't always better. Parents report product satisfaction at both ends of the price spectrum.

Buy either a bouncer seat or a swing. If budget or space are a consideration, choose one or the other. Many parents report that it's overkill to buy both since a bouncer seat and a swing essentially

Sitting pretty: The Maclaren Kate Spade Rocker features jazzy black-and-white striped fabric with red accents and a coordinated toy bar.

Certification

Of all the brands of bouncy seats on the market, nine have been certified by the Juvenile Products Manufacturers Association (JPMA) as meeting the safety standards set by ASTM International. These include Delta Enterprise, Dorel Juvenile Group, Fisher-Price, Graco, Kolcraft, Regent Baby Products Corporation, Sassy, Scandinavian Child (Svan chair), and Summer Infant. The industry standard covers structural integrity, restraint system, and slip resistance and requires that safety instructions be on a permanent label or stamped right on the product. Certified bouncers must also meet standards for small parts, hazardous sharp points and edges, secure latching, and size of openings. Any wood parts must be smooth and free of splinters. Models must also comply with all current federal regulations for lead paint.

Shopping for a second-hand bouncer? Buy certified too, and look for a recent model. The bouncer should be sturdy and stable with a secure toy bar, no ripped fabric, sharp edges, or missing parts—and have its instruction manual. (Current manuals may be on the manufacturer's Web site.) Also check the Consumer Product Safety Commission Web site, www.cpsc.gov, to be sure that any model you may be interested in has not been recalled.

do the same thing: provide a secure and soothing place for your baby to relax and stay occupied while you get some hands-free time to catch up on things around the house, while watching your baby at the same time. If you can, try your baby out in a friend's or relative's swing and bouncer or test store models, to gauge what your baby prefers. If your baby doesn't like the motion of a swing (some don't), go with a bouncer. If your baby seems to need more motion than a bouncer provides, opt for a swing.

What's Available

Some brands of bouncer seats, in alphabetical order, are: BabyBjörn (www.babybjorn.com), Kids II—makers of Baby Einstein, Boppy, and Bright Starts (www.kidsii.com), Combi International (www.combi-intl.com), Dorel—makers of Cosco (www.coscojuvenile.com), Eddie Bauer, and Safety 1st (www.djgusa.com), Fisher-Price (www.fisher-price.com), Graco (www.gracobaby.com), Kolcraft (www.kolcraft.com), Maclaren (www.maclarenbaby.com), phil&teds (www.philandteds.com), Summer Infant (www.summerinfant.com), and Svan (www.svanusa.com). Prices can range anywhere from $20 to $120. Many of them require AA, D and/or C batteries (which are not included) to power music, vibration, and toys.

Features to Consider

Cushiness. Seat padding can vary from basic to extra-thick. Because wet diapers are bound to come in contact with the fabric covering, upholstery should be removable and machine washable (check the label). There also shouldn't be any loose threads or gaps in the seams.

Frame. When you're in the store, give the various display models a "bounce," if possible. Bring your own batteries, in case the display models don't have them. A bouncer seat should have a wide, stable base and be springy. If it seems stiff, it probably won't bounce with your baby in it.

Foldability. Some models fold flat or nearly so, which is handy if you'll be traveling with your bouncer seat.

Canopy. Some models have a canopy to block light. The canopy can be a sunshade if your baby spends time in it outdoors, but be sure to position the bouncer in the shade so your baby won't become overheated or get sunburned. The American Academy of Pediatrics (AAP) recommends that infants under 6 months old not be exposed to direct sunlight. Even with a canopy, keep the bouncer in complete shade and dress your baby in clothes that cover her arms and legs as well as a hat with a brim.

Music and vibration. Some bouncers can play up to 12 songs, with additional sound effects, to stimulate your baby's sense of hearing. These models usually provide a vibration feature along with music since both features are often packaged in the same mechanism. Vibration simulates the motion of a soothing car ride. It's a feature you'll probably use often.

Rockability. As we mentioned, some bouncers, such as the Maclaren rocker and the Fisher-Price Newborn-to-Toddler Portable rocker, are designed to rock as well as bounce, but most infants aren't strong enough to generate a rocking motion, so keep in mind there won't be much rocking movement until your baby is several months old. That's why it's a good idea to buy a rocker-bouncer that vibrates, too.

The Fisher-Price Ocean Wonders Aquarium Bouncer vibrates, and features music and sound.

Be Bouncer-Seat Savvy

An estimated 2,000 infants are injured each year in bouncy seats. Here's how to protect your baby:

◆ **Stick to the weight and development limits.** Most manufacturers specify an upper limit of 18 pounds (a heavier child can tip the seat), and advise that you stop using the seat as soon as your baby can sit up unassisted or attempts to climb out. Some seats do accommodate toddlers and even bigger kids, with weight limits ranging from 28 to 40 pounds. With this style of seat, continue to use the restraint system until your child is able to climb in and out of the chair unassisted.

◆ **Never use a bouncer seat as a car seat.**

◆ **Put the seat on the floor.** Never use it on an elevated surface, such as a table, where the baby's movement could rock it to the edge, or on a soft surface, such as a bed, sofa, pillow, or cushion. The seat may tip and soft surfaces are a suffocation hazard.

◆ **Don't place the bouncer with your baby in it near window-blind or phone cords.** They're a strangulation hazard.

◆ **Don't suspend strings over a bouncer seat or attach strings to toys on the play bar.** They're also a strangulation hazard.

◆ **Don't carry your baby while he's in the bouncer,** even if the bouncer has a carrying handle, and never use the toy bar as a handle.

◆ **Always keep a close eye on your baby,** even if you think he's completely safe and secure in the bouncer seat.

◆ **Make sure the bouncer you select doesn't have any sharp edges.**

◆ **Always secure your baby with the bouncer's three- or five-point safety harness.** A five-point harness is better for infants because it can keep them from slumping.

◆ **Don't use a bouncy seat that's damaged or broken.**

◆ **Don't park your baby in a bouncer.** The AAP says babies who spend excessive time in bouncers (or car seats) may be prone to positional plagiocephaly, also called flattened head syndrome, a persistent flat spot in the back or on one side of the head. The AAP doesn't say how much is too much, so use your best judgement. No more than 30 minutes at a shot seems reasonable to us. Don't substitute a bouncy seat for cuddle time or for tummy time on the floor.

◆ **Register the bouncy seat you buy** so the manufacturer can easily notify you in case of a recall. Many companies now allow you to do that online through their Web sites.

◆ **Read the instructions carefully during assembly.** Many bouncy seats have many parts and assembly steps. If there's something you don't understand, don't guess. Call the manufacturer for clarification.

Seat belts. Most models have a soft fabric three-point crotch strap as a restraint; others have a five-point harness, which is ideal for newborns because they tend to list to the side or slide to the end of the seat. Check all fasteners on models with three-point or five-point harnesses to see that they're strong, secure, and easy for you to work, and that they won't poke your baby. They should be stiff enough to be safe without being so rigid that they pinch or are difficult for you to operate.

Head support. Seats with an adjustable, removable cushioned head support are ideal for newborns.

Seat fabric. Fabric patterns range from kiddy prints and colors to sophisticated solid and patterned color combos like gray and mandarin (orange), chili (red), or wasabi (lime green), which are the featured hues on the Combi Pod bouncer ($90; *www.combi-intl.com*). A cloth seat cover is the norm; make sure it's removable and machine washable.

Seat positioning. Some bouncer seats recline more than others. At least two seatback positions—upright and recline—are a definite plus. The recline feature is necessary for infants, since they don't have the head control that sitting, even on a slight incline, requires.

Toy bar. Besides watching you and your family from the sidelines, your baby may enjoy the sensory stimulation of toys, sounds, and lights that many bouncer seats come with. A toy bar isn't necessary in the early months, since your baby may not want to play with the toys all the time or even know what to do with them. Toy bars come into play around 4 months of age, though music and vibration features will likely be appreciated well before then. Toys usually are suspended from a removable play bar, although some models, such as the Baby Papasan Infant Seat by Fisher-Price ($60), feature a swing-away mobile, which suspends a toy in front of a baby in mobile fashion. Look for spinning, squeaking toys and teethers in bright or contrasting colors. Some models have toys that are pastel colored, which won't make as dramatic an impact on your baby as brighter colors will. If your baby can't reach the toy bar, position it so she can kick at it. Most bouncers allow you to take the play bar off and use just the seat for snoozing and quiet time. Not all models have toy bars, though many parents believe they're a must-have, especially starting at around the 4-month mark. Don't use the toy bar as a carrying handle.

Recommendations

Make safety your primary concern. You'll want a bouncer seat with a base or rear support that's wider than the seat itself for steadiness. Test the stability of models in the store, if possible. When you press down on a bouncer from different positions, it shouldn't tip sideways. When you rock it front to back, it should stay in place. The bottom of the base should have rubber pads or other nonskid surfaces that really work.

If you're buying a seat with toys attached to a toy bar, squeeze and tug them to make sure they won't break off. The bar should stay in place when you bat at it.

chapter

Breast Pumps

If you're planning to breast-feed, a breast pump can be indispensable. But you'll need to choose carefully to get the right pump for your situation, especially if you'll be pumping at work. The right pump can mean the difference between meeting your breast-feeding goals and having to stop short.

Some models, such as the Medela Pump in Style Advanced, come in a shoulder bag that contains everything you need to pump when you're away from home.

As you probably know, these days, "breast is best." The American Academy of Pediatrics, as well as a number of leading professional organizations, recommend breast-feeding for a baby's first six months, unless there's a medical reason not to do so, without supplementing with water, formula, or juice

If you want to continue breast-feeding nonexclusively after that, these groups say all the better. That's because breast milk—custom-made nourishment specially formulated by Mother Nature—offers so many benefits: It boosts your baby's immune system by providing antibodies against illness, promotes brain and vision development and a healthy digestive tract, and may reduce your child's risk of sudden infant death syndrome (SIDS). Plus it may reduce the risk of certain diseases later in life—diabetes, some types of cancer, obesity, high cholesterol, and asthma. Breast milk also changes over time and even during the course of a day to meet the needs of a growing baby. Breast-feeding helps moms return to their pre-baby weight faster, and may decrease the risk of breast and ovarian cancer, and even osteoporosis.

Breast-feeding is convenient—there are no bottles to prepare and warm—and it's free! There's no formula to buy, which can run you about $170 per month, depending on the type of formula you buy. But unless you plan to take your baby with you wherever you go and the process always goes smoothly, you'll probably need a breast pump. In fact, a pump can be indispensable for nursing mothers in a number of sce-narios: You are

A double-electric breast pump like the Ameda Purely Yours with Carry All is a must-have if you'll be returning to work full-time, but still want to continue breast-feeding.

returning to work and want to continue breast-feeding; you need to formula-feed your baby temporarily for medical reasons but want to resume breast-feeding when you get the go-ahead from your doctor; your baby can't physically breast-feed for whatever reason, or you need to miss a feeding occasionally because you're traveling or otherwise away from your baby.

A breast pump may come in handy during those first few days after you've delivered, when the breasts can become so full that a baby may have trouble latching on. Things can be sailing along in the hospital, but when you get home, supply can outpace demand. The solution is to express some milk with a breast pump—and to have one on hand before your baby is born, so you're ready to go as soon as you return home after delivery. A breast pump also allows you to store milk (in bottles or storage bags) for later, then bottle-feed it to your baby or mix it with a little cereal when she reaches the "solid" food stage at around 6 months.

You can refrigerate breast milk safely for 24 hours, or freeze it for three to six months. However, "when you put breast milk on a shelf and let it sit, the fats may begin to break down and a few of the many other components may begin to change," says Miriam H. Labbok, M.D., M.P.H., director of the Center for Infant and Young Child Feeding and Care, Department of Maternal and Child Health, at the University of North Carolina in Chapel Hill. So use expressed milk as soon as possible, with the oldest milk first.

A housekeeping note: Always refrigerate expressed milk as soon as possible. When you're away from home, use an insulated container packed with ice or frozen ice packs to keep your breast milk cool. When freezing breast milk, date it when you freeze it and store it in the back of the freezer, not on the door—that's a warm spot that can prompt thawing every time the door is opened. When the time comes to use it, thaw breast milk in warm water. Don't boil or microwave it; both of those heating methods can destroy valuable immunological components that make breast milk the liquid gold it is. Microwaving can also create uneven "hot spots" that can scald a baby's mouth and throat. Finally, don't add fresh breast milk to already-frozen or refrigerated milk for storage, and don't refreeze breast milk once it has been defrosted. If you can't use it up, throw it out.

There are several types of breast pumps available—large, hospital-grade pumps; midweight personal-use automatic pumps; small, lightweight, and easily portable electric, battery-operated, or manual models that work one breast at a time; and hands-free pumps that strap around your waist, so you can multitask instead of simply sitting through another pumping session. You'll want a pump that's appropriate to your particular situation. Pumping can be time-consuming and just one more

> "Pumping can be time-consuming and just one more thing to do, but it shouldn't be painful or frustrating."

thing to do, but it shouldn't be painful or frustrating. Choosing the right pump can make the difference in breast-feeding success. A baby's natural sucking rhythm is 40 to 60 cycles per minute (one pull per second or a little less). Hospital-grade and personal-use automatic pumps typically operate at 30 to 50 cycles per minute. Other pumps are usually less efficient. As a general rule, the more suction and releases per minute a pump provides, the better it will be at stimulating your milk supply. Consider this: Breast milk naturally changes during each feed in conjunction with a baby's swallowing technique and suction. In the beginning of a breast-feeding session, breast milk is thin and watery. In the middle, it gets fattier, becoming whole milk. Toward the end, it's even creamier, says Labbok. The fat is healthful; it contributes to satiety, among other benefits. Ideally, you'll want a pump that mimics a baby's natural sucking action. Efficiency is important if you plan to save a large quantity of milk. If you're returning to work, for example, you'll need to have much more breast milk on hand than if you stay home with your baby or are supplementing breast milk with formula.

Once you find the right pump, you'll need to learn how to position it correctly and adjust the suctioning to get the best results. Don't worry—with the right pump, you'll soon get the hang of it. Pumps require some assembling and disassembling for cleaning. Use the dishwasher or hot soapy water to clean any parts of the pump that touch your breasts or the milk containers. Drain them dry before each use.

Shopping Secrets

Do your research. Like a toothbrush or lipstick, breast pumps are personal-use items. For hygienic reasons, some manufacturers don't allow returns once the product is opened, unless it's defective. So be as sure as you can be about this purchase before buying. You're on the right track by reading this chapter!

Consider renting. To save money (midweight, personal-use automatic pumps can retail for as much as $380), think about renting a pump, which will typically run you around $55 per month, plus, in some cases, a security deposit. If you plan to breast-feed longer than three or four months, however, buying is the way to go. But check with your rental vendor. Many offer a price break the longer you rent. For referrals to lactation consultants who can advise you on the type of pump you need and where to rent it, contact the International Lactation

- **Myth Conceptions**

Do You Need to Wash the Pump Between Sessions?

We ran across this misguided advice on a popular breast-pumping message board: You don't have to wash a breast pump between sessions. Not having to wash or rinse breast-pump equipment (bottles and shields) during the business day saves time and potentially embarrassing run-ins in the office kitchen or bathroom. And, "human milk is very effective at killing bacteria for about 12 hours after it leaves the breast," says Mary Rose Tully, director of Lactation Services at both North Carolina Women's and Children's Hospitals in Chapel Hill, N.C. "But we don't know what the effect is if it starts drying or is exposed to large amounts of pathogens." If you don't have time to wash breast-pump parts between sessions, place them unwashed in a clean plastic bag, such as a Ziploc, and store them in the refrigerator, Tully advises. But be sure to'wash them thoroughly at least once a day.

Consultant Association (ILCA, *www.ilca.org*). The hospital where you delivered your baby may have a lactation consultant on staff. Medela, a leading breast pump manufacturer, also allows you to search by ZIP code or city and state on its Web site (*http://medela.findlocation.com*) for retailers that rent breast pumps in your area and local breast-feeding specialists.

Shop around. You can find deals on new breast pumps online, and at hospital birthing centers. You also can consult a La Leche League leader (*www.llli.org*) or an ILCA-certified lactation consultant in your area. A little research reveals that there are deals to be had in the online breast pump marketplace once you know what kind of pump you want. (Not sure where to start? Simply type in "breast pump" on a search engine like Google.) A good site for breast pump deals is *www.breastpumpsdirect .com*. The site allows you to compare prices, warranties, suction settings, cycle speeds, and other features of competing-brand breast pumps. The site also has a price match guarantee. If you find the same product on another Web site at a lower price, they'll match that price.

Browse at the hospital. Many hospitals and birthing centers are now in the breast-pump business, offering competitive prices on a variety of pumps, plus advice that can help ensure success. You can also get a recommendation from your hospital's lactation consultant for the right type of pump for you.

BPA and Bottles

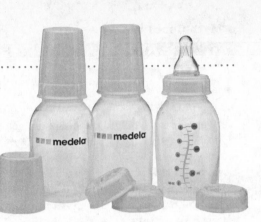

The breast pump bottles that come with most breast pumps are now made without bisphenol A (BPA), a chemical used to make polycarbonate rigid and shatterproof that has been associated with adverse health effects in children. To play it safe, look for "No BPA" labeling on product packaging. For more on BPA, see the Baby Bottles & Nipples chapter beginning on page 37.

Plastic bottles made without BPA (non-polycarbonate) are solid and sturdy, and a safer way to store breast milk than plastic milk storage bags, which can become contaminated with bacteria if they get bumped by anything sharp, such as the edge of an ice cube.

Today, most breast pump breast milk collection bottles such as these from Medela are made without BPA, but check the labeling.

What's Available

Now that breast-feeding has made a comeback (some hospitals organize human breast-milk banks for babies who can't physically breast-feed), the options in breast pumps are dizzying. Some major brands, in alphabetical order, are: Ameda (*www.ameda.com*), Dr. Brown's (*www.handi-craft.com*), Evenflo (*www.evenflo.com*), Lansinoh (*www.lansinoh.com*), Medela (*www.medela.com*), Philips Avent (*www.avent.philips.com*), Playtex (*www.playtexbaby.com*), The First Years/Learning Curve (*www.learningcurve.com*), and Whittlestone (*www.whittlestone.com*).

Breast pumps come in these basic types: large, hospital-grade, dual-action, which typically aren't available for sale (you rent them from the hospital where you deliver or from a lactation or rental center); midweight, personal-use, automatic models that are comparable to hospital-grade pumps and can travel with you; small electric or battery-operated units that double- or single-pump; and one-handed manual pumps. There's even a "hands-free" pump you can strap around your waist that operates while you work, or relax. Here's the lowdown on each:

Hospital-grade breast pumps

These electric powerhouses are about the size of a car battery and can weigh 5 to 11 pounds. Manufactured for users in hospitals and for

Parent to Parent

"My company purchased a hospital-grade pump for the women who were nursing to use in a private room equipped with a refrigerator," says Megy Karydes, a mom of two from Chicago. (Each woman brought all her own attachments including the plastic tubing.)

"There's no way I could have continued to pump without it, since I often had meetings throughout the day and even a few minutes of pumping made the difference for me."

those who choose to rent, they have sensitive controls that allow you to regulate suction rhythm, intensity, and pressure. Some have a pumping action that's almost identical to a baby's natural sucking, which can help build and maintain your milk supply. A hospital-grade pump can cut pumping sessions in half—to just 15 minutes with a dual pump, which empties both breasts at once. These are expensive to buy, but you can rent them from hospitals, medical-supply stores, lactation consultants, drugstores, and specialty retail stores.

Pros: They're fast and efficient. Many are also light, comparable to a midweight, personal-use automatic pump.

Cons: Even though some come with a rechargeable battery and an adapter for use in a vehicle, many don't come with a discreet carrying case. You wouldn't want to lug one to and from work every day because it can be awkward and heavy.

Price: As we mentioned, you can expect to pay around $55 a month to rent one. You may also need to purchase your own breast shields, collection bottles, and tubing, which can run an additional $40 or so. It's prohibitively expensive to buy (in the range of $900 to $1,000), so renting is the only realistic option.

Choose this option if: Nursing is difficult because your baby has trouble latching on; you're not sure how much you'll need a breast pump, but you want one on hand just in case; you plan to pump for three months or less from home; you must dramatically increase your milk supply and need the power of a hospital-grade pump.

Ameda's Elite Electric Breast Pump is a durable hospital-grade pump that's light, too. It weighs only 7 pounds including the battery.

Top brands/models to consider: the Elite Electric Breast Pump by Ameda (*www.ameda.com*); Medela's rental line: Symphony or Lactina Select (*www.medela.com*); and Whittlestone Breast Expresser (the rental version at *www.whittlestone.com*).

Midweight, personal-use, automatic breast pumps

Usually no bigger than a briefcase and weighing around 8 pounds or less, these electric breast pumps typically are lighter and slightly less efficient than the hospital-grade models. Like a hospital-grade pump, a personal-use automatic can slash pumping time because it has a powerful motor and serious suction. Many personal-use automatic pumps have suction that mimics a baby's natural sucking, which typically begins with rapid, high-frequency suction and changes to a slower, suck/swallow pattern. This mimicking fosters faster milk flow, although some pumps use a constant vacuum, with self-adjusting suction settings. Intermittent action better imitates a baby than a constant vacuum—and it's probably easier on you, too.

The Playtex Embrace Deluxe Double Electric Breast Pump System offers 25 speed and suction combinations. The pump fits all Playtex and most other standard reusable bottles.

Many models come housed in a black microfiber shoulder (a.k.a. "Metro") bag or backpack, which is ideal if you're working outside your home. They're often equipped with an adapter for your car's cigarette lighter or a battery pack for times when you're not near an electrical outlet. They may come with all necessary attachments, including removable cooler carrier and cooling element, battery pack, AC adapter, and collection containers, lids, and stands.

Pros: This is a quick and portable way to double-pump and fill up a bottle in minutes.

Cons: It's probably more than you need if you plan to pump only occasionally. The pump can be a lot to lug if you're also carrying other things. "I actually ended up buying two pumps so all I had to bring back and forth to work was a cooler bag with the bottles. This way, I wasn't carrying a huge bag plus my briefcase and my purse each way," says Season Skuro, the mother of a 16-month-old, from Calabasas, Calif.

Price: $150 to $350 to buy.

Choose this option if: You'll be returning to work full- or part-time and you need to pump throughout the day to maintain your milk supply and express milk for missed feedings.

Top brands/models to consider: Ameda Purely Yours Breast Pump (www.ameda.com); Evenflo Comfort Select Performance Dual Auto Cycling Breast Pump (www.evenflo.com); Lansinoh Double Electric Breast Pump (www.lansinoh.com); Medela Pump in Style Advanced (www.medela.com); Philips Avent Isis IQ Duo Twin pump (www.avent .philips.com); Playtex Embrace Double Electric breast pump (www .playtexbaby.com); and Whittlestone Breast Expresser (the personal-use version at www.whittlestone.com).

Small electric or battery-operated units

Using widely available AA or C batteries or household current, these lightweight, compact devices can fit discreetly in your purse or briefcase. They're relatively quiet, but the suction can be sluggish, although the vacuum on some models can be regulated for maximum comfort. Others, though, have a constant vacuum that can cause nipple discomfort.

Pros: They are relatively inexpensive and portable. With the battery pack, you can pump anywhere, anytime.

Con: If you want to use this pump frequently, you may find that pumping takes too long. Consider one of these for occasional use only.

Price: $65 to $150 or more to buy.

Choose this option if: You need to pump only occasionally because you'll be away from your baby now and then—for a night out or for a couple of hours during the day.

Top models/brands to consider: Dr. Brown's Natural Flow Electric breast pump (www.hand-craft.com); Medela Single Deluxe or Swing Breast Pump (www.medela.com); Philips Avent ISIS Uno Handheld Electronic Breast Pumps (www.avent.philips.com); and Playtex Petite Double Electric Breast Pump (www.playtexbaby.com).

Manual breast pumps

With these small pumps, you produce the suction yourself by squeezing a bulb or lever or by manipulating a syringe-style cylinder. There are

> ✔ **Tip**
>
> A few electric breast pumps come with a manual breast pump, so you get two for the price of one.

many designs of manual pumps on the market. Cylinder, or piston-style, pumps usually allow you to control pressure and minimize discomfort. Some manual models can be operated with one hand. They're easier to use than those requiring one hand to hold, one to pump.

Pros: They're less expensive than electric models and don't need an electrical source or batteries, and often are compact enough to fit in a tote or purse.

Con: Manual pumps often are markedly slower than other pumps. We recommend these only for occasional use, such as when you're traveling.

Price: $40 to $65 to buy.

Choose this option if: You're a stay-at-home or work-from-home mom and you need to miss only a rare feeding because of a night out; you're traveling or you have plugged milk ducts or sore nipples. A manual pump is also ideal for pumping on the go, in places where electricity may not be available. Look for one with an ergonomic handle, not a bulb, though any small pump could tire your hand and arm and cause repetitive strain injuries if you use it frequently.

Top brands/models to consider: Ameda one-hand breast pump (*www.ameda.com*); Dr. Brown's manual breast pump (*www.handi-craft.com*); Evenflo Comfort Care or Comfort Select Manual Breast Pump (*www.evenflo.com*); Lansinoh manual breast pump (*www.lansinoh.com*); Medela Harmony (*www.medela.com*); Philips Avent ISIS Manual Breast Pump (*www.avent.philips.com*); and the Playtex Manual Pump (*www.playtexbaby.com*).

Lansinoh Manual Breast Pump features an ergonomic handle and lightweight compact design.

Hands-free pumps

Medela's Freestyle (*www.medelafreestyle.com*), a rechargeable, double electric pump, is the first hands-free breast pump on the market. The breast shields attach to a nursing bra and the hands-free kit attaches to the top clasps of most nursing bras. The pump unit with a battery inside weighs less than a pound and can be worn on your waist with the adjustable belt for mobile pumping, or placed on your lap or a table. It uses Medela's 2-Phase Expression technology, which mimics the feel and sucking pattern of a baby. The product also features an LCD screen with a digital display that can be read during low-light use, which can help you track how long and the level at which you've been pumping. You can also program the Freestyle to repeat your most comfortable pumping pattern so you don't have to reset it every time.

Pros: You don't have to drop everything you're doing. Since your hands are free, you can pump while you're reading, working, e-mailing, talking on the phone, or even holding your baby. "We created this product because we learned from our market research that moms want to multi-task while they're pumping and they don't want to be tethered to a power outlet," says Susan Rappin, director for consumer product management for Medela, adding that although the pump is lightweight, it's powerful enough to empty both breasts at once quickly. "It's versatile, too," she says. "You don't have to use the hands-free option if you don't want to."

Cons: Get ready to get rigged. The Freestyle's setup instructions warn you: "Don't be overwhelmed by the parts and pieces!" We haven't tested this pump, but we found that the setup process, which involves multiple straps and clasps, is complicated. To curtail frustration, don't attempt to assemble when you're sleep deprived or otherwise not at your sharpest. To speed the process, have your partner help you, or get assistance from a friend or relative who is an experienced Freestyle user, or a lactation consultant. Be sure you have the right size breast shields; Using shields that are too small can cause breast soreness. Medela offers sizes from 21 mm to 36 mm. In general, "If it's painful to pump, you should stop and see a lactation consultant who can assess why," says lactation director Tully.

Price: $380 to buy.

Choose this option if: Your schedule is hectic and you like the idea of being able to do something else while pumping. Note: Many regular breast pumps can be made hands-free with a special pumping bra. For more information, see the Nursing Bras chapter, page 257.

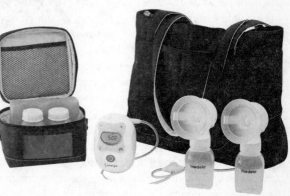

The Medela Freestyle is battery operated. Since you're not tethered to an outlet, it can be strapped around your waist for truly mobile pumping.

Don't Buy a Used Personal-Use Pump

It isn't a good idea to use the same personal-use breast pump for more than one baby or to borrow or buy a used pump. But if you must, wash the parts and replace the tubing.

A used pump can put your baby's health at risk because milk and moisture can enter the tubing and bacteria and viruses can grow there. These potential contaminants can travel through the tubing and lodge in the pump's internal mechanism—the part that connects to the tubing—which can't be removed, replaced, or fully sterilized. With each suction and release, these contaminants can be microscopically blown into the milk you're expressing and possibly infect your baby, says Nancy S. Mohrbacher, a lactation consultant with Ameda Breastfeeding Products in Lincolnshire, Ill., the maker of Ameda breast pumps. That's why manufacturers encourage nursing moms to think of a breast pump as a toothbrush or lipstick—like any personal-use item you wouldn't share with a friend.

However, hospital-grade rental pumps, such as Ameda's Elite and Medela's Symphony and Lactina, are designed for many users and are built to last for years. With these pumps, each mother receives her own milk collection kit to attach to the pump. They're designed so that milk comes in contact only with the collection kit's pieces and not the pump itself, so there's no cross-contamination when the pump is used by more than one mother.

The Purely Yours Breast Pump by Ameda is the first personal-use pump on the market that features a patented silicone diaphragm. This barrier prevents air from flowing between the pump tubing and the breast flange—so you never have to clean the tubing. The diaphragm protects expressed milk from contamination that may exist in the pump and protects the pump from any contamination in the milk. It also prevents self-contamination, which can occur when moisture and/or milk particles enter the pump tubing and organisms, such as bacteria and mold, grow there and get blown back into the milk. Still, even with its unique milk collection system, the Ameda Purely Yours pump isn't marketed as a multi-user pump because it's not as durable as Ameda's rental pumps. Ameda's rental pumps use the same milk collection kit and have the same diaphragm barrier, but they have a heavier-duty motor, Mohrbacher says.

Nonetheless, breast pumps, especially double electric models, are pricey. If you must buy a preowned pump or borrow one from a friend (but again—we don't recommended it because it's very risky), wash all the parts you can with soap and water according to manufacturer's directions, and replace the tubing, says lactation director Mary Rose Tully. This advice also applies if you're planning to use the same breast pump you got new for baby number one for later siblings. "One of the worst cases of mastitis [a breast infection typically associated with breast-feeding] I ever saw was with a woman who had put her breast pump away for four years until her next baby came along," Tully says. Organisms in the tubing got reactivated and some blew back against her and got into her system.

Features to Consider

Suction settings. The best pumps mimic a baby's natural nursing rhythm by automatically pumping in two distinct modes: rapid, to simulate a baby's rapid sucking to begin fast milk flow, and slower, to simulate a baby's deeper sucking to produce the most milk flow. Together, the two phases offer a more authentic breast-feeding experience with greater comfort, increased milk flow, and quicker pumping time. "Closer to nature" brands/models on the market that purport to pump more like a baby include Medela's Pump In Style Advanced, Swing, and Freestyle pumps, its hospital-grade Symphony, and its Harmony manual breast pump. Others, such as Avent's ISIS iQ Duo and ISIS iQ Uno electronic dual and single breast pumps, allow you to automate the pumping rhythm, speed, and suction at the touch of a button instead of relying on preset controls.

Warranty. If you'll be using your personal-use breast pump every day, look for a pump that has at least a one-year warranty on the motor. A generous warranty typically is a sign of quality and durability.

Adapter/batteries. If you're pumping on the road or you don't have access to an electrical outlet (say, for example, you don't have a pumping room at work and you're relegated to a restroom stall), look for a pump that can run on batteries or that includes an adapter that can attach to your car's cigarette lighter. However, even if you have a Freestyle hands-free model, we don't recommend pumping while driving because it can be distracting.

Double-pumping. If you'll be pumping at work or pumping often, get a double hospital-grade or midweight, personal-use, automatic pump. By expressing both breasts at once, you can complete a pumping session in 10 to 15 minutes. Besides being fast, double pumps are better for milk production. Double-pumping increases levels of prolactin, the hormone responsible for milk production. Smaller pumps or a single pump may not be able to maintain your milk supply long-term and can quickly become frustrating to use.

Carrying case. If you'll be commuting or traveling, a professional-looking pump "briefcase," sporty backpack, or "Metro"

The Philips Avent ISIS Twin Electronic breast pump features a gentle vacuum and soft massage cushions that flex in and out to replicate a baby's sucking action and stimulate a fast, natural letdown.

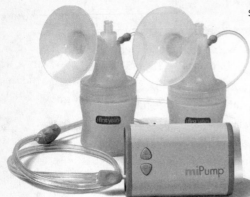

The First Years' miPump Double Pump is light and compact, electric or battery-operated, and has eight suction settings.

shoulder bag is the way to go. Most models, other than the hospital-grade ones, come in a chic, black microfiber case with a shoulder strap. Some models, such as Medela's Pump in Style Advanced, also feature a removable cooling compartment and pump motor, so you can lighten your load by leaving a section at work.

Insulated storage compartments. Look for compartments in the pump's carrying case if you'll be pumping on the go and need to store your milk for later. But be sure to keep an ice pack or two with your breast milk in the storage compartment.

Pump weight. Even a 5-pound breast pump can seem heavy after a while if you have to carry it back and forth to work every day along with a briefcase, a purse, and maybe a diaper bag, if you'll be dropping off your child at day care. If you've got a lot to lug and you'll be traveling frequently with your breast pump, get the lightest pump possible within the range of pump you need to buy. For example, the Ameda Purely Yours with Backpack, a double electric pump, weighs a pound less than the comparable Medela Pump in Style Advanced with Backpack.

LCD display and memory indicator. Some breast pumps, such as the Medela Freestyle, offer an LCD panel and programmable memory that allows you to record your preferred pumping pattern, so you don't have to reset the pump each time you use it.

Recommendations

Consider renting a hospital-grade breast pump if you're not sure how long you'll need to use a pump or if you know you'll need to pump for only a short time and you plan to be home with your baby. If you expect to use a breast pump regularly, especially if you plan to return to work, buy a top-quality midweight, personal-use, automatic model at the best price you can find. This caliber of pump will help you get a significant volume of milk in a given time and will be your best bet for maintaining your milk supply. If you plan to use a breast pump only occasionally, a manual pump or a small electric or battery-operated one will probably be all you need.

Tips for Successful Pumping at Work

Here are tips from moms who've been there, and other experts.

◆ Learn to pump during your maternity leave so you're familiar with your pump and have the system down by the time you return to work.

◆ Don't psyche yourself out. Pumping at work can be challenging, but if you dwell on the negative, you'll talk yourself out of it. And don't feel guilty, either. "Most smokers are taking more breaks than I do," says Hillary Bates, a mom of one from Columbus, Ohio, who has been pumping at work for four months.

◆ Get a double electric breast pump. Don't waste your time single-pumping. "Buy the best, most powerful unit you can afford. Without the right equipment, you're almost doomed to fail," says Jeanmarie Ferrara, the mother of a 10-month-old daughter, from Miami.

◆ Pump in a room with a lock on the door, if possible. You'll need privacy to relax.

◆ "Keep to a strict pumping schedule, a set number of times daily for no less than 15 minutes," says Julie Kupsov, the mother of an 11-month-old, from Farmington Hills, Mich. If you work in an office that uses electronic calendars, mark off time for your daily pumping breaks. It reduces the chance you'll have meetings that conflict with your regular pumping time. Going too long between pumping sessions can be uncomfortable.

◆ "Use the time you pump to catch up on e-mails or do light reading so you can keep working, too," says Tracy Baldwin, a new mom from Chicago. "But don't pump while you're on the phone with coworkers or clients. It puts them in an awkward position: 'What's that noise?'"

◆ Bring your baby's T-shirt from home. A photo of your baby is nice, "but it's the smell that tricks your body into thinking your baby is nearby, which can help with letdown," says University of North Carolina breastfeeding expert Labbok.

◆ Consider skipping the company outing. "A few weeks after I came back from maternity leave, my company had its semiannual outing to a museum and lobster bay cruise. I couldn't find a quiet and private place to pump, so I ended up locking myself in the bathroom of the bus we chartered. While it turned into an interesting bonding opportunity with my colleagues (they were painfully aware of what I was doing), I would probably skip out on this type of all-day event if I had to do it all over again," says Angie Henderson Moncada, the mom of a 12-month-old, from Miami.

◆ Keep ice packs on hand or get a small fridge for your office to keep milk cold (and safe for your baby to consume).

Since using a breast pump can be tricky, most manufacturers now supply informational brochures with their units. You also can call manufacturers' customer-service lines if you encounter problems with a specific pump. Your pump may have a warranty that allows repair or replacement. Check the terms before you buy because they vary. Keep your receipt or the printout from your baby registry as proof of purchase.

There's a host of information on the Internet about breast-feeding in general and specific guidance on such issues as how to get into a pumping routine after you return to work. The La Leche League, at *www.llli.org*, is a good place to start. This Web site offers a mother-to-mother forum, an online community of other mothers you can turn to for ideas on how to overcome breast-feeding obstacles, answers to your most pressing questions, podcasts on breast-feeding and parenting, and information on monthly meetings with experienced mothers in your community who are accredited by La Leche League International. To find a La Leche League group near you, visit *www.lllusa.org/groups.php*.

9

chapter

Car
Seats

A child car seat should be high on your to-buy list. You'll need one to bring your baby home from the hospital and for every car trip with your baby thereafter.

The Chicco KeyFit 30 infant car seat has a removable newborn insert that accommodates babies as small as 4 pounds. The seat can be used until your child weighs 30 pounds.

In fact, hospitals and birthing centers often won't let you leave by car with your newborn if you don't have a car seat. Every state requires that kids up to 3 years of age ride in a car seat; many require booster seats for older children. In this chapter, we'll focus on which car seat to buy when and how to install it properly.

What's Available

Some brands of car seats you're likely to encounter are, in alphabetical order: Baby Trend (*www.babytrend.com*), Britax (*www.britaxusa.com*), Chicco (*www.chiccousa.com*), Combi (*www.combi-intl.com*), Compass (*www.learningcurve.com*), Cosco (*www.coscojuvenile.com*), Eddie Bauer (*www.djgusa.com*), Evenflo (*www.evenflo.com*), Graco (*www.gracobaby.com*), Maxi-Cosi (*www.maxi-cosi.com*), Mia Moda (*www.miamodainc.com*), Peg-Pérego (*www.pegperego.com*), phil&teds (*www.philandteds.com*), Orbit Baby (*www.orbitbaby.com*), Recaro (*www.recaro.com*), Safety 1st (*www.safety1st.com*), and teutonia (*www.teutoniausa.com*). There are also car beds for preemies and other very small newborns if there's a concern that a car seat may not provide a secure fit or that it may exacerbate breathing problems. In addition, there are specially designed car seats for children with special needs. Ask your pediatrician for a recommendation or visit the Automotive Safety Program at *www.preventinjury.org* (or call 800-543-6227). Every model of car seat sold in the U.S. must meet federal safety standards. These are your basic choices:

Infant car seats such as the Britax Companion click into a base that remains in the car, making them convenient to use as a baby carrier.

Infant seats

Unlike other types of seats, these are designed to be used only with the baby facing the rear of the car. They are for babies up to 22 pounds; a few can be used for infants up to 30 pounds or more. Be sure to observe the height limit of the infant seat as well. If your child outgrows the seat in height before his weight, or vice versa, he's ready for the next-phase car seat, a convertible model used in the rear-facing position. Convertible models can be used rear-facing for new

Infant Car Seats

◆ Have your baby ride rear-facing. The American Academy of Pediatrics recommends that all infants should ride rear-facing until they reach, at minimum, 1 year of age and weigh at least 20 pounds; but the AAP prefers that they remain rear-facing until they reach the highest weight or height allowed by the manufacturer. New research shows that, for the best protection from injury, children up to 23 months should remain rear-facing. Many convertible models offer the potential to keep babies rear-facing up until they reach as much as 35 pounds. If your baby outgrows her infant car seat (in height or weight) before age 1, install a convertible car seat in the rear-facing position and keep it that way as long as the seat allows. Don't place an infant seat in a forward-facing position; it always must stay-rear facing.

◆ Never place an infant car seat on a bed or sofa; any soft surface is a suffocation hazard if the seat tips over, trapping your baby's face.

◆ Never put an infant car seat on an elevated surface as it can slide off.

infants, too. However, infant car seats are preferable because they tend to fit small infants more securely and offer the convenience of a carrier that detaches from the base. Many strollers are now also designed to accommodate infant car seats, or you can purchase a car-seat-carrier stroller frame that will accept many infant car seats. For more information on infant car seats and car-seat carrier stroller frames, see Strollers, page 311.

Nearly all infant seats have a base that secures to your vehicle with LATCH connections or a vehicle safety belt. LATCH, which stands for Lower Anchors and Tethers for Children, includes belts that hook or "click" the base to metal anchors in the car. If you have more than one car, buy an extra base for the second one. You can also strap most infant seats into a car without a base, using the vehicle safety belts.

Infant seats have either a three-point harness—two adjustable shoulder straps that come together at a buckle in the seat itself or at a crotch strap—or an adjustable five-point system—two straps over the shoulders, two for the thighs, and a crotch strap. The vast majority of infant car seats now have five-point harnesses, which we recommend.

The handle on infant seats usually swings from a position behind the seat when in the car to an upright position for carrying. When using as a carrier, be sure the seat is properly reclined so that your baby's head doesn't fall forward and inhibit his breathing. Slots underneath

How to Tote an Infant Car Seat

If you opt to use your infant car seat as a carrier, realize that it can be a killer on your wrists, elbows, lower back, and neck if you tote it by the handle or if you put it on your forearm like a handbag. "The greater the horizontal distance from the weight you're carrying to your torso, the more stress on your joints, discs, ligaments, and muscles," says Mary Ellen Modica, a physical therapist from the STEPS program at Schwab Rehabilitation Hospital in Chicago, Ill. "It's equivalent to walking around with three or four full paint cans in one hand—something most people wouldn't do, but yet, they'll carry a car seat that way."

Instead, "Carry the car seat in front of you so that you have both hands on the handle," advises Diane Dalton, orthopedic clinical specialist at Boston University's Sargent College of Health and Rehabilitation Sciences, in Boston, Mass. With the weight of the seat and your baby centered and close to your trunk, the force on your body will be reduced, Dalton says. Another option: Leave the infant seat in your car and transfer your baby to a soft infant carrier (see page 291) or a stroller (see page 311), or use a travel system (see page 115).

Or simply carry your baby in your arms, and your child will benefit. Infants transported in this way use their head, neck, and shoulder muscles to stabilize themselves and, in the process, establish stronger trunk stability.

many seats help them attach to the frame of a shopping cart, but the AAP as well as many manufacturers don't recommend using them this way, and neither do we. (For more on shopping cart safety, see page 283.)

Pro: With an infant car seat, you can move your baby from car to house or vice versa without waking her up—a plus for both of you. But don't let your baby sleep in an infant car seat for long periods of time after you have removed it from the car. Move her to a firm, flat surface, such as a full-size crib, as soon as you can.

Con: Your baby may outgrow an infant car seat quickly and become too heavy for you to use it as a carrier. As a result, you may find yourself having to buy a convertible car seat after your baby is 6 to 9 months old. However, our advice is still to start with an infant seat before moving up to a convertible seat because it's more secure and compact for infants. We consider them the safest way to transport the youngest babies.

Price range: $75 for an individual seat to $300 for a seat and base with the seat pairing up with a compatible stroller; stroller frame sold separately. At least one brand of infant car seat, the Orbit, is sold as a unit—car seat base, infant car seat, and exclusive coordinating stroller frame. We have not tested the Orbit infant car seat/stroller system, which retails for $900.

Travel systems

A travel system offers one-stop shopping, consisting of an infant car seat, a car-seat base for your car, and a separate stroller, all in one. With these systems, you create a carriage by snapping an infant car seat into a stroller. The snap-on car seat is generally positioned atop the stroller so the infant rides facing you—the person pushing. Once your baby can sit up, he can ride in the stroller seat sans car seat. Many car-seat manufacturers offer these combination strollers/infant car seats. And many stand-alone strollers are now designed to accommodate infant car seats from various manufacturers.

The Graco SnugRide with EPS pairs with the Graco Quattro Tour stroller to form a travel system.

Pro: A travel system allows you to move a sleeping baby in an infant car seat undisturbed from car to stroller and vice versa. That's fine for short jaunts, but be sure to give your baby a break from an infant car seat by carrying her in a soft infant carrier or just on your shoulder, if you'll be out all day.

Cons: Some travel-system strollers can be used only with a car seat from the same company. A way around that is to choose a stroller that accepts car seats from a number of different manufacturers. Travel systems can also be bulky, so if you're a city dweller who negotiates more subway stairs than highways or if the trunk of your car isn't too roomy, you may be better off with a separate car seat and a compact stroller that offers a reclined, safely enclosed space that's appropriate for a newborn. For more information on travel systems, see Strollers on page 311.

Price range: $110 to $350.

Convertible seats

With a convertible seat, your child faces rearward as an infant (up to 30 or 35 pounds, depending on the model), and forward as a toddler (generally up to 40 pounds, though some seats have front-facing weight limits

of 65 pounds or more). Models typically have an adjustable five-point harness system, which we recommend based on our tests. A convertible car seat can be a money saver, taking your child from infancy to kindergarten and maybe even beyond. But we advise starting with an infant seat first, as mentioned earlier, then switching to a convertible car seat when your baby outgrows his infant car seat. Choose among convertible car seats in our Ratings (page 125). Keep your child's convertible seat facing the rear of the vehicle until he is 23 months old or until he reaches the weight and height limits specified by the manufacturer. Don't switch the convertible car seat to a front-facing orientation for a child younger than 1 year and weighing less than the seat's minimum weight limit in that mode.

One of our top-rated convertible car seats, the Britax Diplomat, works rear-facing from 5 to 35 pounds, forward-facing from 1 year old and 20 to 40 pounds.

Once your baby reaches the required weight or height, you can turn the seat around, but don't be too quick to do so. "The longer you can keep your baby rear-facing, the better," says Kisha Price, a health educator and certified child passenger safety technician at the Johns Hopkins Children's Safety Center in Baltimore, Md. Some children ride rear-facing beyond their second birthday. Convertible seats aren't compatible with strollers, so you will have to transfer your baby from the convertible car seat to a stroller when you're ready to set out on foot. Such jostling can wake a sleeping baby, which can be problem if you need to take your child on frequent shopping expeditions or other errands.

Price range: $60 to $360.

Toddler booster seats

A belt-positioning booster seat, such as the top-rated Graco backless TurboBooster, can properly position your child for the vehicle's safety belts.

Looking like large versions of convertible seats, these front-facing seats are used with an internal harness for toddlers 20 to 40 pounds. They're either LATCH-attached or can be secured using a vehicle safety belt. Some toddler-boosters can be used with the seat's own harness for weights up to 65 or even as high as 80 pounds, for kids who are heavier or larger than average for their age. Most vehicles limit LATCH installations to 48 lbs. so the vehicle belts must be used to install them beyond that point—and can't be used to secure the child.

Price Range: $44 to $280.

Belt-Positioning Boosters

These are generally for children weighing 40 to 100 pounds. Belt positioning boosters use only the vehicle's own safety belts to restrain the child but are designed to correctly position both the lap and shoulder portions of the vehicle's belt correctly across the stronger parts of a child's body, the collarbone and hip area. They should be used until a child is at least 57 inches tall—the minimum height at which car seat belts will fit a child correctly.

Price Range: $20 to $350.

Built-in seats

Some U.S. and foreign automakers offer on select cars and minivans an integrated, forward-facing child seat that has a harness and accommodates toddlers weighing more than 20 pounds. There are also some booster-seat versions. Built-in seats must meet the same performance standards as add-on child seats. However, they offer little or no side protection and they're usually located next to a door, instead of the safer center position. You may still also need proper child restraint for when your child travels in other vehicles. And of course built-in seats can't be used for infants who must ride rear facing. We recommend against children between 12 months and 23 months facing forward because they are safer in a rear-facing convertible seat.

Toddler boosters, like the Eddie Bauer Deluxe High Back Booster Car Seat, can be used with your vehicle's safety belt (not the seat's internal harness) when kids reach 40 pounds. Kids can ride that way until they reach 100 pounds.

Shopping Secrets

Check car seat features before you buy. Place similar-looking models side by side in the store to compare features. Put your child in the seat to get a sense of the ease of buckling and unbuckling.

Make sure the seat is compatible with your car. Test the fit of any models you're considering in your own car. If possible, bring the floor model to your car for a test installation. Be aware that some vehicle seats are too short, indented, or excessively sloped to allow a good fit of a child car seat.

A Look at the LATCH System

Since September 1, 2002, all child car seats with an internal harness (three- or five-point safety belt) and nearly all passenger vehicles sold in the U.S. have been required to include equipment designed for simpler installation. This system, called LATCH (Lower Anchors and Tethers for Children), consists of child car-seat connections that attach to anchor points in the vehicle—two lower attachments that attach to anchors usually found in the crease of a vehicle's back seat, and an upper tether on a child safety seat that connects with a top anchor built into or near a vehicle's back seat. (Most infant seats don't use the top anchor, nor do convertible seats in rear-facing mode.) LATCH eliminates the need to use a vehicle's safety belts to install the seat. You can still use safety belts to install a LATCH-equipped child car seat— for example, in an older car that lacks LATCH anchors. But we think you're more likely to get a secure connection with LATCH. We recommend using it if your car has it.

LATCH isn't without its problems, though. Anchors in many cars are hard to access. And many vehicles don't have LATCH anchors in the safest seat in the car: the center rear.

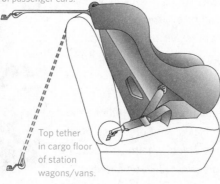

Top tether in rear filler panel of passenger cars.

Top tether in cargo floor of station wagons/vans.

When installing a LATCH car seat, attach the lower anchor and the upper tether. A secure car seat shouldn't be able to move more than 1 inch forward or sideways.

(It can also be tough to adjust safety belts to a car seat located in the center rear.) There are some exceptions as some vehicles have center LATCH anchors. Some Ford models also allow parents to use the inner two LATCH anchors from the outer seats to install a child seat in the center rear if permitted by the child seat manufacturer. A big advantage of LATCH is that once you access the car anchors, the car seat typically fits securely. A tight fit is a major factor in crash protection. With LATCH, our testers are able to get child seats to fit tightly in almost all cars. With vehicle safety belts, a secure fit is harder to achieve in some cars.

But LATCH doesn't trump the rear center seat. If you have the choice between installing your child's car seat in the back middle seat of your vehicle with safety belts (and without LATCH), or an outer (window) seat with LATCH, "it's safer to use the middle seat without LATCH, if you can get a tight fit of the car seat using the seat belt," says safety technician Kisha Price of Johns Hopkins.

Don't Do the Twisted-Car-Seat Lift

Lifting your toddler into and out of a forward-facing car seat can put stress on your knees, lower back, neck, shoulder, elbows, and wrists, leading to injury over time. That's especially true if you twist and lean into the car with both your feet on the ground. You'll probably catch yourself doing this unhealthy stretch once you become aware of it. A better idea: If your car seat is near the door, put one leg into the car and face the car seat as you're putting your child in it, advises Boston University's Diane Dalton. You'll take pressure off your back. If your car seat is in the middle of the back seat, climb in and face it as you lift your child in. Of course, positioning yourself properly can take a few extra seconds you may not always feel you have. Still, "it doesn't have to be perfect all the time," says Dalton. "But the more often you lift correctly, the better you're able to tolerate it when you don't."

Try the floor model of a convertible seat in both the rear- and front-facing positions. Check out the harness release button in the rear-facing position; in some models it may be too low to reach comfortably. If the store won't let you take the seat out to your car to try it, make sure you can return any car seat you buy or, better yet, go to another store.

Check the store's return policy. If you're not happy with a particular car seat for whatever reason, it's important to know that you can return it and try again with another model. Be aware that a badly soiled or damaged seat may not be exchanged.

Features to Consider

"Push-on" style LATCH Connectors. These "click" into the lower anchor bar of the LATCH system. They're often easier to use than hooks, especially if the vehicle's LATCH anchors are hard to reach.

Recline adjustment. This feature allows you to tilt the seat back to reach a safe and comfortable angle. Look for one with a button, knob, or dial that's easy to use on infant seats. Some convertible seats recline to up to five positions, which is handier than using a wedge or rolled towel to get the correct recline when rear-facing or to keep a forward-facing sleeping toddler comfortable.

Level indicator. This feature lets you know when the seat is correctly reclined. The best versions operate akin to a level you might use for a home construction project, making it easy to see if the car seat is at the correct angle. When the angle is right, the bubble in the small indicators on the seat remains between the lines.

Harness height adjustment. Look for seats with more than one set of harness slots (openings that allow you to move the harness position) so your baby has room to grow. The best versions can be adjusted without having to rethread the harness straps and can be moved without having to uninstall the seat. The harness fits properly in rear-facing seats when the top of it is at or below your child's shoulders, and in forward-facing seats when it's in the slots at or above your child's shoulders.

Chest clip and harness adjuster. Besides a five-point harness, look

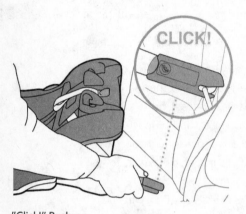

for an infant car seat with a chest clip that's easy to open and a single-step or single-pull harness adjuster. Both help make frequent adjustments to the safety harness correct and secure, and make it easier to get your baby in and out without a fuss.

Fabric. Today's car seats cater to every possible taste—neutral colors, plaids, animal and paw-print motifs, and pretty florals. Remember that, style aside, babies tend to be messy,

"Click!" Push-on LATCH connectors are often easier to use than the hook-type.

so washable fabric is a plus, especially if your car seat will be with you beyond the first year, when sippy cups and juice boxes come into play. Child car-seat fabric from some leading brands, however, requires hand washing and line drying. Most coverings are routed around the harness-strap system and are held in place with elastic so they can be removed for laundering, but in some cases extracting the fabric from the seat can require extensive dismantling. Check the seat's manual and the manufacturer's Web site for how-tos.

Snack accessories. Many convertible and booster seats come with cup holders and snack trays. These are nice, but not necessary. Having your child snack while you drive is risky because your eyes are on the road. If she chokes, you may not know it, especially if she's sitting facing the rear. A juice box or sippy cup for the road is OK, but otherwise plan ahead, and have your child eat before you leave. Besides being safer, having a no-snacking policy can keep your car cleaner, too.

Extras. Add-on seat covers to gussy up your baby's car seat, boots (fabric covers for infant car seats designed to protect your baby's legs from the elements), thicker padding, and adjustable head-support cushions may offer greater comfort. But buy them only if they are sold by the same maker as the seat and for that specific seat. Some models have elastic side pockets for toys, bottles, or snacks. As your baby grows, they can come in handy, but they're certainly not necessary.

Car Seat Installation: Getting It Right

One study estimated that as many as 80 percent of infant car seats may be installed or used improperly, which can dramatically increase a child's risk of injury in a crash. Kisha Price, the Johns Hopkins safety technician, thinks it may be even worse than that. "From my experience, I've seen probably two car seats out of a thousand installed correctly," she says. Car seats are complicated because you have to install the seat in your vehicle and use it correctly with your child in it. There's a lot of room for error, especially considering that not every vehicle on the road is designed the same. That's why it's a good idea to visit a free safety seat inspection station near you and have a certified car seat technician install the car seat you've selected before your baby is born. You can find child safety seat inspection stations through the National Highway Traffic Safety Administration (NHTSA). Visit *www.nhtsa.dot.gov/cps/ cpsfitting/index.cfm*. (You may need to make an appointment with the inspection station.) Encourage grandparents and anyone else who will be transporting your child in their vehicle to do the same.

If that's not convenient or you decide to install your car seat yourself, visit a car seat inspection station to double-check your work as soon as possible afterward (ditto for grandparents and babysitters). You can also find tips about car seat installation and use at the NHTSA site. Many car seat manufacturers also have an installation video on their Web site. Take the time to watch it before you attempt to install your car seat. When installing a seat for the first time, give yourself a good half-hour. If you can recruit a helper, even better. Here are a few more pointers for making installation easier:

Read all about it. Consult the instructions that come with the seat so you're familiar with the seat before you try to install it. For example, whether you choose to install your baby's infant car seat using your

More Tips for Safer Seating

◆ Always use a car safety seat and make sure your child is buckled up every time you drive, even if it's just down the street or crisscrossing a parking lot.

◆ Don't use products that are not approved by the manufacturer for your particular seat, such as an after-market infant headrest or cushions. They may alter the effectiveness of the car seat in the event of an accident. "If it didn't come with your vehicle or in the box with your car seat, you probably shouldn't be using it," says certified child passenger safety technician Kisha Price.

◆ Location, location. The safest place for a child is in your vehicle's rear center seat. The car seat should never be installed on a front seat that has an air bag. Two exceptions: If your car doesn't have a back seat, or if your child has a medical condition that requires constant monitoring, you can have an on/off switch installed for the front-passenger air bag or have the air bag deactivated (but only if there is no airbag on/off switch for the model of car) so the child's car seat can go next to the driver. But to have either done you'll need a letter of authorization from NHTSA. To obtain one, contact the agency via its Web site, *www.nhtsa.gov.*

◆ Insist on new. Although there are many baby items you can borrow or buy secondhand, don't make a car seat one of them if you can avoid it. A used seat may have been in a crash or recalled. The manufacturer's instructions may be missing.

◆ Know the age of your seat. If, for some reason, you must use a second-hand seat, avoid those with an unknown history or that are older than 6 years, because components can degrade over time. If you're considering using the same car seat for your next baby, start over and buy a new one if the seat is more than 6 years old, or close to it. Look for a label on the seat that indicates the date it was made.

◆ Avoid recalled models. You can check for recalled models and sign up to receive e-mail recall notifications of child restraints at *www-odi.nhtsa .dot.gov/cars/problems/recalls.* (About

vehicle's safety belts or with LATCH, with or without the base, you'll need to follow the specific area in the manual that relates to your installation situation. Also, check your vehicle owner's manual for information on how to find and use your car's LATCH anchors or safety belts with that car seat. Some car manufacturers also have a free how-to brochure or video that can help. Keep these instructions handy for future reference. The NHTSA Web site also has downloadable instructional videos on installing the various types of car seats with LATCH (search for "LATCH instructional videos").

eight car seats are recalled each year.) You'll also find monthly recall reports at *www.ConsumerReports.org*.

◆ Send in the registration card that comes with a new car seat. Or register the seat you buy on the manufacturer's Web site. You can also go to the NHTSA Web address above for major manufacturer's registration forms or to have NHTSA register your seat with the manufacturer for you. When your seat is registered, you can be notified by the manufacturer if the car seat is recalled.

◆ Replace the seat after a crash. NHTSA guidelines say that child safety seats do not automatically need to be replaced following a minor crash. A "minor crash" is one that meets all of the following criteria: The vehicle was able to be driven away from the crash site; the vehicle door nearest the safety seat was undamaged; there were no injuries to any of the vehicle occupants; the air bags (if present) did not deploy; and there is no visible damage to the safety seat. However, we believe you should err on the side of maximum safety and replace the seat even after a "minor" crash.

◆ Use the curb side (rather than the traffic side) when putting a child into your car or taking her out.

◆ Put loose items in the trunk, or strap them down with cargo anchors. Loose items can fly around in the car and hurt you or your baby if you stop suddenly or you're in a crash.

◆ Never leave your baby alone in the car, even if he's snoozing soundly. A car can get very hot, even on a cloudy day. And who knows what else might happen when your baby is unattended—even if you leave a baby monitor in the car with your baby.

◆ Don't forget your baby. We've all heard stories of distracted parents who drive to work with their baby in the car, forgetting that it was their day to drop the baby off at day care, especially if this isn't part of the normal routine. To help you remember that your baby is in the car, put a soft toy in the front seat. Or secure something you need, such as a purse or backpack, in the backseat near your baby as a reminder.

Position the seat. As we've mentioned, the center rear seat is the safest spot. You may have to place the seat next to a door if you have more than one small child; if there isn't a shoulder belt in the center (for use with a booster seat); if your LATCH-compatible vehicle lacks lower anchors in the center rear position and you don't want to use the center-seat vehicle safety belt; or if using the center rear seat would make the child seat unstable.

Secure the seat. Use your weight to push the child seat into your vehicle's seat (you may want to use a knee) while pulling the slack out of the LATCH strap or the car's safety belt. With a rear-facing seat, adjust the angle as directed by the manufacturer, using the level indicator or other means to get the backrest to a 45-degree recline. With a front-facing seat for a toddler up to 40 pounds, use the top tether of the car seat. If the top tether is not in use, such as with a rear-facing convertible seat, remove the top-tether strap or secure it so it doesn't fly around and injure your child in a crash. Similarly, if you use the car safety belts instead of the LATCH belts to install the seat make sure the LATCH belts are secure so they can't fly around. When you're securing an infant or toddler seat with a car's safety belt, you may need a locking clip for the lap belt so it remains tight. See the manufacturer's instructions for details.

Check the seat every time you use it. Whenever you buckle your child in, try shifting the car seat from side to side and back to front. It shouldn't move more than an inch in either direction. Make sure the harness straps fit snugly. Your overall goal: The seat must be buckled tightly into your vehicle and your child must be buckled snugly into the seat at all times.

Recommendations

Start out with an infant seat because that is the most secure seat for very young babies. Choose one with a five-point harness. Pay close attention to the height and weight limits of the seat you buy. When your child reaches either one of them, buy a convertible seat with a five-point

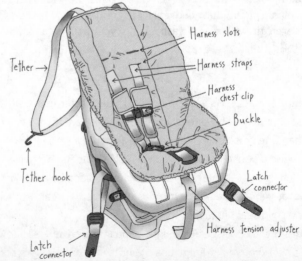

Here are some basic components you should be familiar with before installing a child seat in your vehicle. Shown is a convertible seat.

Tether →
Tether hook
Latch connector
Harness slots
Harness straps
Harness chest clip
Buckle
Latch connector
Harness tension adjuster

harness and use it in the rear-facing orientation up to the seat's limits in that mode, then switch the convertible seat around, and use it front-facing until your toddler reaches the next height and weight limits—at least until he is 23 months old. After that, use a toddler booster and then a booster seat until your child is tall enough to use the car's safety belts (at least 57 inches tall). Use our Ratings as a guide for those seats as well; they can be found at *www.ConsumerReports.org*. Even with a seat belt, all children under the age of 13 should ride in the back seat.

After selecting a car seat, use it safely: Don't wrap your baby up in a blanket, thick coat, or other bulky garment and then strap him into a restraint system. This can result in too much room between the child and the harness. If you need to keep your baby warm on a chilly day, strap her into an infant or convertible car seat and tuck a blanket or coat around her, keeping clear of her face.

Also, the harness chest clip should be fastened and positioned at your child's midchest or armpit level, which positions the shoulder straps correctly. Harness straps should be snug and straight (not twisted). You should not be able to insert more than one of your fingers between the harness and your baby. Position rear-facing (RF) harness straps at, or slightly below, your child's shoulders. On forward-facing (FF) convertible and toddler booster seats, harness straps should be positioned at, or slightly above, your child's shoulders.

Ratings • Convertible Car Seats

	Excellent	Very good	Good	Fair	Poor
	⊜	⊖	○	◖	●

Within types, in performance order.

Brand & model	Overall score	Overall	Price	Test results				Features		
	0 100 P | F | G | VG | E			Crash protection	Ease of use	RF fit to vehicle	FF fit to vehicle	RF weight range (lbs.)	FF weight range (lbs.)	Height range (in.)
40 LB. HARNESS CAPACITY SEATS										
Britax Diplomat	68	VG	260	⊖	○	⊖	⊖	5-35	20-40	22-40"
Cosco Scenera ✓	64	VG	60	⊖	○	○	⊖	5-35	22-40	19-43"
Graco ComfortSport	58	G	90	⊖	○	◖	⊖	5-30	20-40	<40"
Maxi-Cosi Priori	53	G	200	⊖	◖	⊖	⊖	5-35	22-40	19-43"
Safety 1st Alpha Omega Elite	52	G	140	⊖	○	●	⊖	5-35	22-40	19-43"

Brand & model	Overall score 0–100 P | F | G | VG | E	Overall	Price	Test results				Features		
				Crash protection	Ease of use	RF fit to vehicle	FF fit to vehicle	RF weight range (lbs.)	FF weight range (lbs.)	Height range (in.)
40 LB. HARNESS CAPACITY SEATS continued										
Combi Zeus Turn	46	G	300	○	○	○	○	5-22	20-40	19-40"
Safety 1st All-in-One-Deluxe	46	G	140	◑	◑	●	◑	5-35	22-40	19-43"
Evenflo Tribute V	45	G	60	◑	◑	○	◑	5-30	20-40	19-40"
MORE THAN 40 LB. HARNESS CAPACITY SEATS										
✓ **Evenflo** Triumph Advance Premier (manufactured after 12/4/2008)*	70	VG	180	◑	◑	○	◑	5-35	20-50	19-50"
✓ **Evenflo** Triumph Advance LX / DLX (manufactured after 12/4/2008)*	70	VG	135	◑	◑	○	◑	5-35	20-50	19-50"
Britax Boulevard	65	VG	310	◑	○	◑	◑	5-35	20-65	<49"
First Years True Fit	63	VG	190	◑	○	◑	◑	5-35	23-65	<50"
Britax Marathon	61	VG	270	◑	◑	◑	◑	5-35	20-65	<49"
Orbit Toddler	59	G	360	◑	○	●	◑	15-35	20-50	<49"
Sunshine Kids Radian 80	40	F	250	◑	◑	●	◑	5-35	20-80	<53"
Recaro Signo	30	F	290	○	●	●	○	5-35	20-70	<50"

*Some Evenflo Triumph Advance seats manufactured prior to 12/4/2008 exhibited cracking in simulated crash tests with a toddler-sized dummy in a rear-facing position. Although some of these cracks resulted in the shoulder belt leaving the seat's belt path, the seats still would have scored 'good' for crash protection. Evenflo has since modified the seats at issue and samples of the Triumph Advance seats manufactured from 12/4/2008 forward did not crack in our tests. See ConsumerReports.org for more information.

✓ **CR Best Buy** These models offer the best combination of performance and price. All are recommended.

Guide to the Ratings

Overall score is based on the potential for each seat to protect a child in a crash as well as our judgments of how easy the seat is to use and how well it fits in different vehicles. To judge **Crash Protection** we contract an outside laboratory to perform "sled" tests similar to those used to certify the seats to the government standard and that simulate the forces exerted on the seat and the instrumented child dummy in a frontal crash at 30 mph. Depending on the range of size and weight allowed by each seat, dummies representing kids of different sizes from 12-months to 10-years old maybe used to evaluate the potential for injury (to the head and chest) and how much movement (seat angle, head and knee) the seat allows. Convertible models are tested both rear and forward-facing and with different installation methods. **Ease-of-Use** is our judgment of how easy each seat is to use and includes items from how intuitive the labels and instructions are to how easy it is to make adjustments of clips, harnesses and installation features such as LATCH connectors, top tethers and belts, and how easy it is to transition from rear to forward-facing for convertible seat models. **Fit-to-Vehicle** rates how easy it is to securely and correctly install each seat in a variety of vehicles including sedans, SUVs and a minivan and how well they fit each vehicle once installed. Fit-to-Vehicle assesses rear and forward-facing installations separately for convertible seat models that can be installed in either orientation. Installations are done using both the vehicle belts and LATCH.

chapter

Changing Tables & Dressers

If you have the space, a well-stocked changing station will help make diaper duty go more smoothly by giving you a place to keep diapers and other essentials close at hand.

The safest changing tables have barriers on all four sides like this Cascade model from Child Craft.

You can diaper a baby just about anywhere you have room and where the baby is safe from falling, even on the floor. But since you'll change 2,000-plus diapers in your baby's first year alone, your back and your knees will benefit from something made for the task—either a standard changing table or a dresser that doubles as one. You'll be able to diaper your baby at a comfortable level (most changing tables stand 36 to 44 inches high), and have diapers within easy reach.

Unlike the crib or the floor, changing tables also have shelves, baskets, and/or drawers you can use to store other essentials, such as wipes, rash ointment, and a toy or two to keep your baby busy. A vinyl changing pad is usually included, but pad covers are sold separately, available in a variety of colors and patterns.

Changing-pad covers like this one from JoJo Designs can add a decorative touch to the nursery.

Consumers Union believes that a dedicated changing table with barriers on all four sides is the safest way to go. Another option you may see in stores is a removable changing pad that simply affixes to the top of a regular dresser. If you decide to go this route, which is the least expensive ($23 to $60), look for a changing table pad with at least two opposing contoured sides with a baby restraint strap, such as the Contour Changing Pad by Simmons Kids (www.simmonskids .com). With that style changing "table," you simply remove the pad (sold separately) when your baby grows out of the changing table stage (usually around age 2) and the changing table becomes a full-time dresser.

There are wooden, retractable changing tables, such as the Bellini Slide Top Changer (www.bellini.com), which sits on top of a Bellini dresser and attaches to the back of it with hidden L brackets. This mini-changing table has a flat changing surface. But to comply with the most recent industry safety standard, a changing table must have barrier protection on all sides unless it has a contoured pad, in which case barriers are required only on the two opposing long sides. Because the retractable (or slide-top) style has barriers on only the two short sides, we can't recommend it.

Smart Habits to Prevent Changing-Table Falls

Each year an estimated 3,000 babies, on average, are injured in changing table accidents. Some injuries are fatal. In no more time than it takes to turn for a diaper or wipe, an active baby can roll over and tumble to the ground. For a child, a fall from a changing table is like an adult plunging from several stories and could be fatal.

While changing tables with barriers on the two opposing long sides of the top comply with the ASTM International standard if they have a contoured changing pad, we recommend using a table with barriers on all four sides. Whether you use a table with barriers on two, three, or four sides, or you use a contoured pad on top of a dresser, prevent accidents by always using the safety straps on your changing table or pad. Never leave your baby unattended—even for a moment, even if you're using the safety straps, and

even if you're sure your baby is secure. In fact, make it a practice to keep one hand on your baby. When you are shopping for a changing table, make sure that the drawers and shelves are easily accessible so you won't have to let go of your baby to reach something.

Before changing your baby's diaper, be sure that any products you need—diapers, wipes, or the wipe warmer—are within arm's reach but not within your baby's range, and place the diaper pail adjacent to the table. If you run out of diapers or forget your little one's outfit, carry her with you while you get what you need. If you wheel your changing table from room to room, be sure to lock the wheels on a stable, flat surface. Park your changing table away from small objects your baby can grasp and hot objects, such as a radiator. Never wheel the table with your baby on it, strapped on or not.

Shopping Secrets

Size up storage. Most changing tables have open shelves that make it easy to reach diapers and clothing, either stacked or in decorative wicker baskets, but some have drawers or a combination of drawers and shelves. Having at least one drawer, preferably right under the table, can help you quickly retrieve the supplies you need, though some parents prefer open shelving. A drawer offers an advantage over open shelving because it can hide diaper supplies, which look like a treasure trove to the curious crawler and toddler your baby will become—before you know it.

Look for barriers on four sides. A traditional changing table is usually surrounded by a restraining barrier made of rails or solid wood. According to the latest voluntary safety guidelines from standards developer ASTM International, changing tables with a flat surface must have a barrier on all sides, as noted earlier. If only two or three sides of the table are protected instead of four, don't buy it.

The cherry sleigh-style changing table from Badger Basket can be used as shelving for clothes or toys when diapering days are over.

Go for girth. If you're planning to use a dresser as your changing table, think short and fat, not tall and thin. A dresser that's wider and lower to the ground will be less likely to fall forward when you place your baby on top. If you do use a dresser as a changing table, anchor it to the wall or floor if it is more than 30 inches tall. Use furniture restraint straps or other furniture restraints.

Consider convertibility. Some babies won't lie down to have their diaper changed once they become mobile, so you may use a changing table for less time than you think. To get more mileage out of this piece of furniture, some changing tables can be used as a desk, book or toy shelf, CD rack, or TV table, so you can use it well beyond the diaper years. Others become just a dresser once you remove the "changing station" on top. Convertibility makes sense, especially if you won't be using a changing table for more than one baby, though you might pay more for this option.

What's Available

Some major makers of changing tables and dressers that can be used as changing tables are, in alphabetical order: AFG Baby Furniture (*www.afgbabyfurniture.com*), Angel Line (*www.angelline.com*), Baby Mod (available at *www.walmart.com*; not sold in stores), Badger Basket (*www.badgerbasket.com*), Bassettbaby (*www.bassettbaby.com*), Bellini (*www.bellini.com*), Child Craft (*www.childcraftindustries.com*), Da Vinci (found at e-tailers such as Amazon.com), Delta Enterprise (*www.deltaenterprise.com*), Graco (*www.gracobaby.com*), L.A. Baby (*www.lababyco.com*), Pottery Barn Kids (*www.potterybarnkids.com*), Scandinavian Child (*www.scichild.com*); Simplicity for Children (*www.simplicityforchildren.com*), Sorelle (*www.sorellefurniture.com*), South Shore (*www.southshorefurniture.com*), Stanley Furniture (*wwwyoung america.stanleyfurniture.com*), Stokke (*www.stokkeusa.com*), and Stork-craft (*www.storkcraft.com*). Most models have wooden frames, but you may find some made of wicker, vinyl, plastic, and metal. A safety belt—a single strap with a wide buckle—is usually included with the changing pad. If there isn't one, buy a changing pad with a

Furniture Straps Prevent Tipping Accidents

In an average year, 22 people, mostly young children, are killed when household furniture, TVs, or ranges tip onto them, and an estimated 3,000 people, mostly children, are hurt.

The KidCo Anti-Tip Furniture Strap.

Toppling furniture can cause broken bones, bruising, and death from suffocation. But furniture straps can help keep your child safe. They secure a dresser, armoire, or bookcase to the wall to prevent it from tipping over when a child grabs it to balance himself or tries to climb. You'll need to find studs or other wood framing in the wall to drive the screws into. If installed properly, furniture straps are strong enough to provide effective protection for children up to about age 4.

Several manufacturers make furniture straps. We judged the Parent Units Heavy Duty Topple Stop Furniture Fastening System, $15.95 for two, the best model of the three furniture straps we tested (*www .parentunits.com*). Installing the straps requires many steps involving screws and adhesive, and the required tools are not included. When installing the straps on furniture made of particleboard instead of solid wood, it might be necessary to first attach pieces of solid wood to the furniture.

Other products we tested were the KidCo Anti-Tip Furniture Strap, $6.85 for two (*www.kidco.com*), and Safety 1st Furniture Wall Straps, $3.99 for two (*www.safety1st.com*). These fabric straps must be screwed into both the wall and the furniture (or into wood attached to the furniture). The length is adjustable.

safety belt and attach the pad to the table according to the manufacturer's directions.

Changing tables range from $23 (for a simple changing table pad you attach to a dresser top) to $1,200 or more for solid wood and medium density fiberboard (pressed timber with synthetic resin binders) models that convert to a flat-top dresser with drawers/enclosed shelving. For $70 to $130, you can buy an adequate changing table with open shelving and possibly one drawer, but quality is a factor. At the low end, parents have reported drawers that stick, changing pads with plastic that cracks in short order, and lesser-quality wood (typically laminated particleboard), which can become flimsy over time. Still, tables in this

Get Change Back on Your Changing Table

If you're shopping online for a changing table, you can often order directly from the manufacturer's Web site. Badger Basket (*www.badgerbasket.com*), for example, allows you to do that. But for the lowest prices, check *www.walmart.com* and *www.target.com*. These mass merchandisers sell major brands of baby furniture at a considerable discount.

We found a Badger Basket black sleigh-style changing table at *www.walmart.com* and *www.target.com* for $40 less than the price listed on Badger Basket's Web site.

lower price range may be sufficient, depending on your situation. If your baby spends part of the time in day care, for example, the table may hold up well. You'll probably have to assemble the table yourself, which can be tricky if you're not handy, and if the table you select has a drawer that requires installing. Read the instructions carefully and keep them for future reference. At the high end of the price range, changing tables may be custom finished in the paint or stain color of your choice. Drawers, solid-wood construction, and convertibility drive up the price.

With the Stokke Care changing table, you can face your child while you're changing him, which some parents find more comfortable than changing from the side.

Features to Consider

Safety strap. The changing table you're considering should have a safety strap and a pad that securely affixes to the table. Changing pads are also sold separately, but use a pad in a size the changing table manufacturer recommends. Make sure the safety strap is strong, not flimsy.

Sturdiness. A changing table or dresser shouldn't wobble when you give it a light shake. Test the floor model in the store, if possible.

Wheels. Some tables sit on wheels and are designed to be moved from room to room. If you buy a table with wheels, make sure it has brakes that lock so you can keep the table stable when you park it. Keep the wheels locked when you're using the changing table.

Diaper direction. On most changing tables, you have to change your baby from the side. But on a few, such as the Stokke Care (*www.stokkeusa.com*), you can change your baby from head to toe, which some parents deem a more comfortable position.

Look for JPMA Certification

The following changing table companies currently carry the Juvenile Products Manufacturers Association (JPMA) certification seal, indicating that they meet ASTM International voluntary standards: AFG International, Dorel Juvenile Group (Safety 1st), Ever Bright International, Learning Curve Brands, Muu Inc., Scandinavian Child/Cariboo, and Simplicity for Children. Although JPMA certified, Scandinavian Child's Cariboo Changing Table and Cariboo Bassinet Changer were voluntarily recalled in October 2006; a fall hazard could result if the zipper on either table's cloth surface was misaligned. The manufacturer subsequently added a secondary latch mechanism to correct the problem.

Wood. Depending on how much you'll use a changing table, you may want one with a good pedigree. Pricier changing tables tend to be sturdy and constructed from solid birch, beech, and maple rather than particleboard with a wood finish, although there are particleboard changing tables at the high end, too. If this is your first baby, and you plan a larger family, it may make sense to pay more. It's also worth spending a little more if you plan to convert the changing table into a media center, bookcase, or desk (an option with the Stokke Collections, *www.stokke.com* and Badger Basket, *www.badgerbasket.com*). In any event, look for wood surfaces that are smooth and splinter-free and make sure there is barrier protection on four sides.

Height. As we mentioned, changing tables vary in height. Some are as low as 36 inches; others as high as 44 inches. If you're tall, go with a taller table or dresser and secure it to the wall to reduce the risk of tipping. If you're short, aim lower.

Recommendations

Before you buy, consider all the furniture you plan for the nursery. We recommend that you try to find room for a changing table with barriers on all four sides of the top. But if you're tight on space or budget, and decide to use a dresser as a changing table, buy a contoured changing pad with a safety strap and affix it to the dresser, according to the manufacturer's installation directions. If you go with a dedicated changing table, try before you buy. Test the table in the store, as if you were changing a baby. If you see a backache in your future because that changing table is too low, try another. Check drawers

Baby Lotion, Powder, and Shampoo

Baby care products—lotion, powder, and shampoo—may be one source of phthalates in infants, according to a recent study in Pediatrics, the Journal of the American Academy of Pediatrics.

This group of chemicals, which can be absorbed through the skin, is used in personal care products to help stabilize fragrances and enhance a product's color and absorption. Children and adults can also be exposed to phthalates by breathing dust contaminated with them. Some studies suggest that phthalates may affect human development and the reproductive system, but the U.S. Food and Drug Administration has determined that there's not enough evidence to take regulatory action against these compounds.

If you'd like to minimize your baby's phthalate exposure until more is known about the possible risks, use only a small amount of shampoo or baby wash, and don't bother stocking your baby's changing table with lotion or powder.

"Healthy, normal newborns do not need either," says Sheela Sathyanarayana, M.D., M.P.H., acting assistant professor of pediatrics at the University of Washington, the lead author of the phthalates study published in Pediatrics. If, by chance, your baby has really dry skin, go with an unscented, hypoallergenic lotion, she advises.

While you're at it, buy unscented personal care products for yourself and keep the dust bunny level low in your house by sweeping wood floors often, especially under and around beds, and vacuum carpets frequently. Home dust is a major source of phthalates. "House dust can also exacerbate asthma and allergies in children, which is another reason to keep your house clean," Dr. Sathyanarayana says.

and cabinets. They should function smoothly and be easily accessible while you hold onto your squirmy baby. The unit should seem sturdy. Make sure it has safety straps to help prevent your baby from falling, or that you can affix a pad with safety straps. Use the straps every time you change your baby's diaper. If the table comes with a pad, use only the pad that's provided by the manufacturer. Don't use a changing table that's damaged or broken. Whether you assemble the table yourself or it comes that way, check from time to time that screws and fastenings are firmly tightened so parts don't become loose or fall off, which increase your baby's risk of choking and other injury. Stop using your changing table when your baby reaches the manufacturer's age or weight limit, which is typically age 2, or 30 pounds. If you buy a cloth changing pad, make sure it has a waterproof layer on the underside, which helps the changing table stay clean and sanitary. Vinyl changing pads can be wiped clean with soap

Buying a Used Changing Table

Changing tables are popular at tag sales and consignment shops, and a used one can be an acceptable and less-expensive alternative to buying new, provided that the table is in good condition and hasn't been recalled. So go ahead and snag one from a friend, or buy one second-hand. Don't compromise safety or quality; check for recalled models at *www.cpsc.gov* so you don't inadvertently buy or borrow an unsafe model. Look for models that meet our criteria for new changing tables under Features to Consider, page 132.

and water. Purchase two or three covers so you can throw one in the wash and have at least one on hand.

More Tipping Points: Armoires, Bookcases, Dressers, and TV Stands

If there are young children in the house, it's essential to attach any potentially unstable furniture to a wall with tip-over straps or restraints, and keep heavy objects like TVs off dressers. This added step is necessary even though ASTM International has a *voluntary* tip-over standard for chests, armoires, and dressers, and Underwriters Laboratories (UL) has one, also voluntary, for TV stands. Childhood injuries and deaths from tipping furniture and television sets are a growing problem, according to Consumer Product Safety Commission statistics.

The ASTM tip-over standard for chests, armoires, and dressers requires that an empty unit can't tip when any doors are open and all drawers are open two-thirds of the way or to the stop, whichever is less. It also can't tip when one drawer is open two-thirds of the way (or a door is opened fully) and a 50-pound load (to simulate a child's weight) is applied to the center front of each drawer. (ASTM is currently working on a revised tip-over standard.)

The tip-stability section of the UL standard for carts and stands for audio/video equipment mandates that the unit can't tip when holding a load that weighs as much as a television set (using the largest TV size specified by the manufacturer or a standardized weight based on the size of the TV, whichever is greater) and placed on a plane inclined 10 degrees from horizontal.

Those standards, however, are voluntary, and many manufacturers don't even claim to meet them. Our tests revealed that furniture often doesn't meet the standards, and that the standards are inadequate in any case.

We tested dressers, armoires, bookcases, and TV stands in two ways: against applicable standards and then while using the furniture the way you might—with drawers full of clothes and fully opened, and with carpeting underneath, for example. Most of the tested furniture is typical of that used in children's rooms and is sold through retailers found at *www.babydepot.com, www.burlingtoncoatfactory.com, www.ikea.com, www.jcpenney.com, www.kidkraft.com, www.potterybarnkids.com, www.sears.com, www.target.com,* and *www.walmart.com.*

The three dressers passed the ASTM stability test (weight applied when drawers are two-thirds open) but one tipped when all drawers were simply fully opened, and the other two tipped when weight was applied to fully-opened drawers. One armoire passed the ASTM test, the other tipped when weight was applied to the open door. The TV stand didn't tip, but the TV on top of it tilted. The following chart provides specifics.

Ratings • Furniture Stability

Brand & model	Price	Meets standard?	Comments
DRESSERS Covered by voluntary ASTM tip-over standard.			
South Shore Blueberry 5-drawer Chest (Sears.com)	$150	Yes	But tipped with all drawers open all the way.
Kendall Drawer Chest Dresser (PotteryBarnKids.com)	750	Yes	But tipped when 50-lb. weight was applied to drawers opened all the way.
Creative Interiors Reflections Dresser (Sears.com)	160	Yes	But tipped when 50-lb. weight was applied to clothing-filled drawers opened all the way.
ARMOIRES Covered by voluntary ASTM tip-over standard.			
Berkeley Armoire (PotteryBarnKids.com)	900	Yes	Also passed our tests on carpet, with drawers and shelves loaded.
Prepac 3-Drawer Wardrobe (shopping Web sites)	200	No	Tipped when 50-lb weight was applied to door.
BOOKCASES Not covered by ASTM.			
Kidkraft Avalon 3-Shelf (Kidkraft and Target.com)	110	NA	No problems.
TV STANDS Covered by tip-stability section of voluntary Underwriters Laboratories (UL) standard.			
Sauder TV/VCR Cart (Walmart.com)	28	Yes	With 27-inch TV, TV tilted but unit did not.

Clothing

Warning: It will take every ounce of willpower not to load up your shopping cart with mini Levi's, teeny-tiny sailor suits, floral sundresses, peasant smocks, and rompers in every color. Baby clothes, trendier than ever and oh-so-scrumptious, are as irresistible to parents (and friends and relatives) as a pool on a hot day.

Can't resist designer baby wear like these cuddly fleece outfits? Watch for sales and scout secondhand shops and resale sites.

Everyone wants their baby to be well dressed, and manufacturers have responded with micro styles that appeal to our adult fashion sense. Not that your baby cares. All she wants is to be comfortable, and that's important to keep in mind. The basic necessities—even if they're "preowned"—will keep your little cutie content. Still, you may not want to dress your baby in just any old thing.

Shopping Secrets

Expect to get clothes as gifts. During your first forays into the baby department, buy only a few items in newborn size, such as one or two sleepers. Depending on how large your baby is at birth, she may outgrow this size within a few weeks. You'll want to focus on 6-month-size clothing—your baby will grow into it quickly. Even then, try to hold back and fill in after you've reaped the birth-announcement bounty. Clothes from generous friends and relatives may get you through the first year. Rest assured that gift-givers who are already parents, grandmothers, and aunts will buy in bigger sizes—they know how quickly babies grow. You'll find a list of New Baby Basics on pages 18-19. Use your own judgment on how much you want to buy yourself, and what you can expect as gifts.

Watch for sales on brands you like. Sales are everywhere—in stores, in catalogs, and online at the end of each season and in between. Major chain stores that sell baby clothes have regular promotions, sometimes weekly. If your baby is a newborn, resist the urge to stock up, since most babies whiz through this size range. Don't shop too far in advance for larger sizes, either. Infants can have sudden growth spurts that throw off your sizing forecasts. A winter coat you snag for your baby in August may be too small by December.

Consider used. If you've never bought anything secondhand, start now. You can easily get away with it, especially when your child is an infant. Scout for tag sales and watch out for local moms' group sales. Babies go through clothes so quickly that the small stuff is almost always in good condition. It's not unheard of to pay 50 cents for a near-perfect pair of pants that would cost you $12 or more new. Pristine used clothing is tougher to come by in toddler sizes; when messy activities such as finger-painting come into play, clothing gets more wear and tear.

Secondhand shops are prime hunting grounds for special-occasion baby and toddler clothes such as christening and holiday outfits and

Babies Grow Too Fast for Designer Duds

You don't have to spend a bundle on baby clothes and shoes. Here are ways to save big:

◆ Don't buy designer duds or put them on your baby registry. Babies may be able to wear them only once or twice before they outgrow them, which inspires new-parent guilt and the sense that the money could have been better spent on diapers, wipes, or formula. If you can't resist, watch for sales at your favorite baby stores and scout for designer wear at secondhand shops and sites.

◆ Arm yourself with coupons. Before you hit your favorite baby clothing stores or buy anything online, check for printable coupons and codes on websites such as *www.couponcabin .com*. There you can find online coupon codes for retailers that sell baby clothes such as Babies "R" Us, babyGap, Baby Age.com, Gymboree, Sears, Target, and Old Navy. You can also find some printable coupons that can slash even more bucks off your clothing tab, or at the very least, give you free shipping on online orders.

You can also do a quick Google search for "(store name) coupon" or "(store name)

Even in this adorable romper by Tea Collection, the baby makes the outfit.

code." You'd be surprised at how many coupon codes are out there. Or join the e-mail list of your favorite baby and department stores by signing up at the store's Web site for advance notice of sales and coupons sent right to your In-box. Combining a sale item with a coupon can result in impressive savings on top brands—and tingles for you at checkout. One caveat: When you're shopping online with coupons, take note of shipping costs and handling charges. They can sometimes wipe out any savings—and then some. (In addition to using online coupons, zone in on a clothing Web site's sale and clearance sections for serious savings.)

◆ Do your footwork. When buying your child's shoes online, look for sites that charge no sales tax and offer free shipping so you can easily return shoes, if necessary. To reduce your chances of having to return shoes, visit a shoe store first to scope out the selection and to measure your child's foot.

For how-tos on baby-shoe buying, see "The Best Time to Buy Baby's First Shoes", page 143.

fancy party duds that have been worn only once or twice (if at all). You'll likely pay a fraction of the retail cost. Check local tag or garage sales, try browsing Web sites such as eBay (*www.ebay.com*) and craigslist (*www.craigslist.org*) or getting a free membership at Freecycle (*www.freecycle.org*), a Web site through which consumers can give and get free stuff. And don't forget to put the word out among parents you know. You may get quite serviceable clothes delivered by the boxload to your front door. But inspect hand-me-downs carefully for unraveling thread, loose buttons or snaps, or scratchy appliqués and elastic bands. Don't dress your child in anything that's not as good as new or that appears unsafe to you.

What's Available

You'll find "boy" and "girl" baby clothes in every imaginable pattern, color (besides pink and blue, think mocha, powder, buttermilk, safari, camouflage, silver, avocado, Bordeaux, and pistachio), style, and fabric. Cotton, which is soft and absorbent, is still the most common fiber. Organic cotton children's clothes are coming into their own as the trend toward "green" takes hold outside the health food store. Read laundry instructions, though. Organic fabric can be more labor-intensive than regular cotton. Many garments are made of cotton/polyester blends, which dry quickly and resist wrinkles, or cotton/spandex for maximum give. You'll also find thick, soft knits and fleece made of microfiber. At specialty boutiques, you'll see high-maintenance fabrics that require ironing or dry cleaning, such as linen, cashmere, and hand-knit items.

Some brands of infant wear can be found in leading department stores and retail chains across the country, online, and in catalogs. They include, in alphabetical order: babyGap (*www.gap.com*), babystyle (*www.babystyle.com*), Bunnies By The Bay (*www.bunniesbythebay.com*), Carter's (*www.carters.com*), First Impressions Baby, (available at *www.macys.com*), Flapdoodles (*www.flapdoodles.com*), Gerber Childrenswear (*www.gerberchildrenswear.com*), Gymboree (*www.gymboree.com*), Halo Innovations (for sleep sacks, aka wearable blankets, *www.halosleep.com*), Hanna Andersson (*www.hannaandersson.com*), Juicy Couture (*www.juicycouture.com*), Little Me (*www.littleme.com*; available at *www.nordstrom.com*), Old Navy (*www.oldnavy.com*), Pumpkin Patch (available at *www.nordstrom.com*), Ralph Lauren (*www.ralphlauren.com*), Taggies (*www.taggies.com*), and Tea Collection (*www.teacollection.com*). Many

■ **Sanity Saver**

Keep Track of Coupons and Other Stuff

Saving money takes organization. A small accordion file that you stow in your purse or the car can help you stay organized. Label the tabs and use the file to stash coupons, gift and store cards, your grocery and to-do list, library cards, bank deposit slips, and receipts so you always have them when you need them.

A 5-by-7-inch accordion file like this one from The Container Store can help you stay organized.

of these brands can also be found at major retailers and e-tailers such as *www.babiesrus.com* and *www.buybuybaby.com*, as well as at boutique e-tailers such as *www.cutelittleclothes.com* and *www.littleboychic.com*. Organic cotton baby clothes can be found at *www.kee-ka.com*, *www.my goodnessduds.com*, *www.organicbabywearhouse.com*, and *www.sagecreek organics.com* and by Googling "organic baby clothes." As with adult clothing, baby apparel prices run the gamut.

Sizing Demystified

Confused about what size clothes to buy for your baby? Here's help. Baby clothing sizes are usually based on age: preemie, 0 to 3 months (newborn), 3 to 6 months, 6 to 9 months, 9 to 12 months, 12 months, 18 months, and 24 months. However, one manufacturer's 6 to 9 months may be quite different from another's because there are no standard sizes in the industry. Every brand of baby clothing has its own size specifications. Try this general rule: "Double your baby's age," says Vivian G. Reisman, president of Baby Steps (*www.bsteps.com*), a children's clothing manufacturer based in Closter, N.J. For example, if you're buying for a 3-month-old, buy a 6-month-old size; if you're shopping for a 6-month-old, buy a 12-month-old size, and so on. Even though that doubled size may seem a little big at first, your baby will grow into the clothing quickly and you'll have leeway for shrinkage.

You don't always have to double the size, though. It depends on the manufacturer, so experiment. The age-doubling formula ends at around age 2 anyway, Reisman says. Then, buy one to two sizes up, depending

■ **Chemical Caution**

"Green" Baby Clothes

If the label says the garment is 100 percent organic, that means only that the cotton in the clothes was grown without synthetic pesticides and other such chemicals. Since cotton is one of the most pesticide-intensive crops grown, buying baby clothes made of organic cotton may be better for the planet. But keep in mind that an organic label certifies only the growing methods of the fiber in the item, not the way it was processed into fabric. There's no guarantee that clothes marked "organic cotton" haven't been chemically treated. If you want to buy truly "green" baby clothes, check if the tag or manufacturer's Web site has information on how the clothes were processed and dyed.

If you'd like to buy truly "green" baby clothes like this organic ensemble from Kee-Ka, find out how they're dyed by checking the label or the manufacturer's Web site.

on your child's size. For example, an average-sized 2-year-old (a toddler in the 50th percentile for height and weight) can probably wear a size 3. But a large 2-year-old (say, in the 95th percentile) would wear a size 4, she says.

Read the weight and length charts found on the back of many garment packages or consult a size chart, which many baby-clothing stores keep on hand, especially those that sell garments in European sizes. But be sure to know your baby's height in inches—that's key to converting your baby's size to centimeters.

Features to Consider

Your primary concerns for baby clothing should be dressing ease, softness, durability, and safety, and then style. Since most babies dislike having anything pulled over their heads, look for garments that are easy to take off and put on, with front-opening or side-snap tops. Snaps are easier (and faster) than buttons. Quick access to the diaper area is essential, so opt for snap-open legs or loosely elastic waists. Velcro closures are quick and convenient. Before washing, close them so that they don't fill up with lint and threads and lose their holding power.

The Best Time to Buy Baby's First Shoes

Shoes complete the outfit for kids, but wait until your child begins walking— usually at 10 to 14 months— before buying her first pair of shoes. That's when a child really needs them. Jane Andersen, D.P.M., a spokeswoman for the American Podiatric Medical Association, recommends picking a first shoe with flexibility, which helps the foot develop its arch. "Try to bend the shoe in half," she says. "If it bends easily, it's a good shoe."

The best shoes for your little walker bend easily.

The best shoes also have traction on the bottom so your baby won't slip easily. A shoe doesn't have to be expensive to be flexible, but in Andersen's shopping experience, the most flexible shoes are higher-ticket brands. In our opinion, that might include Merrell (*www.merrell.com*), Nina Kids available at leading e-tailers such as Shoebuy (*www.shoebuy.com*), Pediped (*www.pediped.com*), Stride Rite (*www.striderite.com*), and Umi (*www.umishoes.com*). And, adds Andersen, stores that sell higher-ticket brands generally have experienced sales help to make sure you buy the right size. You'll want some room at the toe, but not so much that your child will trip. Also, keep in mind that toddlers kick off anything and everything, so look for flexible shoes that lace. They're harder to take off than shoes with Velcro closures.

To keep your prewalker's feet warm on cool days, look for soft, elasticized baby socks or booties that cling to the feet so your baby can't kick them off. You don't have to buy the leather baby shoes you'll see everywhere, which can easily run you $28 per pair or more, and which your baby will outgrow quickly.

Comfort. Check the seams on the inside of the garment. They should be smooth, not rough, and lie flat rather than sticking out. Don't buy clothes with tight elastic bands on arms, legs, neck, or waist; they can irritate your baby's skin and restrict circulation. Bypass anything that could be scratchy—unpainted metal zippers, appliqués, or snaps with rough or uneven backings. If an appliqué is made of heat-welded plastic, check for rough edges on the back. Give sequins, buttons, and snaps a quick tug to make sure they can't easily come off, posing a choking hazard. But don't pull so hard that you weaken the attachment in the process. And recheck after each washing.

Fabric. Apparel labels must state fiber content and care instructions. All-cotton knits may look large when new, but they can shrink as

■ Sanity Saver
Time Your Shopping Trips

Whether you're going shopping or just need to get some errands crossed off your to-do list, you can make lots of retail headway while your baby naps, so be sure to time occasional outings around your baby's sleep schedule. Sync it so that your baby falls asleep in the car on the way to the store. When you get there, simply transfer him to the stroller and away you go.

much as 10 percent with repeated washing. Polyester/cotton blends are less expensive than pure cotton or organic cotton and more resistant to wrinkles and shrinking. Avoid thin, semitransparent items or garments with poor finishing such as unclipped thread. Although babies grow fast, you'll need clothing that's durable enough to last several months.

Safe Sleepwear

Fabric and fit are important safety considerations for your baby's sleepwear. To protect children from burns, Consumer Product Safety Commission (CPSC) regulations dictate that children's sleepwear sizes 9 months to size 14 must either be made of flame-resistant fabric, which doesn't ignite easily and must self-extinguish quickly when removed from a flame, or the clothing must fit snugly because loose garments are more likely to catch fire. Sleepwear that fits snugly does not trap the air needed for fabric to burn and reduces the chances of contact with a flame. Flame-resistant fabrics may be worn either loosely or snug-fitting; they're often made of polyester, although cotton can be treated to make it flame-resistant.

Flame-resistant sleepwear isn't necessarily treated with chemicals. Some polyester, for example, is inherently flame-resistant, says Patty Davis, a spokesperson for the CPSC. As long as it passes flammability tests that manufacturers must conduct according to children's sleepwear regulations, it can be used in sleepwear without being chemically treated. Under the Federal Hazardous Substances Act, any flame-retardant chemical used is required not to be toxic. However, the CPSC doesn't require, suggest, or endorse any particular chemical that manufacturers must or can use, Davis says. Clothing manufacturers

Children's sleepwear sizes 9 months to size 14 must meet CPSC sleepwear safety requirements for flammability.

■ **Safety Strategies**
Drawstrings Pose Hazards

Although there have been federal guidelines and an industry standard for more than 10 years, clothing with hazardous drawstrings continues to be sold.

Clothing drawstrings are a strangulation hazard because they can get caught on playground equipment and in other places, like bus doors. In 2007 and 2008, the CPSC issued more than two dozen recalls of clothing with such drawstrings, mostly sweatshirts and jackets. The agency continues to track and investigate incidents of deaths and injuries each year in which children's hood and waist drawstrings become entangled.

When your baby reaches size 2T (not uncommon around his first birthday), CPSC recommends removing neck drawstrings from all outerwear, including jackets and sweatshirts. Likewise, before buying outerwear with a waistband drawstring in sizes 2T and up, such as those found at the bottom of a jacket, make sure the drawstring is sewn to the garment at its midpoint so that it can't be pulled out more than three inches from the garment on either side.

Even better, do not purchase children's jackets and sweatshirts that have any drawstrings. Look for snaps, buttons, Velcro, or elastic at the neck and waist instead. Finally, remove toggles or knots at the ends of all drawstrings to prevent them from getting caught on objects or doors and entrapping a child.

aren't required to label the type of flame-retardant chemical used, if any. If you'd like to buy sleepwear that hasn't been chemically treated, look for sleepwear with a prominent warning on the label: "Wear snug-fitting, not flame-resistant." Then buy it in your baby's correct size.

Here's a checklist for buying safe sleepwear for your child:

▶ Don't buy oversized sleepwear that's not flame-resistant. (Look for a label on the garment indicating flame resistance.)

▶ Don't allow your baby to sleep in loose T-shirts, sweatshirts, or other apparel made from non-flame-resistant fabrics.

▶ Don't buy snug-fitting sleepwear a size or two larger for your baby to have growing room. That defeats the purpose of the garment and puts your baby at risk. Snug-fitting sleepwear looks tight, but it stretches. It must have a prominent warning label that states: "Wear snug-fitting, not flame-resistant".

Infant sleepwear smaller than size 9 months is exempt from government flammability requirements, because infants aren't sufficiently mobile to expose themselves to an open flame. For infants, we recommend a wearable blanket, or sleep sack, to replace loose blankets in your baby's crib, which are a suffocation hazard. Sleep sacks don't fit snugly;

there's plenty of kicking room. They're typically made of flame-resistant fabric, but check the garment's label to be sure.

Recommendations

When stocking up on basics before your baby arrives, purchase very little in newborn size. Your baby will outgrow these tiny garments fast—sometimes in less than a month. It's more practical to buy in the 3-to 6-month or 6-to-9-month sizes. If saving money is your mission, do most of your shopping post-baby showers and after friends and relatives respond to your birth announcement. Then fill in any gaps in your baby's wardrobe and buy as she grows.

Consider safety. Be wary of tiny buttons, hooks, snaps, pompoms, bows, and appliqués. They can be choking hazards. Routinely check clothes and fasteners for these loose items. Avoid Carter's brand clothing with heat-transferred or "tagless" labels with a solid background. Such labels have been associated with rashes. Avoid loosely knitted clothes—sweaters, booties, or hats—that look like they might trap a baby's tiny fingers or toes. Cut all dangling threads before your baby wears a garment and avoid clothing that has seams with very few stitches per inch. Before you put socks or booties on your baby, turn them inside out to look for small threads that could capture toes.

Low-priced and mid-priced garments often have soft but sturdy fabrics, competent workmanship, and plenty of fashion flair. And they're usually machine washable—a definite plus. Upscale baby clothes cost more, without a proportionate increase in quality and durability. High-fashion clothes may require hand laundering, even dry cleaning. (Air out any dry-cleaned clothes before your baby wears them.)

Recall Reminder

Clothing has been recalled because of safety hazards such as snaps that come off (a choking hazard), dangerous drawstrings at neck or waist, or failure to meet the federal flammability standard for sleepwear. For updated recall information on infant products, consult monthly issues of CONSUMER REPORTS or visit the CPSC's Web site at *www.cpsc.gov*. To report a dangerous product or a product-related injury, call CPSC's hotline at 800-638-2772 or CPSC's teletypewriter at 800-638-8270, or visit CPSC's Web site at *www.cpsc.gov/talk.html*. You can also send an e-mail to *info@cpsc.gov*.

chapter

Cribs

Of all the items on your baby-shopping list, a crib probably will be among the most challenging to select because there are so many on the market, ranging from economy and mid-priced models to high-end cribs with hand-painted details and European influences that up the style ante.

The DaVinci Emily crib is a CR Best Buy. It has stationary sides and converts to a day bed and full-size bed.

Whatever style you choose, you'll want a crib that's durable, safe, and matches your tastes and budget. Increasingly, you'll find crib styles that adapt as your child grows—from toddler bed to day bed to full-size bed. So making the right choice now means you may not have to shop for your child's bed later.

Basic Is Best

When you're crib shopping, you may be tempted to buy the showiest model, along with bumper guards and blankets that say your nursery is fit for a prince or princess. Resist the temptation. The safest cribs are basic; they have simple lines and no scroll-work or finials—infants can strangle if their clothing gets caught in such detail work. They're bare, too, with nothing but a fitted sheet where your baby sleeps (more on that below). Heeding this advice will get you a safer crib and it will save you money.

Although bassinets, cradles, or co-sleepers are alternatives for the first four months or so, we think your baby is safest in a crib. All cribs sold in the U.S., whether made here or abroad, are now required by law to be certified by an independent testing facility as meeting federal safety standards. Currently there is only a voluntary industry standard for bassinets and cradles and no standard at all for co-sleepers. (See "Crib Alternatives", page 161.)

The best cribs, such as this Babi Italia Pinehurst Lifestyle, are basic and bare.

Shopping Secrets

Buy new. If possible, avoid buying or accepting a used crib. Older models—those manufactured before 2000 (about a year after the latest voluntary standards for slat-attachment strength took effect)—won't meet current safety standards and may be in disrepair. (Check the manufacture date on the crib label, which is required by law.) If you must use or buy a used crib, make sure it's circa 2000 or later.

How Long Should Your Baby Sleep in a Crib?

For safety's sake, monitor your child's development closely and stop using a crib as soon as your toddler can climb out. At that point, consider a bed with child railings or put the mattress on the floor. Don't put your child back into the crib after the first "escape," regardless of his age. According to CPSC records, falls are a frequent source of injury.

Choose a crib with stationary sides. Recent recalls have raised concerns about the safety of cribs with drop sides. We recommend that you look first for a crib with stationary sides until more stringent and comprehensive safety standards are developed. (You'll find cribs with stationary sides in all price ranges.) A crib with no drop sides is safest because there's no hardware or moving parts that could potentially malfunction or be improperly installed, but be sure to test models in the store. Use the mattress's lowest setting to see how easy it is for you to lean in and pick up your baby. Cribs with stationary sides have less hardware (less chance of missing or broken parts), but depending on your height, it can be hard to get to your baby.

Folding sides are safer than drop sides. If you're not tall, you may favor a crib with a folding side—a sensible compromise between a stationary and drop side. We tested only one such crib—the Ocean by Baby's Dream, $450—a heavy wooden model with a simple craftsman look. But the folding side requires two hands to fold and to raise. This is a safety feature, to prevent the child in the crib from operating the folding side, but it's a disadvantage if you're holding a baby.

Cribs with a folding side like this Ocean model from Baby's Dream require two hands to operate.

If you opt for drop sides, check them carefully. If you insist on buying a crib with drop sides, operate them in the store, if possible, to make sure they can be raised and lowered smoothly and quietly. You can't do that if you're shopping for a crib that's only available online. But if it's also available in a store near you, you'll learn a lot about a crib by scrutinizing it in person. Models that open with a lift-and-leg-press action or those with a lift-and-foot-release mechanism (see Features to Consider on page 154) can usually be operated with one hand—an advantage when you've got a baby in the other arm. Still, you'll probably raise and lower the side of the crib only during the first few months. Once babies get bigger and stand up in the crib, many parents pick them up without lowering the side. With two drop sides, you can access your baby from either side of the crib, a plus if the crib is in the center of the room. Of course, if the crib will be against a wall, you'll have no use for a second drop side.

Check construction and workmanship. The simplest in-store test is to shake the crib slightly to see if the frame seems loose. But be aware that display models aren't always as tightly assembled as they could be. Without applying excessive pressure, try rotating each slat to see if it's well secured to the railings. You shouldn't find loose bars on a new crib.

A display-model crib isn't what you'll be taking home (unless you happen to buy it), but it does give you a general idea of the quality and safety of the crib you're considering.

> **Shake the crib slightly to see if the frame seems loose."**

Look for the JPMA sticker. Although cribs are now required to have compliance certification with federal safety standards, durability tests are not currently mandated. Cribs accredited by the Juvenile Products Manufacturers Association (JPMA) certification program do have to pass durability testing of the mattress supports and crib side rails—but not for the strength of spindles or slats or the drop-side hardware.

Still, look for the JPMA certification label on the crib or packaging because you will get an extra degree of safety. The Consumer Product Safety Commission (CPSC) advises, however, that parents should regularly make sure slats and hardware are secure and intact, and that drop sides and hardware are functioning smoothly. As mentioned, we don't recommend buying a crib with drop sides. The JPMA currently certifies certain models from the following full-sized crib brands: Avalon Products, Baby Appleseed, Baby's Dream Furniture, Bassett Furniture Industries, Bella D'Este Ltd., Bellini, Child Craft, Creations, Delta Enterprise, Dorel Juvenile Group (Cosco), Everbright International, Foundations (Shamrock Industries), Green Frog Art, Innovative Crib Designs, Jardine Enterprises, LaJobi, Million Dollar Baby, Muniré Furniture, Inc.,

- **Safety Strategies**

What to Do When Your Baby Starts Rolling Over

The American Academy of Pediatrics recommends that infants be placed on their backs for sleeping to reduce the risk of Sudden Infant Death Syndrome (SIDS).

If your baby starts rolling over onto his tummy on his own when he's sleeping, which is an important developmental milestone, "go ahead and put him back on his back if that won't disturb his sleep," says Laura Reno, vice president of public affairs for First Candle, a national nonprofit health organization dedicated to advancing infant health and survival based in Baltimore. But don't feel compelled to check on him throughout the night to make sure he hasn't rolled over. You need your sleep, too. Instead, accept the reality that he may end up on his tummy, but remain diligent about keeping your baby's crib bare. Babies who are able to roll over can move around even more and scoot near a crib bumper or get a blanket wrapped around their head and suffocate, says Reno.

Also, have your baby sleep with a ceiling fan on or have a small fan blowing in the room, but not directly on your baby. "It will help circulate the air so that any build-up of exhaled carbon dioxide might be more easily dispersed to reduce the risk of SIDS," Reno says. You can add a fan even before your baby starts rolling over, if you want. A recent study published in the Archives of Pediatrics & Adolescent Medicine found that fan use was associated with a 72 percent drop in the risk of SIDS. Fans seemed to help most when sleep-condition factors, like stomach sleeping, would increase the risk.

Muu Inc., NettoCollection, Nurseryworks, Pt. Domusindo Perdana, Simmons Juvenile Crib Furniture, Simplicity for Children, Spot On Square, Stork Craft Manufacturing, Westwood Design, Young America Stanley Furniture, and Yu Wei Co. Ltd. Each crib manufacturer just mentioned has specific styles of cribs that are JPMA certified. For that detailed list, log on to *www.jpma.org* and click on the "Safety Certification" heading.

Buy the mattress at the same time. In the store, pair the mattress and crib you plan to buy to make sure they're a good fit. (Mattresses typically are sold separately.) By law, a mattress used in a full-sized crib must be at least 27¼ inches by 51⅝ inches and no more than 6 inches thick. Still, do a quick check. If you can place more than two fingers between the mattress and the crib frame, the fit isn't snug enough.

What's Available

Some brands of cribs include, in alphabetical order: Angel Line (*www
.angelline.com*), Baby Mod (sold exclusively online at *www.walmart.com*), Baby's Dream (*www.babysdream.com*), Bassettbaby (*www.bassettbaby*

.com), Bellini (*www.bellini.com*), Child Craft (makers of Child Craft and Legacy cribs, *www.childcraftindusties.com*), DaVinci (can be found online at e-tailers such as Amazon.com), Delta Children's Products (*www.deltachildrensproducts.com*), IKEA (*www.ikea.com*), Jardine Enterprises (available at retailers and e-tailers such as *www.babiesrus.com*), LaJobi (which has the Babi Italia, Bonavita, ISSI, and Graco licenses, *www.lajobi.com*), Land of Nod (*www.landofnod.com*), Nursery Smart (*www.nurserysmart.com*), Pottery Barn Kids (*www.potterybarn kids.com*), Simmons (*www .simmonskids.com*), Sorelle (*www.sorellefurniture.com*), Stokke (*www.stokkeusa.com*), Storkcraft (*www.storkcraft.com*), Westwood Design (*www.west woodbaby.com*), and Young America (*www.youngamerica .com*). Crib prices range from $100 for economy models to over $4,000 for solid wood custom models. In general, paying more will get you better quality in the finish, wood, design, and operating mechanism. Still, price and quality don't necessarily correlate. You can find perfectly adequate cribs at the lowest end. In all price ranges, you'll find cribs that change to a toddler bed, day bed, or full-size bed. Some cribs convert to all three configurations. Here's more on what you'll get at the various price points.

The IKEA Leksvik crib is another CR Best Buy. It has stationary sides and converts to a toddler bed.

Economy cribs ($100 to $199). Models at the low end of the price scale can be perfectly adequate. In fact, in our tests, the IKEA Leksvik crib, which retails for $160 and has no drop sides, rated very good overall and excellent for safety and construction. Prices are low because manufacturers use less expensive materials and simpler finishes and designs. These models tend to be lighter than top-of-the-line cribs. White or pastel paint or shiny lacquer-like finish may cover wood defects, such as knots and variations in shading. You may notice minor finishing flaws, such as poorly sanded rough spots, uneven patches of paint, and the heads of metal brads or glue residue at the base of the slats. The metal mattress support hooks at each corner may be loose. The springs supporting the mattress may be lighter in construction than

Where Your Baby Should Never Sleep

A full-sized crib is the safest place for your baby to sleep. Consider most everything else, except for possibly a JPMA-certified bassinet or cradle, off-limits for infants, especially:

◆ **A waterbed, sofa, sheepskin, quilt, soft mattress, air mattress, pillow, or bean bag chair.** The fluffy bedding materials and soft surfaces are a suffocation hazard in themselves for an infant who cannot control her head and can also allow a dangerous buildup of carbon dioxide from the baby's own breathing. Rebreathing exhaled carbon dioxide has been identified as a potential cause of sudden infant death syndrome (SIDS).

◆ **A co-sleeper.** These beds, also called "bedside sleepers," allow infants to sleep near their parents for bonding and nursing. But the Consumer Product Safety Commission hasn't established safety standards for these products, so the American Academy of Pediatrics doesn't recommend them or co-sleeping at all. (For hazards, see next column.)

◆ **An heirloom crib.** It doesn't meet today's safety standards. Even if a crib has been in your family for generations, don't use it.

◆ **Your bed.** In addition to the risk that you might roll onto your baby, adult beds pose other hazards. For example, your movements during sleep could push your baby into becoming trapped between the bed and a wall, headboard, bed frame, or other object, or might even push him off the bed. Accidental suffocation in soft bedding or by a parent is another danger. Although it sounds theoretical, it happens. "I took care of a 1-year-old boy who suffered an oxygen-deprivation brain injury after being accidentally smothered by his father while bed-sharing," says Aaron Lentz, M.D., an emergency room physician at Wesley Medical Center, in Wichita, Kan. The child is now permanently dependent on a ventilator. If you breast-feed your baby in bed, be sure to return him to the crib afterward.

those in pricier models. When you shake the crib, make sure it is sturdy and doesn't rattle.

Midpriced cribs ($200 to $499). At this price level, it becomes increasingly difficult to discern quality differences from brand to brand. You'll find a lot in this price range. These models are sturdier and more decorative than economy models. They come in an array of wood finishes, from Scandinavian-style natural to golden maple and oak shades, reddish-brown cherries, and deep mahoganies. End boards may be solid and smoothly finished, although many models have slats on all sides. The gentle curves of the end boards are well finished with rounded edges. Slats are thicker than those of economy models and may be round or flat, with rounded edges. The mattress supports on these models tend

Avoid Recalled Cribs

Complete and mail in product registration cards so a company can contact you directly in the event of a recall. You can also sign up for automatic e-mail recall notifications at *www .cpsc.gov/cpsclist.aspx*. In 2007, Simplicity for Children recalled more than one million cribs because of drop-side failures resulting from both hardware and crib design. In 2008, Babies "R" Us recalled 320,000 Jardine cribs because the slats and spindles could break too easily. The flaws created entrapment and suffocation hazards. Other cribs have been recalled due to faulty hardware, railings that were too low, posing a fall hazard, and mattress supports that left a gap between the crib and the railing. Staying up-to-date on recalls can help you spot unsafe cribs that may still be in circulation in stores, resale shops, and at tag sales (but again, we don't recommend used cribs).

to be sturdy, the springs heavier. Locking wheels or casters (sometimes optional) provide stability. There may be one or two stabilizer bars—metal rods that extend between the two end rods—running underneath for greater rigidity. The best-made cribs in this category have recessed guides (a grooved channel in each end board for the drop side), no exposed brads or glue residue where the slats are fastened to the rails, and a uniform finish. They may have extra-high posts, canopies, or a storage drawer underneath.

High-end cribs ($500 and up). These models, many of them imported from Europe, have hand-rubbed, glazed, or burnished finishes. They have the look and feel of fine furniture, with high-quality details such as hard wood, rounded edges and curved wood, and dovetail joints. You'll see round cribs (still a novelty, though they've been around for some time), sleigh styles with curved end boards and hand-painted details, and models handcrafted from wrought iron. These cribs have a mattress that's supported by heavy-gauge springs and heavyweight metal frames and may adjust to four heights. At the highest end, you'll find custom-made regular and convertible cribs that may be sold as part of a nursery suite; a fairy-tale canopy may be part of the ensemble.

Features to Consider

Convertibility. Consider buying a crib that converts to a toddler, day, or full-size bed only if you don't plan to have more children soon. Otherwise, you'll need the crib for your next baby and it may be years before you get the chance to convert it. Many convertible cribs can be switched to a "big girl" or "big boy" bed simply by removing one drop side; the basic look of the crib remains. Because the change is so small, some parents report that toddlers have an easier time making the transition to a bed. Keep in mind that some convertible beds require parts that typically aren't included in the original purchase, such as bed rails, stabilizing rails, or support rails (for converting to a full-size bed).

Bottom drawer. Some models include a drawer or two under the mattress support structure. Under-crib drawers usually are not attached to the crib frame. Some are freestanding and roll out from under the crib on casters. Some cribs have a set of drawers attached to the short end of the unit. Before buying, pull any drawer all the way out to inspect its construction. You may find that it has a thin, cardboard-like bottom that could bow and give way when loaded with linens or clothing. A drawer bottom made of a harder material, such as fiberboard, is more likely to hold up.

Drop sides. The newest cribs with drop sides have relatively quiet releases that require you to lift the rail while you push the release with your leg. An older design requires you to lift the side while pressing a metal lever or tab under the railing with your foot. The foot maneuver is awkward because you have to stand on one leg to do it. (Metal components often rattle and squeak too.) A third, though rare, type of release mechanism has latches at each end of the top rail that must be pulled out at the same time. Federal regulations mandate that lowering mechanisms require either a certain force or a double-action release to prevent accidental opening by a baby or sibling. Still, due to recent recalls, we do not recommend buying a crib with drop sides.

The top-rated Child Craft Legacy Kensington Lifetime crib will last your child from babyhood to college. It morphs into a toddler bed and then into a full-size bed. At top it is shown in crib mode; below that, it's shown as a toddler bed.

Finish. Cribs in lighter stains such as natural wood, oaks, and maples tend to be popular, but cribs with dark wood finishes are a trend as more parents want the furniture in the baby's room to blend with the décor of the rest of the house. White, however, remains the most common crib color. Other painted colors include off-whites, washed whites (revealing the wood's grain), and pastel green, blue, pink, or yellow. A little roughness in the finish may not be a problem as long as there are no serious defects such as splintering or peeling paint.

The Bonavita Peyton crib is made from eco-friendly rubberwood.

Mattress height. All full-sized cribs have at least two mattress height positions; more expensive models have three or four. To prevent your baby from falling out of the crib, adjust the mattress support to its lowest height as soon as she can sit or pull up, usually between 6 and 8 months of age, but sometimes before. Many models don't require tools for adjusting mattress height; in some models, screws or bolts are hard to reach.

Mattress supports. Most mattress supports consist of a metal frame with springs. In some cribs, the mattress support is a one-piece board; in others, it's a grid with wood slats. The mattress supports are adjustable so the mattress can be raised or lowered, depending on the size of the child. Mattress supports need to be held securely in place so they aren't dislodged when you're changing a crib sheet or when another child or large pet pushes up from underneath.

Sides and railings. Crib sides are constructed by fitting bars (or spindles or slats) into holes in the top and bottom rails, then securing each bar with glue and one or two metal brads. The small holes made by the brads are usually filled and covered with a finish so they're invisible. The mandatory federal safety standard requires that crib slats be no more than $2\frac{3}{8}$ inches apart, so slat spacing shouldn't be an issue. But check in the store because cribs have been recalled for over-large spacing. Corner posts or finials should be either no higher than $\frac{1}{16}$ inch *or* taller than 16 inches to avoid the possibility of a child's clothing catching on them.

Safety Strategies
Sleeping Dos and Don'ts

Aside from buying a full-sized crib, follow these safety tips for putting your baby to bed safely.

DO

◆ **Think "back to sleep."** To reduce the risk of SIDS and suffocation, place your baby to sleep on his back (unless your pediatrician advises otherwise) at naptime and nighttime in a crib that meets all safety standards.

◆ **Change your baby's head position.** To reduce the risk of plagiocephaly, or flat-head syndrome, in which a baby develops a flat spot on the back of her head (back sleeping may increase the risk of it), make sure your newborn isn't always looking in the same direction. A baby in a crib tends to turn her head so she can look out toward the room, not the wall. Knowing that, "put your baby in her crib so that one day, she's looking toward her right shoulder, the next day, her left shoulder and so on," says Darcy King, an advanced registered nurse practitioner in the Cranio-facial Center at Seattle Children's Hospital, in Seattle, Wash. That will involve placing her in the crib so that her feet are where her head was yesterday, and vice versa. It's safe to face your baby in either direction. The risk of plagiocephaly lessens as babies get older, but changing head position is especially important to do in your baby's first 2 to 4 months.

◆ **Consider using a pacifier at naptime and bedtime.** Several studies have reported a protective effect of pacifiers on the incidence of SIDS. If your baby is breast-fed, wait to introduce a pacifier until 1 month of age, to ensure that breast-feeding is firmly established. But if your baby doesn't like a pacifier, don't force him to take it. Begin weaning your baby off the pacifier after his first birthday.

◆ **Use a baby monitor** to alert you to a situation before it becomes a problem.

DON'T

◆ **Use an electric blanket, heating pad,** or even a warm water bottle to heat your baby's crib. An infant's skin is highly heat-sensitive and can be burned by temperatures comfortable to an adult.

◆ **Dress your baby too warmly.** Over-heating may be a contributor to SIDS. Keep the temperature in your baby's room between 68° and 72° F. Your baby shouldn't feel hot to the touch.

Structural integrity. Sturdiness is a sign of construction quality. One or more stabilizer bars—metal rods fastened to both end boards beneath the crib—help make the frame more rigid.

Teething rails. These are smooth, plastic coverings for the top of the side rails to protect the crib and a gnawing baby's gums. Cribs accredited by the JPMA certification program must pass testing for secure fastening and carry a label stating that the rail must be replaced if damaged, cracked, or loose.

Wheels/casters. Plastic or metal crib wheels can be standard rollers or round, multidirectional, ball-shaped casters that swivel and make it easier to haul a crib from one room to another. Not all cribs come with them, which isn't an issue if your crib won't be venturing out of the nursery. If your baby's crib will be on bare wood or tile floors and you choose a crib with wheels, make sure they lock to prevent the crib from "walking" across the room—and the other children from taking baby on a joyride when your back is turned.

Eco-friendliness. Some crib manufacturers, such as Bonavita (*www.lajobi.com*), are using "eco-friendly" wood that comes from sustainable forests, water-based, nontoxic glues, and biodegradable, recycled/ recyclable packaging. You'll typically pay 10 to 12 percent more for an eco-friendly crib, though, because the materials are usually more expensive and more of them are required. We're told that water-based finishes, for example, require more coats than conventional finishes. In addition, manufacturers must maintain a cost-adding "paperwork trail" that they have used these materials.

Recommendations

Buy a new, full-sized crib with stationary sides made after 2000 that is JPMA certified. Still, certification is no guarantee of safety so parents must be on the lookout for safety hazards. Even when you're buying new, take along a soda can when you shop. If you can pass the can between the slats, they're too far apart. Check for sharp edges and protruding screws, nuts, corner posts, decorative knobs, and other pieces that could catch a baby's clothing at the neck. Buying new will help protect your baby from wear-and-tear hazards such as drop sides, slats, or hardware that may have been weakened by rough use, or excessive dampness or heat during storage. By law, a code indicating the production date of the crib must be displayed both on the crib and on its shipping carton.

Cribs are shipped unassembled, so if you're not certain you can put a crib together correctly (it's typically a two-person job that requires a full hour—from unpacking to complete assembly), recruit a handy friend or relative or ask the retailer to send a qualified assembly crew to your home. This can cost an extra $70 or more unless assembly is included in the retail price, but it can give you valuable peace of mind. But don't think you're off the hook; make sure assembly instructions are followed exactly. Besides saving tempers and fingers, having the store assemble the crib allows you to inspect it on the spot—and reject it if you discover flaws.

If you assemble the crib, put it together where your baby will be sleeping initially, such as in your bedroom (recommended for your baby's first six months). Once it's put together, the crib may not fit through a small door, and you may need to disassemble and reassemble it again in your baby's nursery six months later. That's not convenient, but you'll have the reassurance that your baby is sleeping in the safest possible place. Follow our Safety Strategies in Where Your Baby Should Never Sleep (page 153), and Sleeping Dos and Don'ts (page 157), and tell grandparents and other caregivers who may be with your baby at naptime or nighttime about these safety tips, too.

Ratings • Cribs

	Excellent ⊖	Very good ⊖	Good ○	Fair ◑	Poor ●

Brand & model	Price	Overall score 0 ... 100 P | F | G | VG| E	Safety	Construction	Ease of use	Toddler bed	Day bed	Full-sized bed
STATIONARY SIDES									
Legacy Kensington by Child Craft F38121.80	$600	85	⊖	⊖	⊖	•		•
Bonavita Peyton Lifestyle 01-75	400	85	⊖	⊖	⊖	•	•	•
✓ **DaVinci** Emily 4791	250	84	⊖	⊖	⊖		•	•
Babi Italia Pinehurst Lifestyle 3123035	400	84	⊖	⊖	⊖	•	•	•
Young America myHaven Built to Grow 46120	900	84	⊖	⊖	⊖	•	•	●
✓ **Ikea** Leksvik 601.086.63	160	82	⊖	⊖	⊖	•		
Bella D'Este Claremont Lifetime 0315S00	400	82	⊖	⊖	⊖		•	•
Simmons Ashford Y0795001	430	82	⊖	⊖	⊖	•	•	•
Simplicity Ellis 4-in-1 8676N	250	81	⊖	⊖	⊖	•	•	•
Baby's Dream Serenity 4751-18	350	81	⊖	⊖	⊖	•		•
SINGLE FOLDING SIDE									
Baby's Dream Ocean 4762-9A	450	74	⊖	⊖	⊖	•		•

✓ **CR Best Buy** These models offer the best combination of performance and price. All are recommended.

Brand & model	Price	Overall score (0–100) P|F|G|VG|E	Safety	Construction	Ease of use	Toddler bed	Day bed	Full-sized bed
SINGLE DROP SIDE								
Bellini Bella 4300	$930	82	Excellent	Excellent	Excellent			•
Graco Lauren Convertible 3250282	150	69	Excellent	Excellent	Good	•	•	•
Pottery Barn Kids Dana 221070M	500	69	Excellent	Good	Excellent	•	•	
Land of Nod Jenny Lind 139912	330	60	Excellent	Good	Good	•		
Cosco 2-in-1 Convertible * 10-186	120	59	Excellent	Good	Good			
Jardine Enterprises Olympia 0102B00	250	46	Good	Good	Fair			
Delta Jasmine 4852-2	260	45	Good	Good	Good	•	•	•
DOUBLE DROP SIDE								
Bellini Isabella 2000	620	83	Excellent	Excellent	Excellent	•		
Delta Jenny Lind 4750-1 Note: Some versions of this model have been recalled.**	120	26	Fair	Fair	Fair	•		
RECALLED MODEL TESTED WITH REPAIR KIT								
Bassett Wendy Bellissimo 5545-0521	500	83	Excellent	Excellent	Excellent	•	•	•

*Metal frame

**In October 2008, Delta Enterprise Corp. recalled some models of Delta Jenny Lind cribs due to problems with spring pegs, which can become nonfunctional, causing the drop side to detach from the crib, and creating a gap that can potentially entrap or suffocate an infant or toddler. Check the recall notice for the affected model numbers.

Guide to the Ratings

Safety score incorporates compliance with federal and voluntary safety standards, drop side safety (where applicable) and mattress support security. CR's tests do not address the durability issues associated with recent recalls that could impact safety. **Construction** incorporates drop side hardware; general construction quality (including types of hardware used, e.g. the use of allen bolts, barrel nuts and the like; use of screw insert sleeves rather than placing screws directly into wood, etc); sample and design defects, if any; and ease of assembly (which includes ease of following instructions for assembly). After testing, all cribs were examined for degraded operation (for example, the drop side movement had become stiff or got stuck); wobbliness or other wear. **Ease of use** incorporates drop side operation (where applicable), ease of moving the crib, and ease of adjusting the mattress support.

chapter

Crib
Alternatives

For the first four to five months of your baby's life, you'll find some alternatives to a crib, including bassinets, Moses baskets, co-sleepers, and cradles. But as we mentioned in the Cribs chapter, the best beds for babies are full-sized cribs, so consider all other options with caution.

If you choose a bassinet, get one that's JPMA-certified, like the Cariboo Classic Bassinet by Scandinavian Child.

Bassinets, co-sleepers, cradles, and Moses baskets—a basket with handles, a bottom pad and puffy fabric sides, designed so you can tote your baby from room to room—seem to offer a cozy nest near a parent's bed. And you might think that a newborn or young infant would be more at home in a compact space than in a large, airy crib. But full-sized cribs have long been subject to mandatory federal safety standards and could be recalled from the market if they fail to meet them. In addition, some manufacturers have their cribs certified by an independent testing facility in order to meet a voluntary industry standard set by guidelines developer ASTM International. Certification is indicated by a seal from the Juvenile Products Manufacturers Association (JPMA). Now, the Consumer Product Safety Improvement Act of 2008 requires that all cribs sold in the U.S., whether manufactured here or imported, must be certified as meeting federal and ASTM industry standards.

However, there are currently no federally mandated standards specifically for bassinets, cradles, Moses baskets, or co-sleepers, beyond those for such items as small parts and rough edges, and the spacing of any rails. ASTM does have a standard for bassinets and cradles and has agreed to work on one for co-sleepers, a.k.a. "bedside" sleepers. But we don't recommend using a co-sleeper— or a Moses basket, either.

Bassinet and cradle manufacturers can voluntarily comply with the ASTM standard for these products (again, indicated by a JPMA seal on the package)—and certification can provide a layer of protection— but at present aren't required to. (Ultimately, however, all durable nursery products will require certification.) And makers must now meet other provisions of the new law for all children's products, such as lower lead levels and the ban on certain phthalates (substances that can be harmful to development), plus product labeling.

We don't recommend Moses baskets or co-sleepers.

Bassinet and Cradle Basics

A bassinet is a compact baby bed made of fabric, wicker, or woven wooden splints; some come with wheels and can usually be moved easily from room to room. Many have a rigid hood that can be attached on one end to block the light. Cradles are bassinets that rock from side to side. Both types of baby beds take up little space. Ideally, a full-sized crib should go in your bedroom for at least your baby's first six months, but if you're short on space, a bassinet or cradle (some do double duty) can be another option. A bouncer seat, a swing, or a play yard with a bassinet insert are acceptable for an impromptu snooze, provided they don't have any loose fabric, which is a suffocation hazard. And don't add loose fabric, such as a blanket, comforter, any type of pillow or stuffed animal, or an additional mattress to any place your baby sleeps.

Shopping Secrets

Look for the JPMA seal. Bassinets have had some safety issues, such as rough, sharp inside edges, soft sides that pose a suffocation hazard, and bars widely spaced enough to trap a baby. The ASTM updated the bassinet and cradle standard in 2007, and the new standard is used for certification. The following manufacturers carry the JPMA seal: Amby Baby, Delta Enterprises Corporation, Dorel Juvenile Group (Safety 1st), Hushmok, Ltd., Kolcraft, Learning Curve, Scandinavian Child/Cariboo, and Summer Infant.

Choose a bassinet or cradle with a sturdy bottom and a wide, stable base. There should be no sharp points or edges on the inside or outside, or small parts that could be a choking hazard. If the bassinet or cradle is made of wood, it should be free of splinters.

Check any folding mechanisms. If the legs or frame of the bassinet or cradle collapse for storage, make sure they lock into place when the unit is set up.

Make sure the mattress/pad is smooth and extra firm, and fits snugly. The mattress/pad in a bassinet or cradle should be no more than 1½ inches thick. It's thin for a reason; a thicker mattress/pad is a suffocation hazard.

Size up bassinet/cradle sides. "You want an airy environment. If the sides of a bassinet aren't meshy, there's a potential

The hammock cradle (also known as a motion bed) by Amby Baby, certified by the JPMA, can be used for babies up to 25 pounds. Its slightly upright sleeping position can help babies suffering from colic and reflux.

concern that a baby could suffocate against the side," says Rachel Moon, M.D., a pediatrician and SIDS researcher at Children's National Medical Center, in Washington, D.C. Bassinets have been associated with 53 infant deaths from 1990 to 2004. Suffocation was a leading cause, according to a 2008 study in The Journal of Pediatrics. However, the mesh should not be soft or stretchy. In late 2008, a Playkids U.S.A. convertible crib with a bassinet attachment was recalled when the stretchy mesh allowed a child to became entrapped between the mattress and the side of the crib and suffocate.

If you opt for a cradle, go with one that barely rocks. Cradles with a pronounced rocking motion can cause a small infant to roll against the side of the unit, posing a suffocation hazard. Look for a model with a frame suspended on hooks, or with locking hardware to both stabilize the rocking motion so the cradle won't tilt too much and to stop the rocking when you're not present to check on your child. Do not let a baby rock unattended, especially if you have pets or young children who can exaggerate the rocking motion or even tip the cradle.

The Kolcraft Cuddle 'n Care features mesh side windows for increased air flow.

Consider a bassinet or cradle as only a quick fix. Bassinets and cradles have a short life span. Once your baby can roll over, begin to push up on his hands and knees, or reach the manufacturer's maximum weight (usually 15 to 18 pounds, but sometimes as much as 25 pounds), whichever comes first, it's time to move him to a crib. Although you won't believe it when you bring your baby home, he'll soon be busting out of his bassinet; some babies run out of leg and head room in just three months. So factor that into your buying decision. If your budget is tight, don't go all out for this item—even skip it altogether and use a full-sized crib (placed in your bedroom) from the start.

Keep the receipt and all packaging and materials that come with the product. You'll need those in case you decide to return the bassinet or cradle for any reason.

Bassinet and Cradle Cautions

You can't be too careful when buying or using a bassinet or cradle. Here are more safety considerations to keep in mind when you're looking at these baby beds:

◆ **Buy certified and buy new.** Although it's not a complete guarantee of safety, buying a certified product adds a layer of protection. Certified products must meet the ASTM standard requirements such as correct spacing of side slats or bars. In 2008, for example, 900,000 Simplicity 3-in-1 and 4-in-1 convertible close sleeper/bedside sleeper bassinets (200,000 of which also carried the Graco logo or a Disney Winnie-the-Pooh motif) were recalled because the bassinet has metal bars that can be exposed when the Velcro flap that covers them is not properly secured—and the bar spacing exceeded the maximum 2⅜ inches allowed under the federal crib standard, forming a strangulation hazard. Beware: Some of those bassinets could still be in circulation online and at tag sales and secondhand shops. Always buy new—the maker is required to put the date of manufacture on the product. Send in the registration so you can be notified of a recall.

◆ **Say no to an heirloom cradle or bassinet.** It's a quaint idea to use one that's been in the family for generations, but chances are it isn't up to today's safety standards. Some possible hazards are an overly thick mattress or puffy sides, both suffocation risks, and legs with an old-style latching mechanism that can unexpectedly release.

◆ **Don't leave your baby unattended in a rocking cradle.** Use the hardware to stop the rocking motion before your baby's bed- and naptime if you're going to leave the room, and around pets and toddlers.

◆ **Don't use a bassinet or cradle with wheels unlocked** around stairs or other children. Lock the wheels as soon as you finish moving the bassinet from one room to another—and keep them locked.

◆ **Don't carry or move a bassinet or cradle** with your child in it.

◆ **Use only the mattress/pad provided by the manufacturer** and only the fitted sheet made for the bassinet, or one specifically designed to fit the dimensions of the mattress/pad. Buy at least three fitted sheets so you have one to use, one for the wash, and one as a backup. Don't use a pillowcase or different sized sheet as a substitute.

◆ **Don't add stuffed animals or any bedding,** such as a pillow, comforter, or blanket, or extra padding like an additional mattress/pad, or a sleep positioner to your baby's bassinet or cradle; they're suffocation hazards. Put your baby to sleep in a wearable blanket (swaddle sack) instead of covering her with a blanket.

◆ **Don't let strings, toys suspended from a mobile, or window blind or curtain cords hang into the bassinet.** Don't place a cradle or bassinet near window blind or drape cords (a strangulation hazard). Shorten window blind cords by cutting the looped cords in half and keep them out of your baby's reach. Position the mobile so your baby can't reach it. And don't add any suspended toys on your own. Use only those provided with the mobile.

◆ **Place your baby on his back in a cradle or bassinet,** just as you would in a full-sized crib. Ninety percent of SIDS cases occur during the first six months of a baby's life, which is prime bassinet time.

What's Available

Some brands of bassinets and cradles are, in alphabetical order: Amby Baby (*www.ambybaby.com*), Baby Mod (available exclusively at *www.walmart.com*), Badger Basket (*www.badgerbasket.com*), Burlington Basket Company (*www.burlingtonbasket.org*), Eddie Bauer (*http://eddiebauer.djgusa.com*), Fisher-Price (*www.fisher-price.com*), Kolcraft (*www.kolcraft.com*), Orbit Baby (*www.orbitbaby.com*), PoshTots (*www.poshtots.com*), Pottery Barn Kids (*www.potterybarnkids.com*), Scandinavian Child (*www.scichild.com*), and The First Years/Learning Curve (*www.learningcurve.com*). Prices range from $40 for basic bassinets to $390 (and more) for custom-made deluxe bassinets decked out with elegant, flowing bed skirts and decorative ruffles and bows, or intricate wooden or ornate iron cradles. In general, you'll find a lot to choose from in the basic to slightly upgraded range—$60 to $250.

Features to Consider

The Badger Basket Portable Bassinet 'n Cradle converts to a handy toy box. All parts are included for the alteration.

Convertibility. Some bassinets convert into impromptu changing tables and many include pockets or storage underneath for diapers, wipes, and so on. Others can become a co-sleeper that attaches to an adult bed, but again, we do not recommend that option. Some bassinets even morph into other useful items, such as a toy box, when your baby has outgrown the bassinet function.

Movement. Some bassinets mechanically morph into cradles with a quick-release latch and retractable wheels, allowing the unit to gently rock only when your baby moves. Others, such as the Fisher-Price Zen Collection Gliding Bassinet (*www.fisher-price.com*, $250), glide from side to side at the turn of a dial (four D batteries required, not included) while the unit's wheels stay stationary.

Portability. Some bassinets have a handle so you can carry it from room to room, to keep your baby nearby. Others have functioning wheels so you can roll the entire unit around. Don't move a bassinet or cradle with your baby in it.

Toys. You may also find bassinets/cradles with a detachable mobile or a canopy with attached toys. Some mobiles can be detached and the unit then used on a crib.

Sound effects, vibration, light. Some bassinet mobiles include soothing music and heart-beat, ambient, or nature sounds with volume control, plus lights and rotating toys, all of which can be controlled by a keypad. The bassinets may also feature a soft-glow night-light so you can peek in on your baby without disturbing her. That's a plus. These extras usually run on AA or D batteries (not included).

Shape. Most bassinets and cradles are rectangular, but at least one manufacturer we know of (Badger Basket) makes an oval bassinet. We're not sure this shape offers any advantages, except as a conversation piece.

Bedding. Besides a thin mattress/pad (which should be no thicker than 1½ inches) and a fitted sheet, most bassinets also have a fabric lining. You'll find bassinets with a liner that includes an attached pleated or ruffled hood and some with a bed skirt, often cascading all the way to the floor. These frilly details are standard on most bassinets. The bedding is also sold separately to fit bassinets in certain sizes, like jumbo. At the highest end, these extras can be custom-made. Popular bassinet and cradle bedding fabrics are toile, vintage florals, gingham, white eyelet, and colorful checks and plaids. Undyed, organically grown cotton bedding in natural shades of cream, brown, and green is also a trend. No matter what look you go for, choose bedding that's machine washable. You may need to line dry it to prevent shrinkage (check the instruction manual). And refer to your instruction manual to make sure you always remount the bassinet cover correctly.

An oval bassinet, like this one from Badger Basket, makes a style statement.

Canopy. A canopy can help block the light—so you can read before bedtime, for example, without waking your baby. It may be retractable or removable, which gets it out of the way if you'll be changing your baby in the bassinet. Be aware that although the frilly curtains and canopy may appeal to parents, they are unnecessary, and can pose a strangulation hazard to your child. The risk is less for the tiniest babies who are less mobile.

Storage. A bottom storage basket is useful for stashing a change of clothes, booties, toys, diapers, and wipes. A flowing bed skirt can block access, so get a bassinet with a short skirt.

Recommendations

First, decide whether you truly need a bassinet or cradle. If the crib you've selected fits in your bedroom, have your baby sleep in that from day one, then shift the crib into the nursery when your baby reaches 6 months or so. That's the safest route. If you want to use a bassinet or cradle, consider how you'll use it and how portable you'll need it to be. If you just want a place for your baby to sleep nearby at night, buy a basic model, preferably one that's JPMA certified. View other bassinets and cradles with caution. They may be in compliance with the voluntary safety standard, but unless they've been officially JPMA certified, you can't be sure. As we mentioned, all durable nursery products, including bassinets, will require certification in the future.

When buying and using a bassinet or cradle, follow our Shopping Secrets and Safety Strategies. Be sure to abide by the manufacturer's weight and size specifications and stop using the product when your baby can roll over, push up on his hands and knees, or sit up by himself. There are usually warnings on the product, sometimes a lot of them. A note about assembly: Some bassinets have as many as 23 parts, and you may need a Phillips screwdriver and a good half-hour to put the puzzle together. Follow the manufacturer's instructions exactly. If you need any parts, get them from the same company that made the cradle or bassinet. To order, check the instruction manual.

14

chapter

Crib
Bedding

Right up there on the excitement scale with creating your list of baby names is pondering the endless possibilities for making your baby's room special. The look of your baby's nursery is important. But make safety, not style, your main concern.

These fitted crib sheets by Bamboosa are made from 100 percent organic bamboo fine jersey, which can be surprisingly soft.

Making a big deal out of the baby's room is part of the fun of parenthood (although you can certainly be low-key if you wish). From a fantasy room that clearly stands apart to a subdued space that blends with the décor in your house, your baby's nursery can be anything you want. Keep in mind though, that the American Academy of Pediatrics recommends that your baby sleep in a full-sized crib but nearby, optimally in your own room, for the first six months.

After you've chosen the crib and other nursery furniture as a foundation, a logical place to start in decorating your baby's room is with the crib bedding and crib skirt. Then choose paint or wallpaper and other accessories, such as the fabric for your rocking chair, based on those colors and patterns. It's often much easier to start with the crib linens and then add paint or wallpaper. But as you know from the Cribs chapter, to guard against suffocation, we recommend keeping your baby's crib basically bare—just a tight fitted sheet, and maybe a crib skirt/dust ruffle for a touch of style. Instead of blankets or quilts, we recommend dressing your baby in a one-piece bunting.

A decked-out crib like this one can be a safety hazard.

A fitted sheet and a crib skirt aren't much to work with, but they can get your creative juices flowing. Colors and styles of fitted crib sheets and crib dust ruffles run the gamut—from bears, boats, barnyard animals, and bunnies to prints, checks, florals, polka dots, solids, gingham, toile, and stripes in bold and muted tones. Consider coordinating them with the window treatments and other accessories such as artwork and lighting. Besides conventional fabrics like 100 percent traditional cotton, you'll find fitted sheets in soft, 100 percent organic cotton, cotton fleece, flannel, T-shirtish cotton knit, and 100 percent bamboo, a renewable, fast-growing grass. Bamboo and organic cotton

▪ Safety Strategy

Don't Buy a Crib Bumper

Crib bumpers are designed to help prevent minor injuries a baby might experience in a crib—slight head bumps against the sides or poking an arm or leg through the slats.

But bumpers might not prevent all small injuries (most leave a gap near the mattress which would allow a baby's limb to pass through anyway) and the risks of using them are considerable, according to a study from the Washington University Department of Pediatrics in St. Louis, published in The Journal of Pediatrics. The study, which analyzed three Consumer Product Safety Commission (CPSC) databases for deaths related to crib bumpers from 1985 through 2005, found that 27 children from 1 month to 2 years old died from suffocation or strangulation related to bumper pads or their ties. The authors concluded that the possibly fatal risks from crib bumper pads outweigh any benefit provided by such padding in preventing relatively rare minor bruises and contusions.

Take crib bumpers off your nursery wish list.

Besides suffocation and strangulation, bumpers can also increase the risk of SIDS, says Laura Reno, vice president of public affairs at First Candle, a national nonprofit organization dedicated to advancing infant health and survival. "If a baby gets his face against a bumper, he could rebreathe exhaled carbon dioxide instead of fresh air. The lack of enough oxygen could trigger a SIDS incident in babies who are susceptible to it," she says. To play it safe, keep your baby's crib bare and bumperless.

can also be better for the planet because they're grown with fewer pesticides and fertilizers. You may pay slightly more for these products, though. A 100 percent organic bamboo fitted crib sheet by Bamboosa (*www.bamboosa.com*), for example, costs roughly $25; we found a fitted crib sheet for as low as $5.

Though they often come in sets or "collections," crib linens are also sold individually, but you may have to seek out these separates. And if anything but a "fully loaded" crib (with luxurious, cushy bumpers and so on) leaves you feeling decoratively deprived, think of how much better you'll rest knowing your baby is sleeping in a safe place.

A tight-fitting crib sheet can set the style tone for your baby's nursery.

Going spare is easier on your decorating budget, too. Although we found 4-piece crib bedding collections (sheet, bumper, comforter, and dust ruffle) for as low as $20 in the clearance section on Wal-mart.com, we also saw custom-made crib ensembles for more than $3,000 (at www.poshtots.com). There's a lot to offer in between, but it's easy to find yourself in the "luxury linen" category, even when you didn't intend to be. Beware: Linens, like baby clothes, have a way of blowing the budget because they're so aesthetically appealing.

What's Available

Some brands of crib sheets and dust ruffles that are sold separately (not only as part of a set) include, in alphabetical order: Bananafish (www.bananafish.com), Carter's (available at www.jcpenney.com), Cocalo (www.cocalo.com), Crown Crafts Infant Products (www.crowncrafts infantproducts.com which has the NoJo license), DwellStudio (www.dwell studio.com), Gerber Childrenswear (available at www.babiesrus.com), Kee-Ka (www.kee-ka.com), Kids Line (www.kidsline.com), Koala Baby (Babies "R" Us store-brand linens, www.babiesrus.com), Lambs & Ivy

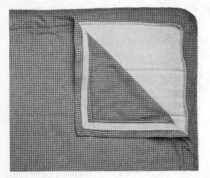

(www.lambsivy.com), MiGi (www.migistyle.com), Pottery Barn Kids (www.potterybarnkids.com), Sleeping Partners (www.sleepingpartners.com), Shabby Chic (www.shabbychic.com), Summer Infant (www.summerinfant.com), Sumersault (www.sumersault.com), and Trend Lab (www .trendlab.com). Many of these brands can also be found at leading retailers such as www .babiesrus.com, www.jcpenney.com, www.target .com, and www.babystyle.com. Prices for fitted crib sheets range from $5 to $44. Prices for crib dust ruffles range from $17.96 to $125.

The QuickZip crib sheet by Clouds and Stars makes changes easier. The fitted base sheet completely encases the mattress; the removable top panel, sold separately, zips in and unzips out.

Bedding 101

Here's a rundown of what you'll need to outfit your baby's crib:

Mattress pad. Buy two waterproof mattress pads so you can have one as a backup. These quilted pads should be thin—one inch or less in thickness. They're usually made of cotton, some-times 100 percent organic cotton, or a synthetic material, and should cover the mattress securely. Most, like fitted sheets, have

It's Tummy Time

Even though you shouldn't use a blanket or comforter in your baby's crib, it can come in handy as a play mat or exercise pad for tummy time under your watchful supervision, so there's no need to ban the blanket altogether. Tummy time—the time your baby spends on the floor during the day doing "push-ups" and turning her head—promotes neck and shoulder development and builds the muscles your baby needs to roll, sit, and crawl. According to the American Physical Therapy Association (APTA), many babies aren't spending enough time on their stomachs. A lack of tummy time

and the resulting developmental delays can affect a child's ability to learn basic skills such as chewing, grasping, crawling, standing, and walking.

The APTA cites a recent survey of 400 physical and occupational therapists, two-thirds of whom had seen an increase in early motor delays among infants under six months in the past several years. (An early motor delay happens when a child isn't able to meet important physical milestones in the first years of life.) More than 80 percent of the therapists listed a lack of tummy time as the number one reason for this increase. By spending

time on their stomach—ideally, as soon as they come home from the hospital and for at least one to two minutes after every nap, diaper change, and feeding, working up to a total of an hour a day—babies can typically develop normal muscle strength and coordination. Tummy time also helps prevent tight neck muscles and the development of flat areas on the back of the head. When babies don't get enough tummy time, they may need therapy to catch up. Tummy time can also be play time. For more information, check out a brochure called Tummy Time Tools, found at *www.apta.org.*

elastic all the way around. Never use a plastic bag as a mattress cover. Plastic is a suffocation hazard.

Fitted sheet. Most crib sheets have fitted corners, which keep them secure. Fabrics range from woven cottons and cotton blends, including 100 percent organic cotton, to lightweight flannel and bamboo. Two or three should get you off to a good start. Don't use fitted sheets that are loose or bunchy; they should fit your baby's crib mattress like a skin. And never use an adult sheet on a crib mattress, not even in a pinch. It can come loose and entangle a child.

A swaddle wrap. This type of sleep sack is made for infants as an alternative to a receiving blanket (a very thin blanket typically made of woven cotton used for swaddling), though that's also an option. A swaddle wrap slips over a regular sleeper or diaper and has plenty of room for little legs to stretch and kick. Use a swaddle wrap or receiving blanket to swaddle your newborn during nap and nighttime for the first few months. Buy four swaddle wraps or a half-dozen waffle-weave receiving blankets made of 100 percent cotton for good absorbency (or put them on your shower gift list). Swaddle blankets are also available in 100 percent cotton muslin, in regular and organic (*www.adenandanais.com*, among others). The loose-weave fiber promotes air-flow to avoid overheating. It's cozy, too; muslin gets softer the more you wash it.

Leading swaddle wraps are the SleepSack Swaddle by Halo ($34.95 for 100 percent organic cotton; $29.95 for regular cotton and for micro-fleece; available at *www.halosleep.com*) and the SwaddleMe adjustable infant wrap by Kiddopotamus ($9.99 for 100 percent cotton, including fleece; $14.99 for bamboo; and $15.99 for 100 percent organic cotton; available at *www.kiddopotamus.com* and leading retailers such as *www.babiesrus.com*). Wraps are recommended by First Candle. Use a swaddle wrap instead of a crib blanket, which we do not recommend because it is an entanglement hazard.

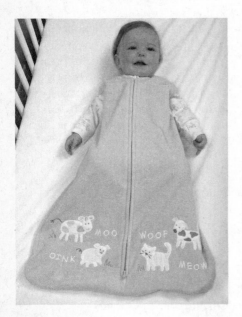

A wearable blanket, like this Halo microfleece sleep sack, is a much safer substitute for a crib comforter, which is a suffocation hazard.

Wearable blanket. After your baby outgrows his swaddler, he'll be ready for a regular sleep sack, a wearable blanket that goes over a regular sleeper or diaper, with lots of leg room for stretching and kicking. Popular brands are the Halo SleepSack ($24.95 to $32.95 for organically grown cotton, *www.halosleep.com*), the Back to Sleep Sack by Prince Lionheart ($24.99, *www.princelionsheart.com*), and the Beddie-Bye wearable blanket by Kiddopotamus ($19.99, available at *www.babiesrus.com*, among other retailers). CPSC regulations require flame-resistant sleepwear in sizes 9 months and up. (Infant garments do not pose a serious risk of flammability.) As your baby grows, you'll want either tight-fitting sleepwear or flame-resistant fabric.

Crib skirt. It's not necessary, but it does add design flair to the crib and your baby's room.

■ Budget Baby

Easy Ways to Stretch Your Decorating Dollar

Get inspired with accessories. Don't limit yourself to linens. A crib skirt or fitted sheet can set the style and tone for your baby's nursery. But you can also pull a color scheme from a patterned rug, which also helps camouflage stains and spills. (To reduce the risk of tripping, make sure the rug has a nonskid back or is secured to the floor with double-face tape.) A piece of artwork can also serve as your creative catalyst, and it doesn't have to be a pricey oil painting. An inexpensive poster will do. Or, if you have older children, involve them in decorating the baby's room by having these resident artists paint or draw a picture that you mat and frame. If you have your heart set on certain colors, give your kids markers or paint in those colors to work with.

Pick paint colors carefully. Instead of using whimsical wallpaper or painting the room a babyish blue or pink, consider a paint hue that your child won't grow out of so quickly, such as yellow, lime green, or lavender for girls, or navy, red, or Kelly green for boys. Then, to update, just change the accessories, such as the artwork.

Consider convertible furniture. Furniture that morphs—a crib that converts to a toddler bed, or a changing table that changes into a desk or dresser—can help you go the distance so that when your baby moves on to the "big boy" or "big girl" stage, it doesn't necessitate a gear and design overhaul.

Recommendations

Whether you decorate your baby's room lavishly or simply, make safety your main concern. Ignore those inviting retail crib bedding displays and over-the-top magazine spreads of celebrity nurseries and buy your linens separately—the crib skirt/dust ruffle and the fitted sheet, rather than an entire collection. Purchase tightly fitting sheets, then recheck the fit after each laundering, since washing can cause shrinkage or weaken the elastic. Check for loose threads that could catch a baby's head, neck, fingers, or toes. Launder sheets twice before the first use to remove any chemical residue from the fabric-treatment process and to ensure correct fit. Consider using a mild liquid or powder laundry detergent such as Dreft, a specially formulated laundry detergent for infants and toddlers.

Remember, bare is best. The safest crib is one that has a firm mattress that meets the federally mandated measurements of at least 27¼ inches by 51⅝ inches, and is no more than six inches thick. It has a snug-fitting mattress pad and fitted crib sheet—and nothing else. Don't buy bumper pads, stuffed animals, pillows, quilts, or a duvet for your baby's crib. Experts have long recognized the suffocation and other risks inherent in such soft crib bedding.

Avoiding Paint Hazards

Paint the nursery at least two months before your baby arrives. That allows time for fumes to subside before your baby comes home. Use a paint that's labeled low-VOC or zero VOCs (volatile organic compounds), VOCs are solvents that are released into the air as the paint dries and may be irritating to a baby (and to some adults).

You may want to wear a mask as you paint, available at hardware stores and home centers.

If it's practical, paint the nursery and other rooms in your house in warmer months so you can keep the windows open, suggests Philip Landrigan, M.D., a pediatrician and head of the department of Community and Preventive Medicine at Mount Sinai School of Medicine, in New York City. To reduce other fumes, thoroughly air out new furniture and anything made of plastic or wood.

If your home was built before 1978, you can presume that it contains lead-based paint. If paint on walls is not chipping or peeling, it's less likely to cause toxic exposure to lead, but even intact paint can be a hazard, particularly on windows and doors that generate lead-contaminated dust when disturbed by impact or friction. Don't sand paint that may contain lead or attempt to remove it yourself; that's a job for a contractor who is licensed for lead removal work. If you have lead-paint sanded, do so several months before your baby is due; both parents should be out of the house for the duration of the sanding, says Dr. Landrigan. For more information on how to safely combat lead paint hazards, go to *www.hud.gov./offices/lead/healthyhomes/lead.cfm*.

15

chapter

Crib
Mattresses

When you're crib shopping, you'll also need to choose a mattress, which typically is sold separately. Don't underestimate the importance of this purchase. Your baby will spend a lot of time snoozing—up to 18 hours a day initially—so it's essential to select the best-quality mattress you can afford.

Whether you choose an innerspring mattress or a foam one like this Moonlight Slumber model, quality of construction is of top importance.

Mattress size and firmness should be your primary concerns. If a mattress is too small, it can leave gaps between the edges of the mattress and the frame of the crib that could trap and endanger your baby. If a mattress is too soft, it can conform to your baby's shape, causing a risk of suffocation or sudden infant death syndrome (SIDS). If possible, try the mattress you're purchasing in the floor model of the crib you're considering to check for a tight fit.

There are two major types of crib mattresses: foam and innerspring. Either is acceptable. Both types—if they're of good quality—will keep their shape well and provide excellent support for infants and toddlers. There are differences, though. Foam—made from polyurethane—tends to be lighter. The densest foam mattress usually weighs 7 to 8 pounds, compared with the 15 to 23 pounds of an innerspring mattress. So, although you're probably just lifting a corner at a time, changing the crib sheets may be easier with a foam unit. Foam is also less springy and therefore less likely to encourage your child to use the mattress as a trampoline down the road. Still, innerspring mattresses remain the most popular, probably because they are what most adults sleep on in the U.S.

The Sealy Tender Vibes Soothing Mattress gently vibrates your baby to sleep; two D batteries are required (sold separately).

Mattresses are a "blind" item, meaning that almost everything that matters is on the inside, where you can't see it. A crib mattress can feel great in the store, but begin to falter once your baby starts to use it. We've learned that you can't depend on sales staff, even at reputable retail outlets, to give you accurate information. One salesperson told us, quite convincingly, that innerspring mattresses are better than foam because foam tends to "break down" after 18 months. That may have been true 25 years ago, but not anymore. "A top-quality foam crib mattress will hold up just as long as an innerspring crib mattress, with normal use," says Dennis Schuetz, director of marketing for Colgate Juvenile Products, a manufacturer of crib mattresses in Atlanta, GA. That's because foam crib mattresses have become much more durable, Schuetz said.

■ Safety Strategies

Don't Buy Used

Buy a new crib mattress, if possible, especially for your first baby. That way, your baby will be protected by the most current flammability safety standards. Buying new also ensures that the mattress you buy is sanitary. If you buy a used mattress, you don't know how it was cared for or stored. Mold can grow within improperly stored crib mattresses, and bacteria can fester on the surface from liquids (diaper leakage, spit-up) that weren't properly cleaned up. In addition, buying new can protect you from buying a recalled model. If you take care of the mattress and it stays firm (check it with the squeeze test mentioned below in Features to Consider), you can save it for your next child, provided that it's not recalled.

Features to Consider

The best foam mattresses

If you decide to go with foam, remember that density is the most significant sign of quality in a foam mattress.

Dense foam. The best foam mattresses are firm and heavy and resilient—they bounce back quickly when you squeeze the center with both hands. To assess foam quality, compare the weight of different models. That's not always easy to do in a store, but if you're able to lift several mattresses (one at a time, of course), do it. In general, the heavier the foam mattress, the denser (and better) the foam. You can give the mattress a squeeze test. Pick it up, place a hand on each side of the mattress in the center, then press palms together. A dense mattress won't allow you to press very far.

The best innerspring mattresses

If you decide on an innerspring mattress, follow this general rule: The more layers and the better quality of those layers, the better the mattress.

Border rods. They go around the perimeter of the mattress top and bottom, and are the thickest pieces of steel a mattress contains. Never buy an innerspring mattress that lacks border rods. They provide extra firmness, durability, and edge support so a mattress won't sag when your baby stands or walks near the edge. Consider border rods a must-have.

High coil count and low steel gauge. Coil count, the number of springs or steel coils a mattress contains, is a popular marketing point. But a generous coil count doesn't always mean a firmer mattress. The cheapest innerspring baby mattresses may have fewer than 80 coils and more expensive models may have more than 280 coils, but a model with 150 coils could be firmer than one with 200. How? The gauge of steel in those 150 coils may be thicker than the steel in the 200-coil mattress. Steel gauge for mattress coils ranges from 12.5 to 19; the lower the number, the thicker the steel. Thicker is stronger. So look for a moderate to high coil count—135 to 150 coils is a good midrange—and a lower coil steel gauge (15.5 or below).

Coir fiber or wrap pad as the insulator pad. On top of the coils is an insulator pad that keeps the coils from poking through a mattress's cushioning layers to bother your baby. The best insulator pad is made from coir fiber—shredded and woven coconut shell—but fiber wrap pad, also called "rag" or "shoddy" pad, which is made from miscellaneous and pressed scraps of cloth, is also acceptable. Coir fiber is more expensive than fiber wrap pad, but either works well. The lowest quality insulator pad is made from woven polyester. Because it tends to form pockets over time, becoming concave where most of the baby's weight rests, it's less durable.

Foam or cotton cushioning layers. The next layer in the mattress sandwich is the cushioning, which may be made of foam, cotton, or polyester. Foam and cotton are signs of quality, though they contribute to the price. Polyester, which is less expensive and increasingly pervasive because the cost of foam to manufacturers has been rising, isn't ideal because of its tendency to form pockets.

Cover. Encasing the entire mattress is a fabric or vinyl cover. Fabric breathes more than vinyl, but ventilation holes in a vinyl cover help air circulate. A thicker or layered vinyl cover better resists leaks, stains, punctures, and tears, so go with vinyl over fabric. Look for at least a triple laminated ("3-ply") cover, which will give a mattress a tougher shell, adding to its longevity. Unlike a cloth cover, vinyl also acts as a barrier to dust mites.

Ecologically Friendly Options

Eco-friendly crib foam, innerspring, and mat (coconut shell fiber, a.k.a. coir) mattresses are a small niche in the increasingly "green" baby product marketplace. These mattresses tend to be made of fewer chemicals, plastics, and PVC (vinyl) and comprise a greater percentage of renewable and sustainable materials, such as cotton, fast-

Is a Waterproof Mattress Pad Necessary?

It's a good idea, even if the mattress you select is leakproof, as mattresses with a vinyl cover will be. Some cloth-covered mattresses are leak proof as well if they have

a plastic (polyurethane) coating. To be sure, check the label on cloth-covered mattresses for key words such as "leak-proof" or "waterproof." The coating may be on the underside of the cloth, not next to a baby's skin.

A waterproof mattress pad on a vinyl-covered mattress will make your baby's sleeping surface cozier. Without it, the chill of the mattress's vinyl is apt to come through, no matter what the thread count of the fitted sheet. For cloth-covered mattresses with underside waterproofing, a waterproof pad will protect the top cloth surface of the mattress from diaper leaks

and stains; it will also absorb the liquid and wick it away from your baby's skin.

If the mattress cover hasn't been waterproofed (which is often the case with natural crib mattresses, discussed in detail below), a waterproof mattress pad is a must to prevent fluids from reaching and staining the mattress cover and seeping into the core of the mattress, helping to prevent bacterial growth.

Should your baby's vinyl or water-proofed cloth-covered mattress get wet or soiled, spot-clean it with a damp cloth and mild soap to reduce the likelihood that bacteria will fester on the mattress cover.

growing bamboo, coir, plant-based foam, and natural, hypoallergenic latex (rubber-tree sap that's been injected with air). Plus, "the manufacturing process for some eco-friendly crib mattresses tends to produce fewer carbon emissions," says crib mattress producer Schuetz. Some manufacturers, such as Natural Mat (*www.naturalmatusa.com*), also use biodegradable packaging for their products.

If you're planning to buy an eco-friendly crib mattress, consider these features:

Cloth cover: Most green mattresses don't have a vinyl cover, which has been used for conventional mattresses for years because it's durable, easy to clean, and cost effective. Instead, you'll find cloth covers in cotton, 100 percent unbleached, undyed organic cotton, or bamboo yarn. Bamboo is fast growing and therefore quickly renewable, and the fiber is naturally antifungal and antibacterial.

The downside? Cloth covers won't stop diaper leaks from soaking into the mattress (a breeding ground for bacteria) unless they have a waterproof layer, typically made of polyurethane plastic. Whether or not you buy such a waterproof natural mattress (it should say on the label if it is), always use a waterproof mattress pad.

Cushioning layers: The more eco-friendly mattresses use foam that is typically made from a blend of petroleum and sustainable plant-based oil, such as soy. It's impossible to make crib-mattress foam without some petroleum, but a percentage of it can be replaced and still maintain the integrity of the mattress.

In lieu of foam cushioning, some eco-friendly mattresses use natural latex rubber, which comes from a liquid extracted from tropical trees. Some babies may be allergic to latex, but because the latex is tucked into the mattress core, it may not pose a problem. If you have any doubts, avoid a mattress made with latex.

Coir: Until the green movement came along, coir—shredded and woven coconut shell husks that are bound with latex adhesive—was typically used as an insulator pad on top of the coils in better quality innerspring crib mattresses. Now you'll find coir in other sandwich layers of natural mattresses. Two mattresses we know of, the Colgate Natural I (*www.colgatekids.com*, $360) and the Natural Mat Coco Mat (*www .naturalmatusa.com*, $399), use coir as the chief filling, in lieu of foam or innersprings, surrounding it with cotton cushioning or mohair fleece. Coir is renewable and sustainable and puts coconut shells to good use, but it also makes a mattress hefty, comparable to the weight of an innerspring. If you choose a coir mattress, follow the same firmness guidelines you would for a foam or an innerspring model.

Shopping Secrets

Know quality—then find it. Don't buy a mattress from a manufacturer or a retailer that doesn't reveal, with in-store information or displays, what the mattress is made of, or the components of each layer. That's especially true if you're in the market for an eco-friendly mattress. In fact, with this sort of purchase, you should also ask the retailer or visit the manufacturer's Web site to determine what percentage of the "natural/organic mattress" really is natural/organic. Here's why: Most "green" mattresses have some conventional (synthetic) components because not all mattress materials can be satisfactorily produced organically or come from nature. Innerspring mattresses, for example, can't be 100 percent organic because there's no such thing as organic carbon-tempered steel, says Schuetz.

Plus, there are no organic standards for the mattress industry. So a manufacturer could conceivably make a mattress with a 100 percent organic cotton cover with everything else conventional, and slap on an

Antimicrobial Covers

Some mattresses are sold with a special antimicrobial additive that's mixed in at the factory when the vinyl cover is in a liquid state. An antimicrobial mattress cover will slow the growth of mold and bacteria, but it won't prevent it altogether. Do you need this trendy feature? Definitely not. To prevent microbe growth, keep your baby's mattress clean by wiping it down after any accidents with soap and water. To store the mattress for your next child, put it in a snug-fitting crib mattress storage bag, preferably one you can see through (light inhibits bacterial growth). Then stow the mattress in a cool, dry place—in other words, not a damp basement or stuffy attic.

"organic" label. It's possible to buy a "natural/organic" crib mattress with just 5 percent organic or natural materials. If that's enough for you, that's fine. But know what you're buying. These mattresses are comparatively pricey, and it's easy, especially since mattress components are hidden inside the mattress, to get duped.

Check for firmness. Firmer is better. Don't worry that it may feel too firm. "If it feels good to you, it's too soft for your baby," Schuetz says. Most babies will get used to sleeping on anything after a day or two. Press on the mattress in the center. It should snap back readily and should not conform to the shape of your hand. If you're buying an innerspring, check for border rods around the edges.

Test the fit. By law, all full-sized crib mattresses must be at least 27¼ inches by 51⅝ inches and no more than 6 inches thick. But bring a measuring tape to be sure and take all three measurements. In 2008, about 20,000 Simmons Kids crib mattresses sold at Pottery Barn Kids and nursery furniture retailers were recalled because some of them were smaller than the minimum width requirement (27¼ inches). There's no minimum requirement for thickness, and some mattresses are skinnier than others. Shop in a store that displays crib mattresses and check the fit before you buy by pairing the mattress with the crib you choose. If you can squeeze more than two fingers between the mattress and the crib frame, the mattress is too small.

Don't worry about warranties. Mattress warranties range from five years to 25 years to lifetime. Don't be swayed by a long warranty, and don't pay extra for a mattress with a warranty. "Warranties are mostly a marketing tool to help make a sale or to entice the consumer to spend more," says Schuetz. More important than the warranty is the quality of the product, the reputation of the manufacturer, and the return policies and reputation of the store. In general, you can expect a good quality crib mattress to last as long as you're going to use it, provided that the cover has not been ripped or torn and that the mattress has been used properly (for sleeping, not for toddler tumbling or as a pet bed).

What's Available

Some major brands of foam, innerspring, and eco-friendly crib mattresses are, in alphabetical order: Colgate (*www.colgatekids.com*), DaVinci (available at retailers and e-tailer locations such as *www.babyuniverse .com*), Dream On Me (*www.dreamonme.com*), Kolcraft (*www.kolcraft .com*), which offers a number of brands, including Baby Prestige, Pediatric, and Sealy), L.A. Baby (*www.lababyco.com*), Moonlight Slumber (*www.moonlightslumber.com*), Natural Mat (*www.naturalmatusa.com*), Baby Natura (*www.naturaworld.com*), Naturepedic (*www.naturepedic.com*), and Simmons Kids (*www.simmonskids.com*).

Prices for conventional mattresses range from $50 to $320. You'll typically pay a higher price for green mattresses because the raw materials used to make them are more expensive. Using bamboo yarn instead of a vinyl cover on a crib mattress can cost the manufacturer five times more. Prices range from $180 for mattresses with natural components that aren't necessarily organic, such as Colgate's Natural line, to $625 for the Mohair Mat by Natural Mat, with raw materials from 100 percent renewable resources.

The Natura World Baby Natura Classic's open-cell interior allows air circulation.

Safer Mattresses

All mattresses sold in the U.S., including crib mattresses, must meet current federal flammability standards. One standard, 16 CFR Part 1632, which has been in place for more than 30 years, covers a mattress's ability to resist ignition from a cigarette. A newer performance standard, which was effective nationally on July 1, 2007, requires that all mattresses pass an open-flame test. The standard is designed to retard the

- **Budget Baby**

Skip the Convertible Option—and Save

If you're planning to convert your baby's crib to a toddler bed, "dual firmness" convertible mattresses are available at the top end (in the range of $220 for conventional mattresses and $400 for natural mattresses). These mattresses are designed to go the distance. They're extra firm for infants on one side, and cushier, with standard foam or springy, "viscoelastic" memory foam on the other for toddlers. (Do not flip the mattress until your baby's first birthday. Memory foam can be a suffocation and SIDS hazard.) But put this added feature in the "not necessary" category. Your baby will still be happy with a firm mattress when he becomes a toddler. If he's exposed to a more forgiving mattress, he probably won't want to go back. So if you buy a dual-firmness mattress, be sure not to flip it too soon.

flammability of mattresses from open flames, such as lighters and matches, reducing the severity of mattress fires and buying you time to get your family out of your home safely in the event of a fire.

Mattress manufacturers don't have to use synthetic flame-retardant chemicals. According to the Consumer Product Safety Commission (CPSC), many fibers—including rayon, acrylics, wool, and some polyesters currently used in crib mattress foams, fillings, barriers, and ticking are flame-resistant enough to meet both standards. That may be true with some natural fibers as well, such as bamboo. One manufacturer, Naturepedic, uses a proprietary FlameBreaker fire protection system, which is based on baking soda and silica bonded to cellulose fiber. Flame-retardant fibers may be used in every component of a mattress—or just one to meet the newer standard. But even if synthetic flame-retardant chemicals are used, they're safe. "The CPSC has extensively tested mattresses for any health problems associated with flame-retardant chemicals and the risk has been proven to be insignificant," says Patty Davis, CPSC spokesperson in Bethesda, Md.

The Natural Mat Mohair Mat crib mattress is constructed with horsetail hair, organic coir, and mohair (hair of the Angora goat).

Do Crib Mattresses Emit Toxic Gases?

Maybe you've heard of the "toxic gas" theory: Toxic fumes can result from a chemical reaction between crib-wetting and a flame-retardant chemical (antimony) used in some mattresses, increasing the risk of SIDS. But Consumers Union agrees with other experts including First Candle, a national nonprofit dedicated to advancing infant health and survival, that scientific evidence doesn't support this theory. Several studies show no link to higher antimony exposure in SIDS kids or evidence of exposure to other agents.

Crib mattresses may contain phthalates, a family of compounds used primarily in vinyl. Some studies suggest that phthalates may affect a child's development and reproductive system. But as a result of the Consumer Product Safety Improvement Act of 2008, three phthalates have been permanently banned in children's products, including crib mattresses. Three more are temporarily banned pending further study.

Recommendations

You needn't spend a fortune to get a good-quality conventional mattress, but don't skimp, either. For conventional mattresses, a good middle range is $90 to $200. Low-priced models (less than $90) tend to be mushy and flimsy. Higher-priced models tend to be firmer, thus safer.

With an innerspring, the number of layers, what each component is made of, and the quality of the covering add to the price and increase comfort. The cheapest foam and innerspring mattresses have thin vinyl coverings and edgings that can tear, crack, and dry out over time. As prices go up, coverings become thick, puncture-resistant, reinforced double or triple laminates. The weight also tends to increase because the innerspring mattress contains more or better-gauge steel and better-quality cushioning while the foam mattress is made of denser, better-quality foam. Dual firmness/reversibility, the presence and number of vents, and thickness are factors that differentiate models.

If you're shopping for an eco-friendly mattress, keep in mind that most mattresses are a blend of organic or natural components and conventional materials. Green mattresses might be easier on the environment. But don't buy one thinking it's healthier for your baby. Despite what you may have read online or heard from other parents, it's not the case. There's no evidence indicating that conventional mattresses aren't safe, as long as they're firm.

Diapers

Y ou'll change thousands of diapers by the time your child is 2 to 3 years old and ready for the potty. Fortunately, diaper quality is better than ever, which makes the task easier.

Although cloth diapers are making a comeback, disposable diapers continue to be a popular choice because they're so convenient.

Your first major decision in the diaper department will be between the cloth (a.k.a. "reusable") or disposable ("single-use") kind. Both types have their benefits and drawbacks. Disposable diapers are undeniably convenient, but they're costly: You can expect to spend $1,500 to $2,000 or more on disposables by the time your baby is out of them. If you use "eco-friendly" disposable diapers, which are biodegradable or not bleached with chlorine, you'll pay even more, an average of $1,600 to $2,500, depending on the number of diaper changes per day.

Cloth diapers can be much less expensive, especially if you wash them yourself. After paying the start-up costs—namely the waterproof covers you'll need to lock in moisture, the diapers, diaper inserts (cloth pads added to increase absorbency), and flushable liners that help contain the mess and eliminate the need to rinse cloth diapers before depositing them in a diaper pail—you'll spend hundreds of dollars less in diapering supplies over the years because you'll wash and reuse them again and again. You might even be able to use them for more than one baby. "People have this leftover image of rubber pants and pins," says Betsy Thomas, co-owner of Bummis, a Montreal-based company that makes washable waterproof diaper covers and sells prefolds and fitted diapers to go with them. But cloth diapers that close with snaps or Velcro can be almost as easy to use as disposable diapers. Yet you still have to wash them. Despite a resurgence in the popularity of cloth diapers, disposable diapers continue to be an accepted choice among today's parents, day-care centers and hospitals.

Disposables Deconstructed

A disposable diaper is an absorbent pad sandwiched between two sheets of nonwoven fabric. The pad typically contains chemical crystals that can absorb up to 800 times their weight in liquid and hold it in gel form. This helps keep liquid away from your baby's skin, so you can leave him in a disposable longer than in a cloth diaper without causing him discomfort. The quality of disposable diapers has improved in recent years. They're generally less leaky, feel less moist when they're wet, and provide a better fit. All the diapers we tested absorb far more liquid than a child is likely to produce during the time a single diaper is worn. But we've also found that all disposables are not the same; you'll see differences from brand to brand in fit, absorbency, and leakage control.

Diapers are often sized according to a baby's weight, beginning with preemie and newborn and progressing to sizes 1 through 7. Some store and "eco-friendly" brands are marked simply small, medium, large, and extra large, and weight ranges are listed on the package. The largest diapers fit children 41 pounds and over. As the sizes increase, you get fewer diapers for the same price. A large package might give you 72 diapers in size 1, but only 40 in size 6. As with many things, buying the largest packages can reduce your per-diaper costs. For example, at one diaper Web site, we calculated a savings of 6 cents per diaper by buying the extra large case of size 3 Pampers Cruisers (160 diapers) rather than the Pampers Cruisers size 3 jumbo pack (35 diapers).

Cloth vs. Disposables

Parents have argued about the merits of cloth and disposable diapers for years, and the arguments will likely continue into the distant future. If you're thinking about going the cloth route to be more environmentally friendly, consider this: Disposable diapers account for only 2 percent of the waste in dumps. At that rate, "disposable diapers aren't clogging up our nation's landfills," says Chaz Miller, director of state programs for the National Solid Wastes Management Association in Washington, D.C. "They're just another pebble on the beach." (The big culprits are large corrugated boxes, newspapers, and food waste.) And although cloth

Pampers and Huggies have scored tops in our tests.

diapers don't contribute to the 2 percent of landfill refuse, you have to wash them—and that requires energy to heat the water. Cloth diapers can be cheaper than disposables if you wash the diapers yourself, but not if you use a diaper service.

Another argument for cloth is that because they lack the high-tech absorption properties of disposables, toilet training will be faster since your child is more uncomfortable in a wet diaper. However, there are no concrete data to support this theory. In any case, products marketed to parents of toddlers who are trying to end the diaper years have a special liner designed to let your child "feel" the moisture. The super absorbent gel matrix in most disposable diapers for younger children can also hold and wick wetness away from your baby's skin, and buffers the alkaline pH of urine, significantly reducing the risk of diaper rash. "It's a great innovation that keeps your baby much drier than cloth diapers," says Ilona J. Frieden, M.D., director of pediatric dermatology at the University of California, San Francisco Children's Hospital. "Because of the gel in disposable diapers, irritant diaper rashes that were once commonplace are now rare," she says.

In the end, let convenience and cost be your deciding factors. A lot will depend on your lifestyle, your situation, what you're comfortable using, and what type of diaper works best for your child. If your baby is in day care, for example, you'll need to use disposables, at least during the day. Some parents at our Babies & Kids Blog (*blogs.consumerreports.org/baby*) report using cloth diapers at home and disposables when they're traveling. Others feel they must use disposables because they live where electricity rates are high and water is scarce.

If you're not sure which type of diaper to use, you could try both types and experiment, as did Cecile Yusilon, a registered nurse and mom of a 7-month-old, from Phillips Ranch, Calif. "For the first six months, we used all-in-one cloth diapers for our son during the day and disposable diapers at night, but now that he's 7 months old, he's exclusively on disposables. I work, go to school, and have a new baby. I couldn't handle all of it, and using cloth diapers is what I chose to cut out. It was too labor intensive to keep up with washing cloth diapers two to three times per week and removing the stains," she says.

But you be the judge. If you decide to use cloth diapers, "Give yourself two weeks to learn how to use and wash them," says Bummis co-owner Thomas, especially if you're transitioning from disposables. If you have any problems, call the manufacturer. You'll want to know how to wash cloth diapers properly so they remain bacteria-free. For laundry instructions, see page 197.

DISPOSABLE DIAPERS
What's Available

Some major brand names of disposable diapers are Huggies (*www.huggiesbabynetwork.com*), Luvs (*www.luvs.com*), Playskool (sold exclusively at CVS, *www.cvs.com*), Nature Babycare (*www.naty.com*), Pampers (*www.pampers.com*), Seventh Generation (*www.seventhgeneration.com*), and Tushies (*www.tushies.com*).

Store brands include Cottontails (Stop & Shop brand, available at Stop & Shop supermarkets and online at *www.peapod.com*, for delivery within select service areas on the East Coast and in the Midwest), CVS (*www .cvs.com*), Kirkland Signature (*www.costco.com*), Little Ones (Kmart's brand; not available online), Simply Dry (another Stop & Shop brand; not available online), Target brand (available in Target stores only), and White Cloud (Wal-Mart; not available online). We have found prices of our tested diapers varying from a low of 17 cents to a high of 24 cents when buying them in the largest-sized package available. Although our tests show that the name brands are the top-rated diapers, because overall they tend to be more absorbent and fit better, you may find store brands more than adequate—and a cost cutter. In our informal research, we calculated a savings of 3 cents per diaper when we compared the cost of size 1 Parent's Choice, Wal-Mart's store-brand diapers, with Pampers, also size 1, from the same store. Saving pennies per diaper may not seem like much, but with 10 changes per day (which is reasonable with an infant), you'd bank about $9 per month and $108 per year using the size 1 store-brand diapers.

Features to Consider

Fasteners. The type of fastener varies from brand to brand. Most now have Velcro fasteners, which, unlike tape, don't lose their sticking power when they come in contact with baby creams or powders.

Store-brand disposable diapers can be a good deal.

Contoured fit. Many diaper brands have elastic around the waist, legs, and thighs to help prevent leaks.

Lotion. Many diapers have a lotion in the liner that is supposed to protect baby's skin. But keep unscented diaper cream on hand for the possible outbreaks of diaper rash. Some babies are more prone to diaper rash than others because their skin is more sensitive.

Stretch sides. These sides help the diaper do a better job of molding to each baby's contours, which can help stop leaks. Diapers with stretch sides may be more comfortable, too.

Ultra-absorbent core. Many diapers have materials in the crotch padding that enhance absorbency.

Wetness indicator. At least one brand of disposables, Pampers Swaddlers Sensitive, has a wetness indicator that lets you know your baby needs a change. Newborn sizes of many brands also have a curved front or cutout to avoid irritating the still-healing navel area.

Recommendations

Plan on using plenty of diapers for your newborn, but don't load up on the newborn size. Unless you're the parent of multiples, it's overkill to buy economy packs, which may contain up to 160 newborn diapers. Your baby is likely to outgrow the newborn size before you use that many. In fact, some babies are too big at birth to ever wear the smallest size. Buy by your baby's weight. Start with one package of 40-count newborn diapers if your baby weighs less than 8 pounds at birth. If your baby weighs 8 pounds or more, start with a package of size 1s, then buy in volume after you find the brand you like best. Don't be afraid to experiment. You'll find a favorite brand in time.

> **Plan on using plenty of diapers for your newborn, but don't load up on the newborn size."**

In general, purchasing the largest-count package you can find is the way to go. Opting for an extra-large case of Pampers Baby Dry, for example, rather than the jumbo-size package, could save you up to 9 cents per diaper, depending on the size of the diaper you buy. You'll save the most money if you buy store-brand diapers in economy-size boxes, which come in counts that range from 92 to 252; you can also find competitive deals on name-brand diapers on sale, in packages of various sizes.

Don't be too quick to jump to the next size diaper. Selecting the smallest diaper your baby can wear comfortably will save you money in the long run because a larger diaper costs more. Manufacturers usually charge the same amount per package regardless of the actual size of the diapers, but they will put progressively fewer diapers in the package as the size gets larger. In addition, a diaper that is too roomy may allow leaks.

Diaper sizes vary from brand to brand. One brand's size 1 may fit children from 8 to 14 pounds, while another's fits those from 8 to 18 pounds, combining sizes 1 and 2 into one package. A brand's weight ranges usually overlap: Size 2 in one brand covers 12 to 18 pounds; size 3, 16 to 28 pounds; and so forth.

There are lots of ways to save on disposables diapers—see Budget Baby, page 194.

CLOTH DIAPERS
What's Available

Cloth diapers are made from absorbent cotton fabrics: cotton fleece, terry (like towels, but softer), bird's-eye (similar to old-fashioned tea towels), gauze (thin and lightweight), and flannel (similar to the material used in flannel sheets and pajamas, but denser and thicker). Flannel is the softest against the skin, and the most absorbent. A combination of terry and flannel is also quite absorbent. Organic cotton cloth and eco-friendly diapers made from bamboo are widely available, but you'll pay a premium—as much as 35 percent more for them, compared to nonorganic cotton. To enhance their absorbency, you may also need to wash organic cotton and bamboo diapers several times before your baby wears them, so check care instructions. There are five types of cloth diaper to choose from. (With the first three diaper types, you'll also need to use waterproof pants.)

1. **Unfolded diapers** are rectangles of flat fabric that you fold to fit your baby's shape, holding them in place with diaper pins or a Snappi diaper fastener, a pinless diaper fastener with T-shaped grips on each end that hook into diaper fabric in three places: the left and right sides, and center (see *www.snappibaby.com)*. Unfolded diapers can also be folded and placed inside a Velcro or snap-closing waterproof cover, which you'll have to buy in different sizes as your baby grows.

2. **Prefolded diapers** are also rectangular, but not nearly as big as unfolded diapers, and because of the precise way that you have to fold them before placing them in a Velcro or snap-closing waterproof cover, they have extra layers in the center. You'll need to buy a different sized diaper and diaper cover as your baby grows. Prefolded diapers are most commonly used by diaper services. They typically come with folding instructions—different ones for boys and girls.

3. **Fitted or contour diapers** are shaped more like disposables, with a narrow crotch and wide wings that wrap around a baby's waist. Some require diaper fasteners, but others have Velcro fasteners or snaps. They may also have elastic at the waist and legs, and a more absorbent layer in the center. With contour diapers, you have to buy different sizes as your baby grows.

4. **All-in-one diapers** are just what the name implies: They combine the diaper and the outer waterproof cover into one piece

Save Dollars on Diapers

Whether you use disposable or cloth diapers, here's how you can cut down on your diapering costs:

◆ If you use cloth diapers, launder them yourself; you can save hundreds of dollars on diapers this way. But you will spend more time in the laundry room, so consider the trade-offs.

◆ Try store-brand disposables. They can offer excellent quality and performance for less than name brands.

◆ Watch for specials. Stores and Web sites often put disposable diapers on sale as "loss leaders" to induce parents to shop there, so take advantage of good deals.

◆ Use coupons combined with store sales. You can find diaper coupons in Sunday newspaper inserts and by logging on to diaper Web sites. Huggies and Seventh Generation also have offers and/or coupons. Some diaper Web sites, such as Diapers.com, accept manufacturers' coupons.

◆ Join a warehouse club, such as Costco or BJ's Wholesale Club.com. Or try Wal-Mart or Target for good prices on store and national diaper brands.

◆ Buy big. You'll save more per diaper by buying larger packages. If you buy online, a bulk shipment may qualify you for free shipping; it typically takes only one or two cases to qualify.

◆ Get a store card. With a preferred-shopper card, you receive automatic discounts on the products listed in the weekly specials or special savings on products without clipping coupons. If you can use your preferred shopper's card with a manufacturer's coupon, that's even better.

◆ Visit *www.amazon.com*, *www.drugstore.com*, and *www.cvs.com* for good deals on name-brand and store-brand diapers (and save yourself a trip to the store). Amazon's Subscribe & Save program offers the best deal if you sign up for regular deliveries; you can save 15 percent and get free shipping, too. You'll find decent prices on reusable diapers at *www.walmart.com* and *www.target.com*.

◆ Call the toll-free customer-service lines of disposable diaper companies, or register at their Web sites, for their new-parent programs, which often include coupons and free samples. If you join Pampers .com, for example, you can earn points for toys and gift cards through the Gifts to Grow program, but it might take a number of purchases to accumulate points. And keep in mind that your name may end up on mailing lists.

so cloth diapering is a one-step procedure. They're convenient for quick changes on the go and, with an extra diaper inside, can work well overnight. However, they're bulky and thick, so they may not dry quickly after laundering. Some all-in-one diapers are one size; instead of having to buy larger sizes as your baby grows, you simply secure the front flaps on the outer snaps as your baby gets bigger.

5. **Pocket diapers** consist of a moisture-resistant covering of nylon or polyester that includes a pocket into which you insert a folded diaper or a disposable or washable liner. Velcro fasteners or several rows of snaps (for different fits) keep the covering closed. The outer cover comes in a range of sizes to accommodate a baby's growth.

Major brands of unfolded, prefolded, fitted, all-in-ones, pocket diapers and/or diaper covers are, in alphabetical order, bumGenius (*www.bumgenius.com*), Bumkins (*www.bumkins.com*), Bummis (*www.bummis.com*), Dundee (available at *www.amazon.com*), FuzziBunz (*www.fuzzibunz.com*), Gerber (*www.gerberchildrenswear.com*), Happy Heinys (*www.happyheiny.com*), Kissaluvs (*www.kissaluvs.com*), Kushies (*www.kushiesonline.com*), Mommy's Touch (*www.mommystouch.com*), Soft Bums (*www.softbums.com*), Swaddlebees (*www.swaddlebees.com*), Tiny Tush (*www.tinytush.com*), and Under the Nile (*www.underthenile.com*).

A Bumpkins All-in-One cloth diaper by Tiny Tush.

Basic cloth diapers cost from 85 cents to $3 (or more) each, and waterproof pants cost $12.99 and up, for a set of three. All-in-ones, pocket diapers and other diapers that are inserted into a waterproof or snap-closing waterproof cover are superior to plain diapers for absorbency, fit, and leak control and spare you the hassle of safety pins. But they're also more expensive, especially in terms of start-up costs. If you decide to use the Bummis system, for example, you'll pay approximately $145 for the cotton diapering kit, which includes three dozen prefold diapers and six diaper covers for an 8- to 15-pound baby. When your baby outgrows those, you'll then spend $118 for the cotton diapering kit for a 15- to 30-pound baby, which includes two dozen prefold diapers and four diaper covers for that size baby. That's a total of $263, but that's basically all you'll spend on diapers, except for the added cost of flushable liners, cloth doublers, which you might need for added absorbency, cloth inserts, and laundry detail (the price of detergent and the electricity

A Swaddlebees All-in-one diaper.

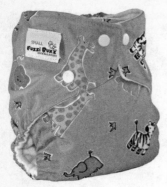

needed to heat the water). You'll pay even more for all-in-ones and pocket diapers, in the range of $11 to $19.95 apiece, and manufacturers recommend buying 12 to 16 of them to get started, which can run you up to $320. But because these diapers are reusable, they're a cost-effective option. Cloth diapers and diapering systems are available at baby and toy stores, via mail-order and through diaper-specific Web sites such as *www.diapers.com* (as well as those mentioned previously).

Pocket diapers like this one by FuzziBunz have an internal pocket for an absorbent cloth insert.

Features to Consider

Cloth diapers are easy to use, but less convenient than disposables because of the laundry involved. If you don't use a diaper service, you have to soak the soiled diapers in a "wet" diaper pail or store them between laundry loads in a "dry," bag-lined diaper pail after flushing the solids and any diaper liner. Don't forget that the demands of a new baby can make keeping up with diaper washing a daunting proposition. But once you get into a routine, it can be more doable than you think, especially if you're motivated by the money savings. Cloth diapers are easier to deal with if you use a diaper service, although you can wind up paying as much as you would for disposables. For that reason you may want to drop hints with friends and relatives that you'd welcome a diaper service as a shower gift.

Recommendations

The type of cloth diaper you choose (as well as whether you go with cloth at all) is a matter of personal preference. Cloth diapers can be a significant money saver, so it can pay to go this route. But don't be a slave to the laundry room. Buy enough to have on hand so you don't have to wash diapers and fabric liners more frequently than every two to three days. If you choose unfolded, prefolded, or fitted cloth diapers, you will need two to three dozen to begin with, plus six to 10 waterproof covers. If you go the all-in-one or pocket diaper route, having 12 to 16 should be adequate in the beginning. Some cloth diapers are sold as start-up kits, which include all the diapers, diaper covers, and flushable liners you'll need for that diaper's weight limit, which can help you make sure you're prepared. Pay close attention to washing instructions until

Caring for Cloth

Many cloth diapers come with laundry instructions, which you should follow carefully. If you don't wash them correctly, they won't get clean; urine crystals can form and bacteria can fester, which can contribute to diaper rash and odor. Here's the basic drill.

Before first use: Wash cloth diapers in hot water with a small amount of detergent to enhance their absorbency. If diapers are made from unbleached fabric, such as organic cotton, you may need to wash them two or three times, drying them in the dryer between washes to remove their natural oils and waxes. Check the label. Test your diaper's absorbency by pouring a small amount of water into one. If the water beads at all, you should wash them again.

For dirty diapers: Knock solids into the toilet (or if you use a flushable liner, toss it with solids into the toilet) and store used diapers in a dry or wet pail. Wet pails can help eliminate diaper stains because dirty diapers soak until you wash them. But the elastic on diapers that have it, such as fitted, pocket, and all-in-ones, will wear out faster when used with a wet pail. Dry pails are the most popular choice among parents. Lining the pail with a washable bag makes collecting diapers for the laundry room easier.

Wash cloth diapers every two days so your diaper pail doesn't get too stinky. On laundry day, unfold cloth diapers before washing. Diaper covers don't need to be washed every time; you can wait until they're wet, soiled, or smelly. Run a cold-water rinse or a short-cycle rinse with no detergent in your washing machine; it helps reduce the chances that stains will set. Then, using your washer's hottest water at the highest water level, wash diapers (and covers) with no more than one half of the laundry detergent recommended on the package. Using too much detergent can leave an irritating residue that can affect a diaper's absorbency and smell.

If you have a front-loading washing machine, set your water levels to the highest settings, and use one-fourth of the amount of laundry detergent recommended on the package. If your detergent is formulated for High Efficiency washers—you'll see "HE" on the package or the instructions label will explain—you can use the lower amount recommended on the detergent package. Seemingly clean diapers can smell right after your baby wets them if you don't wash with enough hot water, which is a common problem with high-efficiency front-loading washing machines. "If you can't adjust the water level on your machine manually, you may have to trick your machine into adding more water by tossing in a wet towel," Bummis co-owner Thomas says. Minimal amounts of hot water won't rinse diapers well enough to eliminate urine.

After the wash cycle, diapers should be rinsed well, in cold water. Don't use straight liquid fabric softener or dryer sheets. Your baby may have an allergic reaction to the fragrance. Fabric softener will leave a buildup on diapers, which blocks a diaper's absorbency.

■ **Spotlight on gDiapers**

Green Hybrid Diapers Take Getting Used To

Designed with the environment in mind, gDiapers (*www.gdiapers.com*) are a "hybrid" diaper, a combination of cloth and disposable diapers. The diaper consists of an outer cotton pant that comes in small, medium, and large sizes, and a snap-in, reusable

gDiapers will cost you more than regular disposables, but they won't tax the environment.

waterproof liner. Inside this outer cover, you insert a disposable, decomposable diaper refill that can be flushed down the toilet (no diaper pail necessary). You can also throw the refills in the trash without "green guilt," or even compost wet ones that contain no solids. gDiapers contain no plastic; they're made from wood fluff pulp, sodium polyacrylate (SAP), which provides absorbency, and cellulose rayon. They are made to decompose within 50 to 150 days. You'll have to get the hang of flushing them, though. The gDiaper Starter Kit (about $26 at *www.amazon.com*), which contains two cotton pants, two waterproof liners, and 10 flushable refills, also comes with a "swishstick" to help the

refills go down. To prevent toilet clogging, you'll need to use the swishstick to separate the inner core of the refill from the outer material.

gDiapers aren't for everybody, or at least not everybody's plumbing. The instructions on the company's Web site say, "Do not flush with tree-infested, faulty or non-standard plumbing, and use with caution with septic systems." The Web site advises you to check your septic system "every few days to make sure the outflow is clear." That's not feasible if you have a buried septic system, so you might want to stick to tossing or composting.

A 4-pack of 40-count gDiaper disposable liner refills will run you roughly $54.

you get a system down and diaper duty becomes second nature. If you go the cloth diapering route, don't think it's all or nothing. Feel free to use disposables when you need or want to, such as when you're traveling with your baby. Browse online to find the most competitive prices and bulk discounts.

Diaper Bags

Although just about any bag will do, a diaper bag with lots of compartments can help you keep it all together when you and your baby are on the go. Consider size, style, comfort, and durability, just as you would with any handbag you carry frequently.

Many of today's diaper bags, like the Ruby Bag by Timi & Leslie, combine function with fashion.

When you're on the go, a diaper bag probably will be your constant sidekick—your changing table away from home as well as a baby entertainment center and portable food court, since many bags have separate compartments where you can stash toys, bottles, and snacks. It might also double as your purse.

But chances are you'll be happier with one that's specifically designed for baby gear. You'll need compartments to keep things organized, and that's what many diaper bags have to offer that generic carryalls don't.

You'll find a lot to choose from in the Daddy diaper bag department.

Diaper bags have come a long way from the traditional rectangular, pastel-colored bags adorned with nursery characters (although these are still an option). In the past few years, there's been an explosion of styles, colors, designs, and functions. Manufacturers recognize that today's parents are active and that Dad, who may be taking on a bigger parenting role, may want his own bag. The trend is to unisex family diaper bags that both parents can use, ones that can be handed from Mom to Dad without embarrassment.

Many of the newest diaper bags are designed to double as an adult backpack, or a satchel for your laptop. Bags aimed at dads come in guy-friendly, rugged fabrics such as camouflage and faux suede. Other diaper bags are designed purely for a mom's sense of style. They look like a purse—you'd never know there were diapers and bottles inside—and feature fun details such as pompom trim; classy colors including raspberry, lilac, olive, and black; and floral or mod prints.

Features such as "parent" pockets for your iPod, wallet, cell phone, and day planner; insulated bottle pockets and compartments for baby wipes; and lightly padded shoulder straps are now standard so you don't have to carry two or three bags. A large, wipe-clean, detachable changing pad is also standard equipment.

Shopping Secrets

Consider how you'll use your diaper bag. There are many styles available: backpack, messenger, and tote are three of the most popular. To decide which is right for you, think about how you'll be using your bag. Do you expect to be a heavy packer, prepared for anything, with extra diapers, changes of clothes, and favorite toys? Do you bottle-feed? Do you want to attach the diaper bag to the back of the stroller? (There are stroller diaper bags designed specifically for that.) Will your partner be the one who carries it? Do you need a diaper bag that blends in, so you feel comfortable carrying the same bag from work to day care? Will you be using your diaper bag on lots of day trips? Do you consider a diaper bag an accessory, like a chic pair of pumps? And perhaps most important, what's your budget? The answers to these questions can help you decide how roomy your bag needs to be, the number and types of compartments you should look for, the style that's likely to work best for your lifestyle, and aesthetic details such as color and type of fabric.

"Test drive" models in the store. You'll be carrying your bag for a while, perhaps more than two years if you tote it until your baby is potty-trained. So, even if you buy online, it's a good idea to go to a store to try on some bags for size, look, and feel. Load up the bags with baby stuff you bring from home. Consider where you'd put diapers, a change of clothes for your baby, wipes, the changing pad, an insulated lunch bag, your keys and wallet, and whatever else you typically carry with you. Bring the baby bottles you use (or plan to use) to make sure the bottle holders on contender diaper bags accommodate that size and type of bottle. Try unfolding the changing pad with one hand; you may be holding your baby in the other. It should be easy to use. Functionality is key; so is comfort.

Don't think bigger is necessarily better. You want a good-sized diaper bag, yes. As your baby grows, bigger diapers take up more diaper-bag space. But you don't want one that's so roomy that you're constantly losing things in its caverns or bumping it into people. A weekender or deep hobo-style diaper bag, for example, may be too big for your everyday needs unless you have more than one child's things to carry with you. And even if you don't have a lot of stuff, there's a tendency to fill the void. Before you know it, a large diaper bag can easily outweigh your baby.

A diaper bag with lots of compartments like this backpack by Baby Sherpa can help you keep it all organized.

The Quest for the Perfect Diaper Bag

You can buy a perfectly "street chic" yet road-worthy diaper bag for around $30. In fact, that's how much the most frequently registered-for diaper bag is on Amazon.com's baby registry. On the other hand, you can also spend hundreds for a designer-brand bag like Juicy Couture or Kate Spade. That's a much bigger investment that doesn't necessarily deliver a bigger return. If you love a designer bag, can afford the splurge, and think you may be using it for years to come, go ahead and go designer, if you want to. (Even then, you might want to hold off on buying a designer bag until you've played the field a while.)

Finding the right diaper bag for your lifestyle and your circumstances can sometimes be a matter of trial and error. By buying a moderately priced bag, at least initially, you'll have more leeway to try different types of diaper bags until you're sold on a particular style or brand.

Look for extra compartments. Babies are a demanding bunch. Trying to find a pacifier, for example, when your baby starts howling can feel like an emergency. Internal and external zippered pockets, toy loops, key clips, and bungee cords offer speedy access to pacifiers, toys, baby wipes, and your keys. Everything should be within easy reach. You want to be able to grab and keep going, without having to break stride or put your baby down to find what you need.

What's Available

Some brands to consider, in alphabetical order, include: A.D. Sutton (*www.adsutton.com*), Baby Sherpa (*www.babysherpa.com*), Bugaboo (*www.bugaboo.com*), Bumble Bags (*www.thebumblecollection.com*), Caden Lane (*www.cadenlane.com*), DadGear (*www.dadgear.com*), Daisy Gear (*www.daisygear.com*), Diaper Dude (*www.diaperdude.com*), Eddie Bauer (*www.eddiebauer.com*), Fleurville (*www.fleurville.com*), Graco *www.gracobaby.com*), Kalencom (*www.kalencom.com*), Kate Spade (*www.katespade.com*), L.L.Bean (*www.llbean.com*), OiOi (*www.oioi.com.au*), O Yikes! (*www.oyikes.com*), Petunia Pickle Bottom (*www.petuniapicklebottom.com*), Reese Li (*www.reeseli.com*), Skip Hop (*www.skiphop.com*), Stork Sak (*www.storksak.com*), and Timi & Leslie (*www.timiandleslie.com*).

Fabrics and patterns run the gamut from classic Mickey Mouse to sophisticated solids, florals, geometrics, checks, plaids, and stripes in leather, rugged nylon, vinyl, microfiber, suede/faux suede, cotton, canvas/laminated canvas, and dry-clean-only rayon/silk. Styles include

Stop Digging Through Your Diaper Bag

If the diaper bag you select—or that's given to you—doesn't have compartments, you can compartmentalize it yourself by placing specific items in their own small plastic bags. "Put toys in one bag, your baby's pacifier in another, and designate another just for baby wipes," says Elizabeth Hagen, a mother of five and a professional organizer from Sioux Falls, S.D. If your diaper bag has a zippered side pocket, designate that area as a home for your keys and cell phone. Then, to find these important items faster, get into the habit of putting them away right after you use them.

"Taking that split second to put things where they belong saves you time and frustration later," Hagen says. Babies demand a certain amount of efficiency, such as when they want their pacifier—*now*. Multiple pockets can help keep a pacifier search from turning into a crisis.

backpacks, tote-style bags that could pass for a briefcase, trendy purses/handbags with shoulder straps, deep hobo bags, fanny packs that resemble tool belts, ultra-hip urban slings, and messenger bags. Some diaper bags are made to attach to the back of the stroller, and can easily make the transition from stroller to shoulder. Diaper bags range from $9 for a low-end fabric or vinyl model to as high as $465 for well-appointed designer bags.

Features to Consider

Changing pad. Most bags come with a rectangular changing pad that folds up, fits in the bag, and can be wiped clean. Many pads fold to fit into a designated pocket. That's a plus; isolating the changing pad can help prevent it from contaminating your diaper bag's contents. Some diaper bags have a semirigid interior that helps maintain the pad's shape. Some pads are cushier than others (cushy is better.)

Construction. Look for wide, padded, adjustable shoulder straps, well-reinforced seams (tug on them to make sure they're strong) and quality hardware—heavy-duty plastic or metal zippers and sturdy closures. Zippers, rather than magnetic closures, ensure that your stuff won't fall out if your diaper bag tips over.

Handles vs. hands-free. The handles of a tote-style bag should be short enough so that the bag doesn't drag on the ground when you carry it like a suitcase, but long enough so it can be slung over your shoulder

If a personalized diaper bag is high on your list, this photo bag from Wal-Mart could be a contender.

The Backpack, Messenger, and Sport Bag diaper bags by DadGear feature an "easy-access wipes window" that fits most brands of travel baby wipes.

or worn on the diagonal. Wide or well-padded straps are more comfortable. A backpack, messenger, or sling-style diaper bag keeps your hands and arms free. A backpack's shoulder straps should be adjustable for proper fit, and a sternum strap, which connects the shoulder straps at the upper chest, helps redistribute the weight to make lugging baby gear more comfortable.

Fabric. Bags made of quilted fabric or silk are often favored by gift givers, but heavy-duty, moisture-resistant nylon or microfiber are more practical, especially if you're planning to have more than one child and you want the bag to go the distance. Beware of vinyl bags if you live in a cold climate. They can crack when the temperature dips. And you'll want a diaper bag that's washable inside and out.

Color. Some manufacturers continue to offer "baby colors"—pastels and light-colored prints. But dark shades are less likely to show stains and soil. And if you go for a more adult look, you can consider using the bag for other purposes when diapering days are over, assuming it has held up well enough. Still, make sure the interior is a light color. Otherwise, you will find yourself digging for items in a black hole.

Storage. Easy-to-access, zippered interior and exterior compartments, which can function as a wallet and as storage for things you constantly need such as baby wipes, pacifiers, and your cell phone, are a convenient plus. Make sure the zippers are heavy-duty so they'll hold up. Clear vinyl or mesh pockets inside can hold diapers, wipes, and other baby gear. If you'll be taking many outings or doing lots of traveling with your baby, look for a bag with an insulated cooler section. Bottle pockets are handy, but make sure they fit your brand of baby bottles or your favorite bottled water or juice for older babies. Always keep bottles and food away from dirty diapers.

The Well-Stocked Diaper Bag

Whether you're going to Grandma's house for the day or on an international business trip with your baby, you want to be prepared, without going overboard. Here are some ideas on what to pack. (Restock the bag as soon as you return home, so you don't forget anything the next time you go out.)

❏ Diapers, of course. At least five or six if you'll be out most of the day.

❏ A travel pack of baby wipes.

❏ A changing pad.

❏ Zinc oxide diaper-rash ointment.

❏ Plastic bags for disposing of soiled disposable diapers.

❏ A leak-proof bag for soiled cloth diapers or wet clothes. (Some diaper bags come with one of these.)

❏ A complete change of baby clothes, including socks, a hat, sweater, and/or jacket if it's chilly out.

❏ Sunblock (if it's summer).

❏ Hand sanitizer for washing your hands after diaper changes, if you won't be near soap and water.

❏ Extra formula and sterilized nonfluoridated water (if you're bottle-feeding).

❏ Snacks, such as cereal and crackers, in lidded plastic containers or Ziploc bags, and/or an insulated bag for cold items such as yogurt or breast milk.

❏ Tissues.

❏ A baby spoon in a Ziploc bag to keep it clean until you use it.

❏ A bib or two.

❏ Two clean pacifiers (if your baby uses them).

❏ A book your baby can hold or chew on.

❏ Teething toys (if your baby is teething).

❏ A small towel to mop up spit-ups and spills.

❏ Baby pain and fever reliever or even a small first-aid kit.

❏ An extra baby blanket.

❏ Reading material for you. If you have a few minutes, you can catch up on that magazine or newspaper you never got to read at home.

If you're going on overnight trips with your baby, plan for unexpected layovers and pack extras of everything, especially diapers, changes of clothes, baby wipes, formula, sterilized water, snacks, plastic bags, and pacifiers. And don't forget to bring your health insurance cards in case you or your baby gets sick.

Recommendations

Opt for a bag that leaves your hands free, such as a backpack or sling or messenger-style diaper bag with a diagonal strap. That way, you won't have to balance your baby in one hand and a bag in the other. When you've got a baby to lug, you probably need more hands than you've got. A hands-free bag also makes it easier to keep up with an energetic toddler (that'll be your baby, in no time). And it's healthier for your neck and shoulders, too, when your torso bears the brunt of the weight you're carrying. Loading up one shoulder can lead to neck and back strain. Another option is a stroller bag, which easily straps to a stroller's handlebars. Many messenger-style and tote baby bags now have a stroller-bar feature. Be careful of overloading your diaper bag. Don't place too heavy a bag (more than 5 or 6 pounds) on stroller handlebars; it may cause the stroller to tip. And don't hang a diaper bag on an umbrella stroller at all.

If value is what you're after, midpriced models (in the $35 to $100 range) offer the best mix of sound construction and generous storage. The best bags have a plastic liner and a durable, wipe-clean shell, since gunk tends to accumulate both inside and out. They also have lots of Velcro or zippered pockets, which can help you stay organized as long as you assign each compartment to a specific task, such as one for baby wipes, one for toys, one for snacks, and so on.

Low-end models (under $35) may skimp on quality and durability, leaving you with a bag that could tear, fray, or get stained or sticky and soon have to be replaced. If you expect to have more than one child and consider diaper-bag shopping a one-shot deal, spending a little more (in the upper end of the $35 to $100 range) will get you a good-quality bag that will last through several siblings.

Designer diaper bags are a class unto themselves. If you want a certain look or designer label, you'll pay for it. You're apt to get a good-quality bag, too. But make sure it's made of a durable fabric and has all the features you're looking for. Diaper bags tend to be mess magnets. They pick up dirt and grime from the outside and may act as temporary receptacles for dirty diapers. So whatever you do, don't buy a bag that requires dry cleaning. Unless you plan to buy two diaper bags—one for dress-up and one for every day—exchange a high-maintenance bag if you get one as a gift for one made of a mom- and baby-friendly fabric. Think washable and waterproof.

Diaper Pails

Changing diapers, of course, is the least glamorous aspect of taking care of a baby. But it must be done many times a day, and the right diaper pail can make the job easier. That's especially true if you have more than one baby at a time in diapers—twins or triplets or children close in age.

The Diaper Dékor Plus has a claimed capacity of 40 diapers, but all diaper pails hold fewer diapers as your baby and his diaper size get larger.

The type of diaper pail you'll want depends on whether you're using cloth diapers or disposables. Cloth-diaper users now favor a "dry" pail, a lined plastic pail you put rinsed diapers in until wash time. "Wet" pails—a plastic pail for soaking diapers before laundering—were once the standard, but are not used much anymore. The typical disposable-diaper pail is also plastic, and it may be rigged with special liners or devices that dispel diaper odors, or with regular garbage bags.

What's Available

For cloth diapers. Wet pails for cloth diapers are strong enough to hold a considerable amount of water but are easy to carry, and have a comfortable handle and a spout for pouring out soaking solution. A dry pail can be any sturdy plastic model that uses a standard plastic garbage bag for a liner, such as Safety 1st Easy Saver or the Simple Step diaper pail (*www.safety1st.com*), both of which can also be used for disposable diapers.

Not your grandmother's diaper pail: The First Years Clean Air Odor-free Diaper Disposal has a carbon filter/fan system to trap and neutralize odors. It requires 4 D-cell batteries (not included); batteries and filters must be replaced about every three months.

For disposables. Models of pails For disposable diapers are, in alphabetical order, Baby Trend Diaper Champ (*www.babytrend.com*; accepts both cloth and disposables), Diaper Dékor (*www.diaperdekor.com*), Diaper Genie II and Diaper Genie II Elite (*www.playtexbaby.com*), Graco Touch Free Diaper Pail (*www.gracobaby.com*), Safety 1st (*www.safety1st.com*), Sassy Hands Free Diaper Pail (*www.sassybaby.com*), and The First Years Clean Air Odor-free Diaper Disposal (*www.learningcurve.com*). Prices range from $16.99 to $50.

Disposable diaper pails are typically simple models that are easy to operate. With the Diaper Genie II and the Baby Trend Diaper Champ, for example, you can open and close the pail with one hand, which helps when you're holding a baby in the other. The Diaper Dékor and the Diaper Genie II Elite offer a "hands-free" design. You simply step on a pedal to open the lid and drop in a diaper. Both the Graco Touch Free Diaper Pail and the Sassy Hands Free! Diaper Pail (batteries required) have a motion sensor that automatically opens the lid when you wave your hand over it. The Diaper Champ, Graco Touch Free!, Sassy Hands Free, Safety 1st Easy Saver, and the First Years Clean Air Odor-free! diaper pails have an advantage because they can be used with regular trash bags. The others require specially made tubular bags specific to each that you have to purchase. Refills range from $5.99 (for a single refill pack for the Diaper Genie II/II Elite) to $14.99 for a Diaper Dékor two-pack refill, which is biodegradable. The Diaper Dékors and the Diaper Genie IIs have built-in blades to cut the tubular bag when it's filled.

" Disposable-diaper pails are typically simple models that are easy to operate."

Features to Consider

Capacity. Diaper-pail makers claim pails hold between 24 and 50-plus disposable diapers, although our tests have shown that capacity is often overstated, so you have to empty the pail sooner than you think. Keep in mind that diaper-pail capacity decreases as your baby grows into bigger diapers.

Child-resistant lid. A disposables pail, which can also be used as a "dry" pail for cloth diapers, should have a child-resistant locking button or a mechanism that makes it difficult for a child to break in, such as a step-pedal opener. Be careful with pail liners, whether model-specific tubular liners or regular trash bags; both are suffocation hazards. A wet pail requires a locking lid to prevent any young child from falling in; children can drown in an inch of water.

Comfort. If you're going the cloth route and choose a wet pail, pick one with a pouring lip and comfortable handles.

Ease of use. Some diaper pails require two steps: You have to open the lid, and then place the diaper into the plastic-bag insert. Others require more steps; still others can be operated with one hand or have a "hands-free" pedal or motion sensor.

Liners or bags. Some pails require special plastic liners, which add to the cost of diapering, while others use regular garbage or plastic bags. The cost of refills will depend on the brand of diaper pail you choose. Standard garbage bags are not specially designed to trap odors, but diaper-pail liners are, which contributes to their cost. Depending on the sensitivity of your nose, you may feel the extra cost is worth it.

The Diaper Genie II Elite is taller than the Diaper Genie II so you don't have to bend to dispose of a diaper. You step on the pedal, drop in the diaper, and go.

Recommendations

The right diaper pail can make diaper duty less of a chore. Pails that use their own liners typically contain odors better than those that use garbage bags, but refills do cost more. However, one pail

Refill liners for the Diaper Genie II and Elite diaper pails are multilayered to act as a barrier, trapping odors better than standard garbage bags.

we know of that takes garbage bags, the Graco Touch Free, has an "isolation design" plus carbon filters to control odors. If you use cloth diapers, dump solid waste into the toilet before depositing a soiled diaper into the pail. (For instructions on caring for cloth diapers, See Caring for Cloth, page 197.) It's a good idea to dump waste from disposables, too; that added step helps cut down on the odor. Look for a secure lid; any diaper pail can be a danger to a young child. Plastic liners in a disposables or dry pail are a suffocation hazard; water in a soaking pail is a drowning peril. And a child who lifts a diaper pail lid and falls in may not be able to get out. Capacity counts too, although we have found in our previous testing that manufacturers may claim a pail holds more than it actually does. But as diaper size increases, any pail holds fewer diapers. And besides, whether you go with cloth or disposables, you will want to regularly empty the pail anyway to minimize odor. A pedal or motion detector opening mechanism makes disposal faster and easier. A taller pail means you won't have to bend as far. When you're changing diapers all day, every day, anything that helps you out is a plus.

Doorway Jumpers

A doorway jumper, which attaches to the top of a door frame with a spring-loaded clamp, is a bit like bungee jumping for babies. As fun as it seems, we consider the product too risky for little ones because there's always the chance the clamp could fail, which could cause injury. A stationary activity jumper is a safer bet.

Jumpers that hang from doorways are not the safest type.

In case you've never seen one, a doorway jumper is a seat connected to a bungee-like cable or cables that attach to the top of the door frame with a spring-loaded clamp. There are also stationary jumpers with cables that extend from the corners of the seat to an independent low stand (typically about 30 to 42 inches tall), making the door frame unnecessary. A variation is the Jolly Jumper Exerciser with Stand. Rather than use cables at the corners, this model suspends the seat from an overhead cable attached to a stand. We think using a stationary model with a sturdy stand is much safer than hanging a free-swinging jumper from a doorway. The stand eliminates the potential hazard of a doorway jumper clamp slipping off the door frame. Models with cables at the corners rather than a single overhead cable eliminate the potential for the jumper to crash into the jumper frame and possibly tip it.

Some doorway jumpers feature a fabric seat with a built-in frame that surrounds a child, while others have a solid, external molded play tray that encircles the baby, with rubberized sides that act as bumpers to protect your baby from crashing into woodwork (and the woodwork, too, from getting nicked or chipped). Jumpers usually lack seat belts, which is something to keep in mind, even though the baby is fairly well contained in the seat.

Most doorway jumpers accommodate babies up to 28 pounds, starting from when they can hold their head up unassisted. Bungee-style cords or springs suspend the seat from a clamp so pre-walking babies can jiggle themselves up and down when they push off the floor. It's a cheap thrill that can delight active babies—and help them burn off steam, priming them for their morning or afternoon nap. Yet while many infants enjoy jumpers, others actually get "seasick" from the motion.

A stationary jumper like the Fisher-Price Rainforest Jumperoo is safer than jumpers that hang from a doorway.

Another major downside: A doorway jumper's straps or clamps can break, allowing the apparatus to fall. Also, babies can bump into the sides of the door frame, either because vigorous jumping causes them to bob around or because a sibling tries to swing them. Doorway jumpers have been recalled because the plastic clamp that attaches the jumper seat to a door frame has broken, allowing babies to fall to the floor. At least 14,000 units were recalled for that reason in 2005. There have also been recalls because clamps detached from the cord.

For these reasons, we think there are plenty of other, safer alternatives to help your baby work off energy and enjoy playtime, including a stationary activity jumper. Some models look much like a stationary activity center, but with a springier seat and a raised platform for a little lift off. Others have a seat attached to a stationary stand with enclosed springs. Like a doorway jumper, stationary activity jumpers require babies to sit upright. Stationary activity jumpers typically accommodate babies up to 25 pounds and 30 to 32 inches, depending on the model. Weight and height maximums vary, so check your owner's manual. To use one, your baby must be able to hold her head upright unassisted, but not be able to climb out of the product or walk.

The Jolly Jumper Exerciser with Stand nixes the need for a doorway.

What's Available

Brands of doorway and stationary activity jumpers include, in alphabetical order: Baby Einstein (*www.babyeinstein.com*), Bright Starts (*www.brightstarts.com*), Bungee Baby Bouncer (*www.bungeebabybouncer.com*), Evenflo (*www.evenflo.com*), Fisher-Price (*www.fisher-price.com*), Graco (*www.gracobaby.com*), Jolly Jumper (*www.jollyjumper.com*), and Sassy (*www.sassybaby.com*). Prices range from $20 to $90.

Features to Consider

Foldability. Doorway jumpers and some stationary activity jumpers, such as the Galloping Fun Jumperoo by Fisher-Price, can be folded to move from room to room, stash in a closet, or even take to Grandma's.

Springs. On stationary activity jumpers with a seat attached to a frame with springs, look for covers on the springs to keep your little one's fingers from being pinched.

■ Budget Baby
Focus Your Baby's Fun

Doorway and stationary activity jumpers as well as walkers and stationary activity centers, essentially serve the same purpose: to keep babies busy who can sit up by themselves but not yet walk. (See page 357 for walkers and page 305 for stationary activity centers.) To save money and living space, buy just one of these products, if you want to (they're not a necessity). To make the selection even easier, choose either a stationary activity center or a stationary activity jumper. They're the safest choices.

Seat. Doorway jumpers have straps that adjust to a child's "jumping height" with a spring-loaded clamp that attaches to the top of a door frame. Some stationary jumpers have up to six height adjustments to grow with your baby. Most doorway and stationary activity jumpers have a removable, washable seat. A plush seat is a plus.

Toys. Some doorway jumpers come with toy loops to attach your child's favorite toy and a console on the play tray that features blinking lights, songs, and other activities for added stimulation. Stationary activity jumpers typically come with a fully loaded toy tray with lights and music as well (two or three AA batteries required).

Recommendations

Buy a stationary activity jumper instead of a doorway jumper. No amount of supervision can keep an infant from crashing to the floor if the doorway clamp fails, or from hitting the side of a doorway or the stand if suspended from above. These things may happen no matter how many times your baby has used the jumper successfully in the past. Look for a jumper with a low stand that suspends the seat from four corners rather than one that suspends the seat from one overhead cable. You'll also find quality differences in the construction of the springs, suspension cords, supports, and seat.

A stationary activity jumper is a safer bet, but don't buy one thinking your baby will shoot ahead in terms of physical development. Even though babies are pushing off the floor, the springy nature of these "exercisers" doesn't do much to strengthen their thigh and back muscles, which are critical to crawling and walking. Follow our safety strategies and stop using the product when your baby can walk, reaches the height and weight maximums, or tries to climb out, whichever comes first.

Less-Risky Exercise

If you decide to use a doorway or a stationary activity jumper, here are a few things to keep in mind:

Doorway jumpers:

◆ Buy a jumper with specifications that match your door frame and moldings. Not all doorframes are constructed in a way that can adequately support a doorway jumper with a spring-loaded clamp.

◆ Adjust it to the proper height; typically, just your child's tippy toes should touch the floor.

◆ Inspect the jumper every time you put your baby inside to be sure the straps are securely fastened; tug on the clamp and the straps to make sure they will hold.

◆ Always keep an eye on your child when he's in the jumper.

◆ Take the jumper down as soon as your baby is done using it. Don't leave it in a doorway when it's not in use.

◆ Never push a jumper as if it were a swing (or let others do it). Even though swinging in the house sounds like fun, it can cause your baby to strike the side of the doorway. Jumpers are not a good choice in a multikid environment.

◆ Limit jumping time to 15 minutes at a stretch, so your baby doesn't become nauseated. To prevent your baby from spitting up, it's best to use a doorway jumper before meals and snacks, not after.

Doorway and stationary activity jumpers:

◆ Don't use a jumper near stairs, pools, hot surfaces, or areas that may be hazardous to a child.

◆ Always keep an eye on your child when she's in a jumper.

◆ Keep a close eye out for trouble and don't leave the room while your child is jumping.

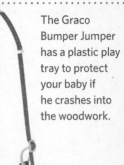

The Graco Bumper Jumper has a plastic play tray to protect your baby if he crashes into the woodwork.

◆ Don't attach toys with strings to a jumper. Strings are a strangulation hazard.

◆ Stop using a jumper when your baby reaches the jumper's upper height and/or weight limit, or when your child can walk unassisted or can climb out of the product, whichever comes first.

◆ Don't use a jumper that's damaged or broken.

◆ Use caution when buying a used jumper by checking the Consumer Product Safety Commissions's Web site (*www.cpsc.gov*). Recalled products that are dangerous for your baby may be available at tag sales and secondhand shops. Even if the jumper hasn't been recalled, check that all parts work and are not worn.

◆ Always place the jumper on a flat, level indoor surface.

◆ Never move the unit while your child is in the seat.

chapter

Formula

I f you can't or don't want to breast-feed, want to supplement breast-feeding, or decide to wean your baby before age 1, you'll need to give him formula, which is usually derived from cow's milk and provides a wide range of nutrients.

Feeding your baby formula may cost you as much as $2,000 by her first birthday.

As the parent of a newborn, you'll have a million things to do. But planning gourmet meals for your baby won't be one of them. Until your child is about 6 months old, breast milk or formula will take care of breakfast, lunch, dinner, snacks, and those middle-of-the-night wake-up calls.

That's all your baby needs to grow healthy and strong. Then you can begin adding so-called solid food to the mix—continuing to breast-feed and/or supplement with formula—until your baby's first birthday or so, when regular cow's milk becomes an option.

As we mention in the Breast Pumps chapter starting on page 95, nursing is good for both babies and moms. Even the infant-formula companies will tell you that, as Nestlé does on its Web site: "Breast milk is the ideal food for your baby during the first year." Breast milk contains a uniquely superior mix of carbohydrates, amino acids, fats, including omega-3 fatty acids, hormones, growth factors, antibodies that optimize the development of the immune system, factors that decrease inflammation, components typically known as probiotics and prebiotics that contribute to a healthy digestive tract, vitamins, minerals, and enzymes that work to give your baby the best possible start.

Breast milk is Mother Nature's liquid gold that commercial formula can simulate, but not equal. Breast-feeding may reduce the risk of sudden infant death syndrome (SIDS) and a range of infectious diseases, including bacterial meningitis and diarrhea, as well as respiratory, urinary tract, and ear infections. It also may enhance your baby's brain power and visual acuity. According to the American Academy of Pediatrics (AAP), babies who are breast-fed rather than formula-fed may have less risk of asthma, diabetes, and certain forms of cancer through adulthood. They're also less likely to be obese as they grow up.

❝Breast milk is the ideal food for your baby during the first year.❞

Breast-feeding protects moms, too. Hormonal changes associated with breast-feeding are thought to lower breast cancer risk; physical changes to breast cells may make them more resistant to mutations. Breast-feeding moms also may be better protected against ovarian cancer and bone-weakening osteoporosis.

Financially, breast milk is a bargain. The cost of formula, on the other hand, can add up. In fact, if your baby is consuming only formula, you're likely to shell out as much as $2,000 by her first birthday, depending on her nutritional requirements and the type of formula you choose. There's

■ **Safety Strategies**
Protecting Your Baby's Teeth

Some infant formulas contain sucrose (a.k.a. cane sugar or table sugar), which can harm a baby's tooth enamel faster than any other sugar, according to Diane M. Paletta, DDS, a dentist in Charleston, W. Va., and a spokesperson for the Academy of General Dentistry.

Sucrose is the sweetener in Similac Organic formula, as well as some protein-hydrolyzed formulas and some lactose-free infant formulas, such as soy formulations. All infant formulas have some added sweeteners, to help infants digest the protein from cow's milk or soy. Along with lactose or sucrose, you might find corn syrup solids and maltodextrin. "Sucrose acts on bacteria in the mouth to produce acid and form plaque, which can begin to erode tooth enamel if it has direct contact with teeth for just 20 minutes," Paletta says. Check the ingredients on the label if you want to avoid a formula sweetened with sucrose.

After every formula feeding, wipe off your baby's teeth with a wet or dry gauze pad so that a layer of plaque never has the chance to form.

You don't need toothpaste, Paletta says. "Just the mechanical action of wiping is enough to get rid of plaque, and that's even true for adults.

Also, never put your baby to bed—or even down for a nap at home or on the go—with a bottle of milk, breast milk, or formula, or give your baby juice or water sweetened with table sugar, all of which can lead to baby-bottle tooth decay.

Similac Organic formula contains sucrose, as do some lactose-free and protein hydrolzyed formulas.

also the money you may spend on doctor bills. One study found that breast-fed infants had fewer hospital admissions.

Still, the decision about whether to go with breast milk or formula (or both) can be complicated, depending on your work situation and lots of other factors. The short answer: Try breast-feeding if you can. The AAP recommends breast-feeding exclusively for a baby's first six months. According to the Centers for Disease Control and Prevention National Immunization Survey, more moms are starting out breast-feeding—about 74 percent in 2005, up from 68 percent in 1999, but only about 43 percent make it to six months. If you can't breast-feed or if you decide to wean your baby before age 1, you'll need to give him formula.

Usually derived from cow's milk, formula provides a wide range of nutrients but not all the crucial components of breast milk. If your baby

Breast-Feeding Tip

is exclusively formula-fed, she will probably drink 2 to 5 ounces of formula every three to four hours during the first few weeks. By six months of age, she may be up to 6 to 8 ounces every five hours or so.

Shopping Secrets

Shop at mass merchandisers. Your formula costs will vary by where you shop, according to a Department of Agriculture report. Formulas sold by mass merchandisers such as Wal-Mart cost the least. Super-

market prices will make a bigger dent in your budget. And drugstores charge substantially more, so don't wait to shop for formula until the all-night drugstore is the only outlet open. Milk-based formula tends to cost less than soy-based formula, so don't buy soy or another type of special formula unless your pediatrician recommends it.

Sign up for savings. Some formula companies offer exclusive offers and savings on their Web sites. Nestlé, for example, promises up to $319 in savings and free offers, including money-saving checks for their Good Start formula (at *www.verybestbaby.com*). However, this includes "partner offers" on products you might not want, so you might save less, and you must provide your e-mail address.

For good deals on infant formula, shop at mass merchandisers such as Wal-Mart, Costco, and Sam's Club.

Similarly, at *www.enfamil.com* you can enroll using your e-mail address in Enfamil Family Beginnings to receive special offers and promotions, including up to $60 in formula checks.

Buy online. Some retailers, including many mass merchandisers such as Target and Wal-Mart, don't sell formula through their Web sites, so you'll have to go shopping and then schlep the stuff home. But you can purchase formula online at many sites including *www.samsclub.com* (Member's Mark, the store brand), *www.costco .com* (national brands and Kirkland Signature, Costco's store brand), www.naturesonedirect.com (Baby's Only), and www.amazon.com. Amazon.com offers Enfamil, Similac, Nestlé Good Start, and Member's Mark, and free shipping on some quantities. Amazon.com also has some organic brands, such as Earth's Best and Baby's Only. You can sign up for Amazon Prime, which entitles you to unlimited "free" standard shipping and two-day shipping on eligible items, as well as other benefits, for an annual membership fee of $79.

Another option is to buy formula online from the manufacturer's Web site. Earth's Best (www.earthsbest.com), Enfamil (www.enfamil.com), and Similac (www.similac.com) offer this convenient option. In some instances, if you buy three or more cases at one time from the manufacturer, you may get a price break and standard shipping may be included—and, unlike Amazon.com, there's no membership fee. Although drugstore formula tends to cost more than formula sold in supermarkets, you can scout for drugstore savings online at www.cvs .com, where you can use a preferred shopper's card to save even more. Shopping online saves on a trip to the store and can be a convenient way to get some hard-to-find formula. The downside? Some sites, such as www.similac.com, don't accept coupons, and the infant formula selection can be limited on other sites.

Use powder, if possible. Powdered formulas are the least expensive option. The USDA reports that liquid concentrate formulas, which are more convenient and easier to mix than powder, tend to cost more. Ready-to-feed is the most expensive option. Here' one strategy to try:

"I bought the small cans of liquid formula to try out the different kinds, then branched out to the powdered formula after I found one my son liked," says Sarah Francomano, mother of one from Foxboro, Mass.

Buy big. Across brands, larger cans of formula, whether in powder or liquid form, cost less per reconstituted ounce than smaller cans. Buy the largest cans you can find.

Consider a store brand. You'll find store brands of formula at major retailers such as Kmart, Target, and Wal-Mart, and the savings can be substantial. "For my second son, we went straight to the generic Target brand formula. The ingredients are nearly identical to Similac Advance. He did great—and we didn't pay through the nose for it," says Kristen Lunceford, the mom of three from Hastings, Minn.

Through our informal research, we found that the store brand of formula at a local Wal-Mart (Parent's Choice) cost at least 40 percent less

Cash in on Formula With Coupons During Sales

Before going to the store for infant formula, scout for savings by previewing weekly store advertisements online. Then capitalize on sales by bringing manufacturer's coupons and load up on the largest cans you can find.

per ounce than a leading national brand (Similac Advance). Is the store brand as good as the national brand? It has to be. According to the Food and Drug Administration (FDA), all formula marketed in the U.S. must meet the same nutrient specifications, which are set at levels to fulfill the needs of infants. Although infant-formula manufacturers may have their own proprietary formulations, brand-name and store-brand formula must contain at least the minimum levels of all nutrients specified in FDA regulations, without exceeding maximum levels, where those are specified.

Check the "use by" date. When buying formula, look for the "use by" date on the label, which is required by the FDA. Until that date, you can be sure the formula will contain no less than the amount of each nutrient declared on the product label and will be of acceptable quality.

Be brand loyal. Although major brands of formula are roughly equal, it's generally recommended that you stick with the brand your baby gets used to. It's fine to use liquid and powder interchangeably.

Features to Consider

DHA/ARA. Almost all brands of formula sold in the U.S. are now fortified with DHA (docosahexaenoic acid) and ARA (arachidonic acid),

synthesized versions of the essential fatty acids that are naturally found in breast milk; the natural versions of DHA and ARA are also concentrated in the cells of the brain and eyes.

The chemical structure of extracted DHA/ARA isn't the same as human DHA/ARA. And even formulas with DHA and ARA aren't a perfect match for breast milk because breast milk contains hundreds of components that can't be replicated. Also, infants can make these fatty acids from other fatty acids in their diet, including those in unfortified infant formula. Although the FDA approved the addition of DHA and ARA to infant formulas, they caution that the scientific evidence is mixed. Some studies in infants suggest that

Nearly 100 percent of all infant formulas now contain DHA.

- **Myth Conceptions**

Why Babies Don't Need Water

Myth: It's okay to give your baby water, especially in summer, or if you think your baby needs it. **Reality:** The answer is no. During the first year of a baby's life, you don't need to supplement formula with bottles of water—even on hot days. In fact, giving infants water can be dangerous because they can easily suffer from water intoxication, a condition in which their developing kidneys can't excrete water fast enough. Water can build up in the body and dilute the electrolyte balance of the blood, which can cause seizures, coma, or even death. Give your baby a little extra breast milk or formula instead of water if you sense that she's thirsty on especially hot days.

including these fatty acids in infant formulas may have positive effects on visual function and neural development over the short term. Other studies in infants do not confirm these benefits. There are no currently published reports from clinical studies that address whether any long-term beneficial effects exist.

In any event, it's tough to find an infant formula without added DHA/ARA, even if you wanted to. (You can still buy Nestlé Good Start without DHA/ARA online at *www.diapers.com*, but that's about the only place we could find it.) In the near future, we expect non-DHA/ARA infant formula to become extinct unless consumer demand keeps it in play.

Iron. The formula that you buy should be fortified with iron unless your pediatrician says otherwise. Although there are low-iron formulas available, the AAP strongly discourages using them because they can increase the risk of infant iron deficiency.

Organic. There's a growing selection of organic formula brands on the market. To date, they include Baby's Only, which makes dairy, soy, and lactose-free formulas for toddlers (the company's philosophy is that breast milk is best for the early months), Bright Beginnings (dairy), Earth's Best (dairy and soy), Parent's Choice (dairy; Wal-Mart's store brand), and Similac Organic (dairy). Each of these formulas includes iron, DHA, and ARA. Organic formula costs slightly more than nonorganic, but there are deals to be had online and by buying the store brand. Using organic formula is a matter of personal preference.

Probiotic infant formula. Nestlé Good Start Natural Cultures (including Nestlé Good Start 2 Natural Cultures, for babies and toddlers 9 to 24 months) is the first brand of infant formula to contain probiotics—the friendly bacteria that normally reside in the gut, where they

Formula Complaints and Concerns

Since 2002, when infant formula began being fortified with the essential fatty acids DHA and ARA, some parents have reported to the Food and Drug Administration that their baby had an adverse reaction to the fortified formula, speculating that the added DHA/ARA was the problem. Reported issues have included spitting up, gas, fussiness, constipation, vomiting, and diarrhea after repeated use.

If you think your baby has suffered a harmful effect from an infant formula, promptly report the adverse reaction to the FDA, which regulates infant formula. Contact them at *www.accessdata* *.fda.gov/scripts/medwatch/* *medwatchonline.htm.*

Your pediatrician can also do it for you via FDA's MedWatch hotline at 800-332-1088 or online at *www.fda.gov/medwatch.* The MedWatch program allows health-care providers to report problems possibly caused by FDA-regulated products.

help break down foods and medicine and keep disease-causing bugs in check. Several studies now suggest that infants on antibiotics or suffering from diarrhea may get some relief when they're fed infant formula containing probiotics. To produce any benefit, a serving must contain at least 100 million live cultures. Talk to your pediatrician to see if you should try a formula with probiotics. If you supplement infant formula with breast-feeding, a probiotic formula isn't necessary since breast milk is a natural source of probiotics.

What's Available

Talk to your baby's pediatrician before giving him a probiotic formula.

The major brands of formula are, in alphabetical order: Baby's Only (*www.naturesone.com*), Bright Beginnings (*www.brightbeginnings.com*), Earth's Best (*www* *.earthsbest.com*), Enfamil (*www.enfamil.com*), Kirkland Signature (*www.costco.com*), Member's Mark (*www* *.samsclub.com*), Nestlé Good Start (*www.verybestbaby* *.com*), Parent's Choice (Wal-Mart's store brand, not available online at Wal-Mart), and Similac (*www* *.similac.com*). Formula comes in three versions: powder, concentrated liquid, and ready-to-feed liquid. There are also ready-to-feed bottles for babies on the go. Besides standard formula, which is cow's milk based, there are special formulas, such as lactose-free and lactose-reduced for babies who have problems digesting lactose, a carbohydrate naturally

Avoid Mixing Fluoridated Water With Formula

Recent research suggests that mixing liquid concentrate or powdered baby formula with fluoridated water may affect a child's baby and permanent teeth as they develop below the gums. The condition—enamel fluorosis—usually results in faint white lines or spots, although pitting or staining may also occur.

While more research is needed, the American Dental Association offers this guidance to lower the risk: If liquid concentrate or powdered infant formula is your baby's primary food source, mix it with water that is fluoride-free or contains low levels of fluoride. Look for water labeled purified, demineralized, deionized, distilled, or reverse osmosis filtered water, usually available in grocery stores for less than $1 per gallon. Your pediatrician may want you to use sterilized water. However, sterilization will not remove fluoride.

You can check the fluoride level in your own tap water with your local water utility. Or go to "My Water's Fluoride" at *http://apps.nccd.cdc.gov/MWF/Index.asp*.

found in milk. Soy and protein-hydrolyzed formulas are available for babies with a cow's milk protein allergy. Soy formula is an option if you prefer that your baby have a vegetarian diet. But first consult your pediatrician about your baby's nutritional needs and get a recommendation. There are also specific formulas to reduce spit-up, diarrhea, fussiness, gas, and colic, and for pre-term and low-birth-weight babies, older babies, and toddlers. Your pediatrician is the best source of advice on what to feed your baby. But your baby's preferences and nutritional needs will affect the choice, too. If your baby doesn't take to the first formula you pick, it often simply comes down to trial and error. If your baby has any reaction to an infant formula, see your pediatrician.

Powdered infant formula is the least expensive option.

Powdered formula

Pro: It's the least costly.

Cons: With both powders and concentrated liquids (see right), you must carefully measure the added water to be sure that your baby gets the right concentration of nutrients. The FDA recommends boiling the water for a full minute and letting it cool before mixing. Also, the FDA advises against preparing several bottles at a time.

The FDA says to boil water for concentrated liquid and powdered formula.

Concentrated liquid formula

Pro: It's slightly faster to prepare than powdered because you don't have to mix a solid with a liquid.

Cons: It's more expensive than powder, and you still have to boil water for a full minute before you mix it with formula, according to the FDA.

Liquid formula

Pro: It's convenient because the water is already mixed in, so it doesn't require any mixing or measuring.

Con: It's the most expensive.

Recommendations

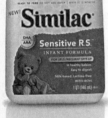

You'll pay for the convenience of liquid infant formula.

If you're planning to use formula, ask your pediatrician for a recommendation, but don't buy much of it until after your baby is born. Many companies are generous with free samples, and the hospital may load you up with samples when you go home. If you register at a baby store for gifts or word gets out that you're expecting, you may receive unsolicited samples or money-saving checks in the mail from formula companies right around your due date. However, you might find that your baby prefers one type of formula or may be able to tolerate only a particular brand, so be prepared to experiment. No matter what brand you settle on, if your baby shows signs of intolerance, such as gas, a rash, persistent vomiting, bloody stool, diarrhea, or any other unusual symptom, consult your pediatrician. You may need to switch brands or change to a hydrolyzed or soy-based formula or to a formula specially formulated to combat your baby's issue, whether it's diarrhea, spit up, or colic.

chapter

21

Gates

Safety gates become key equipment once your little one starts crawling. Use them at the top of stairs, between rooms and as an instant childproofing tool that can travel with you to hotels and to Grandma's house.

It's crucial to get the right type of safety gate for each location.

With an active baby on the loose, a gate or two can make your life a little easier and your child a lot safer by keeping him away from potential danger, such as stairs or a bustling kitchen. You can also use a gate to keep a pet away from a child (and vice versa). Child safety gates are intended for children between 6 months and 24 months of age, not for older children. All the gates CONSUMER REPORTS tested (see page 234 for test results) can be opened and closed by an adult but have various designs to prevent children from opening them. Child safety gates come in two basic types, based on the method of installation.

Hardware-Mounted or Permanent Gate

This type of gate requires screws for installation in a doorway. You drill holes in a door frame or into the studs behind a wall and attach the gate with brackets and screws. If properly secured to the door-jamb or between two walls, hardware-mounted gates are the most secure choice, although no gate can be guaranteed to keep a child in or out. Many hardware-mounted gates are made of wood, enamel-coated steel, or aluminum tubing.

Where you'll need it: At the top of the stairs. Hardware-mounted gates are the only safe choice for stair locations. Most will swing open only one way, although you can decide which way you want a gate to swing. At the top of the stairs, a gate should swing away from the stairs (not over them) for maximum safety.

Gates used at the top of stairs indoors or outside must be hardware-mounted like this Stairway Special by Cardinal Gates.

Installation: You must drill holes into the door-frame or, if the opening doesn't have a wood door-frame, you must drill through the drywall or plaster into the wood framing behind. (You can fill in the holes later with wood putty or wall-patching compound when you no longer use the gate.) You can remove many of these gates from the mounting hardware when you want the doorway or opening free.

Buy a Certified Gate

Located on the frame or packaging, a certification sticker shows that the gate meets the ASTM International voluntary safety standard and that its manufacturer participates in the certification program administered by the Juvenile Products Manufacturers Association (JPMA). The ASTM standard addresses issues such as the bottom spacing—the distance between the bottom of the gate and the floor—so a small torso can't pass through and there's minimal risk of head and neck entrapment; gate height (not less than 22 inches); strength of top rails, slats, and framing components; latching mechanism integrity; and upper-edge configuration—any openings more than ⅔ of an inch deep can be no wider than 1½ inches.

The following brands of gates bear the JPMA seal: Cardinal Gates, Dorel Juvenile Group (Safety 1st), Evenflo, GMI, KidCo, Kolcraft, Lascal/Regal Lager, Learning Curve (The First Years), North States Industries, Inc., Regalo International, Retract-A-Gate/The Creative Frontier, Summer Infant Products, and Tee-Zed Products, LLC (Dream Baby).

Pressure-Mounted Gate

A pressure-mounted gate is held in an opening by pressure against the door frame or walls. This type of gate can have two sliding panels that adjust to make the gate fit the opening. (You remove the panels or slide them to the side to walk through.) A pressure bar or some other locking mechanism then wedges the gate into place without hardware. A swing-style pressure-mounted gate, which has a gate door that swings open, is also an option. Pressure keeps it in place and installation doesn't require drilling. Like hardware-mounted gates, pressure-mounted gates are often made of wood, enamel-coated steel, or aluminum tubing. They may also be made of plastic, wire, or nylon mesh or plastic-coated wire, which may be framed with end tubes and top rails of either wood or coated metal. A few are made with transparent plastic center panels.

You can use pressure-mounted gates like Kidco's Gateway Model G11 at the bottom of stairs and between rooms.

Where you'll need it: Pressure-mounted gates are suitable for less hazardous locations, such as between rooms. They're useful in areas where falling isn't a major concern, such as in a doorway separating two areas with same-level flooring; you might use one, for example, to cordon off your kitchen so you can make dinner without a crawling baby underfoot. You could also use one at the bottom of a stairway to discourage your little climber from venturing upstairs. Many manufacturers recommend not using a pressure-mounted gate at the top of stairs. We believe it is unsafe to use anything but a hardware-mounted gate at the top of stairs.

Installation: To set one up, you adjust it to fit the opening by squeezing it into position. A pressure bar or other locking mechanism wedges the gate in place, leaving no permanent holes, although it may mar the door frame or wall. Basic pressure gates fit openings between 26 and 38 inches, give or take a few inches, depending on the model. Many homes have wider door openings, so manufacturers offer wider models—some as wide as 62 inches. Some models have optional extensions you purchase separately. The Summer Infant Sure & Secure Custom-Fit Gate ($109, *www.target.com*), for example, can expand to fit openings as wide as 12 feet simply by adding more panels.

Shopping Secrets

Decide where you'll use it. A hardware-mounted gate is harder to dislodge than a pressure-mounted gate. That's why it is the only choice anywhere security is paramount, such as the top of a stairway. For less hazardous areas such as between rooms, a portable pressure-mounted gate may do the trick.

Size up the slats. Avoid gates with horizontal slats; they're an invitation for a child to climb. Luckily, there don't seem to be many on the market. Some gates have enough space between their vertical slats to let adventurous toddlers get a foothold on the gate's horizontal bottom rail. They won't be able to climb up the gate, but they may be able to hop onto the bottom rail and go for a ride, which could be unsafe—perhaps even dislodging a pressure gate—or strain the gate's integrity. So look for narrow spaces between the vertical slats. Vertical slats or bars should be less than 3 inches apart to prevent head entrapment, but try to find slats even closer together.

Check construction. Look for sturdy construction and an even finish. Wood surfaces should be smooth, splinter-free, and fashioned with rounded rather than sharply squared edges. Metal is more durable than wood. Some metal gates have a support bar that crosses the floor beneath the gate, which could cause tripping when the gate is open.

■ **What Not to Buy**

Old-Fashioned Accordion-Style Gates

Old-fashioned, accordion-style wooden gates have diamond-shaped spaces between the slats and V-shaped openings at the top that pose an entrapment and strangulation hazard. You may run across them at tag sales, thrift stores, and other secondhand markets. If you have this type of gate, replace it with another model. Although there are newer accordion-style gates on the market that meet current ASTM safety standards—which include smaller openings to reduce the risk of trapping heads and necks—the points formed at the top by the diamond-shaped openings might snag clothing or necklaces. We recommend avoiding these new gates too, unless they have a bar across the top.

We don't recommend accordion-style gates unless they have a top bar, as does the Expansion Swing Gate from Evenflo.

Do your homework. Bring width measurements of doors or openings with you when you shop, and try to avoid gates that will need to be at their maximum width to fit; they may wobble.

Try it before you buy. Most tested models have a dual-action latch that can be opened with one adult hand. If possible, test models in the store to make sure they're easy for you to use. Tip: Once you choose a gate, don't forget to show people who come to your home (workers, babysitters, relatives) how it works. We've heard stories of hardware-mounted gates being ripped from homeowners' walls when frustrated workers couldn't open the latch.

What's Available

Brands of child safety gates are, in alphabetical order: Cardinal Gates (*www.cardinalgates.com*), Dream Baby (*www.dream-baby.com*), Evenflo (*www.evenflo.com*), GMI (*www.gmigates.com*), KidCo (*www.kidco.com*), Lascal (*www.regallager.com*), North States Industries Inc. (*www.north statesind.com*), Regalo (*www.regalo-baby.com*), Safety 1st (*www.safety1st .com*), Summer Infant (*www.summerinfant.com*), and The First Years (*www.learningcurve.com*). Prices range from $12.99 for a basic wooden pressure-mounted gate that extends to a maximum of 41 inches to

$134.99 for a wall-mounted gate of three 24-inch interlocking adjustable sections.

Features to Consider

Gate safety depends on solid construction, reliable hardware, and the absence of entrapment hazards.

Height. To discourage an adventurous child from climbing over, a gate must stand a minimum of three-quarters of the child's height. Most gates measure 22 inches or more from top to bottom. If your child is tall for her age, go with a higher gate. Some, such as the Dream Baby Extra Tall Security Gate, stand as high as 39 inches. Generally, though, when a child is taller than 36 inches or weighs more than 30 pounds (usually at about 2 years of age), a gate is no longer adequate or safe.

Installation flexibility. Many gates can be mounted to odd areas, such as stair balusters, angled banisters, and into drywall where there is no wood framing behind it. (You may, however, need to purchase a specific installation kit for these areas. KidCo has an installation kit for mounting its gates to wrought iron.) Some gates may also adjust to fit irregularly shaped or very wide areas. Some hardware-mounted gates can be slid out of their wall mountings, which is a bonus when, say, you're entertaining and don't want the gate in the way.

The Safety 1st SmartLight Stair Gate lights your way with a motion sensor nightlight that's triggered on approach.

Latches. Many gates have a dual-action latch that can be opened with one hand by an adult. Try different types of latches in the store to make sure they're easy to use, if possible. A gate with a squeezing mechanism opens by compressing parts of the gate, but this type of latch can be difficult to use, so be sure to test it in the store. Other options are a pressure-release handle, which can be lifted with one hand to open the gate. Some models have a foot pedal that requires strong pressure to release.

Some models, such as the Evenflo SimpleEffort and SimpleEffort Plus, both pressure-mounted gates, unlock at the push of a button on a wall console. To open the gate, you won't have to put your baby down; that's a plus. But you still have to push the gate open (your knee can do the job) and close the gate manually. One 9-volt

■ Sanity Saver

Use Gates to Childproof Other People's Homes

A pressure-mounted gate or two is an easy way to make a hotel room or a relative's home more child-friendly. When traveling with a baby or toddler and visiting friends, grandparents, or other relatives, install a pressure-mounted gate at the bottom of stairs and between rooms you consider unsafe, like the living room with a fire roaring in the fireplace or the kitchen when people are busy cooking. Also keep bathroom doors securely closed or blocked off with a gate.

battery for the wall console, or four C batteries for the gate module are required (not included).

Sound and color. Many gates audibly click when they're shut, signaling that they're doing their job. The Sure & Secure Extra Tall Top-of-the-Stairs Gate with Alarm from Summer Infant takes it a step further by sounding an alarm if the gate is tampered with or not closed (adults can deactivate the alarm). Other gates use visual cues to do the job. The Perfect Fit Gate by Safety 1st and some Evenflo gates, for example, have a color indicator showing when the gate is locked.

Let there be light. At least one model we know of, the SmartLight Stair Gate by Safety 1st, features a motion sensor night-light that glows when you approach it—an added safety and convenience feature around stairs for when you're parenting on the night shift.

Recommendations

Whether you choose a hardware- or pressure-mounted gate, look for one that's JPMA-certified (see Safety Strategies on page 229) and install it according to the manufacturer's directions. Never use a pressure-mounted gate or the pressure-mount option on a gate that can be installed either way at the top of stairs—no matter how much you want to avoid drilling holes into your woodwork. Choose a gate with a straight top edge and closely spaced, rigid vertical slats or a mesh screen. Avoid accordion-style gates without a top filler bar (with open points at the top) and gates with horizontal slats or similarly tempting footholds. If you choose a model with mesh panels, look for a fine weave—wide-holed mesh may provide a foothold for climbing or could trap fingers. Follow the safety recommendations for installing and using gates and use our Ratings below as a buying guideline.

Ratings • Gates

Excellent ⊖ Very good ⊖ Good ○ Fair ◒ Poor ●

Within types, in performance order.

Brand & model	Price	Overall score 0–100 P|F|G|VG|E	Security	Design safety	Convenience	Fits openings (in.)	Weight (lbs.)	Installed height (in.)	One-hand open & close	Can be used on uneven surfaces
HARDWARE MOUNTED										
The First Years Simple & Secure Stair Gate	$60	87	Excellent	Excellent	Good	29.5-44	10	29	Yes	Yes
Safety 1st Lift and Lock Security*	20	81	Excellent	Excellent	Good	30-42	7	28	Yes	No
Kidco Safeway Gate G20	70	77	Excellent	Good	Good	25-43.5	7	31	Yes	Yes
North States Auto-Close*	80	76	Excellent	Good	Excellent	29.5-39	13	30	Yes	Yes
Cardinal Gate Stairway Special SS-30A	80	61	Excellent	Fair	Good	27-42.5	6	30	Yes	Yes
PRESSURE MOUNTED										
KidCo Gateway G11	70	74	Good	Excellent	Excellent	30-36	10	30	Yes	Yes
North States Auto-Close*	80	66	Excellent	Good	Excellent	29.5-39	13	30	Yes	Yes
Evenflo Simple Effort Hands-Free Metal	50	40	Fair	Excellent	Excellent	28-37.5	14	29	Yes	Yes
The First Years Hands-Free Gate 3600**	60	28	Fair	Good	Excellent	29-34	11	31	Yes	Yes
Safety 1st Lift and Lock Security*	20	13	Poor	Excellent	Good	28-42	7	27	No	No

* Gate could be mounted with hardware or pressure.
** Hands-free open and close also.

Guide to the Ratings

Overall score is based primarily on security. **Security** indicates how well the gate resisted being dislodged. **Design safety** reflects the gate's adherence to the ASTM standard for gates. **Convenience** reflects features and versatility. **Price** is the approximate retail.

22
chapter

High Chairs

Feeding a hungry baby in a high chair isn't always a picnic. But the right high chair can help contain mealtime madness and make the whole experience a lot more enjoyable for you and your baby.

This new but old-style wooden high chair doesn't meet the latest safety standards because it lacks a center post.

A high chair usually consists of a frame of molded plastic or metal tubing and an attached seat with a safety belt and a footrest. There are still a few old-fashioned wooden high chairs out there with a removable tray, or arms that lift the tray over a baby's head. Some, such as the Graco Classic Wood Highchair ($129.99; *www.gracobaby.com*), have modern conveniences, such as a cushioned, wipe-clean seat pad, a three-point harness, a clear, dishwasher-safe, pull-out tray insert that protects the wood finish, and most important, a center crotch post, which helps prevent a child from slipping out of the chair. But many wooden high chairs aren't always as comfortable or cushy for babies as the latest, form-fitting models on the market now, and many of them may not meet the latest safety standards. Unless a wooden chair is a hybrid of the old (in timeless design only) and the new (see Features to Consider), we say don't use it.

Some chairs are loaded with features, such as adjustable trays with dishwasher-safe inserts that make cleanup a cinch, seat backs that recline to multiple positions, and chair heights that accommodate your growing baby and give you some flexibility to feed your baby at different levels. Others are basic models that don't even fold. At the very minimum, you'll want a stable, sturdy high chair that can stand up to spilling, kicking, and regular cleaning for at least a year. You'll probably use a high chair for less time than you'd think. Although high chairs are intended for infancy up to about age 3 (typical top weight is 40 to 50 pounds), some babies can't bear to sit in a high chair once they become adventurous toddlers.

Fortunately, many high chairs now on the market convert to toddler chairs once your child is ready to sit at the table with the rest of the family. You'll typically make the switch by removing the tray and adjusting the chair height so you can scoot your toddler right up to the table. That's a good thing because a regular kitchen or dining room chair will likely put your child at chin level to the table. You'll need some kind of transitional chair; you might as well get the most mileage you can from a high chair.

Shopping Secrets

Take a hands-on approach to buying a high chair. We suggest visiting the baby store near you that has the broadest selection. Then put the chairs through their paces with these simple tests:

- **Open and close the fastener on the seat's safety harness.** Try it one-handed to make sure it's easy to use. If it's not, you might be tempted not to use it every time your child is in the seat—which is a must. Although the current voluntary industry standard set by ASTM International doesn't call for a five-point harness (waist and crotch restraint with shoulder straps), a three-point harness (waist and crotch restraint) is required for certification. On some chairs, you can convert a five-point harness to a three-point harness, but we don't recommend it. Five-point harnesses are safer because they can prevent a child from standing up in a high chair and possibly falling.

- **Test the tray.** It should be easy for you to engage and disengage, but not for your baby. Ideally, tray latches shouldn't be accessible or visible to your baby.

- **Check for a crotch post.** The voluntary industry standard requires high chairs to have a passive crotch restraint, which is usually a fixed crotch post that may be attached to the tray or the seat of the chair. For more on the crotch post, see Features to Consider.

- **Adjust the seat height to see how well that mechanism works.** Not all chairs have this feature, but some come with as many as eight possible heights. Adjustable seat heights can accommodate parents of varying heights and allow the high chair to be used at the level of your dining table, so your baby can eat with the rest of the family.

- **Assess the seat cover.** Look for a chair with upholstery made to last. It should feel substantial, not flimsy. Make sure upholstery seams won't scratch your baby's legs. Seat covers should be wipe-clean (preferred) or machine washable.

- **Make sure wheels can be locked.** If you're buying a model with wheels, they should lock or become immobilized by the weight of your baby in the seat.

- **Watch out for rough edges.** Examine the underside of the feeding tray to make sure there's nothing sharp that could scratch your baby. Look for small holes or hinges that could trap little fingers.

- **Check for small parts.** Make sure the caps or plugs that cover the ends of metal tubing are well secured. Parts small enough for a child to swallow or inhale are a choking hazard.

▶ **Try folding it.** If you plan to fold up your high chair as often as every day, practice in the store. Some chairs that claim to be foldable can have stiff folding mechanisms. Technically they may be foldable, but they're not user-friendly.

▶ **Give the chair a good shake.** Push contenders around to see how well they hold their ground. A chair should feel stable and sturdy, not wobbly. Look for a high chair with a wide base for stability.

What's Available

Some brands of high chairs are, in alphabetical order: Baby Trend (*www.babytrend.com*), Boon Inc., maker of Flair and Flaire Elite (*www.booninc.com*), Chicco (*www.chiccousa.com*), Combi (*www.combi-intl.com*), Dorel Juvenile Group (Cosco, Eddie Bauer, and Safety 1st, *www.djgusa.com*), Evenflo (*www.evenflo.com*), Fisher-Price (*www.fisher-price.com*), Graco (*www.gracobaby.com*), Kolcraft (*www.kolcraft.com*), Peg-Pérego (*www.pegperego.com*), Stokke (www.*Stokkeusa.com*), Summer Infant (*www.summerinfant.com*), and Svan (*www.scichild.com*). There are three general price categories:

Basic High Chairs

High chairs at this end of the price range (under $55) are simple, compact, and generally work quite well. These models are essentially plastic seats on plastic or steel-tubing legs, and may or may not have tray and height adjustments. They tend to lack bells and whistles, such as wheels, and they don't typically fold for storage or recline, a feature you may not use unless you're bottle-feeding. The seat is usually upholstered with a wipe-clean vinyl covering or bare plastic, and the pad may be removable and washable. Some have a towel rack to hold bibs, towels, and washcloths. In our tests, some basic models have scored higher than some bigger-ticket high chairs, indicating that price isn't necessarily correlated with safety or ease of use. The newest addition to this price category is a "space saver" high chair that attaches to a regular dining room or kitchen chair. It doesn't require the extra floor space a regular high chair would, but still offers a three-position recline, a three-position height adjustment, and converts to a booster seat.

Pros: A basic high chair can serve you and your baby well, but it pays to comparison shop because some brands may suit your needs better

Look for Certification

A certification sticker on a high chair shows that the model meets the ASTM voluntary standard, and that its manufacturer participates in the certification program administered by the Juvenile Products Manufacturers Association (JPMA). Certified high chairs are required to have a passive restraint, such as a crotch post; a locking device that prevents accidental folding; secure caps and plugs; sturdy, break-resistant trays; legs wide enough to increase stability (but not so wide that you trip over them); no springs or scissoring actions that could harm little fingers; and no small parts that could come loose. Safety belts must pass force tests. JPMA-certified high chairs include models by Baby Trend, Bergeron by Design, Chicco, Dorel Juvenile Group (Cosco, Eddie Bauer, and Safety 1st), Evenflo, Fisher-Price, Graco, Kolcraft, Peg-Pérego, Scandinavian Child (Anka and Svan), Stokke, Summer Infant, and Tri-Chair.

than others. This kind—whether freestanding or chair-attachable—may be a good choice to keep at Grandma's house.

Cons: Avoid chairs in this price range with grooves in the seat's molded plastic (a mess magnet); cotton seat pads rather than vinyl, which don't hold up as well; and trays with side-release buttons that are accessible to your baby. Some parents report that their babies can remove these trays—food and all—as early as 9 months of age. Be on the lookout for chairs with protruding or widely spaced legs. They're a tripping hazard to parents and siblings.

Midpriced High Chairs

In this price range ($55 to $200), you'll find chairs with many convenience features, including multiple tray and chair heights; casters for mobility, with a locking feature for safe parking; a reclining, padded seat for infant feeding; a tray that can be removed with one hand; a dishwasher- safe tray insert for easy cleanup; flip-out organizer compartments on the tray that hold utensils, dishes, or baby food jars; easy folding for storage; and a five-point harness instead of a three-point harness. Most have vinyl seat pads that can be removed for cleaning. Although you may see models with cloth covers in this price range, they are a challenge to keep clean. Frames and seats are usually made of molded, rigid plastic or steel.

Pros: Generally, these chairs are sturdier and have more features than the basic high chairs. Chair fabric patterns tend to be more muted and sophisticated, with names like "Pebblestone" and "Lexington." If you're looking for a high chair that fits your home décor, or at least isn't covered with teddy bears or nursery figures, you will have lots of options. There's a lot to choose from in this price range.

Cons: If you're looking for a simple chair that doesn't fold, with a wipe-clean cover, chairs in this price range probably will have more features than you may need.

High-End High Chairs

In this price range ($200 on up) are European imports and traditional solid-wood, custom-made high chairs, some that lack a passive crotch restraint. Chairs at this end of the market tend to have a sleek, upscale appearance. Many have fewer features than midrange models, though, and a much higher price tag. Some, on the other hand, go all out to justify their cost. The Flair Pedestal Highchair by Boon Inc. ($230), for example, is a modern-looking pedestal high chair that has a pneumatic lift for continuous height positioning, much like chairs at a hair salon.

Pros: Top-dollar high chairs may mean top quality, which is important to consider if you want the chair to last for another baby or more. But that doesn't mean a midpriced high chair won't last, too. High-end high chairs tend to be stylish, but don't make looks your deciding factor.

The Flair Pedestal Highchair by Boon Inc. has a pneumatic lift not unlike chairs at a hair salon.

Cons: Chairs in this range aren't necessarily the safest option. In our tests, the Svan High Chair ($250), for example, a wooden high chair manufactured by Svan of Sweden and distributed by Scandinavian Child, passed all ASTM safety tests except one for forward stability. We determined that a child seated in this chair, or a sibling pulling on it, might be able to tip the chair over, possibly causing serious injury.

■ Sanity Savers
Play Along When Your Baby Drops the Ball

By the time your baby is 8 to 12 months old, she'll undoubtedly drop things from her high chair—a spoon, her bottle, or her sippy cup—and squeal with delight when you fetch the object again and again. This game may be exasperating, but it helps reinforce the concepts of object permanence and cause and effect—that when your baby sends her sippy cup on a nose dive, it doesn't disappear; instead, it bounces and rolls across the kitchen floor. It also helps her realize that she can affect her environment and get your attention.

Instead of getting frustrated, play along by giving your baby objects she can drop that won't make a mess, such as a rubber ball, a plastic spoon, a paper cup, teaspoons, measuring cups, or an unbreakable toy. It can make mealtime longer, but it can seem less annoying when you realize your baby's getting something out of it. The payback? You get to enjoy your baby's reaction when objects "clank," "ping," or "thwack" when they hit the floor. To add to the fun, be sure to say "Where'd it go? There it is!" when stuff takes the plunge. And if you're game, give your 8-to-12-month-old opportunities to drop other things throughout the day, such as a ball into a box or toy keys off the dining room table.

Features to Consider

Crotch post. To prevent a baby from slipping under the tray and getting his head caught between the tray and the chair, high chairs must have a fixed center crotch post to comply with the voluntary ASTM safety standard for high chairs. The post is not meant to replace the safety belt, though; a high chair needs both for safety. Check the leg openings that form between the tray/passive crotch restraint and the sides of the high chair. Children have been known to maneuver both legs to one side. The leg openings on the high chair shouldn't be large enough for a child to fit both legs in one.

Foldability. Some high chairs fold for storage. If that's important to you because your home is space-challenged, make sure there's a secure locking system to prevent accidental folding while your child is in the chair or being put into it. Such a locking system should engage automatically when you open the chair.

Safety belt. As we mentioned, this is an important feature. Most high chairs have an adjustable three-point harness, but a five-point harness is safer. The shoulder straps it provides could keep a tenacious, on-the-go baby from standing up or climbing out and falling.

Bon Appétit, Baby

Restaurant high chairs are notorious for having broken safety restraints and other defects.

The Munchkin Feeding Friend Portable Hook-On Chair is JPMA-certified.

They can be dirty too, since chances are the chair you plop your toddler into hasn't been cleaned since the last child used it.

One option: Bring your own portable hook-on chair (keep one in the trunk of your car). The JPMA currently certifies four brands of hook-on chairs: The Graco Travel Lite Table Chair, which retails for around $34.99, Chicco's Caddy Hook-On high chair ($30), the Dorel Eddie Bauer Portable Hook-On Chair, ($39.99), and the Munchkin Feeding Friend Portable Hook-On Chair ($42.99). CONSUMER REPORTS has not tested them, however. Use one with a table top only, not with tablecloths or place mats. If you use the restaurant's high chair, clean it with a baby wipe before putting your child in it. Clean his home high chair after every meal, too.

Seat adjustment. Seats can move up or down to as many as eight height positions on some chairs. They may also recline (in case your baby falls asleep right after eating). However, except for bottle feeding, don't use a seat in the reclining position while feeding your baby—that's a choking hazard. On a height-adjusting chair, the seat slides along the chair frame, locking into various positions. Remember, it's not safe to adjust the height while the child is in the chair. Settings may range from nearly floor level to standard high-chair level. At the appropriate height, the chair (with the tray removed) can be pushed up to a dining table.

Toys. Some high chairs have toy bars or toys that attach to the tray, an option your baby will likely enjoy, although to keep your baby busy, you can certainly buy toys that suction on to high-chair trays. But do not attach strings to them because strings and cords are a strangulation hazard. Make sure the toys are securely fastened and have no small parts that could become detached.

Tray. You'll want a lightweight tray you can take off with one hand or that swings to the side when not in use. Many high chairs have a dishwasher-safe tray insert that snaps on and off for easy cleanup. Some trays have compartments to hold utensils, dishes, jars of baby food, or sippy cups. Those are nice, but not necessary.

Snack tray. Some high chairs have a smaller stationary snack tray that sits beneath the removable upper tray table so you can give your baby snacks without having to use the main tray. It's a nice idea, but a built-in snack tray can limit the space you need to get your child in and out of the chair.

Upholstery. Most models have seat coverings—or entire seat panels—that can be wiped clean, or come off for more thorough cleaning. Opt for a seat cover with a pattern rather than a solid color; patterns are better at concealing stains. Vinyl is easier to spot-clean than cloth.

Natures Purest Complete Comfort High Chair by Summer Infant is a sign of these eco-conscious times.

Wheels. Wheels may make it easier to move the high chair around. That's important if you'll be scooting the high chair from the kitchen to the dining room. On the other hand, wheels can be a nuisance because they may allow the chair to move as you're trying to pull a tray off or put your baby in. Older children may be tempted to take the baby for a joyride when you turn your back. If you decide on a wheeled model, look for locks on the wheels, preferably on all four.

Eco-friendliness. At least one high chair on the market, Natures Purest Complete Comfort High Chair by Summer Infant (*www .summerinfant.com*), claims to be good for your baby because its seat pad is made from organically grown, naturally colored cotton. It's supposed to be less irritating for baby's skin than regular high chair upholstery. To our knowledge, that's not a common complaint. In any case, one side of the Natures Purest Complete Comfort High Chair seat pad is vinyl-coated. In general, when buying "eco-friendly" products, including high chairs, buy with a skeptical eye. That said, the Complete Comfort High Chair has lots of features including a crotch post, five-point restraint, three-position seat that reclines, one-hand tray release, locking casters, and four-position height adjustment.

Recommendations

Look carefully at the high chairs you're considering to make sure the one you want will suit your needs. Midpriced high chairs generally are the best value and have the best combination of useful features, so start there. At just $70, the Evenflo Expressions Plus, for example, has many safety and convenience features. You may not know what high chair will suit you best until you try using one. Keep your receipt or packing slip, or if you register for one, ask for a gift receipt to be included so you can return the chair if it doesn't work out. (For more information on how to return baby products and what your rights are as a consumer, see the Introduction, starting on page 9.) Some high chairs have 26 (or more) parts. If you're not handy, you might want to buy a high chair that comes fully assembled.

23

chapter

Humidifiers

Very dry air, common during the heating season, can irritate your baby's respiratory system, making a cold or cough worse. Using a humidifier to raise indoor relative humidity can help alleviate some of the discomfort.

This adorable Frog Cool Mist Humidifier by Crane can ease cough, cold, and flu symptoms for your baby.

A humidifier is more important than ever now that the FDA issued an advisory in 2008 strongly recommending that over-the-counter cough and cold medications not be given to infants and children under age 2 because of the risk of serious and potentially life-threatening side effects. As a result, the American Academy of Pediatrics (AAP) urges parents to seek safer ways to ease children's cold symptoms.

Using a cool-mist humidifier, saline nose drops, and suctioning bulbs can help relieve your baby's stuffy nose. Your doctor might recommend a humidifier if your baby is diagnosed with croup, a contagious wintertime viral infection, or bronchiolitis, an infection of the tiny lower airways in the lungs. "Almost all kids will get a bout of the most common bronchiolitis by age 3," says Susanna McColley, M.D., division head of pulmonary medicine at Children's Memorial Hospital in Chicago.

A humidifier can help ease itchy skin, respiratory irritation, and other problems associated with dry air. Ideally, indoor relative humidity should be 30 to 50 percent. But in winter, heating the air in your home can cause the relative humidity to drop to 10 percent. Using a humidifier can help increase it. However, in extremely cold weather it may be necessary to reduce the level of humidity in your home to less than 30 to 50 percent by increasing ventilation. If you see moisture condensing on cold interior surfaces like walls, doors, or windows, then the indoor relative humidity is too high; this can encourage mold.

Small room cool mist humidifiers like this one from Holmes can run up to 24 hours per tank filling.

Humidifiers come in three major configurations: small tabletop models, which can humidify one room; large stand-alone console models with substantial tanks that can humidify multiple rooms and small homes or apartments; and in-duct systems that are used in forced-air heating systems to humidify a whole house. In this chapter, we'll focus on tabletop models that can be placed right in your baby's room to ease congestion—and let you breathe easy, too.

Tabletop humidifiers include evaporative models (often sold as "cool-mist" humidifiers), which use a fan to blow air over a wet wick, or filter. When air from the fan blows across the filter, the water in the filter evaporates into the air. Warm-mist models are another option. They use a heating unit to boil water before cooling the steam by mixing it with air, but the AAP doesn't recommend them for use with children because of the risk of accidental burns or scalding. A curious baby or toddler might touch the unit or knock it over.

What's Available

Some brands of tabletop humidifiers are Bionaire (*www.bionaire.com*), Crane (*www.crane-usa.com*), Graco (*www.gracobaby.com*), Holmes (*www.holmesproducts.com*), Sunbeam (*www.sunbeam.com*), Sunpentown (*www.sunpentown.com*), and Vicks (*www.vicks.com*). Most tabletop humidifiers have small tanks that need to be refilled frequently. Evaporative models are noisy, although to a baby, it may sound like white noise; warm-mist models are costly to run. Prices range from $30 to $70.

Shopping Secrets

Be the queen (or king) of clean. Some humidifiers for children's rooms have gotten stuffed-animal cute, but like any pet, think about how much work it'll require before committing to it. In fact, don't buy a humidifier for your baby if you don't think you'll be able to clean and disinfect it regularly. (For cleaning tips, see Recommendations at the end of this chapter.) The standing water in a dirty room humidifier is a breeding ground for bacteria and fungi, which can get blown back into the mist that is released into the room. To make cleaning easier, manufacturers have added handles to the tanks and shaped the tanks to fit underneath faucets. Be on the lookout for a removable tank that fits beneath faucets, and, in general, easy-to-use controls. The filter should be a cinch to replace.

Babies are drawn to animals, even humidifier animals, so keep them out of your child's reach.

Beware of cutesy. From cows and Winnie the Pooh to frogs and penguins, animal-inspired humidifiers can be adorable for a child's room. But they can also be baby magnets as can a humidifier with a night light (many animal humidifiers have that feature, too). If you purchase an animal humidifier, or one with a night light, be especially careful to place it in a location that's out of your baby's reach.

Keep a warm-mist humidifier away from your baby. Warm-mist humidifiers tend to be quieter than evaporative (aka cool-mist) models; some make little or no noise except mild boiling and hissing sounds. But if you choose this option, and your pediatrician is OK with it, make sure you put the humidifier in a spot where your baby can't reach or touch it, or accidentally knock it over. The water in it gets hot.

Features to Consider

Be sure it has a humidistat. Whether it's dial or digital, a humidistat controls humidity levels and automatically shuts the humidifier off when the set level is reached. (We recommend 30 percent to 50 percent unless you notice condensation problems.) Digital displays for room humidity levels and settings are best. Models without a humidistat can allow humidity levels to rise too high, leading to condensation on windows and other cold surfaces. Overhumidification can also lead to mold and bacteria growth. It can also damage furniture and wallpaper.

> "Models without a humidistat can allow humidity levels to rise too high."

Consider your water. Some humidifiers have lower output with hard water. Fortunately, that can be easily remedied. If you have hard water, use distilled water, which has a lower mineral content than most tap water and can help boost your humidifier's efficiency.

Recommendations

No matter what brand of humidifier you buy, clean it regularly. The more you use it, the more vigilant you need to be. Mold can grow within 48 hours on wet surfaces, and mold in the tank or in the water then can be transferred into the air, causing itchy eyes and worsening any breathing troubles your baby may have. For the best results, follow these tips:

Change the water daily. Empty the tank, dry all interior surfaces, and refill with clean water. Don't be swayed by tank size. Generally, the larger the tank, the longer your table-top humidifier can run without running dry. A one-gallon tank may run up to 11 hours; a 1.5-gallon tank may operate up to 20 hours without refilling. But no matter how large the tank, you should change the water daily, so buying a humidifier with a larger tank won't save you a step.

chapter

Monitors

Baby monitors can be an extra set of ears and eyes that allow you to keep tabs on your sleeping baby. Using one can alert you to a situation before it becomes dangerous.

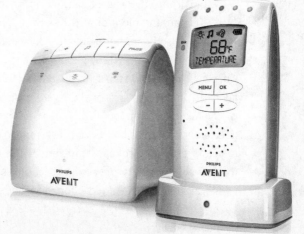

The Philips Avent SCD520, an audio monitor with a display screen, uses DECT technology to cut interference and enhance privacy. It also shows the nursery's temperature.

There are two basic types of baby monitors: audio and video/audio. Both operate within a selected radio frequency band to send sound from the baby's room to a receiver. Each monitor consists of a transmitter (child/nursery unit) and one or more receivers (parent units). Video/audio monitors have a small wall-mounted or tabletop camera to transmit images to a video monitor.

A baby monitor's challenge is to transmit recognizable sound and images over a distance with minimal interference—static, buzzing, or irritating noise—from other nearby electronic products and transmitters, including cordless phones that share the same frequency bands, cellular phones, appliances, and even fluorescent lights.

Is that your baby—or the neighbor's? Video interference can be an issue with analog video monitors.

Audio interference can take the form of hearing someone else's conversation or hearing their baby, which makes it difficult, if not impossible, to decipher the sounds coming from your monitor. If you have a video monitor, interference can mean fuzzy reception or, even more disturbing, being able to peer into other people's homes (and vice versa). "We've been able to see a neighbor's baby on our monitor," says Lyn Mettler, the mom of a 9-month-old, from Mt. Pleasant, S.C. The same thing happened to Robin Kelman, the mom of a 10-month-old, from Lafayette Hill, Pa., who also heard her neighbor's conversation "like it was occurring in the next room." The neighbor happened to have the same audio/video baby monitor on the same channel as Kelman's. That sort of situation can be a security risk or at the very least, an invasion of privacy.

Overall, baby monitors can be as temperamental as a 2-year-old. Interference is probably the biggest complaint parents have about monitors, but they also report problems with video monitor failure (the monitor shutting off for no apparent reason) and low visibility as well as shorter-than-expected reception range and poor battery life on parent units. Choose this product carefully and don't be afraid to return it if it doesn't deliver.

Shopping Secrets

Before buying an audio/video monitor, know thyself. Some parents are reassured by the constant surveillance of a baby's every whimper and movement and feel better knowing they can see their baby at all times with an audio/video baby monitor. Others find it nerve-racking and feel like they have to be hypervigilant. Decide which category you fall into before you go shopping. If you sense that an audio/video monitor will be overwhelming, go with just an audio monitor instead. Having a monitor should make life easier, not be a constant source of worry.

Consider digital if you have nearby neighbors with babies. If you want to be sure the images and sounds transmitted by your monitor are heard and seen only by you and not by neighbors who might have a similar model (or a cordless phone using the same frequency band), go with a digital monitor, not an analog one. Choosing digital will also ensure that the sounds and images you see and hear are coming from your baby and not the neighbor's. Analog monitors operate on a particular frequency band—typically 900 megahertz (MHz) or 2.4 gigahertz (GHz)—much like a radio, sending signals from monitor to receiver in a straight shot. Digital monitors also operate on specific frequency bands, but they encode the signal as it travels between the monitor and the receiver, making it nearly impossible for the sounds to be heard by others. Digital also reduces the possibility of running into interference from other electronic devices. Though they may look high-tech, many monitors are still analog. To find a digital monitor, look for "digital" somewhere on the packaging.

Factor in your phone and other wireless devices. To minimize the possibility of interference, select a monitor (either digital or analog) that operates on a different frequency band from other wireless products in your home. Besides baby monitors, many wireless products—including cordless phones, home networks, and Bluetooth devices—share the 2.4-GHz radio frequency bands. As a result, they're likely to interfere with each other. As we mentioned, interference can cause static on a baby monitor, a cordless phone, or wireless speakers; it can also disrupt a wireless computer network or the video on a home security system or baby monitor. If you buy a monitor and interference is a problem, try changing the channel. Most wireless products, baby monitors included, allow you to change their channels to solve interference problems, which is as easy as pushing a button. If that doesn't work, and you can't take the monitor back (more on that below), try keeping conflicting devices as far away from each other as possible; for example, keep your cordless phone and your baby monitor in different rooms.

Consider your home and lifestyle when deciding which brand/ model to buy. If you're considering an audio monitor, you may appreciate a monitor with both sound and lights, so you can "see" your baby's cries. The louder he cries, the more the monitor lights up. If you'll be taking business calls during naptime, for example, you can turn the sound down low and rely on the lights. A portable handheld or stationary video monitor can serve the same purpose, though we think an audio monitor with lights can suffice. Similarly, if you live in a large house, you may want a monitor with two receivers rather than just one. In general, look for monitors with features that make it easy to move about, such as a compact parent unit that clips onto your belt. Try it on before buying, if possible; antennas have been known to poke the wearer.

Learn the return policy. Before buying or registering for any wireless product such as a baby monitor, be sure the store or online vendor will let you return or exchange it, in case you can't get rid of interference or other problems. If you receive a monitor as a baby shower gift and know where it was purchased, try it before the retailer's return period ends. Return policies are often spelled out on store receipts, on a sign near the register, or on the merchant's Web site. You'll need to return the item before the retailer's return period runs out (usually 30 to 45 days from the date of purchase). But if the return clock has run out, don't feel defeated. Persistence and politeness will often get you into overtime. Keep the receipt and the original packaging. For more information on how to return baby products successfully, see Getting the Right Return on Baby Products, page 15.

Antenna alert: Don't get poked by your parent unit.

What's Available

Some brands of baby monitors, in alphabetical order, are: Agptek (*www.agptek.com*), BebeSounds (*www.bebesounds.com*), Fisher-Price (*www.fisher-price.com*), Graco (*www.gracobaby.com*), Learning Curve (*www.learningcurve.com*), Lorex (*www.lorexcctv.com*), Mobi Technologies (*www.getmobi.com*), Philips (*www.consumer.philips.com*), Safety 1st (*www.safety1st.com*), Sony (*www.sony.com*), Summer Infant (*www.summer infant.com*), and SVAT Electronics (*www.svat.com*). Prices range from $16.24 to $200 for audio monitors and $95 to $269.95 for audio/video monitors. The higher the price, the more features and frills you'll find, such as a high-definition handheld digital color monitor on the parent unit or a vibration feature so you can feel your baby's call. That said, a higher price doesn't always mean higher quality. Even the most sophisticated and pricey models can suffer from typical monitor maladies such as audio and video interference, fuzzy video reception, and parent units that inexplicably malfunction.

Features to Consider

Frequency band. The closer your monitor's frequency is to that of another device, such as a cordless phone, the more likely you'll hear static or cross talk. One manufacturer, Philips Avent, has addressed the interference issue by using the 1.9-GHz frequency band. The frequency, reserved exclusively for voice-only applications by the Federal Communications Commission, is called DECT technology, for Digitally Enhanced Cordless Telecommunications. The Philips Avent SCD520 Baby Monitor ($149.99) and the Philips Avent SCD510 Baby Monitor ($119.99), both audio monitors, use the 1.9GHz-frequency band. Overall, the 1.9GHz-frequency band is still less trafficked than the 2.4-GHz band and can improve your chances of privacy and no interference.

Multiple channels. Some monitors offer only two channels; others, such as the Private Connection monitors by Fisher-Price, offer a choice of 10 channels (the more the better). Multiple channels can be an advantage. If you're getting audio and/or video interference, you can change channels to try to get rid of it.

Some video models, such as the lightweight Graco imonitor, are flip-phone style; the camera also offers real-time digital zoom plus night vision.

Handheld audio/video parent unit. The latest digital and analog video baby monitors feature a color LCD video screen in the portable parent unit so you can watch your baby without being tethered to a video console. That's handy, but make sure the screen is large enough for you to see your baby; screen sizes on portable models range from 1.8 inches to 2.5 inches. An onscreen menu on the parent unit of some models allows you to zoom in on your little one and control screen brightness.

Night vision. Most audio/video monitors feature infrared light or "night vision," which allows you to see your baby on the monitor in the dark. Many also feature a night-light on the nursery unit that you can activate from the parent unit. That comes in handy if your baby stirs, for example, and just needs a little help finding her pacifier before going back to sleep.

Temperature sensor. Some monitors, such as the Philips Advent SCD520, feature an adjustable sensor that monitors the temperature in your baby's room for comfort. If it's too cold or too warm, the monitor alerts you to adjust the climate. The temperature in your baby's room should be between 68° F and 72° F.

Motion and sound sensor. Some audio/video monitors, such as the Lorex Portable Color LCD Digital Wireless Monitoring System ($269.95, *www.lorexcctv.com*), operate intuitively and filter out "normal" sounds and movements; your parent unit turns on only when your baby makes an unusual movement or sound, such as rolling over when he's waking up from a nap or crying. That not only extends battery life (although the receiver should be docked for overnight monitoring to keep the battery charged), it can allow you to have music or a sound machine in your baby's room without you having to listen to it on your parent unit, too.

Sound lights. With this common feature, an audio monitor's parent unit lights turn on when the baby makes a sound; the louder she cries, the brighter the lights get, or more commonly, more lights in a series come on. This is a valuable feature for an audio monitor. It's helpful in a noisy room, plus it lets you turn the volume down and still know when your baby is crying.

Out-of-range indicator. This common feature is a light or beep that lets you know you've reached the range limit of the monitor. Models that lack this feature may let you know you're out of range with static, but that's not as definitive as an out-of-range indicator. Indoor/outdoor ranges on portable video monitors may go up to 650 feet. Audio monitors may go up to 2,000 feet. The greater the range, the better, especially if you plan to take your monitor outside.

Low-battery indicator. Look for a monitor with a light or an icon on an LCD display that lets you know when the batteries in your parent unit are running low.

Extra parent unit. If you have two parent units, you can keep one receiver near your bed and carry the other around with you during the day, or both you and your partner can listen for your baby at the same time.

Expandability. Some monitors, such as the Lorex System, let you add up to four cameras, which can be helpful if you have more than one child to monitor or want the system to cover more areas in your house, such as the nursery and a play room. The Lorex monitor also automatically switches from camera to camera when there's sound or movement in any given room so you don't have to do it manually.

Connectivity. Some audio/video monitors connect to your VCR/DVD recorder or TV so you can watch your baby on the big screen. If you have picture-in-picture, you can watch TV and your baby, too. That's nice, but not necessary.

This video monitor, the Agptek 2.5" LCD Wireless Video Camera Color Baby Monitor, expands up to four cameras, which are disguised as baby-friendly flowers.

Recommendations

Short of DECT technology, which works only for audio, not video, there's no guarantee against interference with either digital or analog monitors, although digital monitors are less susceptible and more private. If you anticipate interference (expect it if you live in an apartment or condo, or otherwise densely populated area) buy a digital model that's not in the same frequency band as other wireless products in your home, and consider models with more than two channels. The Graco imonitor ($90) has two parent units; a similar version with one parent unit is available for $60. Or, if you have two little ones, for $129 you can get two monitors and two parent units. The Summer Infant Secure Sounds ($50) can be a good choice for privacy because the digital technology automatically selects a free and secure channel so you hear only your baby.

An audio/video monitor can help you detect nuances in your baby's movements—is he really up from his nap, or just stirring?—which can prevent you from going into his room and potentially sabotaging naptime. Some flip-phone-style parent units also vibrate when closed, so you can be alerted to your baby's cry and take a look at the video screen. You can also find audio/video monitors that use security-camera technology, but prices are high—$270 for one system we priced.

25

chapter

Nursing
Bras

If you decide to breast-feed, you won't necessarily need bottles, a bottle sterilizer, or formula. But you will need a nursing bra. It will be your key piece of equipment to get the job done quickly and easily.

Look for a nursing bra that's 100 percent cotton or a blend of cotton and Lycra. Want to go green? This soft-cup style by Leading Lady is made from certified organic cotton.

Nursing bras look like regular bras, but the cups open or lower from the front when you pull them aside, or unsnap, unwrap, unzip, or unhook the closure. You should be able to open the cup for nursing quickly and simply with one hand. (You'll be holding your hungry baby with the other. If you can close it one-handed, too, even better.) Most manufacturers have several nursing-bra lines, including models that are comfortable for sleeping or lounging; traditional, seamless "soft cup" and underwire styles; and super-supportive sports nursing bras that can take a pounding on the tennis court. Nursing bras that are built into nylon/Lycra tank tops and T-shirts are also an option; discreet nursing clips offer quick breast-feeding access. You'll also find padded and plus-size nursing bras.

Whichever style you choose, proper fit is the key to breast-feeding success, says Lynne Andrako, R.N., clinical education specialist for Medela, a breast pump and nursing-bra manufacturer. Andrako is also a certified bra fitter and lactation consultant. A poorly fitting bra not only will be uncomfortable but also may increase the risk of plugged ducts and/or mastitis, a breast infection. An ill-fitting bra can put pressure on milk ducts, which can make them vulnerable to infection-causing bacteria.

Andrako estimates that 80 percent of women buy the wrong-size nursing bra. Where do they go wrong? They increase the bra band size and stay with the same cup size. Most women can stay with their original band size—the rib cage expands a bit during pregnancy, but usually not enough to require a larger band size. Some women may want to go up a band size for comfort, which is fine as long as you have a bra with plenty of adjustment hooks in the back. Meanwhile, most women need a larger cup size during pregnancy. If you were a C cup pre-pregnancy, you may go up to an F, or higher; depending on the manufacturer, cup sizes can range from A through D, then DD, DDD, E, F, G, H, and I.

Shopping Secrets

Get fitted by a certified bra fitter. Yes, there's a certification program for bra fitting. When you're a nursing mother, a properly fitting bra is more important than ever. You'll want comfortable nursing bras that provide the right support—ones that don't bind, pinch, hike up in the back or front, or irritate breast tissue. Most women experience changes in breast size during pregnancy and lactation. For optimum size and fit, go bra shopping between four and six weeks before your delivery date.

Best for Breasts

Tempted to use your regular bra for nursing instead of a nursing bra? That's one cost-saving measure you won't want to take. Regular bras aren't designed for nursing and may not give you the extra support you need to be comfortable. Lifting your regular bra up over your breast to nurse can put a lot of pressure on breast tissue, increasing the risk of infection.

Your size may change throughout the rest of your pregnancy and again after you give birth and begin nursing.

You want some give or stretchiness in the cup to accommodate not only these changes in breast size but also normal changes during the course of the day once you begin to nurse. However, though the band should be comfortable, that part of the bra should be firm for proper support. The multiple hook positions will allow you to adjust it if you need to; multiple hooks are the key to comfort. Straps should also be firm—not stretchy—for additional support and stability.

Shop at a maternity store and ask the saleswoman if there's a certified bra fitter on staff. This service is usually free of charge. If a certified bra fitter isn't available, a lactation consultant, perhaps one affiliated with the hospital where you'll deliver, can usually help. Many lactation consultants are also certified bra fitters. The advantage to a bra fitter who is also a lactation consultant is that you can develop a relationship with that person and she can help you address any issues or questions right away. To find a lactation consultant in your area, visit the International Lactation Consultant Association (*www.ilca.org*).

When you're being fitted, you'll be measured under your arms. The tape will also be wrapped around your torso at the fullest point of the bust. The difference between the two measurements is your cup size. Once you get your official size, you can find a style you like and feel comfortable in. Don't be put off by the size the fitter recommends, which could be much different from what you normally wear. Keep an open mind and try it on before you decide whether it's right for you. Once you realize the difference in not only support

The Original Nursing Bra Plus Style by Bravado! stretches to accommodate several cup and band sizes, to support you comfortably throughout the day.

and comfort but also appearance (a properly fitting bra will make you look much better!), you won't be hung up on letters of the alphabet. You may not end up with the bra size you thought you'd wear, but the bra probably will fit well.

After you've settled on a brand and style of nursing bra and you're confident you've got the right size, buy online from the manufacturer or Web sites that sell it, or from a catalog, if you want to avoid a trip to the store. If you're buying a bra you haven't tried on, double-check the retailer's instructions for measuring since brands may be sized differently, and make sure you can return it in case it doesn't fit. Or play it safe by buying all your nursing bras at the maternity store where you were measured.

Buy three to five bras. That should be enough to meet your needs, allowing you to have a couple of bras on deck and one or two in the wash. Plan to buy a sleep/loungewear bra for the early days of nursing when you'll want to wear your nursing bra and pads 24/7 for leakage control.

Shop as early as four to six weeks pre-delivery, as we mentioned, but no earlier. Your breasts may enlarge even more during the end of pregnancy and after your milk comes in, so look for bras with cups that stretch. If you're still not comfortable, you may need to be fitted again.

If you're especially large-breasted, you may need to shop around. Bravado! Designs (*www.bravadodesigns.com*) makes a "Double Plus Style" bra for maximum support and coverage for heavier breasts. Motherwear (*www.motherwear.com*) also offers a plus-size line. If the bras available in your local maternity store aren't large enough, try a specialty lingerie or "foundation" store instead. These shops usually can meet your needs and even custom-make bras in your size, if necessary.

Think twice before buying an underwire nursing bra. The pressure from the underwire support may contribute to breast maladies, such as clogged milk ducts. If you feel you must have an underwire bra, it's vitally important for it be flexible and fit properly. You definitely want to have an underwire nursing bra fitted by a professional.

What's Available

Some of the major brands, in alphabetical order, are Anita (available at *www.breastchester.com*), Bella Materna (*www.bellamaterna.com*), Bravado! (*www.bravadodesigns.com*), Condessa Cassandra and Cassandra Veronica (*www.condessainc.com*), Elle Macpherson Intimates (available at retailers such as Nordstrom, *www.nordstrom.com*), Gilligan

& O'Malley (available at *www.target.com*), Japanese Weekend (*www.japaneseweekend.com*), La Leche League (*www.llliclothes.com*), Leading Lady (*www.leadinglady.com*), Maidenform (*www.maidenform.com*), Medela (*www.medelabreastfeedingus.com*), Motherhood (*www.motherhood.com*), Motherwear (*www.motherwear.com*), and Playtex (*www.playtexfits.com*). Major maternity retailers, such as Mimi Maternity (*www.mimimaternity.com*), have their own brand of nursing bras. Nursing bras range from about $7.99 (just the basics) to about $120 (designer Italian-fabric bras with decorative French lace). You can find deals online, so shop around, once you know the type and proper size of nursing bra you want.

Accessories

In addition to nursing bras, you'll need disposable or washable cotton pads that you can tuck inside to absorb any leakage. The disposable types are usually made of super-absorbent material that wicks moisture away from the skin, They're higher-tech than cotton nursing pads, but both types cost about the same. Both kinds prevent clothing stains and skin irritation and are invisible to the outside world, so it's just a matter of personal preference. You may also need special bra shells that can protect sore nipples from irritation or help draw out inverted nipples. You can find nursing pads and bra shells at drugstores, specialty maternity shops, and baby product stores, and at Web retailers such as *www.drugstore.com*.

Nursing covers like the Privacy Wrap by Learning Curve come in a variety of stylish patterns and colors.

For instant privacy, many women use a baby blanket to cover their baby when nursing in public. But a nursing cover-up can be

Are Nursing Clothes Necessary?

The Essential Nursing Bra Tank by Bravado! Designs is chic and supportive.

You can buy special nursing shirts and nightwear that have strategically placed slits and flaps that give you fast access to your nursing bra, making breast-feeding ultra-convenient. Although nursing clothes make breast-feeding easy, they're not essential.

In our baby products blog (*blogs.consumerreports.org/baby*), moms tells us that they've bought nursing tops they've never used, making do with large shirts and tank tops they can easily maneuver when the time comes.

A button-down-the-front blouse, stretchy T-shirt or sweater, and two-piece pajamas—in other words, your regular clothes—can work just as well. Regular clothes can be even more discreet, if that's important to you.

Because of their front flaps, which consist of two extra pieces of fabric, nursing shirts tend to advertise the fact that you're nursing, although no one, except other mothers, may notice. The newest generation of nursing wear—clingy tank tops and T-shirts—have a built-in nursing bra so you don't have to wear both a nursing bra and a nursing top. They're something to consider for a change of pace. Still, like traditional "nursing" shirts, they're an added expense, and their life span tends to be brief. Many moms, especially those who plan to breast-feed for a while, abandon the nursing duds in short order and breast-feed in whatever they throw on that day.

more secure because it doesn't slip off as easily. Cover-ups have a strap that's worn around the neck, which prevents them from shifting and babies from being able to yank it off. You'll find cover-ups in jazzy prints at *www.bebeaulait.com* for $34.99 each. They're also available at *www.buybuybaby.com*. Learning Curve (*www.learningcurve.com*) makes a basic black cover-up for $11.99 (also available at *www.buybuybaby.com*). Little Carr makes a "Cover-Me strap" ($12, *www.littlecarr.com*), which turns a baby blanket into a nursing cover.

Features to Consider

Support. In the world of nursing bras, support is queen. You'll need it now more than ever, just to feel comfortable. The best nursing bras open in the back but have flaps in the front for access. They also have strong side and undercup support and an extra wide back for a supportive fit that doesn't feel tight. Straps should be non-stretch but adjustable. Soft cup styles usually feature a "no-roll" band, which is a plus. If you're extra ample, you may be a candidate for bras with extra wide, padded shoulder straps and fuller cups. But be sure to try them on before you buy, to see if they're comfortable.

Closures. How you open and close the flaps on your nursing bra is important. The front flap on many nursing bras attaches at the top, near the shoulder strap. Other nursing-bra flaps open and close between the two cups. Some nursing bras don't have a flap at all; the cups just pull down for quick access. Go with whichever type is easier for you to use discreetly one-handed (without having to put your baby down). If you can close your bra one-handed, all the better. Squeeze or push-type latches are easy to operate one-handed, compared with snaps, which usually take two hands to close. Practice in the dressing room at the store.

Adjustability. Near the end of your pregnancy and in the early weeks of nursing, your breasts may enlarge, sometimes dramatically, and then they usually return to a smaller size once breast-feeding gets established. For greatest comfort, you'll want a nursing bra that "grows" with you and springs back again throughout the day—before and after feedings. So although the band and straps should be non-stretch for support, the cups should have some give. In addition, you'll want multiple hook positions on the band—four gives you plenty of versatility—so you can adjust the bra for comfort. After you've found your correct bra size, look for brands made with a blend of cotton and Lycra.

Color and style. Nursing bras once came only in white, beige (taupe), or black. Times are a-changin'. Though white is still the norm, you'll now find nursing bras in brown, teal, florals, and floral animal prints, some with lace and ribbon that fall into the lingerie category.

The Wrap 'N Snap by La Leche League comes in a pretty animal/floral print. The downside? It requires hand washing and line drying.

Recommendations

The best nursing bras are comfortable, absorbent, and don't bind the breasts in any way that could interfere with milk flow. For optimum support, both the band and the straps should be

The Hands Free Pump Bra by La Leche League works with most brands of double electric breast pumps.

Pumping bras are a new addition to the market that replace a nursing bra or are worn over the top of one. They allow you to pump "hands free" with almost any brand of double electric breast pump. The Hands Free Pump Bra by La Leche League (*www.llliclothes.com*), for example, is worn instead of a nursing bra. Once you put it on, unsnap the pumping panel from the bra cup and insert the pump's breast shield into the bra cups. You then attach the pump tubes and collection bottles to the pump shield and you're ready to pump.

Another style of pumping bra on the market, The Easy Expression Bustier ($34) or classic halter ($19.99, *www.easyexpressionproducts.com*), is designed to be worn over your nursing bra. The one-piece halter slips over your head; the bustier zips in the front. A pumping bra costs less than a stand-alone hands-free pump.

made of non-stretchy fabric. However, cups should have some stretch to accommodate changing breast size at different phases of nursing and throughout the day. The band should offer multiple hook positions. Look for bras that are 100 percent cotton or a blend of cotton and Lycra or other stretchy synthetic. Since the right size bra is so important to getting breast-feeding off to a good start and reducing the risk of complications, such as clogged milk ducts, shop at a maternity store or visit a lactation consultant/certified bra fitter for at least your first bra. To find a lactation consultant in your area, contact the hospital or birth center where you'll deliver, or visit the International Lactation Consultant Association at *www.ilca.org*. A professional fitting will ensure a comfortable fit and the correct size. Try on bras for size and feel, and practice with nursing pads in place. After you've bought one properly fitting bra, you can order more of the same style and size online or from a catalog. Many Web sites offer competitive deals. But do stick with the manufacturer and style you were fitted with, or be fitted again, if you'd like to try a different style or brand.

chapter 26

Pacifiers

Whether you call it a "binky," or "paci," a pacifier can help soothe and comfort your baby. And when your baby uses a pacifier at naptime and bedtime during her first year, it may also help reduce the risk of SIDS.

Some babies crave a pacifier while others just spit it out.

A pacifier, a latex or silicone nipple mounted on a wide plastic shield, can be a sanity saver, especially when your baby is fussy. "The sucking action will calm babies and can even help some of their jaw muscles develop properly," says Julie Barna, a doctor of dental medicine and spokeswoman for the Academy of General Dentistry. Pacifiers also may reduce the threat of sudden infant death syndrome (SIDS). In fact, the American Academy of Pediatrics (AAP) recommends that babies up to age 1 use pacifiers at bedtime and naptime because studies suggest that pacifiers cut that risk.

If you're worried that pacifiers can interfere with breast-feeding or damage teeth, consider this: AAP guidelines say there's little evidence that pacifiers harm teeth before age 1 or cause infants to lose interest in breast-feeding. However, the AAP recommends waiting until your breast-fed baby is 1 month old before introducing a pacifier, to ensure that breast-feeding is firmly established.

You can give your baby a pacifier at bed- or naptime during his first year or so, when the risk of SIDS is greatest. Using pacifiers at other times of the day probably doesn't harm your child, provided he stops by age 2, when the practice may cause protruding front teeth and an improper bite, and prevent the jaw from forming properly.

> **" Most pacifiers sold in the U.S. are orthodontically correct."**

For some parents, a pacifier is a godsend. For others, it's a waste of money because some babies, especially those who are breast-feeding, don't like pacifiers and will repeatedly spit them out, no matter which brand or type you try. Will your baby crave a pacifier or be satisfied with the breast or bottle? You'll know soon enough.

So Many Pacifiers, So Little Time

If you find yourself in the pacifier aisle, you'll see a large variety—from angled pacifiers with a wide tip, frequently called "orthodontic," to a basic, round-tipped pacifier, advertised as "most like mother." "Orthodontic means that your baby's top and bottom jaw are in a correct position when he's sucking on it," Barna says. That position doesn't interfere with normal jaw growth and development and, in fact, may promote it. According to Barna, most pacifiers sold in the U.S. are orthodontically correct, whether or not they're labeled "orthodontic." Pacifiers come in several sizes and are classified by age on the package, so it's easy to see which size to buy.

Thumbs Down on Thumb-Sucking

A pacifier is healthier for your baby than thumb-sucking. Why? As a baby sucks on her thumb, she pushes the top jaw forward and bottom jaw backward, which can cause jaw misalignment and malformation over time. And a baby's thumb can be dirty, which introduces bacteria into the mouth that could cause illness. It can also be a tough habit to break because a baby's thumb is always handy. You might want to discourage the habit by giving your child a pacifier whenever you catch her with her thumb in her mouth. Babies tend to thumb-suck when they're tired, which is another reason to have a pacifier ready at bedtime and naptime.

Shopping Secrets

Buy silicone pacifiers only. Babies can develop an allergy or sensitivity to latex.

Be sure the base has ventilation holes. In the highly unlikely event that a baby sucks her pacifier into her mouth, ventilation holes will admit air. Pacifiers are required to have at least two ventilation holes in the shield, but check just to be sure. The holes should be at least 0.2 (about $3/16$) inch wide.

Don't buy pacifiers with strings or anything else attached to it. Babies drop their pacifiers a lot, and clips that attach a pacifier to a baby's shirt are a convenient way to avoid that problem. But babies can find ways to get themselves into all kinds of trouble, so even a short pacifier cord (a.k.a. a pacifier keeper or holder) can be a strangulation hazard. To meet current Consumer Product Safety Commission (CPSC) safety standards, pacifiers can't be sold or distributed with any ribbon, string, cord, chain, twine, leather, yarn, or similar attachment. Also, a short cord can snag on a stroller or carrier, or on something a toddler is walking past or playing near, stopping the child short. We've heard stories of toddlers who get attached pacifier cords caught on end table corners and cabinet drawers, then fall forward and bang their heads on the edge of the table or cabinet. The injuries weren't serious, but could have been avoided. It's a hassle to have to constantly keep track of

We don't recommend using any kind of device to attach a pacifier to your child, even one as cute and innocent-looking as Winnie-the-Pooh.

How to Make Sure a Pacifier Is Safe

The Consumer Product Safety Improvement Act of 2008 requires third-party testing to insure that pacifiers meet federal safety standards. Pacifiers must also conform to limits on lead and phthalates. Any pacifier not in compliance may be recalled.

◆ To prevent choking on a nipple, handle, or small part that may detach from the pacifier guard, the Consumer Product Safety Commission requires that pacifiers be able to pass a "pull test." The pacifier must not come apart if the nipple is pulled away from the guard in any direction with a force of 10 pounds or 10 seconds.

◆ The nipple, along with the handle or ring, must pass this same test after the pacifier has been boiled and cooled six times, which simulates how parents sterilize pacifiers at home.

◆ To verify that the pacifier's shield won't suffocate a child, the CPSC requires that it pass a different pull test. With the pacifier placed in a test fixture, the nipple is pulled at a force of 2 pounds, which is held for 10 seconds. If the shield pulls completely through the test fixture, the pacifier fails.

◆ The pacifier shield must be large enough so that it can't easily enter an infant's mouth. In the highly unlikely event that a baby sucks her pacifier into her mouth, ventilation holes will admit air. Pacifiers are required to have at least two ventilation holes in the shield, at least 0.2 inch in diameter and no closer than 0.2 inch from the shield's outside edge.

◆ Pacifiers must be labeled with this warning: "Do Not Tie Pacifier Around Child's Neck As It Presents a Strangulation Danger." Take that warning seriously. The CPSC continues to receive reports of infants strangling on pacifier cords or ribbons tied around their necks. Never use a cord of any kind, as even short cords can snag on objects, such as crib posts or doorknobs.

◆ Parts cannot stick out more than 0.63 (about $9/16$) inch from the face of the shield on the side opposite the nipple. Pacifiers may not have sharp points or edges. As of August, 2009, paint may not contain more than 90 parts per million of lead, down from 600 parts per million.

◆ Three types of phthalates, a chemical in plastic that may affect development and the reproductive system, are banned from children's products such as pacifiers. Three other phthalates are prohibited pending further study and may eventually be banned.

your baby's pacifier. But cordless is the safest way to go and should definitely be considered.

Check for recalls. Log onto the CPSC Web site, *www.cpsc.gov*, to see if the pacifier or other baby items you plan to buy have been recalled. Even better, sign up for free e-mail notices of recalls at *www.cpsc.gov/cpsclist.aspx*. In the past, pacifiers have been recalled because the pacifier's shield was too small and could easily enter the mouth of an infant. In other cases, the pacifier's ventilation holes were smaller than required and not positioned to accept a tool to remove the pacifier should it get lodged in a child's mouth. Other pacifiers continue to be recalled because the nipple could easily detach or because the pacifier has small parts that can break off, posing a choking hazard. It's up to retailers to remove recalled products from store shelves, but products can fall through the cracks, so it pays to do your homework.

What's Available

Some brands of pacifiers include, in alphabetical order: Evenflo (*www .evenflo.com*), Gerber (*www.gerber.com*), Mam (*www.sassybaby.com*), Parent's Choice (Wal-Mart's store brand, not available online), Philips Avent (*www.avent.philips.com*), Playtex (*www.playtexbaby.com*), RaZbaby (*www.razbaby.com*), The First Years/Learning Curve (*www .learningcurve.com*), maker of the Soothie, popular among hospitals), and Unisar's AlwaysClean (*www.bebesounds .com*). Pacifiers range from $1.30 (basic one-piece GumDrop pacifiers) to $5.99 or so for a package of two. Novelty pacifiers, like those with personalized sayings such as "Momma's Boy," may cost $9.99 or more apiece.

Features to Consider

Handles. Some pacifiers have buttons on the back; others have rings. Babies don't care either way, though some parents do. Ring handles make pacifiers easier to retrieve from the bottom of a diaper bag and other locations where pacifiers land, but they can give your baby a "charging bull" appearance. Button-back pacifiers are easy for babies to grasp.

Snap-on caps. Some pacifiers, like the Avent brand, have a snap-on cap. It's one more thing to keep track of, but it can help keep your baby's pacifier clean when you're out and about and it's not in use. Don't let your baby play with the cap, though; it's a choking hazard.

Illumination. Some pacifier handles glow in the dark, which helps you and your baby find the pacifier in the crib in the middle of the night.

Carrying cases and clip-on ribbons. Short, clip-on ribbons that attach the pacifier to clothing and prevent it from ending up on the floor or the street are available separately. As noted in

The RaZbaby Keep-it-Kleen pacifier closes instantly when dropped.

Shopping Secrets, we don't recommend using any type of clip-on ribbons. To help you keep track of your baby's pacifier, consider a pacifier pod. Skip Hop (*www.skiphop.com*) and JJ Cole (*www.jjcoleusa.com*) are two leading makers of this trendy pacifier accessory, a small pacifier pouch that attaches to your stroller, diaper bag, or anywhere else you need to keep your baby's pacifier within arm's reach.

Self-closing models. Keep-it-Kleen (RaZbaby, $6.98 for 2) and AlwaysClean Pacifier (BébéSounds, $11.99 for a 4-pack) have built-in covers that automatically snap closed if the pacifier is dropped. That's a "neat" idea if your baby will take to it.

Avoid the glitz. Don't buy pacifiers that have been gussied up with anything that could fall off and become a choking hazard, such as faux crystals or beads.

Banning the Binky

Between your child's first and second birthday, it's a good idea to wean him off the pacifier. Cold turkey is one possible method. Out of sight, out of mind. A more gradual strategy is to begin allowing the pacifier only at certain times, such as bed- and naptime—and not during car rides or random moments during the day. Then, after a while, eliminate the pacifier at bed- and naptime, too. You'll save on dental bills later because prolonged use of a pacifier can change the shape of your baby's growing jaw and palate. The sucking action can narrow the jaw in the wrong places and widen it in others. If pacifier use continues into the preschool years, there's a strong possibility that your child will need orthodontic treatment, Barna says.

- **Chemical Caution**

Sippy-Cup Savvy

When your baby graduates to a sippy cup, look for bisphenol A (BPA)-free plastic, such as polyethylene, an opaque, less shiny plastic; it's sometimes marked with recycling code #1 and/or the abbreviation PETE. Other plastics not made with BPA are high-density polyethylene (2, HDPE), low-density polyethylene (4, LDPE), and polypropylene (5, PP). Studies suggest that an infant's exposure to BPA, a chemical used to make polycarbonate plastic, may be associated with possible health issues down the road, such as attention deficit hyperactivity disorder, obesity, and diabetes. Many baby-product manufacturers are taking BPA out of their products, including pacifier shields. Silicone and latex pacifier nipples don't contain BPA. For more on BPA, see the *Baby Bottles & Nipples* chapter, page 37.

There's another reason to ditch the pacifier even closer to the one-year mark. "When a child is sucking on a pacifier, the auditory tube in the middle ear actually opens, allowing bacteria that naturally reside in the mouth to pass through, which increases the chance of infection," Barna explains. If your toddler wants something to suck on, Barna recommends graduating to a water-filled sippy cup with a collapsible rubber straw, rather than the rounded, plastic-spout style. The suction action required with a straw helps promote normal facial muscle development and won't lead to ear infections. It also helps children learn to drink from a cup, because sucking through a straw and sipping from a cup use the same muscles. In general, using a sippy cup helps develop hand/eye coordination. But don't fill that spill-proof cup with juice, soda, iced tea, lemonade, energy or sports drinks, or even milk between meals. They create acids in the child's mouth that can foster tooth decay. Water is your best bet. It's safe to give toddlers small amounts of water after their first birthday. They can drink as needed without the risk of water intoxication, a condition in which an infant's developing kidneys can't excrete water fast enough to prevent diluting the blood's electrolyte balance.

Recommendations

If you decide to go the pacifier route, buy several in infant size, then buy more according to the manufacturer's age recommendations, as your baby gets older. Try different brands and nipple shapes until you find one your baby likes (you'll know), but don't force your baby to use a pacifier if she doesn't want to. Bright-colored pacifiers are easier to see inside a dark diaper bag, so the color can serve a purpose beyond making the pacifier your baby's first fashion accessory. Some brands of newborn bottle sets come with a pacifier or two, so you might start there. Don't worry about buying the same brand of pacifier as the bottle your baby is using. Pacifier and bottle nipples may resemble each other, but they're not always exactly the same.

We recommend silicone over latex pacifiers because some babies can develop an allergy or sensitivity to latex. Silicone eliminates that potential problem and also tends to hold up longer. Over time, pacifiers can crack, tear, and swell. They can also become grainy or sticky, losing their original smooth texture. Check them carefully and often, and if you discover these problems, throw them away. Pull on the bulb portion from time to time to make sure it's firmly attached. If it's not, toss it. Some manufacturers recommend replacing a pacifier every four weeks. Use a pacifier between meals when you sense your baby needs something but isn't hungry. Don't sweeten the deal by dipping a pacifier in juice or anything sugary. If you want to dunk it in something, use water. Giving a pacifier to a baby who wants food isn't a good idea, however. It can make a baby so distraught that he may have trouble calming down enough to eat.

Once you settle on a brand/type, buy several so you don't waste time scouring the house for that precious pacifier—or running to the 24-hour pharmacy in the middle of the night to get your baby's favorite brand and model. Keep two in the diaper bag—it's nice to have an extra in case you drop one or your baby spits it out onto the floor and you don't have access to soap and water. (If you're near a drinking fountain or a restroom, give your baby's pacifier a quick rinse-and-dry before giving it to her.) Disperse several in key locations—the baby's car seat, near the changing table, by the rocking chair—so you always know where they are. And on family trips, make sure your partner is armed with one, too.

Before you use a new pacifier, boil it for five minutes to remove any chemical residue. After that, wash your baby's pacifiers often with warm soapy water by hand and squeeze the bulb to remove excess water. Although silicone-nipple pacifiers are dishwasher-safe (top rack only), latex pacifiers are not and deteriorate faster when heated. So hand washing will help lengthen the life of your baby's pacifier. Frequent washing is particularly important for pacifiers used by babies younger than 6 months, whose immune systems are especially immature.

chapter

Play Yards

Play yards—updated versions of playpens—are for more than just playing. They can also provide babies with an enclosed place for napping and some can function as a portable changing table, saving you from having to run to the nursery for every diaper change.

Some play yards, such as this Disney Care Center from Safety 1st, are multifunctional, with a bassinet, changing area, and storage.

How necessary is a play yard? You can certainly live without one. But a play yard can fill a need you may not know you have until you start using it. Of course, a play yard gives your baby a place to play. Some play yards have extras to amuse your baby, including a mobile, a detachable toy bar, or an entertainment center that features music, nature sounds, and/or dancing lights, some activated by remote control. As a portable changing station, some play yards come with a changing table insert or an attached changing table that flips into position from the side and an organizer or built-in storage shelves for diapers and baby wipes. Although a full-sized crib is the safest place for your baby to doze, a play yard with a bassinet attachment can also double as a portable crib for home or travel for babies 15 pounds or less. The latest versions offer a night-light and a vibrating mattress pad (batteries not included).

This well-appointed Graco Suite Solutions Pack 'n Play offers everything from a bassinet with a vibrating mattress to calming nature sounds and a nightlight to a flip-away changing table and built-in storage shelves. Needless to say, it's at the top end of the price range.

Most play yards originally were designed for portability—to fit through a door, be moved from one room to another, or folded up to fit in the trunk of your car. Many are a standard rectangular size, usually 28x40 inches. But some of the latest versions are bigger, measuring nearly 30 inches wide, which is about the same as a standard-sized door, so scooting them from room to room in the set-up position may be a tight squeeze, if not impossible. Still, many manufacturers also make travel play yards that are designed to move. They roll on wheels and fold easily and compactly into their own tote that resembles a short golf bag for vacations, business trips, and jaunts to Grandma's. A typical play yard weighs around 24 pounds without the bassinet and changing station, and nearly 33 pounds with them. Travel play yards, though, tend to be smaller (around 23 inches wide) and lighter (around 20 pounds) because they're not loaded with extras.

Play yard frames are typically made of metal tubing. Mesh on three or all four sides provides ventilation and allows you to keep an eye on your baby. Most models have hinges and lock buttons in the center of the top rails. To set up a play yard, you'll need to pull the top rails up so they're locked, then push the floor down. To fold this design, you'll need to pull the floor up, and then raise the top rails slightly while pressing the release buttons to unlatch and collapse the top rails. When assembling your play yard, read the owner's manual carefully and keep it handy for future reference.

Shopping Secrets

Think about how you'll use your play yard. If it's going to function mostly as a playpen or you're on a tight budget, you can probably go with a basic model, such as the Cosco Funsport ($43.38 at Wal-Mart), which scored excellent in our Ratings (see page 282), and skip the extras. A pair of lockable wheels or swivel casters on one end will make it easier to move from room to room. If you'll use it for travel, you'll want a play yard that's lightweight, folds quickly and compactly, and has its own carrying case. You may even want to roll the packed unit. A carrying bag that allows the play yard's own wheels to roll when it's packed is ideal.

If you plan to have your newborn take naps in the play yard compare the bassinet options. Most play yards offer a full-sized bassinet, which runs the entire length and width of the play yard. Some feature a full-sized bassinet that rocks or locks in place. Other models have a canopy to help shield your baby from light while in the bassinet only, which can be helpful for nap- and bedtime.

Know when to fold 'em. Some manufacturers claim their play yards fold compactly and easily, which is especially important if you'll be traveling with the play yard and assembling/disassembling it often. See for yourself by practicing on the floor models in a store, if you can.

Select the play yard yourself. Play yards are popular shower gifts; if you're planning to include one on your registry list, select the model yourself and consider the features you'll need for your situation. If you'll be using the play yard as a changing station, for example, go with a model with a changing table and multiple storage compartments. Make sure they attach to the outside or are positioned so they're out of your baby's reach.

Be sure to check the floor pad. It should be one that the manufacturer supplied for the model. It should also be no more than 1 inch thick, snug-fitting, and firm enough to protect your baby from falling or rolling into the loose mesh pocket that can form between the edge of the floor panel and side of the play yard (a suffocation hazard). We judged safer models that have slots on the floor that allow the mattress's Velcro strips to be inserted and secured on the outside of the play yard, making it difficult for a baby or toddler to lift the mattress and possibly become trapped under it. Avoid models with a mattress that attaches to the bottom of a play yard only with Velcro pads that a child can access from the inside.

Think about "the look." Some play yards feature understated and neutral color combinations that could seemingly blend into the décor of any home. Others offer stylish contrasting colors that make the play yard a standout. Still others come in gender-specific color selections, such as pink polka dot with coordinating plaid. Your baby won't care what the play yard looks like, but you might, especially after a while, so decide which way you want to go: neutral, high-contrast, or with fabrics that signify "baby zone."

Check the production date and packaging. Buy the play yard with the most recent date. Make sure the model has a certification sticker from the Juvenile Products Manufacturers Association (JPMA) indicating that it meets current voluntary standards of ASTM International for play yards, The play yard standard addresses design problems of earlier models, such as inadequate locking devices or protrusions that can snag clothing and pose a strangulation hazard.

The Combi Jazz Sport is an example of a play yard with a contemporary look. It features stylish colors and fabrics and a sleek, contoured shape.

Don't buy used. For safety's sake, don't use a hand-me-down or garage-sale play yard. Older models may have a top-rail hinge that can collapse, forming a steep, V-shaped angle that puts children at risk of being trapped or strangled. They may also have changing-table restraint straps that can form a loop beneath the changing table, posing a strangulation hazard to a child in the play yard. In 2007, 425,000 Kolcraft play yards were recalled for that reason by the Consumer Product Safety Commission (CPSC). And in January 2009, the CPSC recalled 200,000 Fisher-Price Rainforest

Certification

Portable Play Yards manufactured by Simplicity Inc. and SFCA Inc., after reports of 1,350 injuries caused by side-rail collapse, including cuts, bruises, and broken bones. In the past, incidents of side-rail collapse have resulted in more serious injuries and some deaths. Even if you plan to buy new, protect yourself by signing up for e-mail recall notices at *www.cpsc.gov/cpsclist.aspx*.

What's Available

Some major brands, in alphabetical order, are Baby Trend (*www.babytrend.com*), Chicco (*www.chiccousa.com*), Combi (*www.combi-intl.com*), Cosco (*www.coscojuvenile.com*), Delta Enterprise Corporation. (*www.deltaenterprise.com*), Eddie Bauer (*http://eddiebauer.djgusa.com*), Evenflo (*www.evenflo.com*), Fisher-Price (*www.fisher-price.com*), Foundations (*www.foundations.com*), Graco (*www.gracobaby.com*), Kolcraft (*www.kolcraft.com*), Safety 1st (*www.safety1st.com*), Simplicity for Children (*www.simplicityforchildren.com*), and Summer Infant (*www.summerinfant.com*). Play yards range from about $43 for the most basic to about $250 for premium models.

Features to Consider

Removable bassinet. This gives newborns a place to nap. If you have older children or plan to use this play yard for your next baby, look for a bassinet that is secured to the play yard in a way that older children can't tamper with. Some of the units we tested had bassinets that attached to the play yard with easily disengaged bars or by bars and exposed plastic clips. Older siblings could easily outwit these fasteners, which could cause the bassinet to fall to the play yard floor. But one play yard we tested, Chicco Lullaby LX ($160), had bassinet clips that are covered by the bassinet's fabric flaps that button on the play yard, hiding the clips from view. It was judged safe. Look for a design that's

Play Yard Precautions

Although the voluntary standard for play yards has been regularly revised and tightened since requirements were added in 1997 for automatically locking top rails and in 1999 for latch strength, play yards were still responsible for an estimated 1,960 injuries to children each year, on average, from 2000 to 2006, according to CPSC data.

Play yards have also been associated with 47 infant deaths due to suffocation, strangulation, or entrapment, between 1999 and 2004 (the most recent CPSC statistics). Product failure was only one cause. Deaths and injuries also happened because of product misuse, including the use of soft bedding, incorrect assembly or altering the play yard in some way, ill-fitting mattresses, and cords or rope, such as window blind cords, near the playpen. Like a crib, using a play yard can be a matter of life and death because babies can get themselves into trouble even when they're sleeping. To keep your baby safe:

◆ Read and follow all safety precautions in the owner's manual (and on the play yard itself).

◆ Always follow the manufacturer's instructions for assembly, and double check that all latching features and hinges on the play yard are in place and secure. Before using a play yard, confirm that all top rails and the center floor are locked in position; the floor pad should also be in place. Never put your baby in a play yard with the sides down.

Keep your owner's manual for future reference.

◆ Don't put two or more babies in a play yard that's designed for only one.

◆ Stop using the bassinet feature when your baby either reaches the manufacturer's recommended weight limit or can sit up, pull up, roll over, or push up on hands and knees (at about 3 months and 15 pounds).

◆ Stop using the changing table insert when your child reaches the manufacturer's weight or height limit, which may be 15 to 25 pounds, 25 inches in height, or 4 months old, whichever comes first. It varies per manufacturer so check your owner's manual.

◆ Stop using the play yard once your baby has reached the maximum height and weight recommendations—usually 35 inches and 30 pounds.

◆ Choose a play yard with mesh holes smaller than one-quarter inch. Those that are JPMA certified will meet this standard.

◆ Inspect your play yard regularly and stop using it if the mesh sides or vinyl- or fabric-covered rails get torn or punctured, or any rivets on the rails begin to protrude. Don't use a play yard with broken hinges.

◆ Remove the bassinet and the changing station, or flip the changing station to the outside, when your baby is playing in the play yard. A baby's neck can get trapped between the side rail and the bassinet or changing station. The safety straps on the changing station insert can also be a strangulation hazard if they form a loop beneath the changing table, which is another reason to remove a changing table when your baby is in the playpen portion of a play yard.

◆ Don't move a play yard with your child in it.

◆ Don't tie any items across the top or corner of the play yard or hang toys from the sides with strings or cords. These can be a strangulation hazard.

◆ Don't add a second mattress, pillows, or comforters to the play yard or bassinet feature. When your baby is sleeping in the bassinet or play yard, remove all toys, too.

◆ You don't really need a sheet (mattresses can be cleaned) and the bassinet is probably safer without this extra piece of material, in which a baby could become entrapped. But if you do use one, make sure it is tight-fitting and specifically made for the bassinet insert you choose. Never use a sheet made for a crib mattress or twin or other size bed.

◆ If you use the bassinet, place your baby to sleep on her back, as you would in a full-sized crib.

◆ Never leave your baby unattended in a play yard, which means your baby should always be in view, even when he's sleeping in the bassinet or in the playpen area.

◆ When you're using a play yard's changing table, always keep a hand on your baby and use the safety harness.

◆ Don't place a play yard near stoves, fireplaces, campfires, or sources of heat and wind, or close to heavy furniture or a wall.

◆ Stop using a play yard, play yard changing table, or bassinet if they are damaged. Don't try to patch holes in the mesh with tape, for example. Don't use a changing table or bassinet with broken or missing attachment clips.

◆ Don't place a play yard near a window where your baby can reach cords from window blinds or curtains. They're a strangulation hazard.

◆ When your baby can pull to a standing position, remove large toys and other objects that can serve as a stepping stool for climbing out of the play yard. Remove mobiles and toy bars when your child can roll over or push up on hands and knees.

◆ If your child uses a play yard at a daycare facility or at someone else's home, be sure it's a recent model, preferably manufactured in 2008 or later. Also check its condition as your would any item your child might use.

easy to use. Stop using the bassinet when your baby reaches the manufacturer's recommended weight limit (typically 15 pounds) or can sit up, pull up, or roll over.

Canopy. Many play yards with bassinets have a canopy to shade your baby from harsh light. Some canopies have attached toys that act as a mobile. Remove the canopy when you are no longer using the bassinet.

Carrying case. Most cases are fabric bags that all the components of the play yard fit into. The four sections of the folded-up floor provide support for the bag by surrounding the unit's other components. A carrying case with a shoulder strap can make life easier. Two tested play yards, the Chicco Lullaby LX and the Kolcraft Jeep Trek Easy-Travel ($170), had the added convenience of rolling while folded.

Changing station. Most attach to the top of the top rail although some are suspended from the side and can be rotated down to hang at the side of the play yard. We think the side-suspension design is safer because parents are less likely to leave it in place. When using a changing table, always keep your hand on your baby and use the safety straps. Two units we tested, the Graco Silhouette Pack 'n Play ($170) and the Kolcraft Jeep Trek Easy-Travel, didn't have restraining straps. We think you should avoid such models. Remove the changing station or flip it out of the way once your baby is in the play yard itself to avoid potentially fatal entrapment between the station and the yard's top rail, and to avoid entrapment by any loop from the changing table restraint strap, although the loop should not be present in a play yard that meets the ASTM International standard.

Foldability. If you'll be traveling often with your baby, you'll want a play yard that folds and reassembles easily.

Storage. Some models provide storage for toys and other baby items in zippered side pockets, hook-on fabric storage pouches, and clip-on parent organizer bags. They should be big enough to actually hold something. Look for a model with storage compartments that attach or are built into the outside so they're out of your baby's reach.

Double the fun. The Graco Pack 'n Play Playard features cozy twin bassinets so two babies can nap side by side. The play space is meant for only one child, though. What will you do with your other baby at play time?

Toys, music, lights. Some play yards feature a mobile with suspended hanging toys or a detachable toy gym that can also be used with the bassinet mattress on the floor as a separate play mat for tummy time. These are a bonus, as are entertainment centers with music, soothing sounds, and lights. But all will contribute to the price. They usually require C or AA batteries (not included). Toys may not be necessary if you intend to use your play yard as just a portable nursery.

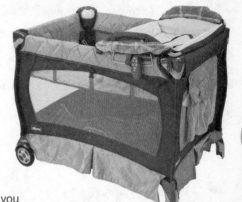

But if you use a play yard as a mobile activity center, toys and sound effects can be helpful.

Wheels or casters. A pair of lockable wheels or swivel casters on one end makes moving the play yard easier. Make sure the wheels lock. Some designs can be rolled when folded. That's a definite plus.

The Chicco Lullaby LX Playard features a remote control to activate music, vibration, and a nightlight; 4 AA batteries are required (not included).

Recommendations

Look for a new play yard that's certified by the JPMA, one that offers the best combination of useful features, such as an attachable bassinet where a newborn can nap, a diaper-changing station, and a parent organizer pouch. A pair of lockable wheels or swivel casters on one end will make it easier to move the play yard. Keep safety in mind. Be sure to check the floor pad: It should be no more than 1 inch thick and snug-fitting. Practice our Safety Strategies (pages 278-279). If you use a play yard for overnight sleeping, keep in mind that the bassinet mattress is thin for a reason: to prevent a child from becoming wedged between the pad and the sides. Never add extra mattresses or padding, and don't use blankets or other types of soft bedding, which pose a suffocation hazard. Keep stuffed toys out of a play yard, too, at nap- and bedtime. Like cribs, "bare is best" when a play yard is used for sleeping. Instead, layer your baby's clothing for warmth with a onesie or T-shirt and a footed sleeper or wearable sleeper sack. Stop using a play yard when your child attempts to climb out or when he reaches the height and weight limits (typically 35 inches and 30 pounds). Stop using the bassinet attachment when your baby reaches 3 months or 15 pounds or can sit up, pull up, or roll over. Do the same when your baby reaches the weight and height limits for the changing table component (check your owner's manual). Register your play yard online at the manufacturer's Web site or by completing and returning the product registration. That step helps ensure that you'll be notified in case of a recall, which isn't uncommon with this product category.

Ratings • Play Yards

	Excellent	Very good	Good	Fair	Poor
	⊖	⊖	○	⊖	●

Within types, in performance order.

Brand & model	Price	Weight (lb.)	Overall score 0 ··· 100 P | F | G |VG| E	Safety	Ease of use	Portability	Bassinet
PLAY YARD / BASSINET / CHANGING TABLE								
Chicco Lullaby LX	$160	23	86	⊖	⊖	⊖	⊖
Graco Silhouette Pack 'n Play 9B10CAD	170	19	64	○	⊖	⊖	⊖
Kolcraft Jeep Trek Easy-Travel Playard	170	25	53	⊖	○	⊖	⊖
PLAY YARD / BASSINET								
Graco Travel Lite Crib 9C01BET	80	16	69	⊖	⊖	⊖	⊖
Evenflo Baby Suite Classic Portable Playard	70	18	58	⊖	⊖	⊖	○
PLAY YARD								
Cosco Funsport Travel Play Yard	45	22	83	⊖	⊖	○	NA

Guide to the Ratings

Brand & model shows the models listed in order of overall performance based on safety tests and convenience judgments, by type. We tested models from the major manufacturers: a mix of simple play yards and others with accessories such as a bassinet, changing station, or electronic light/sound/vibration. **Price** is what we paid. **Overall score** is based on safety assessments, ease of use, and portability. **Safety** assessments mean that all six models tested met the requirements of the ASTM F406-08a Standard Consumer Safety Specification for Non-Full-Size Baby Cribs/Play Yards. The safety score shown consists of whether the model has a changing table strap, whether the bassinet is easy to dislodge—by an older sibling, for example—and whether the mattress is securely attached and cannot be easily dislodged from the bottom of the play yard by the child occupant. The **Ease of use** score is based on our judgment of ease of set-up and closure, and accessibility and ease of use of the latches. **Portability** is based on our judgment of how easy it is to pack and carry or transport the packed play yard. **Bassinet** is our safety assessment of the means of attaching the bassinet to the play yard.

28
chapter

Shopping-Cart Covers

$\mathcal{S}$ome parents may buy a shopping-cart cover in the hopes of shielding their baby from germy cart handles. However, cart covers don't really protect against germs. They will give your baby a cushy ride when you're shopping. So comfort is the main reason to buy a cart cover, if you decide to buy one at all.

A shopping-cart cover itself can be a germ carrier, so wash it after every use.

Shopping-cart covers—decorative fabric or disposable plastic covers that fit over the seat of a shopping cart—are designed to shield children 6 months to 3 years of age from illness-causing germs innocently transferred to the cart by other shoppers, or by children who've touched or gnawed the handle or sat in the seat with a leaky diaper. Cart covers have been around for a few years, but now, due to growing demand, they've come into the mainstream. Much of their appeal stems from the general protectiveness you feel as a parent. The last thing you want is for your baby to get sick; even a stuffy nose can make him miserable.

Fact is, shopping-cart handles are germ magnets, according to a recent University of Arizona study published in the International Journal of Environmental Health Research. But, it's not only cold or flu bugs you need to worry about. It's blood. "We suspect it may be coming from packages of raw meat that shoppers handle, and then they touch their shopping carts," says Kelly Reynolds, Ph.D., associate professor at the College of Public Health at the University of Arizona in Tucson, the lead author of the study. Blood from raw meat can carry salmonella, *E. coli*, or campylobacter, and may infect children who may gnaw on or touch the cart handle, then put their fingers in their mouths.

Still, as awful as that sounds, you don't have to consider a shopping-cart cover a must-have. In fact, using one may be more trouble than it's worth. Remember that the covers themselves can harbor harmful germs—from blood as well as mucus and feces—longer than a bare cart handle because the germs can get embedded in the fabric. That's why Reynolds recommends washing a shopping-cart cover in hot water and a bleach-based disinfectant and drying it completely after every time you use it.

Many supermarkets supply sanitizing wipes for cleaning the cart handle. If not, keep a supply in your diaper bag."

Another reason we put shopping-cart covers in the "optional" category: These days, many supermarkets supply sanitizing wipes for cleaning the cart handle and seat when you walk in, which can do a good job of reducing the germ load there. If wipes aren't provided, keep a small supply of disinfecting wipes in your purse or diaper bag. Even after wiping, keep your baby from gnawing on the handle by bringing her favorite teething toy.

Cleanliness aside, shopping-cart covers can make for a cozy ride. If that's important to you for your child, make it your primary reason for buying one.

Shopping Secrets

Key in on comfort. Since that's a major reason for buying a shopping-cart cover, look for a deluxe model, which usually has extra cushioning and maybe even an attachable pillow.

Think about where you'll use the cover. Shopping carts come in different sizes and shapes. If you decide you need one, be sure the one you buy suits the type of cart you'll use most often. Some brands specify right on the package which type of carts they fit. But if they don't, ask the salesperson for specifics: "Does this shopping-cart cover fit the double-seater cart at Costco?" (Some cart covers are made for the double-seaters found at warehouse clubs.) Keep your receipt and know the store's return policy just in case it doesn't fit.

Shopping-cart covers can make a bare cart cozy and cushy.

Look for a safety belt. An estimated 21,407 children under age 5 are treated in U.S. hospital emergency rooms for shopping-cart-related injuries each year, according to Consumer Product Safety Commission (CPSC) data. Falls from shopping carts are among the leading causes of head injuries to young children, according to the CPSC. Injuries result when children climb or fall out of shopping carts because the restraint system was not being used, children unbuckled or wiggled out of the restraint, or the restraint was missing. Falls from shopping carts most often occur when children stand up in the child seat or the cart basket.

Since the cart cover you buy probably will override the built-in safety belt on the shopping-cart seat, buy a cover that has its own durable safety belt as well as a belt to fasten the cover to the cart—ones that are easy to use, so you'll be more likely to strap your baby in every time.

Check for ease of use. Before you buy, find out how the cover attaches to the cart—with Velcro, a buckle, or elastic. Since inserting a cart cover while holding your baby will be a challenge, you'll want

Do Kids Need to Get Sick to Build Their Immune System?

Your baby does not have to become ill to develop a robust immune system. Preventive care is a much better option. "Routine vaccinations, including a yearly flu shot, will boost the immune system enough," says Philip M. Tierno, Jr., Ph.D., director of clinical microbiology and immunology at New York University Langone Medical Center in New York City and author of *The Secret Life of Germs*. Contact with germs themselves—from people, plants, or animals—will also boost immunity. Of the 60,000 germs we potentially run into, only about 2 percent are overtly pathogenic. Most are innocuous and act to stimulate the immune system without making us sick.

to be able to do it quickly with one hand. Read the instructions before you buy. Once you buy the cover, try it out at home so you'll know exactly what to do in the store. The cover also should be easy to store in your car.

Some cart covers like this one from Just Peachy Baby make a style statement.

What's Available

Shopping-cart covers run from basic to high-end, ranging in price from $15 (for a basic cart cover) to $90 for covers with stylish fabric, organic cotton, bacteria-, mold-, and mildew-resistant padding and other features. Some major brands are, in alphabetical order: Buggy Bagg (*www.buggybaggs.com*), Clean Shopper by Baby Ease (*www.cleanshopper.com*), Eddie Bauer (sold at *www.target.com* and *www.amazon.com*), Floppy Seat (*www.floppyseat.com*), Infantino (*www.infantino.com*), Itzy Ritzy (*www.itzyritzy.com*), Just Peachy Baby (*www.justpeachybaby.com*), and Leachco (*www.leachco.com*). You can also order custom-made cart covers online at *www.kozypalcartcovers.com* with extras like leg flaps, a cup holder, and a diaper pocket.

Avoid Cart Catastrophes

To prevent shopping-cart injuries from falls and tip-overs, the American Academy of Pediatrics (AAP) recommends that you avoid putting kids in shopping carts entirely by:

◆ Leaving your child home with another adult on your grocery shopping days.

◆ Having your child walk once he gets older.

◆ Having another adult come with you to watch your baby while you shop.

◆ Using a stroller, wagon, or soft carrier instead of a shopping cart.

◆ Shopping online for groceries so you don't have to trek to the store with your baby.

If food shopping with your children can't be avoided and you decide to use a shopping cart, the CPSC recommends that parents always use seat belts to restrain their child in the cart's seat. The AAP also issues these don'ts:

◆ Leave your child alone in the shopping cart.

◆ Let your child stand up in a shopping cart.

◆ Place an infant carrier on top of the shopping cart.

◆ Let your child ride in the cart basket.

◆ Let your child ride or climb on the sides or front of the cart.

◆ Let older children push the cart when there's another child in it.

Features to Consider

Versatility. Some cart covers have attached plush toys; pockets for storing sippy cups, your cell phone, keys, and coupons; and loops for attaching toys and teethers. Some convert to a play mat or diaper bag, or can be used on high chairs, park swings, public strollers, or even as an emergency changing pad. You can pay more for these extras, so consider how much you'll use them before you buy.

Fabric. Patterns run the gamut from toile, plaid, and paisley to animal prints, florals, and popular cartoon character motifs. Machine-washable materials are standard, though some fabrics can only be wiped clean. Some covers offer extra-long leg flaps to prevent pinching.

Safety belts. You'll find two basic safety belt/strap options: One is a cover that features one detachable strap that threads through the back of the seat to secure the baby to the cart; and, the safer option, a cover that features two straps, one to secure your baby to the cart and one to secure the cover to the cart.

Padding. Higher-end covers have plush, thick batting for a luxurious ride. Lower-end models have quilted cotton fabric without batting.

Pillow. Covers at the high end have a pillow at the handlebar so a baby can rest her head.

Bag/tote. When not in use, some cart covers fold into a duffel-shape diaper bag with one large compartment for diapers, wipes, toys, and snacks. Others roll up and become their own carrying bag. Some have a separate vinyl carrying case. Shopping-cart covers are just one more thing to carry, so choose a cover that has the portable system you think you'll use most often.

The Buggy Bagg cart cover folds to become its own carrying case.

Germ Defense

Besides shopping-cart handles, bad bugs are everywhere. Here's the dirt on some of the sneakiest places nasty germs commonly lurk and what you can reasonably do to guard against them.

BUG MAGNET: The playground. It's more germ-infested than a public restroom, according to the University of Arizona study. Why? "Restrooms tend to get disinfected and cleaned often," says Kelly Reynolds, the university's public health professor. Playground equipment doesn't, which means harmful germs—mostly from mucus that gets on equipment after kids wipe their noses with their hands—accumulate. Because dirt can protect these bad bugs from drying out and dying, they can survive on equipment for up to three days.

Germ Defense: There's no way you can keep up with all the germs that get spread when kids play. But eventually, you can teach your child to *not* touch his mouth, nose, or eyes when he's outside so the germs he picks up can't gain entry. While hand washing is best, if there are no facilities, bring alcohol-based hand sanitizer gel and have your child use it when you both leave. For the greatest germ kill, make sure your child rubs his hands together with gel for a full 20 seconds—to the tune of "Happy Birthday" twice. It takes that long to dislodge stubborn germs.

BUG MAGNET: Your pediatrician's waiting room. Don't be fooled by the antiseptic smell. With all the runny-nosed, coughing, sneezing little patients who visit the doctor, especially during cold and flu season, you can bet your pediatrician's waiting room is a virtual petri dish.

Germ Defense: Wash your baby's hands with soap and water or hand sanitizer before visiting the doctor so she'll be less likely to pass something along to other kids. Even if she's well, she could be harboring an infection but not yet showing symptoms. Use the well-child waiting room if she's just coming in for a checkup. There's bound to be less germ load there than in the waiting room for ill kids.

If your child is ill, bring along toys to keep him occupied in the waiting room instead of playing with the toys provided. "Your own toys will be infected with germs from your house, but at least they won't be infected with someone else's germs, which could expose your child to a different illness," says Andrew Nowalk, M.D., Ph.D., an assistant professor of pediatric infectious diseases at the University of Pittsburgh School of Medicine.

BUG MAGNET: Petting zoos. They've been responsible for major outbreaks of *E. coli*. The microbes invade when traces of animal feces from a pet's fur or saliva get on your child's hands and then into her mouth.

Germ Defense: Don't bring a child younger than 3 to a petting zoo. Children this young "are more likely to suck their thumb or automatically put their hands in their mouths, no matter how much you warn them not to," says Nowalk.

BUG MAGNET: Bathroom towels. Fecal bacteria from your child's hands and body after a bath or shower or going to the bathroom, as well as mold, can grow on towels. In addition, rotavirus, hepatitis A, and bacteria that cause staph skin infections won't grow but can remain for days on towels. These germs are tough. "Given the right conditions, they can survive your laundry's wash and dry cycle," says Reynolds.

Germ defense: Wash your towels in hot water and disinfect them with diluted bleach during the wash cycle; follow the manufacturer's instructions so your towels don't discolor. Then dry them in the hottest cycle of your dryer until there's no hint of dampness. Replace any towels that smell mildewy. That's a sign they're incubating mold and bacteria, Reynolds says.

BUG MAGNET: Pet fur and paws. An affectionate lick from your family dog on healthy skin isn't likely to make your child sick. Dogs have cleaner mouths than many other animals and their lack of exposure to agricultural situations where other animals might acquire *E. coli* means they are generally harmless, Dr. Nowalk says. But pets can track germs from feces into the house on their fur and paws.

Are Hand Sanitizers Poisonous?

Reports of people who've intentionally ingested hand sanitizer (for its alcohol content) have surfaced on the Internet, scaring parents unnecessarily into thinking that hand sanitizer is poisonous.

But with normal use, "Hand sanitizers are safe for children and their benefits far outweigh any very small risks," says Erica L. Liebelt, M.D., FACMT, professor of pediatrics and emergency medicine and director of toxicology services at the University of Alabama at Birmingham and Children's Hospital and a spokesperson for the American Association of Poison Control Centers (AAPCC), in Alexandria, Va. Hand sanitizer is a valuable defense against the spread of colds and flu, and is responsible for significantly reducing the spread of infections in hospitals. Its germ-fighting ingredient, ethanol, kills germs on contact and no significant amount gets absorbed into the skin. It's a convenient and safe alternative to soap and water, she says. Nonetheless, alcohol-based hand sanitizer, like any household cleaner or medication, should be used according to label directions. Here's how to keep your kids safe when you've got hand sanitizer around:

◆ Always supervise your children when using hand sanitizer. If your child pumps it into her mouth, call the AAPCC's Poison Help Hotline: (800) 222-1222. You'll probably be told to wash your child's mouth out and watch for specific signs or symptoms, Dr. Liebelt says.

◆ Keep large refill packs of hand sanitizer in a locked cabinet, just as you would other household cleaners and medication.

◆ Don't transfer hand sanitizer to unmarked or more familiar containers, such as an empty Cool Whip tub. That can tempt a curious toddler to eat it.

Germ Defense: Make sure your child washes his hands properly after contact with pets, especially before eating. Disinfect your home's entryway, especially if you have an indoor/outdoor pet. "That's where most pet germs in the home get deposited," says Reynolds, adding that germs come in on shoes as well.

Recommendations

Since comfort should be your primary reason for buying a shopping-cart cover, go with one that has ample padding and provides good cart coverage (no exposed metal or plastic) for your baby. Buy a cover with a dual safety-belt system, and use both belts every time you shop. To prevent germ spread, wash your shopping-cart cover after every time you use it. If you don't think you can make that commitment, skip buying a cover and use the sanitizing wipes a store provides or bring your own to wipe the shopping-cart handle before placing your child into the cart.

chapter 29

Soft
Infant
Carriers

Babies love and need to be held, and carriers can be a great, hands-free way to keep your baby close and cozy, whether you're on the go or doing odd jobs around the house. But be careful if you're considering a sling because that style of carrier can be risky.

We consider strap-on carriers like the BabyBjörn pictured here to be safer than a sling.

With a soft infant carrier, you wear your baby (in a sense), which may make him feel secure and ease any fussiness. Some carriers even allow you to position your baby to discreetly breastfeed. If you like using a carrier (and your baby likes it, too—and that's important), you may even be able to postpone buying a stroller for a few months, until your baby can sit up. (Of course, you'll still need an infant car seat any time your baby rides in a car.)

The Scootababy, for babies from 5 months to 40 pounds, can be adjusted so that you can carry your baby on either hip.

There are three major types of soft infant carriers. A front strap-on model holds a baby in an upright position; an infant faces in and an older baby faces out or in. The carrier consists of a padded fabric pouch with leg holes attached to an adult shoulder and waist belt, which supports the baby.

A sling—also called a wrap—is your second option, although we don't think it is a good one due to safety concerns (See Sling Savvy, page 294.) It consists of a length of fabric you wear over one shoulder and around your waist. With a marsupial feel to it, a sling forms a comfy, portable nest for an infant, but babies should not be completely enclosed in a carrier. In the beginning, you'll wear your baby in front. As your baby gets bigger and can hold her head up—at around the 6-month mark—the sling and your baby can shift to your hip, with your baby sitting up.

Hip carriers such as the PortaMEe (*www.portamee.com*), and Scootababy (*www.scootababy.com*) are your third option. They're a cross between slings and strap-on carriers because they've got adjustable straps and they're designed to be worn on your hip. With a hip carrier, your baby faces toward you, just like you'd naturally carry a baby sans carrier, only it's easier because your arms don't have to do the work. Some front infant carriers can be worn on the hip as well.

Most soft infant carriers specify a minimum and maximum weight limit, which we discuss in the following pages. You'll probably find your baby will be too heavy to carry comfortably before he reaches the upper limit. "Slings and other soft infant carriers can pull your body weight forward, which isn't a natural carrying position," says Anne Coffman, a physical therapist from New Berlin, Wis., a member of the American

Physical Therapy Association, and mother of two. By the time your baby can sit up, or around the 20-pound mark, you may want to graduate to a backpack carrier, which provides more structural support than a strap-on carrier or sling. Carrying a load on your back puts less stress on your body. "Make the change before it gets uncomfortable," says Coffman. "If you wait too long, you're asking for muscle strain."

There are pluses and minuses to every type of soft infant carrier, which we'll discuss throughout this chapter. For information on backpacks, see the Backpack Carriers chapter, page 61.

Strap-On and Hip Carrier Strategies

Strap-on carriers are designed for babies weighing 7 or 8 pounds to 25 to 32 pounds, depending on the brand. The Kelty Kids Wallaby and Kangaroo strap-on carriers ($59.95 and $79.95, respectively, *www.keltykids .com*), can be used from infancy (minimum is about 8 pounds) in the inward-facing position, then outward facing for children with full head control up to 25 pounds. Weego, makes the Weego Baby Carrier (*www .weego.com*) that can be used for full-term babies who weigh as little as 6 pounds, and the Weego Preemie, for babies who weigh as little as 3½ pounds. Expecting twins? The same company also makes a strap-on carrier for two; both babies are carried together on your front, which sounds ambitious, but perhaps no more than navigating the supermarket or the mall with a double pram or stroller. Weego says the carrier can be used until the twins are about 5 or 6 months old, but they may get too heavy for you before then.

Hip carriers, unless they have a headrest, are generally designed for babies who can hold their head up unassisted and weigh at least 15 pounds or are at least 4 to 5 months old. Their upper weight limit tends to be higher than front strap-on carriers—35 to 40 pounds—depending on the brand, but to avoid back and neck strain, you should probably stop using one before then, if your baby will let you. (Hitching a ride on mom's hip can be a tough habit to break.) Hip carriers have been subject to recalls because the shoulder strap could detach from the hammock, posing a fall hazard to a baby. It's always a good idea to make sure all

The Weego Twin is designed for twins who weigh in at 3 pounds each or more.

strap supports are secure before putting your baby in any carrier. Front strap-on models with leg openings big enough for a child to slip through have also been recalled. Some models now come with a seat insert for newborns to guard against that. Other models have straps or other ways to narrow the openings so they fit snugly around the legs. In any event, adjust leg openings to the smallest size that is comfortable for your child.

Some soft infant carriers, like the Evenflo Snugli By My Side Soft Carrier, offer three carrying positions: front face in or face out, and hip.

Pros: With a front strap-on or hip carrier, you'll fit better in cramped elevators and other places where strollers can't go. And in some instances, it can also be safer. In supermarkets, for example, wearing your baby in a strap-on or hip carrier and pushing the cart is preferable to placing your baby's car seat carrier on top of a supermarket shopping cart, which we don't recommend. And because strap-on and hip carriers offer supportive infrastructure and your baby sits upright, we think they're safer than slings, which we discuss in the next section.

Cons: Some infants don't like being "worn" in the upright position (and if they get upset, they're literally in your face about it). Some dislike any carrier that feels too confining around the head, which is necessary in the beginning months with front strap-on carriers and hip carriers with attachable head supports. Also, if your baby falls asleep in a front strap-on carrier, you can feel stuck. Since your baby must exit from the top of the carrier, it can be tough to get her out of the carrier and put her down for a nap without waking her. Some front carrier manufacturers have addressed that problem by modifying their design to include a side exit feature, which is handy.

Sling Savvy

Made of fabric (sometimes pleated or padded), a sling forms an over-the-shoulder hammock for holding a young baby across your front in a semi-reclined position, as you'd naturally carry your baby and, like a front or hip strap-on carrier, frees your arms. Many makers claim that their slings can be adjusted to tote a toddler up to 35 pounds. You can transport your child lying down or upright, facing in or out. Some slings can also be worn with your baby on your back or hip.

Strap-On and Hip Carrier Cautions

When using a strap-on or hip carrier, follow these safety tips:

◆ Read the instruction manual and the warnings on the product before you first wear it to make sure you're using it properly.

◆ Before using a carrier at any time, take your time putting it on. Check that the straps are fitted and adjusted correctly, and the buckles, snaps, straps, and adjustments are safely fastened into position and secure.

◆ Sit down when placing your baby in the carrier and when taking him out.

◆ After your child is seated in a carrier, with her legs securely in the leg openings, adjust leg openings to the smallest size possible without cutting into her thighs or seat.

◆ Make sure your baby can breathe easily when in the carrier. His nose and mouth shouldn't be obstructed in any way, and his chin should not be pressed against his chest, which carries a risk of asphyxiation.

◆ Don't transport your child in a carrier on your back unless it's made to be worn that way. Note that infants who can't hold their heads up should never be carried on an adult's back under any circumstances.

Until your baby can hold his head up on his own, he should ride in a strap-on carrier facing toward you.

◆ Use the carrier according to the manufacturer's weight recommendations. To avoid back and neck strain, stop using a front carrier when your baby reaches 20 pounds, or anytime you feel uncomfortable.

◆ Until your child can hold her head upright (around 6 months old), she should ride facing toward you with head support.

◆ Be careful when bending, leaning forward, or going through doorways when wearing a carrier. If you have to reach down, bend at your knees to make sure your baby stays upright. Don't bend over at your waist.

◆ Use a carrier only for standing or walking. Don't use it for sporting activities like running or bicycling or when cooking, cleaning, carrying a load, or driving.

◆ Don't use a carrier to hold your baby in a car instead of a car seat.

◆ Don't put a carrier on or take it off with your baby in it.

◆ Don't put your baby in a carrier that's not attached to you or another caregiver.

◆ Stop using a carrier if any parts or components are damaged, missing, or broken.

Get His and Hers Carriers

Pros: Like a front or hip carrier, a sling allows you to get around easily in spaces where a stroller can't go, such as an escalator at a shopping mall or a grassy park. Many manufacturers also claim that wearing your baby can enhance baby bonding.

Cons: Just as some babies don't like being carried upright in a front or hip carrier, others don't feel comfortable being carried in a sling in a reclining position. Also, carrying your baby's weight diagonally in front may be uncomfortable, especially if you're petite and your baby is large.

More important, baby slings raise safety concerns. Over the past 10 years, there have been at least 22 reports of serious injury associated with the use of sling-type carriers. They include skull fractures, head injuries, and contusions and abrasions; most occurred when the child fell out of the sling. Moreover, a number of recalls of sling carriers in recent years has prompted ASTM International, a voluntary standards-setting organization, to start a standards development process for sling carriers. (Currently, there is no standard.) Concerns raised by manufacturers, who requested the review, included not only the fractures and bruises but also the risk of smothering. The Consumer Product Safety Commission (CPSC) has documented a risk of death caused from "positional asphyxia," particularly in infants three months or younger. There are two scenarios: When the infant assumes a position with the head bent forward, chin touching the upper chest, and the body forming a C-shape, and/or when the infant is completely contained by the carrier, with head turned so his face is pressed against the caregiver's body. Both can cause airway blockage and suffocation.

The man sling by z'fina is designed especially for dads who want to get in on the action.

Like strap-on carriers, slings have been recalled. About 1,200 Ellaroo Ring Sling baby carriers, sold from June 2007 through February 2008, were recalled in 2008 because the aluminum rings on the sling carrier could bend or break, allowing the fabric to slip through the rings, creating a fall hazard for infants. In 2007, about 100,000 Infantino SlingRider infant carriers, sold from July 2006 through February 2007, were recalled because of a similar malfunction in a plastic slider. Don't buy or accept as a gift any secondhand carrier or sling because defective ones could still be in circulation.

Some slings can be simple to put on and wear. Others resemble a fabric version of origami, which leads us to believe that some of the incidents with sling carriers are likely due to improper wearing or assembly, or failure of rings or other hardware. It's uncertain how an ASTM International standard can help make these products safer or error proof. For now, we think there are better ways to transport infants, including strollers, hand-held infant carrier/car seats, and strap-on carriers. If you insist on using a sling, follow our Safety Strategies for slings on page 299.

Getting the Hang of It

You may feel a little awkward the first few times you use any type of infant carrier. You have to figure out how to put it on or wrap it around yourself and your baby (if you're using a sling). You have to adjust the straps or fabric so the carrier will fit your body comfortably. In our tests, we've found that some slings, such as The Ultimate Baby Wrap by Parents of Invention, have a steep learning curve to put on and use. For maximum comfort with a sling, a baby should ride above your waist and below your bust line.

Make fit adjustments before putting your baby in the carrier or sling. Mastering the adjustment of rings and folds so everything fits correctly takes time, even with clear, printed directions. But getting it right and frequently checking the hardware (again without your baby in the sling) is critical to keeping your baby safe. If your back or neck hurts from carrying most of a baby's weight on one side, give that shoulder a break and put the sling on with the strap on the other shoulder.

It's a wrap! Some slings can be complicated, which can put your baby at risk if you don't take the time to learn how to wear it correctly. In general, we don't think slings are the safest way to carry the youngest babies.

Last—and this is the fun part—you have to get your baby inside the carrier without provoking a fuss, then learn to trust the carrier and get used to the initially uneasy feeling of having your baby suspended. Our advice is to read the directions carefully, then practice. Some manufacturers recommend that you rehearse with a teddy bear or doll until all steps become natural. That's not a bad idea.

Learning how to move with a sling, front, or hip carrier can take practice. You can't lean over too much, and your back, shoulders, and legs must adjust to the added weight. You'll also have to be mindful of your extra dimensions when you go through doorways and around corners so your baby won't bump into anything. With slings and front carriers, since your baby is carried in front of you in the beginning, tripping—even over something minor like a crack in the sidewalk—is a major issue since you can't see your feet. Although many carriers are designed to adjust and "grow" with your baby, some parents complain of lower back pain with carriers once their baby reaches about 20 pounds. A simple rule is to stop using any type of soft infant carrier when you sense you're approaching your own physical limits. You'll know.

Shopping Secrets

Decide if you're the type who'll use a soft carrier. If you're not sure, wait until after your baby is born before you buy one. Better yet, borrow one first. Try on a friend's carrier to see if it is comfortable for you and how your baby fares in one. If your baby constantly wants to be held, a soft infant carrier may be just the ticket for relieving your tired arms.

By the same token, don't buy one secondhand. Since strap-on carriers and slings have been subject to recalls, buy new to ensure that you're carrying your baby safely. To play it even safer, make sure any new carrier you're considering hasn't been subject to a recall. For the latest recall information, check the CPSC Web site at *www.cpsc.gov* or sign up for free e-mail notices of future recalls at *www.cpsc.gov/cpsclist.aspx*. As an added precaution, send in the registration card for the soft infant carrier you select so you will be alerted to any recalls.

Try on the floor model with your baby, if possible. But take another adult along to help, especially if you're not familiar with soft infant carriers. We've discovered in testing that not all carriers and slings fit all builds. Doing a test run in the store will give you a quick take on sizing and the features each carrier or sling offers.

■ **Safety Strategy**

Sling Carrier Cautions

If you insist on using a sling, take these necessary steps to keep your baby safe:

◆ Don't wing it. Read the instructions (most sling manufacturers have detailed how-to instructions on their Web site) and watch the video demonstration, too, if it's available, so you have a clear understanding of the product and how to wear it before transporting your precious cargo.

◆ When trying a sling on for the first time, recruit an assistant or practice in front of a mirror with a doll or stuffed animal. Try putting your baby in for the first time when you're both fed and well rested (or as well rested as you can be considering your new-baby circumstances). Sit down to do it and don't stand until you feel your baby is secure.

◆ Avoid carrying your baby lying down or completely contained by the carrier; his chin can press against his chest, blocking his airway. His face should be free, not pressed against your body.

We don't recommend slings, but if you insist on using one, avoid carrying your baby lying down or completely within the carrier (left). Your baby's head should be free, her face and nose not pressed against your body (right).

To reduce the risks, why not wait a few months until your baby can hold his head up and be carried in an upright position? The "front" (tummy to tummy) or "hip" carry positions are safer.

◆ Don't wear your baby in a sling in a moving vehicle. Your baby should be in a safety-approved car seat any time he's in a car.

◆ Don't wear your baby while cooking or near open flames. The fabric may not be flame resistant, plus your baby could burn or hurt herself by reaching for something sharp or hot, and any splashes or splatters would probably hit her first.

◆ Squat instead of bending over when your baby is in a sling so your baby doesn't fall out.

◆ If wearing a sling hurts your back, try shifting your baby to your other hip, or stop wearing it and use a stroller instead.

Consider a framed (backpack) carrier. This is an option when your baby can sit up unassisted and has full head and neck control (about 6 months) These carriers are basically backpacks with a fabric baby seat and structured frame. Usual weight limits are about 40 pounds, which would accommodate a typical 3-year-old plus assorted gear.

The Jeep 2-in-1 baby carrier by Kolcraft has a locked-latch indicator and reflective trim.

Know you can return it. Some babies need time to adjust to an infant carrier; others never come around. Your baby's verdict is unpredictable, so keep your receipt and the packaging the carrier came in, and know the retailer's return policy. If you or your baby dislike the carrier or sling you select, take it back.

What's Available

Some brands of front and hip carriers are, in alphabetical order: BabyBjörn (*www.babybjorn.com*), Belle (*www.bellebabycarriers.com*), Chicco (*www.chiccousa.com*), Evenflo Snugli (*www.evenflo.com*), Fisher-Price (*www.fisher-price.com*), Infantino (*www.infantino.com*), Kelty Kids (*www.keltykids.com*), Kolcraft Jeep carriers (*www.kolcraft.com*), Lascal M1 Carrier (*www.regallager.com*), Maclaren (*www.maclarenbaby.com*), Munchkin (*www.munchkin.com*), PortaMEe (*www.portamee.com*), Scootababy (*www.scootababy.com*), and Weego (*www.weego.com*). Prices range from $18.96 for a very basic carrier to $130 for carriers with enhanced shoulder and back support.

Some brands of slings are, in alphabetical order: Baby K'Tan (*www.babyktan.com*), Balboa Baby (*www.balboababy.com*), Blue Celery (*www.bluecelery.com*), Ellaroo.com (*www.ellaroo.com*), Hotslings (*www.hotslings.com*), Infantino (*www.infantino.com*), Maya Wrap (*www.mayawrap.com*), Moby Wrap (*www.mobywrap.com*), Munchkin (*www.munchkin.com*), My Baby Nest (*www.mybabynest.com*), NoJo (*www.nojo.com*), Parents of Invention (*www.parentsofinvention.com*), z'fina (*www.zfina.com*), and ZoloWear (*www.zolowear.com*). Prices range from $30 to $540 for slings in luxury and designer fabrics.

Features to Consider

Fabric. Slings, strap-on, and hip carriers are typically made of 100 percent cotton, a cotton/Spandex blend, nylon, or moisture-resistant polyester microfiber, and come in fashionable colors and patterns. At the highest end, you'll find slings made from fashion-forward brocade, Japanese prints, silk, and French jacquard. Organic cotton and hemp are also trends. Carriers designed to be used in water may be made of neoprene wetsuit material, which may irritate a baby's delicate skin. Slings and strap-on carriers should be completely washable.

Fasteners. Carriers have a variety of buckles and fasteners for shoulder and waist straps and babies' seats. Snaps should be sturdy and require a lot of force to unfasten. Buckles that hold shoulder and waist straps should be easy to adjust and keep straps firmly fastened when the carrier is in use. Buckles and fasteners should be easy for an adult to use, but not so easy that a baby could undo them, and should fasten tightly, but not in a way that could pinch your fingers. If you get pinched, your baby could be pinched, too. And you might not properly secure the buckles when using the carrier for fear of being pinched, which isn't safe, either.

Cup or bottle holders. Cup holders are de rigueur in cars, and some strap-on carriers, such as the Snugli By My Side Soft Carrier by Evenflo, feature this extra so you or your baby can sip anywhere.

Lumbar support. Well-made carriers may have a special padded waist strap that helps distribute a baby's weight from your shoulders to your hips and pelvic area. This is a definite comfort advantage. When you're shopping, try on a floor model and fasten the belt/waist strap to see if it's long enough and neither too high nor too low when the carrier is in place. Padding should be firm, not mushy.

Shoulder straps. Shoulder-strap padding should be firm and wide so the straps won't dig in. Straps should be positioned so they won't slip off your shoulders or chafe your neck, and they should be adjustable while you're carrying your baby.

Side-vent insets. Babies can get sweaty in an infant carrier. To help keep them cool, some carriers have a panel of meshy material designed to promote air flow, or side insets that can be unzipped or unbuttoned to serve the same purpose. Look for either of those features if you'll be having a summer baby or you live in a warm climate.

Side entry. Many front strap-on models, including most of the carriers we tested, have dual side-entry buckles so you can get your baby out from either side. That exit strategy may be

If you want to use your strap-on carrier outside in cooler months, consider getting a carrier cover like this one from Brooks Pond. It slips over most brands of strap-on soft infant carriers so you don't have to stuff your bundled-up baby into a carrier or zip your coat around him.

Certification

To date, the Juvenile Products Manufacturers Association (JPMA) has certified fourteen brands of soft infant carriers, which are Baby King Products, BabySwede LLC (BabyBjörn), Chicco USA, Clene LLC, Dorel Juvenile Group (Quinny, Safety 1st), Fisher-Price, Kelty Kids, Kids Line LLC, Kolcraft, Learning Curve, Maclaren, Munchkin, Scandinavian Child/Lillebaby, and The Ergo Baby Carrier. Certified soft infant carriers are in compliance with the voluntary guidelines set by standards developer ASTM International. Included in the guidelines are rules for leg openings created to minimize the risk of babies falling through those openings. Certified carriers must also pass dynamic and static load tests, to verify the limits on the amount of weight the carrier can safely support. They also have warning statements on the product and in the instruction booklet stating, for example, that small children can fall through a leg opening and that the product should be used only if your baby's weight is in a specific range, such as 8 to 26 pounds.

a good idea if you want to move your sleeping baby to a crib without waking him.

Pacifier and toy loops, and storage pockets. These are handy for the essentials.

Recommendations

There are parents who like soft infant carriers and there are those who mostly leave their carriers hanging on a hook in the closet. Because it's impossible to predict how you or your baby will react to one, it doesn't pay to register for a soft infant carrier or buy it ahead of time. Wait to buy until your baby is born. Ideally, you've gotten a little practice with a friend's carrier first. For the safety reasons we mentioned, we recommend a front or hip carrier over a sling, especially for the youngest infants who typically will be riding in the sling lying down. If you decide to buy a sling anyway, follow our Safety Strategies on page 299 and make sure the fabric is machine washable.

If you decide to buy a front or hip carrier and your baby is amenable, look for a comfortable, machine washable carrier that can be fitted for your torso, with sturdy, adjustable straps that secure your baby snugly, one that evenly distributes her weight and supports her head. Check the carrier periodically for sharp edges, ripped seams, and missing, loose, or defective snaps, buckles, or rings.

With any type of carrier, follow the manufacturer's instructions carefully to make sure you use the carrier properly and be sure to send in the registration card so you can be notified in the event of a recall. Think about how much you'll use it before you buy one. That will help you determine what to spend, though price isn't necessarily an indicator of quality. A low-priced version may be fine if you plan to use the front or hip carrier or sling only occasionally. If you foresee long jaunts with your baby or expect to be using your carrier a lot around the house, consider a higher-end model, which may give you more support and be more comfortable. Don't use a soft infant carrier for activity more rigorous than leisurely walking. If you want to pick up the pace, a jogging stroller is your best bet.

chapter

Stationary Activity Centers

These all-in-one, molded-plastic play stations typically resemble traditional walkers—but without the wheels, which makes them a less risky way for your baby to have fun and get a little exercise.

The Baby Einstein Discover & Play Activity Center has nine interactive toys to keep your baby busy.

A stationary activity center keeps your baby relatively safe in one spot while you do other things, such as make dinner—and maybe even eat some of it, too. Most activity centers have a circular frame with a rotating seat recessed in the center and a surrounding tray with attached developmental toys that introduce your baby to color, shapes, texture, animals, nature, and language. Another style, the walk-around version, features a seat that rotates around a central pivot or table so your baby can walk in a circle if she wants to, but not actually travel. A stationary activity center can be used as soon as your baby can sit up unassisted (some start at about 4 months and most by 6 months).

Most stationary activity centers adjust to three or more heights. Your baby will outgrow it when he's 30 to 32 inches tall or weighs 25 to 30 pounds; that's the maximum height and weight recommendation for most activity centers. You should stop using the activity center when your child can walk or even stand up by himself. A standing or walking child can tip it over and get injured or trapped.

Shopping Secrets

The Evenflo ExerSaucer Triple Fun Active Learning Center has loads of toys plus music for your little multitasker, but requires 9 AA batteries (not included).

Do your in-store research. Look for a sturdy frame; no accessible sharp edges or hardware underneath or on top; comfortable, soft fabric edging on the sides and legs of the seat cushions; and well-designed, well-secured toys for little hands. The seat should swivel smoothly without any hitches, and there should be no gaps in the rim between the edge of the swivel mechanism and the tray. Such gaps could capture small fingers. If the activity center's bottom is a saucer, its flip-down braces, which prevent it from rocking, should be sturdy.

Look for an activity center that folds if you want to take it along when you travel or if you need the extra room. We know of at least four that do, all from Evenflo: the ExerSaucer SmartSteps Active Learning Center (a tested model), the ExerSaucer Mega Active Learning Center, the Exersaucer Triple Fun Active Learning Center, and the ExerSaucer 1-2-3 Tea for Me Active Learning Center. Practice collapsing display models in the store, if possible, to make sure the folding mechanism works well.

More isn't always better. Most activity centers offer activities that attract a baby's attention and promote her developing motor skills, including electronic toys, lights, sounds, songs, and a rotating seat. One of the most fully loaded we found, the Baby Sit & Step 2-in-1 Activity Center by Kolcraft ($100; *www.kolcraft.com*), includes 20 activities and 9 toys; lights, music, and whimsical sounds; and a springy seat that also spins and rocks. One with fewer gadgets and toys, the Bright Starts Bounce Bounce Baby Activity Zone ($39.99; *www.brightstarts.com*), has only five toys, plus an electronic piano with lights and six melodies. Depending on the baby, that may be enough to keep her busy.

You'll pay more for a high-octane model, but more isn't always better. Although many babies enjoy a wide range of options, some find all that motion, sound, and light too stimulating. So go with an activity center with fewer bells and whistles— in other words, at the lower end of the price spectrum— if you suspect that your baby doesn't have a multitasking temperament.

What's Available

The major brands, in alphabetical order, are: Bright Starts (*www.brightstarts.com*), Evenflo (*www.evenflo.com*), Graco, sold under the Baby Einstein name (*www.graco baby.com*), and Kolcraft (*www.kolcraft.com*). Models come with either a solid flat base with four legs that contain the seat, a rocking base (three legs with a center brace below the seat), or a pedestal support (walk-around models); some, including all Kolcraft models, become a walk-behind walker (beginner walkers can push it in front of them), although we don't recommend using it in that manner because a baby could easily push one down the stairs. Prices range from about $39.99 (Bright Starts) to $130 (for the Evenflo ExerSaucer Triple Fun, a play mat and activity center in one that converts to an activity table).

The Kolcraft Baby Sit & Step 2-in-1 Activity Center offers a carnival of fun, but don't use it in walk-behind mode (below), which we consider to be unsafe.

Certification

Five stationary activity center brands have been certified by the Juvenile Products Manufacturers Association (JPMA), which signifies that they meet the requirements of standards developer ASTM International: Dorel Juvenile Group (Safety 1st), Fisher-Price, Graco (Baby Einstein), Kolcraft, and Summer Infant.

The adjustable seat of Bright Start's Around We Go! Activity Station rotates completely around the base; remove it later and have a toddler play table.

Features to Consider

Motion. Some activity centers offer merely a stationary seat. Others feature a seat that swivels 360 degrees, with springs that allow the unit to bounce when baby moves, and create a rocking motion, which active babies may enjoy.

Stabilizers. These anchor the frame in a stationary position. They're a must to keep a rocking activity center from becoming too turbulent or if you want to feed your baby in his activity center. The stabilizers should seem sturdy.

Adjustable height. Many models offer legs that adjust to three heights, so the activity center can grow as your baby grows. The height of the play tray is the key. When the tray is at the proper height, your baby's feet will touch the floor and her legs will be straight when she's seated. If your baby is on her tippy toes when she's seated, the tray is too high. If her knees are bent when she's seated, it's too low. You may have to adjust the legs (without your baby seated in the activity center) every month or so, just to keep pace with your baby's growth.

Seat. More expensive models have cushy seat padding. Seat pads are typically removable for machine washing, which is a real plus. You might have to air-dry them, though. Check the care and maintenance requirements on the label or in the instruction manual.

Toys. All activity centers feature a play tray with attached interactive toys, such as a fun house mirror, a spinning stoplight, picture books, and bead toys along with lights, songs, sounds, and sometimes bilingual

Use Activity Centers with Care

A stationary activity center can keep your baby occupied and happy and give you a much-needed break. But you're not off the hook. Here's what you should do to help keep him safe.

◆ Keep an eye out. Even though a stationary activity center can give you a chance to grab a bite (without a baby in your lap), take a quick shower, or check your e-mail, always keep your baby in view while he's in it.

◆ Resist the urge to park your baby. Keeping your child in a stationary activity center for more than 30 minutes at a time can tax her naturally weak back and leg muscles.

◆ Don't use a stationary activity center that converts to a walk-behind walker in the walker mode.

◆ Keep the activity center away from hot surfaces, dangling appliance cords, window blind and curtain cords, stairs, sources of water such as a swimming pool, and anything else that might injure a child. Even though it is technically stationary, this play space can creep across the floor as your baby plays. Watch for movement and make sure your baby stays away from hazards.

◆ Don't carry an activity center with your child in it.

◆ Place the product on level ground and make sure the legs are the same height. (The tray should be level.) That's the best way to avoid tip-overs.

◆ Follow the manufacturer's age or weight or height recommendations and keep the owner's manual for future reference. Don't use the activity center before your baby can sit up unassisted, and stop using it when your baby reaches the height or weight maximum and can walk or even stand up by himself, which means he could easily tip it. And, as a general rule, if your child can tip over the activity center by just leaning over the edge or can climb out of it, it's time to retire it.

◆ Don't attach strings to the activity center or to its toys. They're a strangulation hazard.

◆ Stop using a stationary activity center if it's damaged or broken.

voices. To make these gizmos work, you'll need up to 12 AAA batteries, depending on the model. In general, more expensive models are loaded with exciting options and have lots of ways to bounce and rock so your baby feels like she's on the go. They also require more battery power.

Recommendations

Stationary activity centers with a solid, flat base or walk-around models with a stable center pivot or table are the most secure. Examine attached toys for size. They shouldn't be able to fit through a toilet paper tube. Should they happen to break off, they could be a choking hazard.

The Bright Starts Bounce Bounce Baby is loaded with toys, lights, and music.

Although most babies enjoy being in these play spaces, some don't. If you can, have your baby test drive a unit in the store or during play dates at other parents' homes to get a sense of how he fares. If you decide to buy one, look for an activity center with a thick, solid frame, no accessible sharp edges or sharp hardware underneath or on top, and comfortable, soft fabric edging on the sides and legs of the seat cushions. Also, the flip-down stabilizers, which may be available to prevent the saucer from rocking, should be sturdy. You shouldn't get the feeling that they could release during use.

Some activity centers come with lots of bells and whistles—and lots of parts. (We counted 19 on one brand.) You'll need a screwdriver and a good half an hour to assemble. Read the instructions beforehand and keep them for future reference. Routinely check your baby's activity center for loose screws or toys, worn parts, and torn material or stitching, and replace or repair as needed. You can usually order replacement parts from the manufacturer. Stop using a stationary activity center if it's damaged or broken.

Follow our safety recommendations (do your in-store research, page 306). Register the product online or by sending in the product registration card so you can easily be notified in the event of a recall. Stay alert for recalls by checking *www.cpsc.gov* before you shop, or before purchasing a stationary activity center secondhand.

chapter

Strollers

Having a new baby can be a walk in the park—with the right stroller, of course. In fact, a stroller is one of the most important pieces of baby gear you'll buy. And as your baby grows, you may end up with more than one.

The UPPAbaby G-LITE is a CR Best Buy; it's for babies 6 months and over.

Many parents buy a traditional stroller for everyday use and a lighter-weight one for traveling. You may even want a more rugged stroller for jogging or simply negotiating uneven sidewalks and curbs. (City streets are deceptively hard on strollers.) There are dozens of choices on the market—everything from the lightest-weight umbrella strollers to heavy-duty, midsized strollers, carriages, jogging strollers, and models designed to carry two or more children. For a newborn, you can find a basic frame with no stroller seat of its own that can support almost any infant car seat. Or consider a fully reclining stroller with leg holes you can close, so your baby doesn't slip and get trapped.

Another option is a travel system, which consists of an infant car seat, a car-seat base for your car, and a stroller. Some jogging and traditional strollers also function as travel systems by allowing you to attach an infant car seat. All Peg Pérego strollers—the Pliko P3 Classico, Aria OH Classico, Pliko Switch Completo, Uno, and Skate—are designed to anchor a matching Peg Pérego car seat, which is sold separately. When babies reach 6 months old or can sit up and control their head and neck movements, you can use the stroller alone, without the infant seat snapped in. The downside? Until then, you have to push your baby in a car seat mounted on a stroller, which can be unwieldy, depending on the circumstances, such as the terrain you're navigating.

Another CR Best Buy: The Chicco Cortina; it fully reclines and is car-seat compatible, so you can use it from day one.

A final option is a combo stroller—such as most Mutsy models or the Bugaboo Frog or Cameleon—which functions as both a carriage and a stroller. This stroller is a hybrid that consists of a stroller chassis with wheels that can be used with various manufacturers' car seats. There are options such as an attachable bassinet, which converts the stroller into a carriage, so your newborn baby can fully recline, and an attachable stroller seat to use when your baby is ready to sit up. Some systems include the bassinet and/or the stroller seat; with other systems you must purchase these accessories separately. Your stroller options are dizzying. Here's what you need to know to buy the right wheels for you and your baby.

Shopping Secrets

Select it yourself. Strollers are popular baby gifts and shower presents. Still, you should shop for a stroller yourself because you're the best judge of how you intend to use it—then register for it at a department or baby store if you want to receive it as a gift. If you receive a stroller you didn't select yourself, make sure you want to keep it. Strollers, like cars, are highly personal items. You'll probably use your stroller often, and your baby will spend a lot of time in it. You should love the one you end up with.

Let your lifestyle be your guide. City dwellers who rely on subways, buses, and cabs will need a lightweight but sturdy stroller that folds quickly and compactly. A travel system, for example, probably isn't your best bet because the car seat-stroller combination is heavy to push and unwieldy on stairs and public transportation. For suburbanites who plan on long walks with baby and have a vehicle big enough to accommodate a larger stroller model, a stroller with sizeable, air-filled tires is recommended. Besides being more shock-absorbing, these strollers typically have cushier, more supportive seating.

If you'll be strolling through snow, on unpaved roads, or on the beach or taking your baby to soccer games in the park, a stroller with large wheels is the way to go. Under those conditions, a stroller with small wheels may be difficult or impossible to push.

If you're athletic, you might want an all-terrain or jogging stroller for walking or jogging workouts. If you're not, you might want a lightweight stroller so you can lift it more easily in and out of the trunk of your car. Our top-rated single stroller, the Graco Quattro Tour Sport, for example, weighs 27 pounds. Some of the other top-rated strollers weigh in at 10 to 22 pounds. Even five pounds more may make a difference, depending on your build. If you're torn between strollers, weight can be a deciding factor.

Give it a test drive. Take the models you're considering for a spin in the store, even if you plan to buy online or expect to get a stroller as a gift. Compare maneuverability and practice opening and closing

The Graco Quattro Tour Sport, our top-rated single stroller and a CR Best Buy, is easy to maneuver and car-seat compatible. It has a five-point harness.

it—with one hand as well as two. See how easy it is to adjust the backrest, lift and carry the stroller, and apply the rear brakes. Make sure you can stand tall when you push the stroller and that your legs and feet don't hit the wheels as you walk.

If both you and your spouse will use the stroller, you should both try it out. Some models have adjustable handles, an important feature if one parent is taller than the other. If possible, take the floor model you're considering out to your car to make sure it will fit in your trunk when it's folded. Also, jiggle the stroller. The frame should feel solid, not loose.

Consider your baby's age. Newborns can't sit up, so they need a stroller that lets them lie on their backs for the first few months, or one that can hold an infant car seat. Don't use a traditional stroller that doesn't fully recline—including an umbrella-style stroller—until your child can sit up, usually at about 6 months of age. If you buy a stroller that fully reclines for an infant, make sure it has a wall surrounding all sides above the retention space (where your baby lies). In addition, you can use the cover or stroller boot—protective snap-on fabric leg coverings that the manufacturer sometimes supplies for the foot area/legholes so your baby can't possibly slip through—or use the bassinet that may come with the stroller or be purchased separately as an attachment.

Size up the storage. A stroller with a large shopping basket makes life easier for parents who get around town mostly on foot. If you opt for a model that reclines, make sure you can reach the basket if the seatback is fully reclined, or, if it's a travel system, when the infant car seat is in place.

Evaluate warranties and return policies. Most stroller manufacturers and retailers have warranties that cover poor workmanship and inherent flaws, but they won't necessarily take the unit back if it malfunctions. Manufacturers may refer you to the store for a replacement or insist that you ship the stroller back for repair—at your expense—leaving you stranded without baby wheels. Your best bet is to purchase the stroller from a store, catalog, or Web site that offers a 100 percent satisfaction guarantee.

Keep the packaging the stroller comes in until you're sure you want to keep the stroller and ask about a store's return policy (usually 30 to 45 days). It's not uncommon to buy a stroller many months in advance. If you're shopping that far ahead, you'll want to buy from a store with a flexible or long-term return policy.

■ **Budget Baby**

What Makes One Stroller $100 and Another $750?

As you'll discover when you're stroller shopping, there's a wide price range among types and brands. Several things drive up the price tag, including the cachet of a higher-end brand name as well as differences in quality.

Some higher-end strollers are made of high-grade, lighter-weight aluminum, which makes them easier to lift in and out of a car. The seat is cushier and is likely to be made of high-quality fabric. Higher-end strollers may be easier to push, especially over rough terrain, which includes anything from uneven sidewalks to bumpy dirt paths and grass, so babies get a smoother ride.

Bigger-ticket strollers also often have such comfy amenities as adjustable handles, which can save your back if you're tall, but so do a number of cheaper models. In fact, a lower-end stroller may serve you well. For infrequent travel or trips to the mall, an umbrella stroller (less than $100) may be all you need for a child 6 months or older. But if you're going to be strolling more often and through all kinds of weather and conditions, consider spending more. Good quality all-purpose strollers start around $150.

That said, a higher price doesn't always mean higher quality. Though stores are full of pricey strollers, you don't need to spend a bundle to safely wheel your little bundle around. CONSUMER REPORTS' tests have shown that some economical strollers can perform as well as or even better than models costing hundreds of dollars more. Even the most sophisticated models can suffer from flaws such as malfunctioning wheels, frames that bend out of shape, locking mechanisms that fail, safety belts that come loose, or buckles that break.

You don't have to spend a lot to get a good stroller. The Evenflo Journey Elite performed better in our tests than much pricier models.

Check certification. Somewhere on a stroller's frame or carton there might be a certification sticker showing that its manufacturer participates in the certification program of the Juvenile Products Manufacturers Association (JPMA). The program requires the product to be third-party tested for compliance with the voluntary guidelines set by standards developer ASTM International.

The key tests are for brakes, load-bearing strength, stability, restraint system, leg openings, impact resistance, and the security of any car seat attachment and of locking mechanisms that prevent accidental folding, as well as for the absence of sharp edges. Many manufacturers participate in the program and we believe that all manufacturers should. The seals are reassuring, but they don't guarantee that a product is safe. Models from uncertified companies may be as safe as those from certified ones. But all things being equal, choose a certified model. Companies that are JPMA-certified are: Baby Planet, Baby Trend, Bergeron by Design, Britax, Bugaboo, Chicco, Delta, Dorel Juvenile Group, Evenflo, Go-Go Babyz, Graco, Hauck Fun for Kids, Joovy, Kolcraft, Maclaren, Mia Moda, Peg Pérego, Scandinavian Child/Micralite, Summer Infant, Thea & Company, and UPPAbaby.

What's Available

Some brands of single- and multiseat strollers are, in alphabetical order, Baby Jogger (www.babyjogger.com), Baby Trend (www.babytrend.com), Bertini (www.bertinistrollers.com), Bob (www.bobstrollers.com), Britax (www.britaxusa.com), Bugaboo (www.bugaboo.com), Bumble Ride (www.bumbleride.com), Chicco (www.chiccousa.com), Combi (www.combi-intl.com), Dorel Juvenile Group (which features the Cosco, Maxi-Cosi, Eddie Bauer, Safety 1st, and Quinny brands, www.djgusa.com), Evenflo (www.evenflo.com), Fisher-Price (www.fisher-price.com), GoGo Babyz (www.gogobabyz.com), Graco (www.gracobaby.com), Inglesina (www.inglesina.com), InStep (www.instep.net), Kelty (www.keltykids.com), Kolcraft (www.kolcraft.com; it carries the Jeep license), Learning Curve (www.learningcurve.com), Maclaren (www.maclarenbaby.com), Mia Moda (www.miamodainc.com), Micralite (www.scichild.com), Mountain Buggy (www.mountainbuggy.com), Mutsy (www.mutsy.com), Orbit (www.orbitbaby.com), Peg Pérego (www.pegperego.com), Phil & Teds (www.philandteds.com), Silver Cross (www.silvercrossamerica.com), Stokke (www.stokkeusa.com), Stroll-Air (www.stroll-air.com), Tike Tech (www.tiketech.com), UPPAbaby (www.uppababy.com), and Zooper (www.zooper.com).

For Babies Younger Than 6 Months

Because newborns can't sit up without support, they can't ride in a standard stroller—that is, one that doesn't fully recline. You'll find the following basic choices for this age group:

Car seat carrier frames

These lightweight frames have no seat of their own. Instead, you attach an infant car seat for strolling.

Pros: They're compact and convenient and inexpensive because your car seat does double duty. They let you smoothly get a sleeping baby in and out of the car. When you move a baby in an infant car seat to the stroller frame or into the house, you're less likely to wake him.

Cons: The car seat and the frame can no longer be used as a stroller once your child outgrows the seat (at about a year).

Price range: $48 to $75 for just the frame (single) or around $95 for a stroller frame that holds two infant car seats.

Combo strollers

These are a combination carriage and stroller. Before your baby can sit up, you can use the stroller's bassinet or "carry cot," snap an infant car seat into the stroller chassis, or, depending on the model, fully recline the seat and close the leg holes. After that, use the stroller seat attachment to wheel your baby around.

The Baby Trend Snap N Go is our top-rated car seat carrier frame.

Pros: You can start using the stroller from day one, and because it's designed for infants through toddlers (to 40 pounds or so), you may not have to buy more than one stroller.

Con: Combo strollers tend to be pricey. Bugaboo, which is a popular brand of combo stroller, for example, will run you from $760 (the Frog model) to $899 (the Cameleon). That price includes the chassis which weighs 19 to 20 pounds, bassinet, and reversible seat, plus a mosquito net, rain cover, and underseat bag for storage items. But you'll still need to buy an infant car seat for your car.

Price range: $360 to $1,199.

Travel systems

These combine a stroller and an infant car seat; the baby rides in the car seat snapped into the stroller until she can sit up, and then you use the stroller without the car seat.

Pros: Like an infant seat with carrier frame, a travel system allows you to move a sleeping baby in the seat undisturbed from car to stroller. Some also have a seat that fully reclines, so you can use it as a carriage (without the infant car seat).

Don't Park Your Baby in an Infant Car Seat

It's convenient to tote infants in an infant car seat, using it as a carrier and a stroller, but long stretches spent there can contribute to positional plagiocephaly (flat-head syndrome). "Car seats are a contributing factor because you can move your baby from the car to the stroller and go from there, not picking her up very much at all," says Darcy King, an advanced registered nurse practitioner in the Craniofacial Center at Seattle Children's Hospital, in Seattle, Wash. "Some kids develop flat spots because they're not off the back of their head." To give your baby's developing head a break, King recommends using a soft infant carrier when you're not in your car, but out and about with your baby, especially with babies under 3 months old. That's a critical time for head development, when the risk of plagiocephaly is greatest, she says.

Cons: With travel systems, a car seat and stroller are typically sold together. But you can also create your own by combining a car seat and stroller. If you select the car seat first, you have to live with the stroller it works with (and vice versa). An alternative is to choose a stroller that can hold car seats from a number of manufacturers. With all travel systems, you have to push around a car seat and a stroller, which can be bulky and unmanageable on stairs.

Thrift tip: It can be cheaper to buy a travel system as a unit rather than as separate components. We estimate you can save $60 to $100 that way. Plus you won't have to match the car seat and stroller yourself. But be sure to evaluate the stroller as a stand-alone item first, since you'll be using that longer than the infant car seat that goes with it.

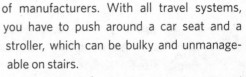

The Graco Quattro Tour Deluxe accepts three Graco car seats.

Price range: $110 to $350 for travel systems (sold as a unit).

Carriages/Prams

These models provide sleeping space for infants. Some have large spoked wheels and bassinets that can be removed to make way for a compatible stroller seat (sold separately).

Pros: They can be used for newborns and they're convenient for sleeping.

Cons: They're pricey and not very portable or user friendly. If you get the kind with large, spoked wheels, it'll be nearly impossible to maneuver on public transportation, and you'll still need a car seat. Traditional prams, the kind that don't convert to a regular stroller, aren't very popular and few manufacturers produce them. If you want your baby to lie flat when strolling, consider a combo stroller.

Price range: From $1,000 to $2,995.

Multiseat Strollers—Infants to Toddlers

Similar to other strollers, multiseat strollers give you a relatively efficient means of taking twins, triplets, or young siblings of different ages for a ride. Most companies that make single strollers for one also make a version with two or more seats. Multiseaters offer the same features as strollers for a single rider, but are bigger. Options include strollers with a standing platform or small seat in the rear that lets a second child hitch a ride. If you choose a model with a platform where your older child can ride, be extra vigilant and warn your child to hold on and keep their feet on the platform at all times. Multiseat strollers usually come in one of two configurations: tandem or side-by-side.

Tandem models

These strollers have one seat directly behind the other. They're the same width as single-passenger strollers and easy to fit through doorways and get around enclosed spaces, such as retail stores. However, while the backseat can recline, the front one usually can't without limiting the space of the rear passenger. On some tandem strollers, you can set the seats so that the children face each other; others have a "stadium seat" that allows the child in back to see over the one in front, as long as the sun canopy isn't covering the front seat.

Pros: Tandems easily go through standard doorways and fit through tight spots, such as an older apartment building with a narrow elevator door. A folded tandem takes up just a little more space than a folded standard midsized stroller. Many tandem models accept an infant car seat in one or both stroller seats, but check which brands of car seats are compatible before you buy.

Cons: Steering can be difficult, and it can be tricky getting over curbs. Some models have limited leg support and very little leg room for the rear passenger. The rear passenger typically has to turn his head to see anything but the back of the first seat. A tandem can often be quite heavy, making it difficult to manage if you're small in size.

Price range: $95 to $380 or more for double tandem strollers; tandem strollers for triplets, such as the Inglesina Trio Domino (there's not a lot to choose from), will cost in the range of $230 to $1,030.

The Maclaren Twin Triumph is tops in our side-by-side double stroller tests. It's lightweight for a double stroller and folds compactly.

Side-by-side models

The other configuration, side-by-side, has two seats attached to a single frame or a unit resembling two strollers bolted together. You can create your own side-by-side by joining two umbrella strollers with a set of screw-on brackets—available at baby discount chains and specialty stores. The features on side-by-side strollers are similar to those on single-passenger models. This type of stroller works best for children of about the same weight, such as twins. Each seat has an independent reclining mechanism.

Pros: A side-by-side model goes up curbs more easily than a tandem. Some side-by-side models accept an infant car seat, though some brands limit it to one seat only. That may be fine if you'll use the stroller for a newborn and an older child. If you'll use it for infant twins and you want a side-by-side, look for one in which both seats accept an infant car seat (that's rare) or recline, such as the Combi Twin Sport 2 ($200), and use the infant boot, or the fabric flap, that covers leg openings to keep an infant from slipping through the holes when the seat is fully reclined.

Cons: If children of different weights ride in the stroller, it can veer to one side. Most side-by-side models can't be used with two infant car seats so unless it fully reclines, it can be tough to find a side-by-side that will accommodate babies of the same age. A folded side-by-side stroller typically requires twice as much space as the equivalent single-occupant version. Although manufacturers may claim that a stroller is slender enough to go through a standard doorway, it can be a tight squeeze, and the stroller may not fit through some doorways at all.

Price range: $85 (for lightweight models that don't accept an infant car seat) to more than $1,000 (for deluxe models with independent reversible seats with multiple reclining positions and air-filled tires).

Down the Road

Stroller types appropriate for babies older than 6 months include:

Umbrella strollers

These are named for their curved, umbrella-like handles, and usually weigh less than 12 pounds. They may have a one-handed release for folding.

Pros: They're lightweight and convenient.

Cons: The compact size of umbrella strollers may cramp infants and toddlers, especially when they're dressed in heavy winter clothes. Because these strollers may lack suspension and seat support, they don't always provide a cushy ride.

Price range: $25 to $350.

Traditional strollers

This category runs the gamut from lightweight strollers to heavy-duty models that weigh 17 to 35 pounds. The heavy-duty strollers are some-what bulky but stable, deep, and roomy. Higher-end models may have shock absorbers on all wheels as well. Many strollers have a two-step, one-handed release for folding.

Pros: Many are lightweight and convenient. They have more features than lower-end umbrella strollers, such as a snack tray and a roomy storage basket, and some may accommodate an infant car seat or fully recline and have a wall around all sides above the retention space, so it's possible to use this type of stroller from day one.

Cons: Heavier models are difficult to carry on public transportation and to lift into car trunks or minivan cargo areas. Small wheels don't perform well on uneven sidewalks or rough terrain. The compact size of lighter-weight models may cramp some toddlers, especially when they're dressed in heavy winter clothes.

The Mountain Buggy Urban all-terrain stroller works for newborns as well as older babies. It reclines fully and, with an adaptor (bought separately), will accommodate other manufacturers' car seats. Also nice: a five-point safety harness and large storage basket.

Price range: $90 (lightweight strollers that are an upgrade from an umbrella stroller) to $635 or more (high-end traditional strollers, with contemporary styling and such features as single-spoke wheels and pneumatic tires.

All-terrain strollers

These three-wheel strollers or traditional-style strollers, with a rugged, outdoorsy look and heavy-duty suspension or larger air-filled tires, let you push your child on a variety of surfaces, from mall floors to pavement and off-road. Many all-terrains have bicycle-type air-filled tires, and larger wheels than a traditional stroller. The larger wheels make the stroller easier to push. All-terrain strollers have a three-wheel design that mimics jogging strollers. Some can be used for jogging; check the manual and manufacturer's Web site. (See Jogging Strollers, next page, for recommended jogging age.)

All have a front wheel that swivels for easier maneuvering on smoother surfaces but can be locked for use on rougher surfaces. Many all-terrains do not fully recline, and therefore are unsuitable for babies under 6 months of age. A few exceptions: BumbleRide Indie ($400), which accepts an infant car seat, and the Zooper Zydeco (about $520), which reclines flat to support an infant's head and shoulders.

Pros: They're good for off-road use and provide a relatively smooth ride over rocks, potholes, and uneven sidewalks. Some all terrain strollers can accommodate heavier children than other strollers can. Several companies offer double and triple all-terrain strollers with a total weight limit of up to 100 and 150 pounds, respectively.

Cons: Three-wheel designs may be unstable when the rear wheels are rolled over a curb. Many all-terrains are not suitable for infants younger than 6 months. They are often large and heavy; some may require you to remove the front and/or rear wheel to fit in a car trunk. Air-filled tires can go flat and require reinflating with a bicycle pump or a gas-station hose.

Price range: $220 to $1,200.

Jogging strollers

These three-wheel strollers with front hand brake, nonswivel or lockable front wheel for serious runners, and large, air-filled tires let you push your child while you run or jog. Larger wheels make it easier for the runner who's pushing, and the air in the tires helps provide a smoother ride for the little passenger. The long, high handlebar is designed to give running feet and legs more space to avoid bumping into the stroller's frame. A wrist strap should be attached to your wrist and the stroller at all times when you're running with a child in the stroller; this will give you some control and keep the stroller from getting away from you if you fall or trip. Make sure that any model you buy has this strap.

The appropriate minimum age for a child to ride in a jogging stroller is a matter of debate. Most manufacturers suggest a child should be 8 weeks or older, but our medical consultants say a baby should be at least 6 months, able to sit up, and have some head support to withstand the potentially jarring ride. Some jogging strollers are made to accommodate the youngest babies, however. Baby Jogger makes a bassinet/pram to work with its Baby Jogger City Series single strollers, so your baby can lie flat while you're logging the miles. The stroller is also car seat compatible. The seat or bassinet faces the rear of the stroller so you can see your baby at all times. But that doesn't mean you should sprint with your newborn; brisk walks are a better idea.

Pros: Jogging strollers can also be used for off-road walks. Many jogging strollers have a longer life than traditional strollers, because they can accommodate heavier children, typically 50 pounds per seat.

Cons: The fixed (nonswiveling) front wheel is good for running but can make steering difficult. Some three-wheel designs may be unstable when the rear wheels are rolled over a curb, or if a child tries to climb into the stroller. Jogging strollers are often large and some are heavy; you may need to remove the wheel(s) to fit the stroller into your car trunk. Bicycle-type

The Jeep Overland Limited Jogging Stroller from Kolcraft features a Music on the Move parent tray for attaching your own portable electronics such as a CD or MP3 player or iPod.

air-filled tires can go flat and require reinflating with a bicycle pump or a gas-station hose.

Price range: $90 (single jogging stroller) to $1,300 (for a triple jogging stroller).

Features to Consider

Restraint system. Get a stroller with a sturdy safety belt and crotch strap, which keep a baby or a toddler from slipping out. Most safety harnesses are made of thick nylon webbing. Look for buckles on the harness that are easy for you to operate but difficult for small hands to unfasten. If you're shopping with your baby, check the seat belt to make sure it's strong, and fits snugly around your child. Some strollers have only waist and crotch straps and this is all the ASTM standard requires, but many come with an adjustable five-point harness (two straps over the shoulders, two for the thighs, and a crotch strap), which keep a baby from climbing out or slipping or falling out if the stroller tips. The straps should be height-adjustable for proper fit, and securely anchored.

Wheels. Most strollers have double wheels on the front that swivel to make steering easier. Front wheels feature two positions: full swivel for smooth surfaces or locked in one forward-facing position for rough terrain. Some three-wheel strollers have a front wheel that doesn't swivel; these can be hard to maneuver. The larger the wheels, the easier it is to negotiate curbs and rough surfaces. But big wheels eat up trunk space. Misaligned and loose wheels are a chronic stroller problem. One sign of good construction is wheels that sit on the floor uniformly when a baby is inside. Pneumatic (air-filled) tires are relatively new in stroller design. You'll need a pump, which is not supplied with some models. Some manufacturers have created wheel assemblies that can be completely slipped off the frame, which makes it easier to replace a damaged wheel, fix the tire, get it filled, and transport the stroller in compact spaces, such as the trunk of a car.

Leg holes. Fully reclining carriages and strollers that are designed for newborns or young infants, must have leg holes that close so an infant can't slip through. Manufacturers use mesh or fabric shields or hinged, molded footrests that raise and clamp over the leg holes. According to the industry's standard, any stroller that can recline must have a non-detachable way to enclose the leg holes. The device can be detachable as long as the stroller can only recline when the device is attached.

Brakes. Check that any stroller you intend to buy has a good parking brake, one that's convenient to operate and locks one or two wheels. Parking brakes on two wheels provide an extra margin of safety. Some two-wheel parking brakes are activated in a single stroke by a bar in the rear of the stroller frame. Others require two actions and have foot-operated tabs above each rear wheel. When brakes are activated, plastic cogs engage with the sprockets of the rear wheels. Avoid models that can hurt your feet when you engage or disengage the brakes with light shoes or bare feet. In addition to parking brakes, most jogging strollers have bicycle-type hand-operated brakes that work on the front or rear wheels. A hand brake is important to help you slow down when cruising at a fast clip.

Canopy. A canopy is a must-have for protecting your baby, especially in glaring sunlight or inclement weather. Canopies range from a simple fabric square strung between two wires to deep, pull-down versions that shield almost the entire front of the stroller. Reversible "180-degree travel" canopies protect the baby from sun or wind from ahead or behind. Some canopies have a clear plastic "peekaboo" window on top so you can keep an eye on your baby while you're strolling. The window (or viewing port) is a nice feature; you'll use it more than you'd think.

Handlebars. Handles may be padded, even thickly cushioned, on more expensive models. Adjustable handlebars can be extended or angled to accommodate people of different heights. Reversible handles can swing over the top of the stroller, then be locked into a front position so baby rides facing you. A single crossbar not only allows one-handed steering, if necessary, but may make the stroller more stable. Umbrella strollers and other models with two independent handles almost always require two hands to maneuver.

One-handed opening/folding mechanism. This is essential for when you need to open or fold the stroller with one hand while holding your baby with the other. The best strollers fold compactly in a matter of seconds.

Play tray. Strollers may have a tray where babies can play with toys, keep snacks, or rest their hands. If the tray comes with attached toys, check their size and make sure they are securely fastened. Some strollers have been recalled because small parts on their play tray toys pose a choking hazard. No toy part should be smaller than the diameter of a toilet-paper-roll tube. To make it easier to get a squirming baby or toddler

Dos and Don'ts for Safe Strolling

◆ Never leave your baby unattended in a stroller, especially when she's asleep.

◆ Buckle up. Always use the safety belt or harness to restrain children from climbing out of the stroller and to reduce the risk of a child leaning over to far and tipping it over.

◆ Don't overload the stroller with a child heavier than the manufacturer's weight limit, and don't put more children in the stroller than its design allows.

◆ Don't jog with a stroller that's not a jogging stroller or with an all-terrain stroller not recommended for jogging.

◆ Don't run with an infant younger than 6 months old in a jogging stroller.

◆ Listen up. If you buy a combo stroller, which includes a bassinet and seat attachment, make sure you hear a "click" when installing these components to the stroller chassis, to ensure that each is installed properly. (Most combo strollers are designed this way.) Likewise, when installing an infant car seat to a stroller frame or to a travel system, make sure the seat is safely "locked" in by jiggling the seat to see that it's secure, or listening for the audible click, if the seat is designed to provide one. Use the instruction manual as your guide for correct installation.

◆ Lock before loading. Make sure the stroller is fully locked into its "open" position when you unfold it before strapping in your child. Listen for that all-important click when you open the stroller, or the stroller might collapse.

◆ Use the parking brake when you're stopped, especially on an incline. It only takes a slight incline to send the stroller rolling away from you. Put your foot on the brake when you take your hands off the stroller, even if you're stopping for just a moment.

◆ Keep your child away from the stroller when you're folding and unfolding it to avoid pinched fingers.

◆ Don't add padding. Never use a pillow, folded quilt, or blanket as a mattress in a stroller or baby carriage, and don't add an extra mattress or cushioning to a carriage/pram bassinet. They're a suffocation risk.

◆ Don't use a hand-me-down stroller without checking its history. A stroller purchased years ago for an older child might have since been recalled. Before dusting it off for reuse, check with the manufacturer or the Consumer Product Safety Commission (*www.cpsc.gov*) for product alerts. Even if it hasn't been recalled, there are other reasons you might want to consider buying a brand-new set of wheels. Stroller safety standards are regularly reviewed, so newer models might be safer. They might also have new features that make them easier to use.

◆ Return the stroller warranty card so you can be notified of a recall and sign up for the Consumer Product Safety Commission's e-mail subscription list at *www.cpsc.gov/cpsclist.aspx*. Updated recall information will be sent directly to you via e-mail.

◆ Don't pull a stroller backward up stairs with your baby in it. Opt for an elevator or ask someone to help you lift it up stairs. And be sure that you don't use your stroller on escalators.

seated, the tray should be removable or swing open rather than be permanently attached to both sides. Instead of a tray, some models have a front bar to keep a baby restrained with the attached crotch strap.

Footrest. A footrest can help a child sit more comfortably without legs dangling, but many are too low to help any but the tallest toddlers. Make certain that the seat rim is soft and won't press uncomfortably into the back of your child's legs.

Cup holders/parent tray. Many strollers have a cup holder for you and one for the small passenger. They're a welcome feature for both. The parent tray is usually molded with a cup holder or compartment for keys, cell phone, and so on.

Leg Coverings. A few strollers have protective leg coverings, or "boots," made of a matching fabric that can snap over baby's legs for warmth. That is not to be confused with the fabric flap, also sometimes called a boot, that closes leg openings for safety when a stroller is fully reclined.

Shock absorbers. Air-filled tires or tires molded from foam can help give baby a smoother ride. So can shock absorbers—covered springs or rubber pads above the wheel assemblies. Such softer suspension is a newer feature that offers a smoother ride, but a too-soft ride can come at the expense of steering control.

Fabric and upholstery. You'll want to be able to sponge off spills and splashes and launder the upholstery without worrying about shrinking, fading, or puckering. Look for a removable seat and laundry instructions, usually on an attached tag or on printed instructions inside the packaging.

Reflectors or reflective trim on fabric. Many strollers have this important safety feature. If yours doesn't, wear light-colored or reflective clothing so you can be seen on cloudy days. Even with a stroller that has reflective trim, we don't suggest strolling near traffic in twilight or in the dark.

Large shopping basket. Sizes of baskets vary. Choose one that's at least big enough to accommodate a diaper bag. When shopping for a stroller, press on the storage basket's floor—it shouldn't drag on the ground when loaded. Some strollers have storage pouches, with elastic top edges, in back. Don't hang heavy bags on handlebars. And never hang any bag on an umbrella stroller. Follow the manufacturer's recommendations for all storage areas. Overloaded strollers can tip.

Recommendations

The right stroller for you depends on many factors, like when you plan to use it and the age of your child. For many people, a fully featured, combo stroller is the best all-around choice and offers the best value. But if you plan to jog or travel with your baby, you may find that your needs are best met by more than one stroller.

For a newborn, using a car seat carrier frame with an infant car seat is an inexpensive way to go. You'll only use it for a short while, but it'll buy you time to figure out what your stroller needs are as your baby gets older. Start with that if you're undecided about which stroller type will be right for you and your lifestyle. Once your child is 6 months old and able to hold his head up, you can use a lightweight or heavier-duty stroller independently of an infant car seat. Spend some time taking practice runs with various models at baby stores. (Even if you ultimately buy online, there's no substitute for "kicking the tires.") If you'd rather have a stroller that multitasks from the start, go with a combo stroller that can carry a car seat or carry cot (bassinet) and later convert to a conventional stroller. If you'll be using a stroller from day one, look for a model that reclines or accepts an infant car seat. No matter what your baby's age, follow our Safety Strategies on page 326 when using a stroller.

Ratings • Strollers

	Excellent	Very good	Good	Fair	Poor
	⊖	⊖	○	◕	●

Within types, in performance order.

Brand & model	Price	Overall score	Test results						Features						
		0 100 P | F | G | VG| E	Ease of use	Maneuverability	Safety	Durability	Folded size	Weight (lb.)	5-point harness	One-touch brakes	Suitable for 6 mo. and under	Car-seat compatible	Trays for parent, child	Extra storage	Adjustable handle	Stands folded
SINGLE STROLLERS																
✓ **Graco** Quattro Tour Sport	$170	83	⊖	⊖	○	⊖	S	27	Yes	•	Yes	Yes	•	•		•
Micralite Toro	580	82	⊖	⊖	⊖	⊖	S	21	Yes		No	Yes			•	•
✓ **UPPAbaby** G-Lite	100	80	⊖	⊖	⊖	⊖	S	10	Yes		No	No				•
✓ **Evenflo** Journey Elite	70	78	⊖	⊖	⊖	⊖	M	21	No		No	Yes	•			•

Brand & model	Price	Overall score 0–100 P | F | G | VG | E	Ease of use	Maneuverability	Safety	Durability	Folded size	Weight (lb.)	5-point harness	One-touch brakes	Suitable for 6 mo. and under	Car-seat compatible	Trays for parent, child	Extra storage	Adjustable handle	Stands folded

SINGLE STROLLERS continued

Brand & model	Price	Overall score	Ease of use	Maneuverability	Safety	Durability	Folded size	Weight	5-pt harness	One-touch brakes	Suitable 6 mo.	Car-seat compat.	Trays	Extra storage	Adj. handle	Stands folded
✓ Chicco Cortina	$160	77	⊖	⊖	⊖	⊖	M	22	Yes	•	Yes	Yes	•		•	•
Mutsy Spider	200	77	⊖	⊖	⊖	⊖	S	21	Yes	•	Yes	No		•		
Zooper Waltz	300	76	⊖	⊖	○	⊖	S	19	Yes	•	Yes	No	•			•
✓ Maclaren Techno XT	280	76	⊖	⊖	⊖	⊖	S	16	Yes	•	Yes	Yes				•
Graco Quattro Tour Deluxe	150	74	⊖	⊖	⊖	⊖	M	27	Yes	•	Yes	Yes			•	•
✓ Bugaboo Bee	530	74	⊖	⊖	○	⊖	S	19	Yes	•	Yes	No		•		•
Mia Moda Facile	60	73	⊖	⊖	⊖	⊖	S	16	Yes		No	No				
✓ Zooper Salsa	130	72	⊖	⊖	⊖	⊖	S	12	Yes		No	No				
Silver Cross POP	200	71	⊖	⊖	⊖	⊖	S	17	Yes	•	No	No	•			•
Mia Moda Cielo	110	71	⊖	⊖	⊖	⊖	S	16	Yes	•	No	No				•
Jeep Cherokee	50	71	⊖	⊖	⊖	⊖	S	19	No		No	Yes	•	•		•
Peg Pérego Pliko P3	340	71	⊖	⊖	○	⊖	S	20	Yes	•	No	No				•
Graco Ipo	80	71	⊖	⊖	⊖	⊖	S	17	Yes	•	No	No				
Graco Mosaic	110	69	⊖	○	⊖	⊖	S	19	Yes		No	No				•
Stokke Xplory	900	68	○	⊖	⊖	⊖	L	28	Yes	•	Yes	Yes		•		
Inglesina Zippy	350	67	⊖	⊖	○	⊖	S	22	Yes		No	Yes				•
Cosco Altura	50	66	⊖	⊖	○	⊖	S	18	No		No	No	•			
Quinny Zapp	200	65	⊖	⊖	○	⊖	S	18	Yes	•	No	Yes				
Bugaboo Frog	760	65	○	⊖	⊖	⊖	S	22	Yes	•	Yes	Yes				
Baby Planet Max Pro	400	62	○	⊖	⊖	⊖	M	24	Yes		Yes	Yes	•	•	•	
Baby Trend Trendsport Lite	40	61	⊖	○	⊖	⊖	S	15	No		No	No	•			
Cosco Deluxe Comfort Ride	35	59	⊖	○	⊖	⊖	S	10	No		No	No				
Maclaren Volo	115	43	⊖	⊖	◐	⊖	S	10	Yes	•	No	No				
Combi Torino DX	180	43	⊖	⊖	○	⊖	S	16	Yes		Yes	Yes	•	•	•	
Combi Cosmo ST	55	39	⊖	◐	○	●	S	11	No		No	Yes	•			•
Bumbleride Flyer	330	28	⊖	⊖	◐	⊖	S	23	Yes		Yes	Yes	•	•	•	
Kolcraft Contours Options 3 Wheeler	140	14	○	⊖	●	⊖	M	30	Yes	•	Yes	Yes	•			
Peg Pérego Aria OH Classico	200	11	⊖	◐	●	⊖	S	14	Yes		No	Yes				•

Brand & model	Price	Overall score 0–100 (P|F|G|VG|E)	Ease of use	Maneuverability	Safety	Durability	Folded size	Weight (lb.)	5-point harness	One-touch brakes	Suitable for 6 mo. and under	Car-seat compatible	Trays for parent, child	Extra storage	Adjustable handle	Stands folded
SINGLE CAR SEAT CARRIER																
✓ **Baby Trend** Snap N Go	$ 55	82	⊖	⊖	⊖	⊖	S	12	NA		NA	Yes				•
Combi Flash EX	60	80	⊖	⊖	⊖	⊖	S	11	NA		NA	Yes			•	
DOUBLE SIDE-BY-SIDE																
✓ **Maclaren** Twin Triumph	245	69	⊖	⊖	○	⊖	S	24	Yes		Yes	No			•	
✓ **Chicco** C5 Twin	200	68	⊖	⊖	⊖	⊖	M	29	Yes		No	No			•	•
✓ **Combi** Twin Sport	200	66	⊖	⊖	○	⊖	M	23	Yes		Yes	Yes, one seat			•	•
Peg Pérego Aria Twin 60/40	330	64	○	⊖	⊖	⊖	S	20	Yes	•	No	Yes, one seat			•	•
Inglesina Twin Swift	250	60	○	⊖	○	⊖	S	28	Yes		No	No				
Jeep Wrangler Twin	85	58	○	○	⊖	⊖	S	21	No		No	No			•	
Joovy Groove 2	300	56	○	⊖	○	⊖	M	31	Yes	•	No	No			•	
Zooper Tango	430	55	○	○	○	⊖	M	30	Yes	•	Yes	No				•
DOUBLE TANDEM																
✓ **Graco** Quattro Tour Duo	240	59	⊖	○	○	⊖	L	39	Yes	•	Yes, one seat	Yes			•	•
Kolcraft Contours Options Tandem	200	49	○	◐	○	⊖	L	43	Yes		Yes	Yes			•	•
Safety 1st Two Way Tandem	150	43	○	●	⊖	⊖	L	41	Yes, one seat		Yes, one seat	Yes		•	•	•

✓ **CR Best Buy** These models offer the best combination of performance and price. All are recommended.

✓ **Recommended** These are high-performing models that stand out.

Guide to the Ratings

Overall score is based primarily on ease of use, maneuverability, and safety. The displayed score is out of a total of 100 points. **Ease of use** is based primarily on ease of safety harness use, folding and unfolding, adjusting backrest, lifting and carrying, engaging wheel brakes and car seat removal and installation (only for compatible strollers). **Maneuverability** was assessed by trained staffers on how well the strollers maneuvered S-turns through cones, narrow sections, grass, dirt trails, uphill, downhill, and curbs while walking. **Safety** for each stroller was assessed by our testing applying the ASTM F833-07a—an industry voluntary standard—and stability and usage tests designed by Consumers Union. We assessed **durability** by rolling the strollers 19 miles over 150,000 bumps with a 40-pound bag in the seat, then each stroller was folded and unfolded 10 times to check for mechanical failure or unusual wear. **Folded size** is relative to each other. **Weight** of stroller included accessories and stroller seat installed (if removable).

chapter

Swings

A baby swing can work wonders, soothing a fussy baby, lulling her to sleep at night or naptime, or occupying her for a few minutes while you get things done nearby or grab a bite to eat.

Plug-in swings like this Power Plus from Fisher-Price eliminate the expense of batteries, which swings can devour.

A swing provides a gentle rhythmic motion, which babies are accustomed to from their months in the womb. If you're like countless parents, you may consider a swing a godsend, especially for calming a colicky newborn and de-frazzling your nerves. It also comes in handy if your baby needs to sleep in a semi-upright position because she has a stuffy nose or other breathing issues.

Full-sized baby swings designed for indoor use from birth to 25 or 30 pounds (depending on the model) typically consist of a seat suspended by a pair of arms attached to a frame with wide-standing, tubular-metal legs. Most swings move from front to back, though several models also swing from side to side, cradle-style. Portable travel swings are popular with on-the-go parents. These swings sit low to the ground and are designed to be moved from room to room or stowed in the car for a trip to Grandma's. Most swings on the market today are battery-operated and driven by a motor that uses four C or D batteries (not included), which may provide up to 200 hours of swinging time. Such models emit a low churning noise with each swing, which can be soothing for some babies but may irritate others.

Several Fisher-Price swings, including the Power Plus Swing, the Zen Collection Cradle Swing, and the Starlight Cradle 'n Swing, among others, feature a plug-in option, eliminating the constant need for batteries. Electric and battery-powered standard-size swings are lightweight, yet they're cumbersome to move, which is why they're typically a fixture in the living room or kitchen for a while.

The Fisher-Price Rainforest Open-Top Cradle Swing moves side to side as well as front to back, and plays music, too.

They eat up a fair amount of room, so they may not be for you if floor space is scarce. You'll use the swing the most in your baby's first few months of life. After that, you'll probably use it less, or maybe even abandon it altogether (save it for your next baby) unless your baby is addicted to motion. Keep in mind that some babies don't like the rocking of a swing, no matter which type you buy, although they may change their minds after a few tries. Windup swing models, in which you crank a handle at the top or side of the frame to propel the swinging action, are relics in the marketplace; we don't know of any new models for sale. If you happen to buy one at a tag sale and it stops working, don't try to remove the spring housing to fix it. The spring is under tension and could injure you if it's released.

Shopping Secrets

If you can, try your baby in a friend's or relative's swing first, to see if he likes it. Or take your baby to the store with you for test runs. Take along your own C and D batteries and try the floor models. Your baby's reactions may help you decide on a brand, or whether he's even a candidate for a swing in the first place.

Decide between a full-sized swing or a travel model. If you want the option of moving your swing from room to room often and taking it on road trips, or if you're short on living space, a travel swing may be right for you. Travel swings take up about as much space as a bouncy seat, and many have a sturdy carrying handle. The downside? Because you have to crouch down to put your baby in the swing and take her out again, using the swing can be uncomfortable or impossible if you have a bad back or are recovering from a C-section. It also can be tricky to maneuver a squirmy baby into the swing from a sitting position.

On a full-sized swing, decide if you want side-to-side movement as well as front-to-back motion. Because of their construction—a seat held in a frame—standard swings, both full-sized and travel models, move only front to back. However, cradle swings, with a cradle-seat suspended from a frame, can move both side to side and front to back. All you have to do is turn the seat. Both standard full-sized and cradle models recline, but cradle swings are positioned so your baby can lie down for the ride, which newborns tend to prefer. But the useful life of a cradle swing is shorter than a traditional swing's, since the seat can't be adjusted to a full upright position. As soon as your baby can push up on his hands and knees, he'll want to sit up and see out. That's when it's time to retire a cradle swing.

Portable swings, like this Boppy Rock in Comfort Travel Swing, fold for travel.

Look for a five-point harness. Full-size swings are required to have a fixed restraint system, which may include a waist and crotch belt (three-point harness) that must be used together so that your baby can't slip out, or a passive crotch restraint and a waist belt, such as a tray with a crotch post and a waist belt. Some models feature an over-the-shoulder, five-point harness. This type of harness is best because it keeps your baby from climbing out of her seat and plunging to the ground, which can happen much quicker than you think possible. Travel swings don't have a tray with a middle post, just a safety harness; most have a three-point harness but five-point is better.

Consider comfort. Seating ranges from deep, padded, womblike cradles to a wider chair with an adjustable infant head support. For the infancy stage, you'll want a seat that reclines or has an angled back because your baby won't be able to hold his head up. An infant head-rest is a bonus; it will help keep your baby's head positioned properly. To increase the chances that your baby will use the swing after 3 months of age, look for a seat with an infant head support that's removable and that has several seatback positions. Older babies will want to sit upright and reach for the toys on the toy bar, if the swing has that feature. If the swing has a front tray, make sure it pivots from side to side, flips up, or is detachable. You'll have a much easier time sliding your older baby in and out of the seat with the tray out of the way.

Check the store's return policy. Try the swing within the time limits of the store's return policy (usually 30 to 45 days), so you have the option of taking it back. Keep the receipt and the packaging. A noisy motor may be a deal-breaker for you. A motor that conks out after a short while, such as after just a month or two of use, is also a reason to return a swing. See Getting the Right Return on Baby Products, page 15.

What's Available

Some major brands are, in alphabetical order: Boppy (*www.boppy.com*), Cosco (*www.coscojuvenile.com* and available at *www.walmart.com*), Evenflo (*www.evenflo.com*), Fisher-Price (*www.fisher-price.com*), Graco (*www.gracobaby.com*), Safety 1st (*www.safety1st.com*), and Summer Infant (*www.summerinfant.com*). Prices range from $42 for a portable swing to $210 for full-sized swings with multiple speeds and features, such as the Zen Collection Cradle Swing by Fisher-Price. The following companies make swings certified by the Juvenile Products

Swing Savvy

An estimated 1,800 infants are injured each year in baby swings, according to Consumer Product Safety Commission (CSPC) data, with an average of about one fatality a year. To protect your baby from falls and other hazards when using a swing:

◆ Assemble the swing according to the manufacturer's setup instructions and keep them for future reference. Give yourself a good half hour to get the job done adequately.

◆ Don't use a swing with parts that are missing or broken.

◆ Never leave your baby unattended in a swing.

◆ Always use the safety harness provided. Don't rely on the play tray to restrain your child.

◆ Never place a portable swing on an elevated or soft surface, such as a bed or sofa. If it tips over, it can be a fall or a suffocation hazard.

◆ Place your baby's swing away from heat sources, such as a stove or radiator, and from cords, such as window blind cords, drapes, and phone cords, which are a strangulation hazard.

◆ Don't let older children "push" your baby in the swing. If your child starts trying to "push" himself by jumping around in the seat, it's time to retire the swing.

◆ Limit the amount of time your baby swings; we recommend no more than 30-minute intervals, even if your baby seems content. More swinging time can make some babies dizzy. If you're drowsy while your baby's swinging, turn off the swing before you fall asleep and put your baby to bed in his crib. You don't want to wake up and find that your baby has been swinging unattended for hours.

◆ With multispeed swings, start with the lowest setting; high settings may be too rough for your baby. Very young babies tend to prefer slower speeds; older babies often like a quicker pace.

◆ To prevent falls, always follow the manufacturer's age and weight specifications. Stop using a full-sized or portable swing when your baby reaches the maximum weight limit, or becomes really active and appears to be able to climb out of the swing, whichever comes first. Stop using a cradle swing when your baby can roll over or push up on her hands and knees.

◆ Don't transport your baby in a swing or use a portable swing as an infant carrier unless the swing offers a detachable-seat carrier option, which some do.

◆ Watch out for recalls. Some models of baby swings have been recalled in recent years. Problems have included a risk of entrapment between the swing frame and the seat; loose screws on the swing's arm support that caused the seat to separate and drop to one side, harnesses that failed to hold a child securely, or could entangle him, posing a strangulation risk, and hazardous toys. One recalled model could be easily misassembled, resulting in a loose seat that flipped forward. For a list of baby swing recalls, go to the CPSC Web site at *www.cpsc.gov*. Send in the product registration card or register your swing online at the manufacturer's Web site, if possible, so you can easily be notified in case of a recall.

SWINGS

Manufacturers Association (JPMA): Dorel Juvenile Group (Cosco and Safety 1st), Fisher-Price, Graco, Kolcraft, and Summer Infant.

Features to Consider

Frames. If you opt for a full-sized swing, look for one with strong posts and a stance that's wide enough so it won't tip, even if your baby leans one way or another. It should also fold or dismantle easily for storage.

Easy access. Portable and full-sized swings are available without a top crossbar, typically called an "open-top design." They dominate the marketplace and it's a good thing. This design can be easier to use because there's no top crossbar to clear. You have access to your baby from the top, instead of having to crouch down to wriggle your baby in. Easy access can be a plus when you're just home from the hospital.

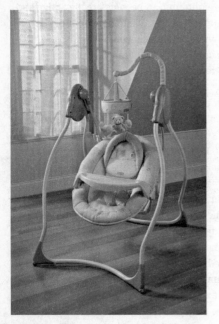

Seat cover. Look for plush padding that's machine washable and a removable infant-head support. At least one swing we know of, the Natures Purest Hug Me Complete Comfort Collection swing ($100), features a seat pad made from naturally grown fabric. Of course, choosing "natural" or organic over conventionally grown materials is a matter of personal preference and your budget.

Seat settings. A swing with at least three reclining positions can help you find the most soothing posture for your baby, which is important if your baby likes to nap while swinging. Some swings also feature two seat-height settings—a raised position for newborns, and a lower position for older, more active infants.

Green seating: The Natures Purest Hug Me Complete Comfort Collection Swing by Summer Infant features a seat pad made of naturally grown and colored cotton.

Speeds. Some battery-operated and electric swings have up to eight speeds, but more than four is overkill. The faster speeds may annoy rather than relax your baby. In general, start with the lowest setting, and see what your baby prefers. The heavier the baby, the more slowly a battery-powered model will swing, so expect to use the high setting more often as time goes on.

Entertainment. Many swings come with mobiles, toy bars, or trays, options your baby may enjoy. Your baby may not be able to reach the toy bar at first or even want to until around 3 months of age. Check that all toys are securely and safely attached and have no small parts that could cause choking. Nice-but-not-necessary extras are a light display and sound (classical music, lullabies, and nature sounds) with volume control, and storage baskets on the side for toys and accessories.

Convertibility. Some swings, such as the Graco Swing 'N Bounce 2-in-1 Infant Swing ($139.99), double as a swing and a stand-alone bouncy seat. The Fisher-Price Smart Stages 3-in-1 Rocker Swing ($93) has a removable seat for toting your baby around the house; it also converts into a toddler rocker. Since you won't use a swing for long (6 to 9 months, tops), getting more mileage out of it makes sense, especially if you don't have room for lots of baby gear. Convertibility ups the price though, so if you're on a budget, consider getting either a bouncy seat/rocker or a swing, since both products serve the same function—to soothe and entertain your baby, especially in the first few months.

Recommendations

Look for a swing that has a sturdy, stable frame with strong posts and legs and a wide stance to prevent tipping. The bottom of the legs or frame should not protrude so far that you're likely to trip over them, however. Examine the seat. It should be well padded, washable, and have a crotch post with a waist belt (if it's not a travel version) or a secure three-point or preferably) five-point harness. It should also have a partially reclining position for snoozing and a position for sitting up. If you buy a cradle-style model, make sure it's firmly mounted underneath; the cradle-to-frame connection shouldn't feel loose or flimsy. To find the safest swing possible, look for the JPMA certification seal, which means the model meets the latest requirements of product-safety standards developer ASTM International. Give yourself a

Double the fun: The Graco Swing 'N Bounce 2-in-1 Infant Swing features a removable seat you can use as a bouncer.

good half hour to assemble the swing. Make sure it's stable by swinging it without your baby in it, pushing down on the seat a little to make sure it's secure.

Buy new, not used. Older swings may not have an adequate restraint system or have broken or loose parts, which can put your baby at risk of falling.

33

chapter

Thermometers

"What's your baby's temperature?" is one of the first things your pediatrician will likely ask when you suspect your baby isn't feeling well. To answer accurately, you'll need the right thermometer. Consider it a must-have for your medicine cabinet.

Many digital thermometers like this one from American Red Cross/Learning Curve are designed for oral, rectal, or underarm use.

U nfortunately, babies sometimes get sick, and a fundamental clue that things are amiss is a fever—a body temperature that's higher than normal. Most pediatricians consider any thermometer reading of 100.4° F or higher a sign of fever. A fever can be alarming, but except in the case of heat stroke (a dangerous rise in body temperature caused by a sweltering environment, like a car with the windows rolled up in August), a fever by itself isn't an illness. It's the immune system's way of signaling that it's working to fight an infection.

Still, fever is often the first sign of illness, and your baby's temperature reading—coupled with your baby's other symptoms (if any)—will help your pediatrician diagnose the cause of a fever. But accuracy is key. For babies under 3 months old especially, every tenth of a degree counts. The difference between a temp of 100.3° F and 100.4° F, for example, can determine whether you stay home or take your baby to the emergency room. Any fever in this age group is typically considered an emergency. If your baby is under 4 weeks old, and has a fever of 100.4° F or greater, call your pediatrician immediately. A baby that young with a fever of 100.4° F or higher will most likely need to be hospitalized to rule out serious infection. For babies 4 weeks to 3 months old, it's still an emergency that needs prompt medical attention.

The Summer Infant 5 Second rectal thermometer features Fever Alert: When a temperature reading is complete, the digital screen will glow red if the temperature registers 99.9° F or higher, but keep in mind that 100.4° F and up is considered a fever.

Rectal Thermometers: Tops for Temps

Due to the toxic risks of mercury, digital thermometers have replaced the glass thermometers you may have grown up with. In fact, if you have a mercury thermometer, get rid of it, advises the American Academy of Pediatrics (AAP). But don't just throw it away. Your doctor or local health department can tell you how to dispose of it properly.

Digital thermometers are easy to read and they don't expose your baby to the mercury in a glass thermometer, which is dangerous if the thermometer breaks. Get a digital thermometer that can be used rectally. You can also take a baby's temperature by mouth, by ear, on the forehead, or under the arm, but the AAP considers rectal readings to be the most precise way to take a temperature in infants

■ **Proactive Parent**

What to Do When Your Baby Has a Fever

When your baby has a fever and you're worried, call your doctor. Be prepared to report your baby's temp, the method you used to take your baby's temp, how long your baby has had a fever, and any other symptoms your baby has. Wait to give acetaminophen (Tylenol) or any fever-reducing medication to a child under 2 until your pediatrician gives the OK. Ibuprofen, for example, should not to be given to children under 6 months or who are vomiting or dehydrated. Don't use aspirin to treat your child's fever. It has been linked to side effects such as intestinal bleeding, and most seriously, Reye's syndrome, a severe neurological disorder.

and children younger than age 3. (We've found in our tests that forehead models are especially imprecise.) After your baby's first birthday, your pediatrician may allow you to use a different temperature-taking method, so be sure to ask what's acceptable at that point, if you want to switch.

A popular option you'll see in stores and online is digital ear (tympanic) thermometers, which measure body temperature inside the ear. "They aren't recommended for young children because there are lots of chances for error," says Paul Horowitz, M.D., a founding pediatrician at Discovery Pediatrics in Valencia, Calif. We've found that you have to align them in the ear canal perfectly to be accurate. Temps taken orally, with a pacifier thermometer (a digital oral thermometer that looks like a pacifier; it displays a reading after your baby sucks on the pacifier for 90 seconds), may seem to be another way to go. But oral thermometers tend to be as much as 1° F lower than rectal thermometers and aren't considered as accurate for children under age 3.

Shopping Secrets

Check features. Simple as digital thermometers are, some have bells and whistles that you might find convenient, such as soft or curved tips, or beeps that tell you when they're in the right spot or when they've finished.

Price and performance don't necessarily correlate. Extrapolating from our tests of oral, ear, and forehead thermometers in 24 adults and 21 children ages 5 to 14, we've found that paying a high price doesn't guarantee a top performer; some inexpensive models we've tested do a better job.

Digital pacifier thermometers seem easy to use, but rectal thermometers are the "gold standard" for children.

Myth: Any Temp Over 98.6° F Equals Fever

Reality: Most pediatricians consider any thermometer reading above 100.4° F a sign of a fever, not 98.6° F as you might suspect. That's because "normal" body temperature fluctuates in each of us throughout the day, depending on our age, general health, activity, how much clothing we're wearing, and the time of day. It's usually lower in the morning and higher between late afternoon and early evening. There's a "normal," healthy temperature range for everyone. For children, it can run between 98.6° F or so and 100.3° F. Accuracy can vary depending on the temperature-taking method you're using, so mention whether you took your baby's temperature rectally or some other way. Your pediatrician probably will ask anyway.

Think long-term. Since you'll probably be changing temperature-taking methods soon, go with a digital thermometer that can be used rectally and later orally. Your pediatrician may have a preferred brand, so be sure to ask. Use a disposable thermometer cover to keep it clean. You can find them at *www.cvs.com* and *www.safety1st.com*.

What's Available

Some brands of digital thermometers are, in alphabetical order: BD Digital (*www.bd.com*), Braun (*www.braun.com*), Exergen (*www.exergen.com*), Graco (*www.gracobaby.com*), Learning Curve (American Red Cross brand; *www.learningcurve.com*), Omron (*www.omronhealthcare.com*), Safety 1st (*www.safety1st.com*), Summer Infant (*www.summerinfant.com*), Timex (*www.timexhealthcare.com*), and Vicks (*www.vicks.com*). Digital thermometers retail from $5.49 to $44.99. Digital thermometers are available at leading pharmacy and baby product Web sites such as *www.amazon.com, www.buybuybaby.com, www.babiesrus.com, www.toysrus.com,* and *www.target.com*.

Features to Consider

Speed-reading. When you're trying to take a wiggly baby's temperature, you don't have much time to get the job done. Some thermometers claim to display a reading in as fast as five seconds, but in our opinion, a reading in 20 to 60 seconds is fine.

Positioning gauge. To take the guesswork out of insertion, some rectal thermometers feature an indicator or design that makes it easy to know if the thermometer is positioned properly—a definite plus.

■ **Sanity Saver**

Worry-Free Temperature-Taking Tips

If you're not comfortable taking your baby's temperature rectally, you're not alone. Most parents don't relish the thought. But most babies don't mind it as much as you'd think they would. Plus, many pediatricians consider a rectal temp the gold standard and insist you measure it that way. It gets easier with practice. Here are some pointers:

◆ Clean the end of the thermometer with soap and water or rubbing alcohol (whatever the instructions direct). Rinse it with cool water; don't use hot.

◆ Apply the probe cover if you are using one and put a dab of petroleum jelly on the end of the cover, or on the thermometer if you are not using a cover. Place your baby tummy-down on your lap or a firm surface. Hold him with your hand on his lower back. With your other hand, turn on the thermometer and insert it one-half to one inch (or to the length indicated on the thermometer) into your baby's bottom.

◆ Wait until you hear the thermometer beep or until the required amount of time has passed, such as 5 to 90 seconds. (It varies per thermometer.) Remove the thermometer and check the reading. Write the temperature down so you'll remember, in case your pediatrician or the nurse asks for it (they will).

Sound effects. Thermometers that beep when they're done are useful; that way, you won't leave the thermometer in any longer than necessary.

Durability. Life with an under-the-weather baby is unpredictable. You'll want a digital thermometer that can withstand dropping, being submerged in water, even being gnawed on by your little one.

Brains. Some thermometers "remember" the last temperature read. That can be useful, especially in the middle of the night when you're sleep-deprived and trying to determine in which direction your baby's fever is going. Some also feature an automatic shut-off to preserve battery life. That's a plus, too.

✔ **TIP**

WHAT NOT TO BUY Digital ear or forehead thermometers are expensive and not recommended for children under age 3 because they're imprecise.

Recommendations

For your baby's first thermometer, go with an inexpensive digital model. Look for an LCD display that's easy to read and a start button that's easy to press. But don't be swayed by digital thermometers that claim to take a reading in an instant. A reading in 20 to 60 seconds is quick enough.

34

chapter

Toys

Y our baby may look like he's simply having fun when he coos at his rattle or tries his hand at stacking plastic "donuts." But make no mistake—what looks like playtime to us is work to babies, and toys are the tools for getting the job done.

Playing is your baby's work— and giggle-inspiring fun, too.

TOYS

Playing helps develop a baby's social, emotional, language, intellectual, and problem-solving skills, says Marilyn Segal, Ph.D., dean emeritus and director of the professional development program at Mailman Segal Institute for Early Childhood Studies at Nova Southeastern University in Fort Lauderdale, Fla. Batting at a mobile, giving a musical ball a shove, or transferring a rattle from one hand to another all help babies learn about the world. Such play also helps them connect sight, sound, touch, taste, and smell to objects; to recognize shapes, patterns, and colors; develop hand-eye coordination and memory; and bond with you and others. "It's how your baby learns, and so much more," Segal says.

When you choose toys and activities that enhance your child's development, you're speaking your baby's language and helping her foster cognitive and social skills she can build on. "I always tell parents if you could see inside your child's brain you'd notice that every time he plays, connections are being made," says Roni Leiderman, Ph.D., the current dean at Mailman Segal. "It would look like a Christmas tree, with thousands of sparkling lights going off."

But don't give toys all the credit. You're a key player. "The most important toy is the parent and other caregivers because babies crave one-on-one social interaction and need the security it provides," Segal says. The right toy, though, can make key developmental stages more fun—for your child and for you. Here are some ideas about age-appropriate toys for your baby—and what you can do to play up their important lessons. Note: Retail prices vary widely, so the prices listed here may not match those in the store. Age recommendations are those of the manufacturer. (CONSUMER REPORTS has not tested these particular products.)

Newborn and Up: Shake, Rattle, Manipulate

Babies are born with natural curiosity and gather information about the world through their senses. "The more of the five senses a particular toy commands, the more rewarding and appealing it is," says Sally Goldberg, Ph.D., professor of education, consultant, and author of six parenting books, including "Baby and Toddler Learning Fun." Babies enjoy looking at the world around them—lights, shapes, patterns, and colors. At around 3 months, they begin to swipe at objects and may try to reach for them.

Suggested toys: Brightly colored rattles and infant toys with colors that make interesting sounds, such as the Infantino Giggle Ball

Toy Set ($9.99, 3 months and up) and Sassy's Whirly Twirly Twosome ($15.53, birth and up), and musical crib mobiles with bright, primary-color objects and high-contrast patterns that attract and hold your baby's attention, such as Fisher-Price's Precious Planet 2-in-1 Projection Mobile ($49.99, birth and up). Keep toys out of the crib. However, mobiles can be suspended near or above the crib as long as they're safely mounted. The mobile should be out of your baby's reach so he can't become entangled or pull anything off of it. Remove the mobile when your baby can push up on his hands and knees, at about 6 months.

Babies can see shapes and colors of rattles and play keys. Babies under 4 months are most attracted to bright and vibrant colors, especially reds and yellows, and high contrast patterns, such as black and white swirls. They can also feel the smooth or nubby texture, hear the rattling or clinking sound, and mouth rattles and play keys, which stimulates brain development. In the best rattles, the source of noise is visible so your baby can see the beads inside and link sound with sight. That helps babies learn about cause and effect—if they shake a rattle or keys, they make a sound.

The best rattles, like the Bobble Bee by Munchkin, teach cause and effect by allowing your baby to see the source of the sound.

Game plan: Play is mostly parent-driven for about 6 months; after that, your baby takes over. Mold your newborn's fingers around a rattle or key ring and have her shake it or help her make the sound. Shake a rattle or other toys at various points in your baby's sight lines so she'll enjoy the surprise of hearing the toy's sound from different angles. At that point, have your baby grab for toys with either hand to help develop and integrate both sides of her brain; sometimes present toys on her right side and have her grab with the left hand, sometimes on her left and have her grab with the right hand. While some babies may start reaching for items at 3 months, the norm is more like 4 to 6 months. However, your baby probably won't show true hand dominance until about 18 months to 2 years, and many children remain ambidextrous until 3 to 5 years old.

Organic and Natural Toys

Toys made from sustainable sources, including renewable wood with water-based finishes, natural and organic-cotton plush toys, and toys colored with vegetable dyes instead of paint are among the latest toy trends. But buyer beware: Some "eco" labels carry more weight than others. Not all "green" toy claims can be substantiated.

There's no standard definition for the term "natural," for example, except as it applies to meat and poultry. And fabric toys labeled "100 percent organic" are only required to meet USDA organic standards that refer to how the fiber was grown, not to the processes by which it was made into cloth.

Some manufacturers have obtained special certifications to differentiate their natural or organic products so you can be more assured of their meaning. Summer Infant's Natures Purest line, for example, which includes fabric rattles and stacking toys, is certified Oeko-Tex Standard 100, which means that the finished fabric, not just the original cotton, is free from harmful levels of substances known to be detrimental to human health, such as formaldehyde. We haven't tested any "organic" toys, though, to determine if they're, in fact, healthier for babies. Similarly, Toys "R" Us has a line of Natural Wood Toys made from materials certified by the Forest Stewardship Council (FSC), a nonprofit organization that sets standards for forest management. FSC certification means that the wood was grown according to the group's 57 environmental, social, and economic criteria, and that a third-party certifier verified those criteria were met. According to Toys "R" Us, 100 percent of the wood in the toys is FSC certified and can be traced back to its source.

Consumers Union, the publisher of this book, considers the FSC label to be only somewhat meaningful in terms of the environmental impact of a product with this designation. Keep in mind, so-called "natural" wood is in no way healthier or safer for your child, although it might be more sustainable.

For more information about the Forest Stewardship Council and other eco-labels, see the Eco-labels center at *www.greenerchoices.org*, Consumers Union's Web-based resource for information about environmentally friendly products and practices (no subscription required).

The Sassy Simply Natural rattle is hand-crafted using hardwoods and water-based finishes. It has a gently curved handle that's easy for a baby to grasp.

You can also try tracking: Hold a toy 6 to 12 inches from your baby's face, which is where babies 4 months and under see it best, with your baby sitting in your lap or lying down, and move it side to side slowly. This technique helps visual development and eventually hand-eye coordination. Later on, take turns playing with the rattle to instill the idea of taking turns and sharing, which your child will understand at about age 3.

4 to 10 Months: Gym Time

By now, babies can track moving items with their eyes, reach for and grasp objects, move them from one hand to the other, and play with their feet. They'll search for the source of sounds.

Suggested toys: A takeoff on overhead mobiles, activity gyms such as the Baby Einstein Baby Neptune Ocean Adventure Gym ($69.99, birth and up), Gymini Monkey Island by Tiny Love ($64.95, birth and up), and the Fisher-Price Rainforest Melodies & Lights Deluxe Gym ($65, birth and up) feature brightly colored floors and hanging detachable toys that make sounds, play music, and have tantalizing textures; some may include unbreakable, embedded mirrors, a definite plus.

"Babies love to look at their own image," says author Goldberg. Like rattles and play keys, activity gyms help babies explore their environment through their senses of sound, touch, sight, and taste. Their fine-motor skills get a tune-up when they bat, reach, and grab for toys. (Safety note: Never place an activity gym in a crib or playpen. Never add strings or ties or secure your own toys to the gym.) Babies of this age also tend to enjoy soft balls with sounds inside, musical toys sized for their small hands, washable baby books, and toys with flaps or lids that can be opened and closed. They'll still be fascinated with rattles, and the more their pick-up skills develop, the more they'll reach for and play with them.

Game plan: Use your creativity to help your baby enjoy the activity gym. Take turns scrunching the crinkle toys and helping

Activity gyms, like the Gymini Monkey Island by Tiny Love, help babies explore their environment through their sense of sound, touch, sight, and taste.

New Toy Safety Standards

The Consumer Product Safety Commission regulates toys sold in the U.S., and toys have long been subject to recall if they did not meet certain federal safety standards.

For example, the safety list for toys meant for children under 3 years has prohibited small parts, such as small balls or marbles, that could pose a choking, ingestion, or inhalation hazard; any small wires that could poke through; and any pinching parts, or sharp surfaces or points. In addition, toys could not exceed flammability limits. The Consumer Product Safety Improvement Act of 2008, signed into law in August 2008, has added other safety measures. All toys sold in the U.S., whether domestically manufactured or imported, are now required to meet lower thresholds for lead paint and lead content. As of August 2009, permissible lead levels in paint will fall from 600 parts per million (ppm) to 90 ppm and permissible lead content will go down from 600 ppm to 300 ppm. In addition, three types of phthalates, a chemical in plastic that may affect a child's development and reproductive system, are permanently banned under the law. Three other phthalates are temporarily banned in any toy a child can put in his mouth until their effect can be further studied, at which time they may be permanently banned, too.

As of August 2009, the law also requires manufacturers to permanently label their products with the maker's name, contact information, the model name and number, the date of manufacture, and any other identifying characteristics. The label must be on both the product and the product packaging so it will be easy to tell if the product is a recall.

him squeeze the toys that beep. Detach his favorite toys and have him reach for them, either when he's lying down or supported by you or a Boppy, a horseshoe-shaped infant-support pillow. At first, your baby might just make general movements in the direction of a specific object, but eventually, he'll be able to reach out and pull objects to him.

9 Months and Up: The Nesting (and Stacking) Instinct Kicks In

Starting at about 9 months, babies play by shaking, banging, throwing, and dropping toys. They enjoy searching for hidden objects, taking objects out of containers, and poking their fingers into holes. Your baby will be able to grasp objects with her fingers and put one object on top of or into another, such as a ball into a box. At around age 1, she'll also start trying to put shapes through their designated slots on a shape sorter, and by 15 to 18 months, you'll see a marked development in hand-eye coordination. Stacking and nesting are other ways babies develop eye-hand coordination and learn about spatial relationships—how things fit inside and on top of one another. Stacking and nesting also help babies develop the fine-motor skills of grasping and releasing, and the visual ability to align one object with another. Sorting helps babies understand the relationship among objects—how they fit together and spatially relate to one another and how they differ in size and shape. "It lays the groundwork for organizing and categorizing, which are basic mathematical concepts," says Goldberg.

Suggested toys: Lightweight balls; nesting and stacking blocks and cups with rounded edges, such as the Friendly Firsts Surprise Inside Cups by Fisher-Price ($9, 6 months to 2 years); pop-up toys that require sliding, toggling, pulling, and/ or turning, such as Playskool Busy Basics Busy Poppin Pals ($9.99, 9 months and up); squeeze and bath toys such as Sassy's Scoop Pour N' Squirt bath toy ($6.99, 12 months and up); soft dolls, puppets, and baby books; musical toys, such as the Lock N Rock Linking Musical Shakers by International Playthings ($14.99, 9 months and up); toy telephones and push-pull playthings, such as the Tonka Wheel Pals Chaser Chuck & Tow-nee Vehicles by Hasbro ($5.99, 12 months and up).

Shape sorters help babies learn about spatial relationships—how things fit together.

Game plan: Play with your child with shape-sorting toys and puzzles and hide another toy inside a nesting block to see if your baby can find it. "That adds the element of surprise and builds on the concept of object permanence," says Goldberg. You can enrich the experience by helping balance the block creation when it gets too high or even just commenting, "Oh, what a big tower!"

"Talking to young children as you're playing helps them assimilate words and concepts," says Jay Cerio, Ph.D., professor and director, Child and Family Services Center at Alfred University in Alfred, N.Y. Even though your child may not say his first words until 12 to 18 months, he's taking it all in.

The Buzz on High-Tech Toys

Step into any baby store and you'll see that a generation of microchip-based toys is beeping, jingling, vibrating, flashing, and wailing its way into the nursery.

Stimulating, tech-driven kid products aren't new, of course. What's newsworthy is the range of such offerings for babies—from an infant-sized "interactive play center" that entertains with microchip-powered songs, sounds, and flashing lights to stuffed animals that sing and vibrate when you press their paws.

High-tech baby products can stimulate and entertain the older diaper crowd, but the chips inside aren't likely to add value for infants. As for those electronic toys that claim to stimulate infant development or creativity, researchers say there's no credible supporting evidence regarding their long-term effects. "If it's a new toy, then for an hour or so, they're a little more alert and involved," says Jerome Kagan, Ph.D., a research professor emeritus of psychology at Harvard University. "But you wouldn't want to make profound predictions, such as, 'If my baby plays with electronic toys, he'll be smarter.'"

Kagan says the typical American household already provides enough sensory stimulation to make such toys unnecessary. "We should view the toys like an ice-cream cone," he says. "It's a brief source of pleasure that vanishes quickly."

Children will get far more meaningful stimulation from the sounds of the people, animals, and objects around them, notes Jane M. Healy, Ph.D., an educational psychologist in Vail, Colo., and author of "Your Child's Growing Mind." There's also a need for quiet time, when the brain consolidates what it has learned. "If there's nothing that's entertaining, it gives the brain time and space to learn to manage itself," Healy says.

> Babies may be drawn to electronic toys, but they're not a must-have. Babies get plenty of stimulation from their environment.

Ages 1 to 2: Babies Get Their Fill

Playtime can get messy starting at age 1, when children begin to take an interest in emptying, transferring, and rearranging their environment. Turn your back and you're likely to find your toddler emptying the salt shaker, overturning the dog's dish, or upending the baby wipes. Filling and dumping are organizing skills that help your toddler experience how things work and relate to each other. They also enhance hand-eye coordination and teach basic spatial concepts like "in" and "out."

Starting as early as 9 months, your baby may also begin walking, although the average age is around 12 months.

Suggested toys: Those that encourage your child's budding ambulatory skills, such as the Fisher-Price's classic Counting Corn Popper ($15, 12 months and up) and Step2's WaterWheel Play Table ($32, 12 months and up).

Game plan: During play and other times, encourage your baby's cruising confidence with plenty of praise as she stands and pushes her way across carpeted or hardwood floors. Bathtime is a good time to encourage filling and dumping by adding spoons, a plastic pitcher, measuring cups, and bath toys, such as Funny Face Bath Beakers by International Playthings ($11.99, 12 months and up), to the mix so your child can fill and pour without a mess.

There are literally hundreds of toys to choose from for every age. Browse stores, catalogs, and Web sites for possibilities. You can also get an idea of the toys your child might like by noticing what toys he gravitates to on play dates and at day care, and by asking other parents who have children of similar ages.

Shopping Secrets

Millions of toys have been recalled, many due to lead, and recalls continue, so don't let down your guard. The Consumer Product Safety Improvement Act of 2008 has made safety standards stricter for lead paint and content, phthalates, and product labeling. But even so, you may find that tainted toys could still be out there. To keep your baby safe, follow these toy-buying tactics.

Buy according to your child's age. Look for manufacturer's recommended age ranges on the toy package—and take them seriously. More than a friendly hint, age grading can alert you to a possible choking hazard, the presence of small parts, and other dangers. It also relates to a toy's play value. Don't assume your little genius is ahead of the curve or that buying more advanced toys will enhance your child's growth. They could be a source of frustration if they're inappropriate for your child's stage of development.

Never buy toys with small magnets even if they're safely contained within the toy. If the toy breaks and the magnets fall out, they could be accidentally swallowed, perforating a child's intestines and stomach lining when the magnets are attracted to each other inside the body. Children have required emergency surgery to remove such magnets and at least one child died.

Think twice before buying toys with small parts for your older children. Your baby will probably find a way to get the toys. Babies experience much of their world through sucking, so expect that most toys will go straight to their mouths.

Check for recalls. Before shopping, visit the CPSC's Web site at www.cpsc.gov, to see if the toys you plan to buy—or the toys already in your home—have been recalled. Or save yourself a step and sign up for free e-mail notices of future recalls at www.cpsc.gov/cpsclist.aspx. Also, a toy may have a registration card; be sure to fill it out and send it in. That way, you can be notified directly by the manufacturer if the item is recalled. But keep checking the CPSC Web site anyway.

Your baby sees bright colors and contrasting patterns best, but can still enjoy these soft, squeezable, texture-y blocks.

Watch where you shop. Be leery of drugstores, airports, and dollar stores. They may be more likely to carry recalled and flimsy toys with dangerous sharp edges or small parts that can break off easily.

Look beyond the logo. Some of the most popular toys for babies and toddlers tie in with characters like Elmo and Dora the Explorer. To assess what you're really buying, ask yourself, If I took Elmo off this package, what do I have? "If a toy has nothing to offer beyond the character, don't buy it," says Richard Gottlieb, a toy-industry expert in New York City. Similarly, do the same when assessing "natural" or "organic" toys. Ask yourself: Beyond being organic or natural, what does this toy offer my baby? Some organic/natural toys are beige, for example, which begs the question of whether they can attract your baby's attention as well as toys with contrasting or primary colors (which may or may not be organic).

What's Available

Some brands of toys for newborns, infants, and toddlers are, in alphabetical order: Alex (*www.alextoys.com*), Baby Einstein (*www.babyeinstein.com*), Bright Starts (*www.brightstarts.com*), Edushape (*www.edushape.com*), Fisher-Price (*www.fisher-price.com*), Haba (*www.habausa.com*), Infantino (*www.infantino.com*), International Playthings (*www.intplay.com*), Kids II (*www.kidsii.com*), LeapFrog (*www.leapfrog.com*), Learning Curve (which includes Lamaze, *www.learningcurve.com*), Little Tikes (*www.littletikes.com*), Manhattan Toy (*www.manhattantoy.com*), Melissa & Doug (*www.melissaanddoug.com*), Munchkin (*www.munchkin.com*), Playskool (*www.hasbro.com*), Sassy (*www.sassybaby.com*), Small World Toys (*www.smallworldtoys.com*), Step2 (*www.step2.com*), Toys "R" Us (*www.toysrus.com*), Tiny Love (*www.tinylove.com*), and Vtech (*www.vtechkids.com*). Prices typically range from under $10 for basic toys, such as blocks, play keys, toy phones, and shape sorters, to $80 or more for deluxe activity gyms and sizeable stuffed animals. (For information on stuffed animals, see Zebras & Other Stuffed Animals, page 363). Natural and organic toys can cost more than conventional toys, though not necessarily substantially more; it varies by manufacturer.

Recommendations

When toy shopping, follow the manufacturer's age recommendations displayed on the package. Sometimes age recommendations can be difficult to find (or nonexistent) even though they are required. You can test an item for safe size by doing the toilet-paper-tube test: If the toy is small enough to pass through the tube, it's too small for a baby to play with. Look for anything that could be bitten or chewed off, such as hard, sewn-on parts like eyes, buttons, or wheels, and soft, small pieces, such as strings, ribbons, and stuffed animals' ears. All can be choking hazards. Avoid any toy with magnets inside that could dislodge and become an injury hazard. Use our Shopping Secrets on page 353 as buying guidelines.

Check all toys for breakage and potential hazards each time you give them to your baby. If they can't be repaired, throw them away.

If you've had a bad experience with a toy, call the CPSC at 800-638-2772 or visit *www.cpsc.gov/talk.html*. Your call may lead to a recall.

Which Batteries are Best for Toys and Baby Gear?

You may not go through as many batteries as diapers during your baby's first couple of years, but it will seem pretty close. Batteries usually aren't included when you buy toys and baby gear with music, lights, vibration, or sound effects, and some toys or baby products may require more than one size battery. Not every battery is right for every job. Here's a rundown of what to consider before your next visit to the battery aisle, based on our recent tests of AA batteries, the most common type—and the most typical type used in toys.

Buy rechargeable batteries for high-use items. Our tests of AA rechargeable batteries show that rechargeables are the best type of battery for some toys and other devices that draw bursts of power or are used often. The downside? These batteries discharge when they're not in use, so they're not the best choice for battery-powered toys that sit idle. You also may have to charge the battery before the first use. Don't mix rechargeable and disposable batteries, and use a suitable recharger.

Keep disposable batteries around as a backup, even if you plan to use rechargeables. Among disposables, lithium batteries, which are expensive, are the best for getting the most shots from your digital camera; the least expensive high-scoring alkalines are fine for everything else.

Follow manufacturer recommendations. No disposable battery is a deal if the toy or baby products manufacturer recommends another type. Be wary of knockoff brands that seem like a great value. Some have been defective.

Ratings • Batteries

	Excellent	Very good	Good	Fair	Poor
	◒	◒	○	◓	●

Brand & model	Price for 2	Score
SINGLE USE		
LITHIUM		
✔ Energizer Ultimate	$4.00	◒
NICKEL OXYHYDROXIDE		
Duracell Power Pix	3.00	○
✔ Panasonic Oxyride Extreme Power	2.40	○
ALKALINE		
✔ Kirkland Signature (Costco)	0.43	○
Energizer e2 Titanium	3.00	○
Walgreens Ultra Supercell	2.25	○
Radio Shack Digital Plus	2.50	○
Duracell Coppertop	2.25	○

Brand & model	Price for 2	Score
ALKALINE continued		
Duracell Ultra Digital	$3.00	○
Rayovac	1.50	○
Panasonic Digital Power	1.60	○
CVS	1.75	◓
Energizer Max	2.25	◓
RECHARGEABLE		
NICKEL-METAL HYDRIDE		
✔ Duracell (2650mAh)	7.50	◒
Energizer e2 (2500mAh)	6.00	◒
✔ Duracell Precharged (2000mAh)	8.00	◒
Sony (2500 mAh)	6.00	◒

✔ **Recommended** These are high-performing models that stand out.

35

chapter

Walkers

The American Academy of Pediatrics (AAP) thinks walkers should be banned from the market, and they are banned in Canada. Walkers can allow your baby to scoot into danger and may even delay development.
If you insist on using a walker, this chapter will help you purchase a model that is as safe as possible.

Babies have been clocked to move in walkers at about 3 feet per second, which doesn't give you much time to react if danger pops up.

A wheeled walker, consisting of a molded plastic or metal frame with a suspended center seat and wheels attached to the base, gives a baby an all-too-quick way to get around before he can walk. It's designed for babies who can hold their heads up and sit up unassisted (typically at around 6 months of age) to whenever they begin to walk, usually by around one year of age, or reach the manufacturer's weight maximum (up to 35 pounds), whichever comes first. Check the owner's manual.

Walkers can keep a child entertained and let her follow you around the house, but they also raise concerns about safety and a child's normal development. Despite the name, a walker lets a baby simulate walking, but doesn't help her acquire walking skills. Indeed, according to several studies, walkers can delay normal motor and mental development. In fact, one study found strong associations between the amount of walker use and the extent of developmental delay.

More important (because "delayed" kids do catch up), walkers pose a significant risk of injury. Older walkers, manufactured before new safety standards were established in the late 1990s, are the most prone to falling down stairs or steps. But even a new or certified walker can take a tumble. Any walker can turn over when their wheels get snagged, or can roll up against hot stoves and heaters. Outdoors, they fall off decks and patios, over curbs, and into swimming pools. Walker accidents can occur despite a safety gate, either because the gate is closed incorrectly or can't withstand a walker's impact.

Walkers, even those that meet the industry standard, are not a safe option. This one is shown folded for storage.

In 1997, a new safety standard was issued for walkers to protect against stairway falls. Since then, walkers must either have a bottom friction strip made of rubberized material that acts as a brake to stop the walker if its leading wheels drop over the edge of a step or the walker must be too wide to fit through a 36-inch-wide doorway. Walker-related incidents have declined since that standard was introduced. According to Consumer Product Safety Commission (CPSC) data, there were an estimated 16,487 walker injuries in 1997. By 2007, estimated injuries had fallen to 4,100, a 75 percent reduction. Some of this sizeable drop may be the result of stationary activity centers supplanting wheeled walkers as the product of choice. Still, we think 4,100 injuries are too many—and there continue to be fatalities, although they are fewer.

We don't consider walkers a safe option. Our testing has found that friction strips don't always work, and they may wear out or come loose. Moreover, baby walkers that don't meet the nationally recognized stair-fall safety standard continue to be sold and recalled in the U.S. They may fit through a standard doorway or lack a friction strip—or both.

The AAP urges parents not to use wheeled baby walkers, and has long recommended that the U.S. government ban wheeled walkers. New and used baby walkers are already prohibited from being imported, advertised, or sold, even second hand, in Canada. We agree that walkers can pose a safety hazard—even if they meet the safety standard. The simple fact remains: Babies can move with surprising speed in walkers, and as long as they have wheels, no standard or testing can make them safe.

There are plenty of safer exercise alternatives, including stationary activity centers and stationary activity jumpers. For more on stationary activity centers and stationary activity jumpers, see pages 305 and 211, respectively.

Shopping Secrets

If you still want to buy a walker, keep these shopping tips in mind:

Check for stability. Select a model with a wheelbase that's longer and wider than the frame of the walker to ensure stability.

Practice folding display models in the store. Make sure the folding mechanism works well. We have tested models that could pinch a finger.

Don't buy a walk-behind walker. Some walkers, such as the Kolcraft Tiny Steps 2-in-1 Activity Walker ($70), can be converted to a walk-behind walker; once they're able, babies have the option of scooting around on foot by pushing the walker from behind. We consider walk-behind units dangerous because a baby can move too fast and could

Instead of a walker, we recommend a stationary activity center like the Evenflo ExerSaucer SmartSteps Active Learning Center (see Stationary Activity Centers, page 305).

push the walker down stairs. Avoid these models or simply don't convert them into walk-behind mode.

Watch the fit. When you're shopping, make sure your baby's feet can touch the ground from the seat's lowest setting.

Examine attachments. Look for small toys or parts that can break off or screws that can loosen. Toys and parts should be firmly attached and all parts should be smooth. Walkers have been recalled because of toys that broke or detached, posing a choking hazard, or had sharp edges.

What's Available

Some major brands of wheeled baby walkers are, in alphabetical order, Baby Trend (*www.babytrend.com*), Chicco (*www.chiccousa.com*), Combi (*www.combi-intl.com*), Dream on Me (*www.dreamonme.com*), Kolcraft (*www.kolcraft.com*), and Safety 1st (*www.safety1st.com*).

Walkers usually have a rectangular base, with a seat that may be round, seat-shaped, or novelty-shaped, such as the sports car and SUV models. Unlike stationary activity centers, your baby's feet touch the floor, not a platform, so he can scoot. Many have optional toy bars and toys, with or without sound and lights, and sometimes a mock steering wheel. Some also have a large snack and play tray. Prices range from $39 to $95. The following walker brands are currently certified by the Juvenile Products Manufacturers Association (JPMA): Baby Trend, Chicco, Delta Enterprise Corporation, Dorel Juvenile Group (Safety 1st), Graco, and Kolcraft. Keep in mind that we have found certified models that failed our testing.

Features to Consider

Foldability. Some models fold flat for easy storage, a convenience if you live in a small space or plan to travel to Grandma's with your child's walker in tow.

Friction strips. They touch the floor when the wheels fall away on stairs or uneven pavement, making it difficult for a baby to push the walker farther. Most walkers now meet the safety standard for

Some wheeled walkers convert to a walk-behind walker, but we don't recommend those, either.

■ **Safety Strategies**

You Can't Be too Careful with a Walker

If you insist on using a walker, always keep an eye on your baby when she's in it. You'll need to be extra vigilant. Walkers can give babies access to things that would normally be out of reach, such as a pot on the stove or a lamp waiting to be pushed off an end table. Here's what else you'll need to do to keep your baby safe in a walker:

◆ If you'll use a walker in rooms with doorways that are wider than 36-inches, look for a walker with a friction strip that's supposed to stop the walker at the edge of a stairway.

◆ To play it even safer, use a walker only in a room that doesn't have access to stairs leading down, and block access to stairs and the outside while the walker is in use.

◆ Don't use a walker around swimming pools and other sources of water.

◆ Clear objects off tables, counters, and stovetops that a baby in a walker might be able to reach, such as a letter opener or paper clips on the desk, a knife on the table, glass figurines on the bookshelf, or myriad other dangerous things waiting to be grabbed.

◆ Make sure any springs and hinges on the walker have protective coverings.

◆ Don't carry a walker with your baby in it. It's too easy for you to trip.

◆ Don't use a walker once your baby can walk or reaches the manufacturer's weight or height limit. Check the owner's manual.

◆ Don't leave your baby in a walker for extended periods. Keep to short stints, such as less than 20 minutes.

◆ Check the walker regularly to make sure it's not damaged or broken. Stop using if so. To assemble the walker correctly, consult the owner's manual and keep it for future reference.

◆ Buy new. A used model is too risky, and this product is risky enough as it is. Recalled models, older models, or any that lack the required safety features, might very well be found in the second-hand marketplace.

friction strips, but our tests have shown that's not a fail-safe design.

Parking stand. This allows the wheels to be lifted off the floor so the baby can't scoot. Or look for a walker with wheels that lock.

Seat. Some seat covers are removable and machine washable. Seat height can be raised or lowered using a locking mechanism located under the front tray, slots in the base of the walker, or adjusters on the seat.

Toys. Most walkers have rimmed trays, often with toys attached, some of which are equipped with lights and/or electronic sound effects.

Lockable bounce feature. Some walkers, such as the Combi Activity Walker ($95), also bounce, making them a combination jumper and walker. When your baby doesn't feel like bouncing, the seat can be locked in place.

Recommendations

We think that even with a friction strip or a frame too wide to fit through a standard doorway, a wheeled walker is still not a safe option. Consider a stationary activity center or a stationary activity jumper instead.

Walkers do poorly on carpet, so reconsider if your house doesn't have hardwood, tile, or linoleum flooring. Babies on wheels can be surprisingly swift. Keep a close eye on your baby when he's in a walker. If you insist on buying this product despite the easy availability of safer products, follow our Safety Strategies and register the walker online or by mailing in the registration card so the manufacturer can easily notify you in the event of a recall.

The Combi Activity Walker converts to a stationary activity center.

36
chapter

Zebras &
Other Stuffed
Animals

After your baby's born—or even before—your home is likely to resemble a zoo of stuffed animals. Although your baby probably won't show an interest in a stuffed animal at first, this plush toy is likely to become his first friend.

A stuffed animal will likely
be your baby's first friend.

Stuffed animals can help your baby to make sense of the world; to discover how something feels, sounds, looks, and tastes. She can see its bright colors and shape, feel its smooth or nubby texture, hear its rattling sound or music, and mouth its fur—sensory stimulation that paves the way for brain development. Down the road, into the toddler and preschool years, a favorite stuffed toy can become an essential companion at bedtime.

Consider yourself warned: Stuffed animals make popular baby gifts. Once your baby starts playing favorites (some babies gravitate toward certain types of stuffed animals), you're likely to spend hours in the toy store looking for just the right stuffed kitty, bear, alligator, or puppy to add to his collection. You may also find yourself back at the store searching for the twin of a beloved stuffed toy that has been lost. Duplicates can come in handy if your baby's best furry friend gets tattered or dirty; your baby can play with one, while you keep the other one in reserve or launder a soiled twin, so consider buying two of a favorite stuffed animal once it's established "who" that is. (Hint: Your baby will likely take it everywhere.)

Shopping Secrets

Stuffed toys are disarming because they're so squishy and cuddly, but they can pose safety hazards. When buying stuffed animals or introducing them to your baby, follow these guidelines.

Buy plush toys according to manufacturer's age recommendations. This helps ensure the ones you choose are safe and user-friendly. Plush toys meant for kids age 3 and up may have small parts, such as eyes that are glued rather than sewn on, which can be a choking hazard for babies. You may not see a reason for age grading for this product, but don't ignore it. It's there for a purpose.

Keep stuffed animals out of the crib. They're a suffocation hazard.

Make sure toys are washable and biteproof. The label on the product should give care and cleaning advice. Many are just surface washable. In our opinion, that's not good enough. Lightly pull on fur to be sure it won't shed and fray. Fur is not specifically covered by federal small-parts regulations, but it can still cause choking.

Choose soft toys. Buy animals with the softest plush rather than those with scratchy fur.

Pick toys with contrasting or bright colors and noises. Because of a baby's vision limits, a stuffed zebra or Dalmatian stands out more than a cute pastel bunny. Stuffed toys with securely embedded, unbreakable mirrors tend to be a hit with the youngest set since children that age are naturally enamored of their own image. Squeaky, rattling, or jingly stuffed toys, or those that reward baby with a song (or a "moo" or a "baa") if she pulls, pushes, or jiggles them, provide an element of surprise and can be more entertaining than those toys that are simply cuddly.

Don't forget the background check. Before buying any toy, check the Consumer Product Safety Commission's Web site at *www.cpsc.gov*, for recalls or its toy recall list, which is a more direct route, at *www.cpsc.gov/cpscpub/prerel/category/toy.html*. Or sign up for free e-mail notices of recalls at *www.cpsc.gov/cpsclist.aspx*. Toy recalls have been announced practically every week over the past few years. Staying up to date can help keep you from buying a toy that has been recalled—and remedy the situation if you bought a recalled toy.

Plush plus: As your baby squeezes the legs of the Baby Einstein Octoplush, it names the color of the leg in English, Spanish, or French; two AA batteries required (included).

What's Available

Some brands of plush toys for babies are, in alphabetical order: Aurora (*www.auroraworld.com*), Baby Einstein (*www.babyeinstein.com*), Gund (*www.gund.com*), Haba (*www.habausa.com*), Jelly Cat (*www.jellycat.com*), Kaloo (*www.kaloo.com*), Kids Preferred (*www.kidspreferred.com*), Lamaze (*www.learningcurve.com*), Manhattan Toy (*www.manhattantoy.com*), Mary Meyer (*www.marymeyer.com*), miYim (*www.miyim.com*), Ohio Art (*www.ohioart.com*), Taggies (*www.taggies.com*), and Ty (*www.ty.com*). Plush toys come in conventional textiles such as polyester and cotton as well as organic cotton. Prices generally range from $4.50 to $130 or more, depending on the size of the plush toy and whether extras like music come with it.

Index